# LUTHER

# And The

# OLD TESTAMENT

by HEINRICH BORNKAMM

Translated by Eric W. and Ruth C. Gritsch

Edited by Victor I. Gruhn

SIGLER PRESS

MIFFLINTOWN, PA

*Dedicated to*
THE RIGHT REVEREND
FACULTY OF THEOLOGY IN MONTPELLIER
in Respectful Gratitude for the Bestowal
of the Honorary Degree of Doctor of Theology

Second English Edition

SIGLER PRESS 1997



*Library of Congress Catalog Card Number 96-5998*
*ISBN 0-9623642-8-2*

# Preface To The Second English Edition

After almost half a century this book has remained a milestone in Luther research. Its English edition has instructed Luther scholars on various levels of scholarship, ranging from seminarians, who needed to become acquainted with Luther, to seasoned Luther scholars, who needed to fill an important gap in their work. Heinrich Bornkamm has summed up Luther's work with the Old Testament in such a comprehensive manner that no other summary is needed; and he has distilled Luther's theological evaluation of the Old Testament in such a way that contemporary discussions of issues can proceed with clarity and objectivity.

Heinrich Bornkamm anticipated more work on lingusitc and philological aspects of Luther's work with the Old Testament, especially by Old Testament scholars. Although some such work has been done, with reference to particular books of the Old Testament, a complete study still remains on the agenda of Luther research. But this kind of study can build on the basic principles elaborated by Bornkamm.

I have used this book as a basic resource for teaching and as a general reference in more than three decades of teaching and work with Luther

*Eric W. Gritsch*

# EDITOR'S PREFACE

The task of editing this magnificent work has been a complex one. Many of the difficulties common to all Old Testament studies remain, and I can only hope that I have helped the reader to appreciate Luther's understanding of the Old Testament. I have tried to lighten the task for the reader so that he may not only comprehend Luther's approach, but also share Luther's zest and zeal for the Old Testament.

I call the reader's attention to the following technical points:

*Anfechtung* is the word Luther used to render his soul struggle. A Christian is embattled, contending with all the forces that assail him in his service of God. We here translate this word with "temptation," or with "conflict" or "trial," remembering the temptation of Jesus, involving not the onslaught of personal drives, passions, and emotions, but rather an attack on the very goals toward which his ministry was directed.

*Heilsgeschichte,* translated here as "salvation history," asserts that biblical history has a special character. Salvation history is the history of divine deliverance, quite distinct from the chronicling of events, which also appears. Four chief wonderful acts of Yahweh are seen in the exodus and passover, in the desert of Sinai, in the covenant and giving of the law, and in the entry into the Promised Land. Creation, patriarchal narrative, and other biblical events have their natural relationship with this theme.

*Schwärmer* was a term applied disparagingly by Luther to the radical reformers of his time. It is related to our English "swarm." It really means dreamers or visionaries or enthusiasts.

VIG

# TRANSLATORS' PREFACE

What Luther once said about the translation of the Book of Job may also be said here: "We had to sweat and toil." And yet the significance of this book, lauded by many scholars, has demanded an English translation for some time, although both the complex language and subject matter presented the translators with innumerable difficulties.

The titles of Luther's writings have been translated, dated, and followed by the original German title in parentheses. Existing English translations of Luther's works were used as guides in the translation of the numerous quotations from the Weimar edition. Since a significant number of Luther's writings are available in English, they are usually cited together with the German sources in the footnotes. The author's preferences regarding the choice of texts in the Weimar edition have been faithfully preserved, sometimes at the expense of stylistic clarity. Thus Luther's peculiar style of writing is also reflected in the translation.

EWG and RCG

# AUTHOR'S PREFACE

Luther's great scholarly legacy is his work in interpretation of Scripture. He occupied himself with the Old Testament far more than with the new Testament. Yet, there has never been a comprehensive study of his Old Testament exegetical work. Clearly, therefore, a significant portion of Luther's life work still needs research. Portions of his Old Testament work have been treated in recent essays.[1] The present study does not claim to fill the gap finally and completely in the research on this material. The primary purpose of this book is to clarify Luther's theological concept of the Old Testament. Linguistic and philological insights from his commentaries and translations are included where they are pertinent. But this is a separate great area of study, as Theodor Pahls' work demonstrates.[2] Such a complete study would be much more detailed than the present work. Basic principles are rather described here. It may be hoped fondly that some Old Testament scholar, familiar with Luther, will undertake this larger task. Such a scholar would thereby erect a monument to his most famous colleague.

Previous exegetical studies have dealt mostly with Luther's theological development in his controversy with scholasticism. The

[1] I name especially: Johannes Hempel, "Das reformatorische Evangelium und das Alte Testament," *Lutherjahrbuch,* XIV (1932), 1 ff.; by the same author, *Luther und das Alte Testament,* 1935; Theodor Knolle, *Luthers Glossen zum Alten Testament nach der Ordnung seiner Lehre* ("Die Lehre Luthers," 2 [München, 1935]); by the same author, "Luther und das Alte Testament," *Allgemeine evangelische lutherische Kirchenzeitung,* LXX (1937), 100 ff., 125 ff.; Hermann Steinlein, "Luther und das Alte Testament," *Luthertum,* XLVIII (1937), 172 ff., 193 ff.; Gerhard Schmidt, "Luther und das Alte Testament," *Junge Kirche,* XXV (1937), 712 ff.; Volkmar Herntrich, "Luther und das Alte Testament," *Lutherjahrbuch,* XX (1938), 94 ff.; Arnold Schleiff, "Luthers Deutung des Alten Testaments aus seiner Sicht der Geschichte," *Luther,* XXI (1939), 75 ff.

[2] Theodor Pahls, *Quellenstudien zu Luthers Psalmenübersetzung* (1931).

present study emphasizes the writings and Old Testament works of the mature Luther. This emphasis results from the task of presenting his basic and enduring understanding of the Old Testament, which he contributed to Protestant theology. It is not necessary to retrace the exegetical development of the young Luther, since recent research has produced some definite results. But, it is necessary not to restrict the theme to the question of law and gospel as the brief sketches always do. Rather, we first describe Luther's understanding of the Old Testament world and then proceed to analyze his concepts. At the same time, I would like to develop here what I began in my work, *Das Wort Gottes bei Luther (The Word of God in Luther)*,[3] with reference to the basic theological problem.

The question of the Old Testament confronts evangelical theology once again, for a new biblical theology, based on the Reformer's understanding of Scripture, has been struggling with modern historical-critical interpretations. The voice of Luther is very frequently heard in this lively debate, but almost always random words and thoughts are singled out. In my detailed description of Luther's concept of the Old Testament I would stress the desire expressed by Gerhard von Rad that interpreters of the Old Testament should "use great restraint in the use of ever so beautiful quotations from Luther and Calvin."[4] For I too am convinced that the discussion has been more confused than clarified by citing numerous contradictory individual points and interpretations of Luther, while his whole concept was not at the same time kept in mind. It is not my vocation to enter into the controversy regarding the Old Testament itself. Through this presentation I hope only to show what can be gained by reflection upon Luther's view.

I am indebted to my colleague Albrecht Alt for his kindness in providing information, and to the Rev. Werner Vogel for devising the survey of Luther's Old Testament interpretations added in the Appendix. This survey should provide easier access to the wealth of material scattered throughout the Weimar edition; at the same time, it warns against an uncritical use of the texts by indicating the kind of transmission (edition or copy). Those citations in which such an indication is not given are entirely Luther's, word

[3] München, 1933.
[4] *Theologische Blätter* (1935), p. 251.

for word. This survey also intends, as an integral part of this book, to have Luther's citations read not as single pieces, but in the context of his entire concept of the Old Testament. I am indebted to Otto Plöger, Old Testament lecturer at Heidelberg, for his kind help in the reading of the proofs.

Although this book has been finished for years, it could not be published—despite various efforts to do so—because its printing was not allowed by the *Reichsschrifttumskammer.*[5] In the meantime, Gerhard Ebeling's book, *Evangelische Evangelienauslegung (Evangelical Interpretation of the Gospels),*[6] the most thorough study of Luther's hermeneutics to date, has appeared. I hope that our studies complement each other to produce a more comprehensive picture of Luther's interpretation of Scripture, since we concur in the essential basic results. Thus I could subsequently limit references to Ebeling's expositions.

HEINRICH BORNKAMM

[5] An agency of censorship in Nazi Germany.
[6] München, 1942.

# AUTHOR'S ACKNOWLEDGMENTS

I really must express my heartfelt thanks to Dr. and Mrs. Gritsch for the great effort they took upon themselves in translating my book. I know best how many "logs and stumps" (as Luther comments on the Book of Job) they had to clear away in my own text as well as in the Luther quotations. I am especially grateful to them for having made Luther's own voice heard more clearly than in my book. As a consequence of the postwar poverty in 1948, Luther had been almost completely banished into the cellar of small-print footnotes. The translators have brought him back into daylight and have with affection linked his words to the text. Thus he is able to speak up for himself much more strongly than he could in the original edition. This is a great gain.

Fortunately, in the last twenty years a large number of special studies have appeared in this field, which had hardly been investigated previously. I am adding them in a bibliography. The regular bibliography in the *Lutherjahrbuch* presents the opportunity to observe the further progress of research.

Until now my book has not contained a dedication. That is why I may dedicate this new English edition to the Faculté de Théologie in Montpellier, as my expression of sincere gratitude for the bestowal of an honorary degree of Doctor of Theology. The problems of biblical hermeneutics have always played a great role in the history of this honorable institution reaching back to 1598, as well as in the whole history of French Protestant theology. To me it denotes not only a personal honor and pleasure that the Faculty bestowed upon me this distinction and allowed me to lecture on Luther at the Theological Faculty and at the University of Montpellier in November, 1967; it also indicates to me that in Protestantism as a whole more and more doors are opening to Luther's words.

Heidelberg, Autumn 1968 HEINRICH BORNKAMM

# CONTENTS

# ABBREVIATIONS

*ANF*—*The Ante-Nicene Fathers,* ed. Alexander Roberts and James Donaldson (Buffalo and New York, 1885–1896, American reprint of the Edinburgh edition).

*CR*—*Corpus Reformatorum,* ed. C. G. Bretschneider and H. E. Bindseil (Halle, 1834–1860).

*EA*—*D. Martin Luthers sämmtliche Werke* (Frankfurt and Erlangen, 1826–1857).

*LCC*—*The Library of Christian Classics,* John Baillie, John T. McNeill, and Henry P. van Dusen, gen. eds. (Philadelphia, 1953– ).

*LCS*—*Luther's Correspondence,* 2 vols., ed. Preserved Smith and C. M. Jacobs (Philadelphia, 1913 and 1918).

*LE*—*The Precious and Sacred Writings of Martin Luther,* ed. John N. Lenker (Minneapolis, 1904–1909).

*LW*—American Edition of *Luther's Works,* Jaroslav Pelikan and Helmut T. Lehmann, gen. eds. (Philadelphia and St. Louis, 1955— ).

*MPG*—*Patrologia, Series Graeca,* 161 vols., ed. J. P. Migne (Paris, 1857–1866).

*MPL*—*Patrologia Series Latina,* 221 vols. in 222, ed. J. P. Migne (Paris, 1844–1904).

*PE*—*Works of Martin Luther,* Philadelphia Edition (Philadelphia, 1915–1943).

*PNF*—*The Nicene and Post-Nicene Fathers of the Christian Church.* First Series: ed. Philip Schaff. Second Series: ed. Philip Schaff and H. Wace (New York, 1886–1900).

*RE*—*Realencyklopädie für protestantische Theologie und Kirche,* 3rd ed. rev., ed. Albert Hauck (Leipzig, 1896–1913).

*St. L*—*D. Martin Luthers sämmtliche Schriften,* 23 vols. in 25, ed. Johann G. Walch, in modern German (St. Louis, 1880–1910).

*WA*—*D. Martin Luther Werke.* Kritische Gesamtausgabe (Weimar, 1883– ).

*WA,* BR—*D. Martin Luthers Werke.* Briefwechsel (Weimar, 1930–1948).

*WA,* DB—*D. Martin Luthers Werke.* Deutsche Bibel (Weimar, 1906–1961).

*WA,* TR—*D. Martin Luthers Werke.* Tischreden (Weimar, 1912–1921).

1

# THE RELATION OF JUDAISM TO THE OLD TESTAMENT

Luther's quarrel with the Judaism of his day must not be treated as a repudiation of the Old Testament. To do so would prevent any understanding of what the Old Testament meant to him. Luther made a clear and sharp distinction between the two. No one who has even superficially looked into his writings can doubt his passionate opposition to the Jews as blasphemers of Christ on the one hand, and his deep love for the Old Testament on the other. He had no difficulty maintaining both, as paradoxical as this may appear to some people today. Both of these views closely interact upon each other. They originate in his particular insight of faith, and so are pivotally related. The promise and expectation of Christ and his gospel were the reasons for Luther's affirmation of the Old Testament; the rejection of Christ by the Jews was the reason for his separation from later Judaism. The faith of the Jews had contained the promise. Yet the very same faith became unbelief because it did not accept the coming of the Messiah. As Luther expressed it with classical conciseness in a thesis for a disputation in 1542, "The Jews still believe in vain in a God who promises a Messiah, although their fathers once correctly believed this."[1]

Their eternal sin was that they misunderstood God's action which changed the face of the world. Thus Luther saw a sharp break, rather than a continuity, in the history of Judaism. For Luther, the separa-

[1] Thesis 16 of *The Licentiate Examination of Heinrich Schmedenstede,* 1542 (*Praesidente reverendo D. Doctore Marti Luthero Respondebit ad haec M. Henricus Lünaeburgensis pro Licentia*), *WA* $39^{II}$, 188:17; *LW* 34, 304. See also below, pp. 113–14.

tion of nations by Christ's cross was also the turning point from the old to the new Israel.

In this connection, one should not overlook Luther's judgment of faith which was broad enough to encompass other viewpoints besides this religious one. It will be shown how many historical and literary treasures he mined out of the Old Testament. Yet, his writings on the Jews illustrate clearly enough the fury with which he denounced the Jews' usurious practices. These viewpoints are not to be taken by themselves and are not decisive; rather, they are clearly linked to his primary judgment of faith. Beauty and wisdom in the Old Testament are adornments of the Holy Spirit; but the spirit of profiteering and the murderous plans of the Jews were the expressions of their mad messianic arrogance.[2] In Luther's opinion, they would have liked to treat Christians as they treated the Persians at the time of Esther.

Luther took pains to show distinctly this contrast between the old pious Israel to whom God's promise had been given, and Judaism upon whom God's curse lay. These distinctions arose from the fact that the Jews do not understand the Old Testament, either the meaning of its law or its promise, and have polluted it with worthless rabbinical propositions.[3] Their decisive mistake is that they separate the formal commandments and signs of election of the Old Testament from the Word of God, on which all this rests. This is where their lies come from, as Luther listed them in his tract of 1543. They boast of their noble descent from the patriarchs. And, even if Luther will not give up his nobility of being descended from Noah—according to Gen. 10:32—it is nevertheless decisive that we are all, Jews and pagans, sinners before God.[4] They harp upon their circumcision and do not know that "where God's Word no longer exists, circumcision is dead."[5] They appeal to the law and forget that "not he who has the commandments should boast . . . but he who keeps them should boast."[6] They boast of having possessed Canaan, Jerusalem and the temple, and therefore expect to possess them again. "But they do

[2] *On the Jews and Their Lies,* 1543 (*Von den Juden und jren Lugen*), *WA* 53, 433:15.
[3] *Ibid.,* 511:20.
[4] *Ibid.,* 425:20 ff.
[5] *Ibid.,* 439:30.
[6] *Ibid.,* 444:27.

not give a thought to why they have it," namely, because they should dwell therein to the glory of God; otherwise they have forfeited it.[7] With all this, the later Jews only carry on much of what had already appeared in the nonbelieving sections of the old Israel. Their arrogant bragging about their ancestry under the old covenant had already brought them many a defeat and severe rebuke from the prophets, and from John the Baptist.[8] Thus their difference from the ancient times is not a moral one, but rather one of faith. The Israel of ancient times had the promise, and many trusted in it; the later Israel refused to believe in its fulfilment.

The rabbis are particularly to blame for this distortion. But as much as Luther emphasized this, and collected examples of distorted rabbinical interpretations of Scripture in his writings on the Jews, he was still no rationalist portraying the Jews as a people betrayed by its priests. Other factors are involved here. The tortured interpretation of the Talmud and of the rabbis was for Luther a sign of how severely God had punished the people of Israel for their unbelief. Luther thought not only of the abstruse magical formula of *Shem hammephorash,* the clarified NAME, the Holy One, which he mocked harshly, of the Tetragram, the Hebrew four consonants of Yahweh,[9] of the Talmudic speculations regarding the androgynous Adam,[10] or countless other exegetical fantasies, which he took apart again and again in all his interpretations; but rather, he thought of the essential—their distortion of the law as well as of the gospel. They invert the one when they invalidate Moses' commandments in their relations with non-Jews,[11] and the other when they refuse to apply the messianic prophecies to Christ.[12] Since their loss of the gospel is plain for all to see,

[7] *Ibid.*, 447:18.
[8] *Ibid.*, 420:17 ff.
[9] *On Shem hammephorash and the Genealogy of Christ. Matthew 1,* 1543 (*Vom Schem Hamphoras: Und vom Geschlecht Christi. Matthei am 1. Capitel*), *WA* 53, 579–648.
[10] *Lectures on Genesis,* 1535 (*In Primum Librum Mose Enarrationes*), *WA* 42, 53:14; *LW* 1, 70.
[11] *On the Jews and Their Lies,* 1543, *WA* 53, 489:25 ff.
[12] This inverting of law and gospel is the theme of all of Luther's writings against the Jews. See the following works on Luther and Judaism: Reinhold Lewin, *Luthers Stellung zu den Juden. Ein Beitrag zur Geschichte der Juden in Deutschland während des Reformations-zeitalters* ("Neue Studien zur Geschichte der Theologie und Kirche," 10 [Berlin, 1911]); Theodor Pahls, *Luthers Auffassung von Staat und Volk. Die Grundgedanken Luthers über Staat, Kirche und deutsches Volk in systematischer Anordnung untersucht und dargestellt*

Luther often emphasized strongly that the law has also been taken from them and that they no longer have a "true understanding of the law."[13] No wonder, for they no longer know anything about what the ancient Jews still sensed, that the law points ahead to the Savior.[14] Again and again horror gripped him when he thought of this fall of Israel from the height of the commandments and promises. What a sign of divine wrath that the exegetes of the Jews apply Isa. 53:4 ("Truly he bore our sickness . . .") to their people suffering among the pagans. "The wrath of God against this people is terrible. What a fall it is that even the greatest scholars among them teach this way!"[15] He also thought he found an obvious change in the Jewish messianic concept. The Jews at the time of Christ still knew, according to John 12:34, something about the eternity of the Messiah, and therefore refused to hear anything about the crucifixion; while the Jews today, according to assertions he found in Lyra, believed in an earthly future kingdom and in a mortal king.[16]

When the Jews failed to recognize the prophesied Messiah in the person of Jesus and thus fell away from the commandments and promises of the Old Testament, not only their relationship to God but also their status among the nations was changed. Not only was the proclamation of the divine Word taken from them, but they also lost the historical-political tasks God had given them earlier. Luther here thought not only of the sentence they had to inflict upon the Canaanites,[17] but he even saw in Deut. 15:6, "You will lend to many peoples," a special task given to the ancient people of Israel to bring, with their usury, divine punishment upon other nations. They certainly would not have been allowed to do

(2nd ed.; Halle/Saale, 1927); Erich Vogelsang, *Luthers Kampf gegen die Juden* ("Sammlung gemeinverständlicher Vorträge und Schriften aus dem Gebiet der Theologie und Religionsgeschichte," 168 [Tübingen, 1933]); Walter Holsten, *Christentum und nichtchristliche Religion nach der Auffassung Luthers* ("Allgemeine Missionsstudien," 13 [Gütersloh, 1932]), pp. 99 ff.

13 *The Prophet Zechariah*, 1527 (*Der Prophet Sacharja*), *WA* 23, 640:28.

14 *Epiphany Sermon on Isa. 60:1 ff., Church Postil*, 1522 (*Kirchenpostille*), *WA* 10I,1, 537:5 ff.; *LE* 7, 324.

15 *Lecture on Isaiah 53*, 1544, 1550 (*Enarratio 53. capitis Esaiae*), *WA* 40III, 714:25, 713:33 ff., 718:7 ff.

16 *Lecture on Isaiah 9*, 1543–1544, 1546 (*Enarratio cap. noni Esaiae*), *WA* 40III, 606:10 ff. Nicholas of Lyra (d. 1340) was a French exegete who stressed the literal as opposed to the allegorical sense of Scripture. Luther frequently cited him in his interpretation of the Bible.

17 See below, pp. 72–73.

so on their own, they did it under a higher law; God himself is really the great usurer who plagues the nations.

But the people of the Jews had a fuller and higher law, not only with regard to the repayment of loans but, as he says here, with regard to lending to the Gentiles on interest and practicing usury—namely, by divine authority, which establishes and permits this very thing. For he is God and the Lord of all. He takes away not only money and goods but also kingdoms and empires from whomever he wills and however he wills, and gives them to whomever he wills. If, therefore, for the sake of vengeance on the Gentiles, God wants to punish them through usury and lending and commands the Jews to do this, the Jews do well to yield themselves obediently to God as his instruments and to fulfil his wrath on the Gentiles through interest and usury. . . . They themselves were no better than any Gentiles, as I have said above; but God only chose and received them out of his mercy. Thus if you view the matter properly, it is not the Jews themselves who are usurers, but God, who persecutes the Gentiles through the usury of the Jews.[18]

This has all changed completely since the Jews stopped being the people of God. The law of Moses is abrogated, and they are now subject to the laws of the nations among whom they live.

Today, however, since the Jews have ceased to be the people of God, when the law is nullified, and when, through their godlessness and blasphemy they have deserved the wrath of God, usury is not to be permitted to them; but they are instead to be controlled by the laws of the people among whom they live.[19]

This is why Luther later occasionally differentiated between the Mosaic Jews, who had permission to collect interest, according to their law (Deut. 23:19–20), and the imperial Jews, who acknowledged the emperor as their lord before Pilate himself and had to obey the laws of the empire. For the law of Moses is not valid outside of Canaan, as examples from the Old Testament itself already prove.[20] "Neither Naaman the Syrian, nor Job, Joseph, Daniel, or other pious Jews have obeyed or used the law of Moses outside their country, but rather the laws and rights of the Gentiles among whom they lived."[21] That is why their usury can no longer

[18] *The Deuteronomy of Moses, with Notes,* 1525 (*Deuteronomion Mose cum Annotationibus*), *WA* 14, 655:35 ff.; 656:15 ff.; *LW* 9, 145–46.
[19] *Ibid., WA* 14, 656:26 ff.; *LW* 9, 146.
[20] *On the Jews and Their Lies,* 1543, *WA* 53, 524:28 ff.
[21] *Table Talk* (from various years), *WA,* TR 6, 128:4 (No. 6693).

bring them permanent advantage. Instead, the terrible prophecy that Christ spoke about them through the mouth of David in Ps. 109:11, "May the usurer bleed him white of all that he has; may strangers plunder the fruits of his toil," has been fulfilled against them time and time again.

It would seem that the opposite of what this verse says ought to happen, for the Jews are notorious usurers and bleed everyone white. But the psalm means to say that they will have no good fortune, only misfortune—in body and soul, in children, property, and honor. Great usurers that they are, an even greater usurer is to come along and take it all away from them, as the second part of the verse says, "May strangers plunder the fruits of his toil!" For this is what happens to the Jews; when they have saved for a long time, disaster strikes them; they are hounded, robbed, punished, and deprived of what they have. They know that this will happen, and they bemoan it daily.[22]

The contrast between the period before the monarchy and the later monarchical period, between the astonishing justification for the collecting of interest among the ancient people of Israel and its sharp repudiation among the later people of Israel, once again shows particularly clearly, in the few examples we wish to cite here, the great differentiation Luther made between the Old Testament and the Judaism of his own day. The curse-laden history of later monarchical period, between the astonishing justification for grace which Israel once experienced under the leadership of the divine Word. And that is why Luther refused to let his judgment of the Jews in his day confuse him in his conviction of the incomparable particularity of the history of the Old Testament people of God. Even though the people of Israel had exactly the same experiences as other nations, victory and defeat, hardship and rescue, there is nevertheless a colossal difference between their history and that of the pagans. What is at stake is not human works but the Word of God, which directs everything. That is why, to Luther, all historical events of the rest of mankind seem of infinitely less value than the history of Israel.

But note that even the history of this nation, if viewed according to appearances, seems similar to the histories of the Gentiles, for now they gain victories, then they are defeated; now they have abundance,

[22] Psalm 109, *The Four Psalms of Comfort,* 1526 (*Vier tröstliche Psalmen*), *WA* 19, 602:1 ff.; *LW* 14, 264. See also below, pp. 75–76 and p. 202.

then they are in want, and whatever wonders are celebrated, God still so hides himself that everything seems to be carried out by human prudence and chance. It doubtless seemed so to all those godless Gentiles. Hence they resisted and treated them as though there were no God of Israel. But the history of this nation is to be separated from the histories of all the Gentiles as far as heaven is separated from earth. In the histories of the Gentiles one can see either the greatness or the insignificance of works; but in the history of Israel, one thing is to be viewed with admiration and reverence: the Word of God. By his guidance and his will everything is carried out. In fact, these are truly called sacred histories, not because those things were done by holy men but because they were accomplished according to the holy Word of God, which hallows everything, and by the holy name of God, which upholds all things. Therefore, even though the deeds of all the Gentiles are themselves sheer wonders and acts of God, they do not have the testimony of the Word and the good will of God. Thus their affairs and history are only testimonies to his wrath, very terrible signs of the fearful judgment of God. When the history of the whole world is taken together, it is still incomparably less significant than even a single insignificant occurrence in Israel. This is why the proud and carnal are deceived by the simplicity of things in the Scriptures, for they take no notice of the Word of God, but value only material things.[23]

So much for Luther's differentiation between emergent Judaism and the central concerns of the Old Testament. To say more would convey the impression that Luther saw this as a problem. Luther's whole interpretation of Scripture must tell us, better than all the distinctions between the situations of ancient Israel and the later Jews, that the question of Judaism on which he took such a passionate stand did not obscure his approach to the Old Testament. A glance at what this meant in his own life will make this clear in the simplest and most direct way.

If one could divide Luther's professorship of the Bible, in his time united, into two fields as now done, one would have to call Luther a professor of Old Testament rather than of New Testament exegesis. He devoted only three or four years to the New Testament out of his thirty-two year career as a lecturer, and all the rest was spent on the Old Testament.[24] He was able to com-

[23] *The Deuteronomy of Moses, with Notes,* 1525, *WA* 14, 566:37 ff.; *LW* 9, 33.
[24] See Hans von Schubert and Karl A. Meissinger, *Zu Luthers Vorlesungstätigkeit* ("Sitzungsberichte der Heidelberger Akademie der Wissenschaften. Philosophisch-historische Klasse," 11, 9 [Heidelberg, 1920]), p. 21. Schubert

plete his translation of the New Testament within three months in the quietude of the Wartburg, but the more difficult and extensive Old Testament took him ten (with the Apocrypha almost twelve) years, though often interrupted.[25] The ratio is the same for the laborious and time-consuming revisions of his translation.[26]

The situation is exactly reversed with regard to preaching. Although Luther preached thirty times as many sermons on New Testament texts as on Old Testament ones,[27] we should not forget that Luther held largely to the Gospel and Epistle pericopes in his choice of sermon texts, no matter how much he criticized them. On the other hand, the ratio of Old to New Testament sermon series is about five to seven. Luther preached through the five books of Moses to the Wittenberg congregation for about six years (1523–1529). Most of his Old Testament sermon texts are from Genesis and the Psalms, the books he considered the richest treasuries of the gospel in the Old Testament. These sermons show that he seldom picked single passages as witnesses to the gospel. He preferred to trace God's dealings with mankind in the interrelationship of commandment and promise.

Any of Luther's sermons or lectures or descriptions of the patriarchical tradition in the Old Testament or of the inner conflict *(Anfechtung)* and consolation of the prophets shows clearly how he lived in that world, how he walked among patriarchs and prophets like one of them.[28] The story of Samuel's mother (I Samuel 1) impressed him deeply in his youth and awakened

presents a brief survey of the chronological order and literary transmission of Luther's academic lectures. See also the supplements in Johannes Ficker, *Luther als Professor* ("Hallische Universitätsreden," 34 [Halle/Saale, 1928]), p. 26.

25 See Wilhelm Walther, *Luthers deutsche Bibel* (Berlin, 1917), pp. 55 ff.

26 See Otto Reichert's introduction to the edition of Luther's revised German Bible (*WA,* DB 3–4), *WA,* DB 4, XI–LVIII. Examples of the revision are cited in Walther, *op. cit.,* pp. 77 ff.; Hans Schmidt, "Luthers Übersetzung des 46. Psalms," *Jahrbuch der Luther-Gesellschaft,* VIII (1926), 98 ff.; by the same author, *Luther und das Buch der Psalmen. Ein Beitrag zur Frage des Werdens des Alten Testaments* ("Sammlung gemeinverständlicher Vorträge und Schriften aus dem Gebiet der Theologie und Religionsgeschichte," 167 [Tübingen, 1933]), pp. 35 ff.; and Pahls, *Quellenstudien zu Luthers Psalmenübersetzung,* pp. 91 ff., 100 ff.

27 See the tabulation in Ebeling, *Evangelische Evangelienauslegung,* p. 456.

28 This closeness to the Old Testament world is immediately communicated through a reading of excerpts from Luther's sermons on Genesis (1527) and his lectures on Genesis (1535 ff.). See, for example, Oskar Ziegner, *Luther und die Erzväter. Auszüge aus Luthers Auslegungen zum ersten Buch Moses mit einer theologischen Einleitung* (Stuttgart, 1936).

in him the desire to own this book himself.[29] He owed to the Vulgate translation of Isaiah the formulas by which the mystery of divine action and nature seemed to him from the very beginning to be expressed in an incomparable manner: the word about the strange work through which God performs his own work (Isa. 28:21) and the "hidden God" *(deus absconditus)* (Isa. 45:15).[30] The words of the prophet Isaiah (54:7; 55:11) often consoled him. "This is a very beautiful consolation, of which I have made frequent use."[31]

He repeatedly expounded and preached, prayed and imitated the "little Bible,"[32] the Psalter, more than any other biblical book, indeed, far more than any New Testament book. He was guided and comforted in the important crises in his life by the words of the Psalms.[33] As he testified, he had hated Ps. 2:11, "Serve the Lord with fear," during his monastic life.[34] The word about the "righteousness" of God, which he repeatedly found in the Psalms (Ps. 9:5 ff.; 31:1; 71:2), threw him into desperate conflict (*Anfechtung*) which can be discerned in his lectures on the Psalms.[35] He clung

[29] *Table Talk,* 1531, *WA,* TR 1, 44 (No. 116); *LW* 54, 13–14; and Otto Scheel, *Martin Luther. Vom Katholizismus zur Reformation* (2nd ed. rev.; 2 vols.; Tübingen, 1917), I, 92.

[30] *Lectures on the Psalter,* 1513–1516 (*Dictata super Psalterium*), *WA* 3, 246:19; 4, 87:23; 331:11; *scholia* to *Lectures on Romans,* 1515–1516 (*Divi Pauli apostoli ad Romanos Epistola*), *WA* 57, 193:15; *LCC* 15, 241; *Sermon on St. Thomas' Day on Ps. 19:1,* December 21, 1516, *Sermons from 1514–1517, WA* 1, 112:24, *LW* 51, 19; glosses to *Lectures on the Epistle to the Hebrews,* 1517–1518 (*Divi Pauli apostoli ad Hebreos Epistola*), *WA* 57, 79:16; 128:7 ff.; *LCC* 16, 233, 59; *Explanations of the Ninety-five Theses,* 1518 (*Resolutiones disputationum de Indulgentiarum virtute*), *WA* 1, 540:23; *LW* 31, 99; *Lectures on Isaiah,* 1527–1530 (*In Esaiam enarrationes*), *WA* $31^{II}$, 169:5 ff.; 364:21 ff. See also Karl Holl, "Was verstand Luther unter Religion," in *Gesammelte Aufsätze zur Kirchengeschichte* (2nd ed.; 3 vols.; Tübingen, 1923), I, 41 ff.; Ferdinand Kattenbusch, "Deus absconditus bei Luther" in *Festgabe für Julius Kaftan* (Tübingen, 1920), pp. 170 ff.

[31] Luther's remark concerning Isa. 54:7, *Lectures on Isaiah,* 1527–1530, *WA* $31^{II}$, 445:20.

[32] *Preface to the Psalter,* 1531 (*Vorrede auf den Psalter*), *WA,* DB $10^{I}$, 99:24–25; *LW* 35, 254.

[33] See H. Schmidt, *Luther und das Buch der Psalmen,* and Volkmar Herntrich, *Die Psalmen als Kraftquelle Luthers. Ein Beitrag zur Frage nach dem lutherischen Bekenntnis heute* (Gütersloh, 1934).

[34] *Lecture on Psalm 2,* 1532 (*Enarratio Psalm secundi*), *WA* $40^{II}$, 295:8; *LW* 12, 80.

[35] *Lectures on the Psalter,* 1513–1516, *WA* 3, 91:10; 163:14; 453:4. See the improved text in Erich Vogelsang (ed.), *Neue Folge: Der junge Luther* (*"Luthers Werke in Auswahl,"* ed. Otto Clemen *et al.* [8 vols.; Berlin, 1930–1933], Vol. V), pp. 64:12; 90:5; 149:18; on *Anfechtung,* see also Vogelsang, *Die Anfänge von Luthers Christologie nach der ersten Psalmenvorlesung, insbeson-*

that much more passionately to the Psalter which earlier had caused him so much misery; he prayed it and sang it, again and again, as his only song of comfort and joy until the day he died with Ps. 31:5, "Into thy hand I commend my spirit; you have redeemed me, God of truth."[36] Especially did he cling to "his" Psalm 118, the "beautiful *Confitemini.*"[37] Ps. 130:4, "There is forgiveness with you, that you may be feared," always witnessed to him anew that God could be honored only by faith. "This verse repeatedly made Luther conscious of the theocentric meaning of justification. It was his decisive scriptural base."[38]

Luther knew of no better way to thank the hereditary marshal of Electoral Saxony, Hans von Loeser, who entertained him at Pretzsch, than by dedicating the exegesis of Psalm 147 to his host. Luther called his work on this psalm "spiritual game," which he had killed in the carriage while his host was hunting in the field. Afterward, Luther "carved" the psalm at home and sent it to von Loeser. This still allowed Luther to retain the psalm whole for himself.[39] Psalm 64 seemed to him especially written against Henry of Wolfenbüttel, and so he incorporated it into his tract *Against Hanswurst* as his most potent weapon.[40] Thus for Luther the Psalter lived in a myriad of relationships with his own world; one could continue giving examples of this indefinitely.[41]

---

*dere in ihren exegetischen und systematischen Zusammenhängen mit Augustin und der Scholastik* ("Arbeiten zur Kirchengeschichte," 15 [Berlin and Leipzig, 1929]), pp. 31 ff. See also my own essay, "Die iustitia Dei in der Scholastik und bei Luther," *Archiv für Reformationsgeschichte,* XXXIX (1942), 31 ff.

36 *On the Departure of D. Martin Luther from this Deadly Life. Report, Briefly Summarized by Justus Jonas and Michael Coelius, and Others who Were Present,* 1546 (*Vom Christlich abschied aus disem tödlichen leben des Ehrwürdigen Herrn D. Martini Lutheri, bericht, durch D. Justum Jonam, M. Michaelam Celium, und ander, die dabey gewesen, kurtz zusammen gezogen*), *WA* 54, 490:14.

37 *Psalm 118, the Beautiful Confitemini,* 1530 (*Das schöne Confitemini, an der zal der CXVIII. Psalm*), *WA* 31$^{I}$, 66:4; *LW* 14, 45, 47.

38 Paul Althaus, "Gottes Gottheit als Sinn der Rechtfertigungslehre Luthers," *Lutherjahrbuch,* XIII (1931), 19. On Ps. 130:4, see *Lectures on the Fifteen Gradual Psalms,* 1532–1533 (*In Quindecim Psalmos Graduum Commentarii*), *WA* 40$^{III}$, 356:14 ff.

39 *Psalm 147,* 1532 (*Der CXLVII. Psalm*), *WA* 31$^{I}$, 439–40; *LW* 14, 110.

40 *Against Hanswurst,* 1541 (*Wider Hans Worst*), *WA* 51, 565; *LW* 41, 252–53.

41 For more examples of Luther's personal use of the Old Testament, see Knolle, "Luther und das Alte Testament," *Allgemeine lutherische Kirchenzeitung,* LXX (1937), 101.

# 2

# THE OLD TESTAMENT AS MIRROR OF LIFE

Luther made an immediate, direct, and personal response to the Old Testament world. He did not need the help of a cultural-historical imagination to reach this world. Rather, he transferred that world into his own cultural setting better than anyone else since. He was very much at home there because it was a peasant world with many characteristics which he knew full well. It had breadth of scope and varied folk life and genuine folk religion. This setting gave him much livelier examples, warnings, and admonitions for the proclamation of his message to his own people than the New Testament setting did. Note that by contrast the New Testament church detached itself from the ethnic group and related itself to individuals and the congregation.

The Old Testament offered to Luther a mirror of life which was of primary importance to him. Here he nourished his hunger for religion in relation to human experience. Indeed, he could have more deeply explored the reality of the world in the New Testament than he did. If he had lectured on the Acts of the Apostles, he probably would have found the mirror there. As it was, the Old Testament offered him an almost unlimited abundance of images and teachings. He was a passionately political man, although he separated the spiritual realm from the worldly realm; he was as vividly moved by the great events of history as by what happened at court and in government circles on the city and village level.

## 1. THE POLITICAL WORLD

The patriarchs, prophets, and psalms gave Luther a fabulous picture of the manners and destinies of political authorities, the true leaders as well as the charlatans; these gave him a lively picture of life at court and among the common people in peace and in war. In all of these sources, Luther saw the rise and fall of nations. No one was as much the prototype of the true sovereign for him as David. He was intrigued, not only by the unspoiled boy and courageous warrior, but also by the wise, experienced king from whose spirit in the Davidic psalms Luther believed he had obtained rich and immediate fruits. David was one of those charismatic men whom God now and then sends to a people. They stand apart. Luther found them in the Old Testament: Samson, David, Jehoiada, Naaman, Joseph; also among the pagans: Cyrus, Themistocles, Alexander the Great, Augustus, Vespasian, Hannibal, Hercules; and in his own time: Frederick the Wise, Fabian of Feilitzsch. No one had to teach charismatic men like these the arts of government and warfare. "Before they can be taught what to do, they have already done it."[1] "To demonstrate his power and wisdom, God does many extraordinary things through heroic men whom he himself calls in a special way even though they are rare and few."[2] The most important thing about David's rule was his readiness to yield himself obediently to God's will. Although the Jews at that time clung tenaciously to idols, he re-established the ancient cult. Many of them became his enemies because of this.[3] He kept his rule free from lies and murder,[4] and knew, as Ps. 116:11 teaches, "All men are false," applying this to the solicitousness of courtiers.[5] That was why he fought the slanderers, "that happy and dear courtier called Envy,"[6] and did not mince words in the process. "That is why David must not only have been a brave hero with his fists but also a fellow free with his tongue. . . . Follow his

[1] *Psalm 101,* 1534–1535 (*Der CI. Psalm*), *WA* 51, 207:21 ff.; *LW* 13, 155. Here are the richest examples among all of Luther's writings.
[2] *Lectures on Genesis,* 1535, *WA* 43, 62:35; *LW* 3, 262. See also *WA* 43, 643:17. Otto Scheel, "Der Volksgedanke bei Luther," *Historische Zeitschrift,* CLXI (1939–1940), 495, n. 5, correctly emphasizes that Luther does not refer only to religious heroes. They are found in all stations of life, even among "lads and apprentices" (*WA* 51, 209:27; *LW* 13, 157). Luther used only the names of those who were already dead, as was correctly observed in Rudolf Hermann, "Zur Frage: Vorsehungs- und Heilsglaube bei Luther," *Zeitschrift für systematische Theologie,* XVI (1939), 216.
[3] *Psalm 101,* 1534–1535, *WA* 51, 216:22; 218:19; *LW* 13, 166, 169.
[4] *Ibid., WA* 51, 233:29; *LW* 13, 188.
[5] *Ibid., WA* 51, 205:13; *LW* 13, 152.
[6] *Ibid., WA* 51, 245:14; 250:16; *LW* 13, 207–08, 212.

example."[7] He kept himself free from pride and tyranny.[8] Luther believed that David possessed the "miraculous virtue," the ability to mind his own business, which was one of his exceptional secrets of success in governing. He did not succumb to *polypragmosyne,* which Luther wittily translated as sloth.[9] David also knew how to nip trouble in the bud.[10] When Luther asked at the end of his exegesis of Psalm 101 whether the reign of David had more blunders and sins than the boastful king admitted in the psalm, he did not leave David with all his contradictions to God alone; instead, he mightily defended his favorite king, at least against this question.[11]

How wise Solomon was too. He knew that more than strength was needed to wage war, and more than cleverness to become wealthy; "time and luck" were necessary (Eccles. 9:11).[12] The Old Testament also abounded in pictures of evil spirits at the kings' courts: Ahithophel (II Sam. 16:23), the evil swindler who cheated David for so long;[13] and the disloyal Ziba (II Samuel 9; 16; 19:17–18);[14] "that treacherous rascal Doeg" (I Samuel 22), "a fine kitten, who can lick in front and scratch in back."[15] Urbanus Rhegius wrote an exegesis of Psalm 52, with a foreword by Luther, against the "Doegites,"[16] especially represented by the figure of Henry of Wolfenbüttel.[17] Jesus Sirach too must have taken a good look at court life when he complained bitterly in his "mighty word" (Ecclus. 26:28): "There are two things that annoy me, and the third makes me furious: if one finally permits a valiant man to suffer poverty, if one finally despises the wise counselor, and if one departs from the true faith."[18] In Luther's

7 *Ibid., WA* 51, 262:7; *LW* 13, 221–22.
8 *Ibid., WA* 51, 254:4; *LW* 13, 212.
9 *Ibid., WA* 51, 222:15 ff.; *LW* 13, 174.
10 *Ibid., WA* 51, 262:12 ff.; *LW* 13, 222.
11 *Ibid., WA* 51, 263:9 ff.; *LW* 13, 223–24.
12 *Ibid., WA* 51, 215:27; *LW* 13, 165.
13 *Ibid., WA* 51, 219:21; *LW* 13, 170.
14 *Ibid., WA* 51, 227:11; 249:27; *LW* 13, 180, 206.
15 *Ibid., WA* 51, 229:17; 247:40; *LW* 13, 183, 205. See also *WA,* DB 3, 54:2.
16 *Ibid., WA* 51, 229:31; *LW* 13, 183.
17 *Against the Godless, Bloodthirsty Saulites and Doegites of These Last, Dangerous Times. An Exegesis of Psalm 52,* 1541 (*Wider die Gottlosen blutdurstigen Sauliten and Doegiten dieser letzten ferlichen zeiten, der LII. Psalm ausgelegt*), *WA* 51, 573 ff.
18 *Psalm 101,* 1534–1535, *WA* 51, 228:5; *LW* 13, 181.

misgivings about the right and value of political alliances, it was comforting for him nevertheless to find a few good examples of such alliances in the Old Testament: Abraham and the three Amorite brothers (Gen. 14:13), Isaac and Abimelech (Gen. 26:26 ff.), David and Jonathan (I Sam. 18:1), Asa and Benhadad (I Kings 15:18–19), the oath of the people under Nehemiah (Neh. 10:30). It is true, on the other hand, that Isaiah warned against trusting in military alliances (Isaiah 30–31).[19]

Luther became just as aware of the nature of law in Old Testament phrases and narratives as he had of the life and dealings of political authorities. All human law is patchwork, "a real beggar's coat." There are always ten exceptions to every law, for the lawmaker can never take all the factors into consideration. Whatever does not derive from the "healthy" law of nature, but must be enforced by human laws, is always a "sick law," just as the world is "a sick thing" which one has to keep mending.[20] That is why the "straight scepter" (Ps. 45:6), a symbol of unbroken and all-inclusive order of law, can belong only to the perfect kingdom of Christ.[21] David very wisely ties mercy and law together in Ps. 101:1, for each, by itself, destroys human order. Luther put the insight "strict mercy is the greatest mercilessness" alongside the "strict justice is the greatest injustice" *(summum ius summa iniuria)* of the ancients.[22] The art of the judge is to balance law and mercy. He stands above the law, and in interpreting it, he is not bound to the letter but only to his conscience; he must always remember Deut. 1:17, "The office of judge belongs to God," to carry out his office correctly. This is at once admonition and consolation for him.

But this is said for the comfort and encouragement of magistrates. They should know that they are carrying out God's business, not their own. They should be certain that they are the servants of God and the executors of a divine work, and that they are in a blessed estate. Therefore they should have that much more courage to judge justly and with integrity. Look at this too: before he gave laws he established judges in order to impress equity upon us. For judges are living

[19] *Table Talk* (from various years), *WA*, TR 5, 508 (No. 6138).
[20] *Psalm 101,* 1534–1535, *WA* 51, 214:14 ff.; *LW* 13, 164.
[21] *Lecture on Psalm 45,* 1532 (*Praelectio in Psalmum XLV*), *WA* 40$^{II}$, 526:2 ff.; 527:13 ff.; *LW* 12, 243, 245.
[22] *Psalm 101,* 1534–1535, *WA* 51, 206:1 ff.; *LW* 13, 153.

laws and the souls of the law. Therefore they are before and above laws, just as they are before and above the sword.[23]

And yet the word of the prophet Habakkuk (1:3), "Might is above right," discloses "the true color of the world,"[24] in spite of the system of justice instituted by God amidst the world's confusion. This is why God must take the sword out of the hand of every political authority after awhile and give it to another. Old Testament history is an unbroken chain of examples of this. "Thus the sword of political authority always remains in the world. But the persons sitting in political authority must always turn somersaults and stagger around, according to their merits."[25] To Luther, Babylonians and Assyrians were examples of such might. This was also the way bishops and nobles vented their anger on the peasants, but their intemperance and lust for vengeance would end in the same manner.[26] The history of big powers presents a depressing picture: everything big ends badly; the tragedies of classical antiquity knew this already. Luther gathered this painful knowledge even from the "message of salvation" of Isa. 14:2, which predicted the return of the people of Israel but at the same time presupposed the breakdown of the proud Babylonian power. This moved him very much every time he scanned the history of nations.

> But this passage corroborates what we learn from the tragedies associated with political life: that the end of even the best political causes is certainly sad. For great empires create great injustices; even though kingdoms and empires exist through the ordination of God and are good creations, human foolishness cannot use them properly. For it is difficult to administer the best causes even as well as one is able to do. Therefore it is better for everyone to live content with his own lot, and not strive for higher things; he to whom great things are given, receives much trouble and affliction in addition. Yet God sends these things so that he himself will be praised and seen as being very close at hand. But human foolishness turns everything into abuse and uses everything for its own purpose; this is the cause of all perdition and desolation. Kingdoms are not instituted for the benefit of the

[23] *The Deuteronomy of Moses, with Notes,* 1525, *WA* 14, 554:34; *LW* 9, 19–20. See also the passages cited in Hermann W. Beyer, *Luther und das Recht. Gottes Gebot, Naturrecht, Volksgeist in Luthers Deutung* (München, 1935), pp. 49, 54 ff.

[24] *The Prophet Habakkuk,* 1526 (*Der Prophet Habacuc*), *WA* 19, 361:14.

[25] *Ibid.,* 360:26.

[26] *Ibid.,* 367:25 ff.

masses, but for those persons and magistrates who are responsible and fit to rule, truly, for those who depend upon God alone and always seek his power. Magistrates should not be deposed, except through foreign powers, and not even then, unless God commands it. This is what we learn from this passage concerning political life.[27]

Nothing reveals the deep social concern with which Luther studied the world of the Old Testament better than his political interpretation of complete Old Testament books. To these belong his allegorical interpretations, such as of the Song of Songs, which he interpreted in 1530 as the song of the true social system. He thought that Solomon described the well-set-up state and the rightful system of law for the people of God in the picturesque language of love songs, almost in the same manner as Emperor Maximilian had in his *Teuerdank*.[28] But he also picked out, with a certain delight, the political passages of the Old Testament: the psalms on political authority, Psalm 82[29] and 101, out of which he made the wonderful mirror for regents that he held up before his young elector John Frederick with disarming candor equaled only by one of the prophets of the old covenant.[30] His view of the preacher Solomon is unique and the most thoughtful political insight that Luther gained from the world of the Old Testament. He had wrestled especially hard with Solomon, but now thought he had something special to say about him. He could say, "I never had such great pleasure in having a book printed as my Ecclesiastes."[31] Luther wanted to entitle it, "The Politics or Economics of Solomon," in strong contrast to the monastic interpretation, based mainly on Jerome, which made it a witness to the monastic flight from life and disgust for the world. He chose this title, not because Ecclesiastes contained laws for state and family, but because

27 *Lectures on Isaiah*, 1527–1530, *WA* 31$^{II}$, 96:39 ff.

28 Preface to *A Brief, Yet Clear Exposition of the Song of Songs*, 1530–1531 (*In Cantica Cantorum brevis, sed admodum dilucida enarratio*), *WA* 31$^{II}$, 587:24 ff. *Teuerdank* is the name of a fictitious knight whose life is narrated in an allegorical work of Emperor Maximilian I (1493–1519). See M. O'C. Walshe, *Medieval German Literature* (London, 1962), p. 354.

29 *Psalm 82*, 1530 (*Der LXXXII. Psalm*), *WA* 31$^{I}$, 189 ff.; *LW* 13, 39 ff.

30 *Psalm 101*, 1534–1535, *WA* 51, 197 ff.; *LW* 13, 143 ff. See also *Appendix to Psalm 101*, 1534 (*Nachtrag zu Psalm 101*), *WA* 53, 659 ff.

31 Preface to *Ecclesiastes, a Well-Founded Interpretation of Holy Scripture by D. John Brenz, Preacher in Hall, Swabia*, 1528 (*Der Prediger Solomo mit hoch gegrunter aus heyliger Göttlicher geschrifft, ausslegung durch D. Johann Brentzen, Prediger zu Schwebischen Hall*), *WA* 26, 621:3.

Solomon looked for strength and consolation therein to bear the misfortune striking the state and the people.[32] Luther's interpretation is based here upon Ecclesiastes' strong connection with the life of the people in the political and domestic world. This is quite different from finding society mirrored in the Song of Songs by reading it allegorically. Luther saw in Ecclesiastes more the mirror of the world and of human life, than the melancholy "I" which is usually noted there. Within the portrait of life, which he could not prove untrue, he sensed the consolation and support of the poet through faith.[33] Luther might well have treated Ecclesiastes as a book against free will.[34] He showed how he expected to find knowledge there such as he needed to maintain the power of his faith, whereas others saw only pessimistic resignation there. He did not find the injustice and foolishness of the ever self-destroying world and its inevitabilities which defeat all our efforts in Ecclesiastes alone; he also encountered these misfortunes in the patriarchs and prophets, the pagans and the Jews. He did so with such overpowering clarity that he needed only to reach into this rich treasure chest repeatedly for examples. He based his opposition to usury on Ecclesiastes' teaching about the world's bondage to death and the vanity of our human endeavors "unless God is drawn into them, so that man fears him and is content with the present, and rejoices in that."[35] He did not form his attitude by a "pro" or "con" method of written proofs (as Calvinism did later),[36]

[32] *Preface to Ecclesiastes, with Notes,* 1532 (*Ecclesiastes Solomonis, cum Annotationibus*), *WA* 20, 7:29 ff.; 8:19 ff.

[33] Luther's lecture on Ecclesiastes, which is available not only in the edition he himself criticized (*Table Talk,* 1532, *WA,* TR 3, 232 [No. 3242]), but also in Rörer's excellent copy, the first we have from him, would deserve a special analysis. Luther's translation and its differences in meaning from the original text should be included in it. Jacob Burckhardt, saddened by the political and intellectual fate of Europe, received the exact opposite impression about Ecclesiastes when he wrote, in a letter to Friedrich von Preen on September 10, 1891—out of a vision of life similar to that of Luther, yet himself skeptical and therefore unable to feel the same nerve of the book—"It is one of the most astonishing books and basically rather godless." See Jakob Burckhardt, *Briefe an seinen Freund Friedrich von Preen, 1864–1893* (Stuttgart and Berlin, 1922), pp. 276 ff.

[34] *Preface to Solomon's "The Preacher,"* 1524 (*Vorrede auf den Prediger Salomo*), *WA,* DB 10$^{II}$, 104:24; *LW* 35, 264.

[35] *Trade and Usury,* 1524 (*Von Kauffshandlung und wucher*), *WA* 15, 300:14; *LW* 45, 255.

[36] Karl Holl ("Die Frage des Zinsnehmens und des Wuchers in der reformierten Kirche," in *Gesammelte Aufsätze zur Kirchengeschichte,* III, 385) cites Ps. 15:5 and Ezek. 18:7–8, besides the Sermon on the Mount, as the basic passages in the Calvinist discussion.

even when the Mosaic tithe seemed to show him an acceptable way.[37] Instead, he based his opinion on the insight that God does not want to have secure what he made insecure—we should receive solely from his hands.[38]

These should be enough examples of Luther's political viewpoints on life. They could be multiplied infinitely, if one would add Luther's descriptions of the patriarchal families with everything that could be learned from them for household and labor, marriage and education, and if one would collect the innumerable references to single biblical passages, especially in Ecclesiastes and Proverbs, with whose civic wisdom Luther associated his own experiences.

## 2. THE INNER WORLD

An immeasurably rich inner world opened to Luther, in addition to the outer world. Faith and doubt, consolation and temptation *(Anfechtung)* are not only taught and described in the Old Testament, but are presented in innumerable examples: patriarchs and prophets, Job and the Psalter.

> Then you look into the hearts of all the saints as you would look into beautiful and gay gardens, yes, as into heaven itself; what fine, hearty, and gay flowers blossom there from all sorts of beautiful and happy thoughts toward God because of his blessings! On the other hand, where will you find deeper, sadder, more pitiful words of sorrow than in the psalms of lamentation? There you again look into the hearts of all the saints, as into death, yes, as into hell itself. How gloomy and dark it is there, with all kinds of troubled forebodings about the wrath of God! And when they speak of fear and hope, they use such words that no painter could paint fear and hope for you in this way, and no Cicero or orator could express them like that.[39]

To Luther mankind always remains essentially the same; so also, in every age similar questions confront man in his life and in his faith. Therefore, he was firmly convinced that everything that people in the Bible did, said, and experienced could be used as examples for life in his own day. That is why he never shrank from

[37] *Trade and Usury,* 1524, *WA* 15, 321:14; *LW* 45, 308–09.
[38] *Ibid., WA* 15, 299 ff.; *LW* 45, 253–54. What Luther said regarding surety is equally valid regarding interest.
[39] *Preface to the Psalter,* 1531, *WA,* DB 10$^{I}$, 103:14 ff.; *LW* 35, 255–56.

finding himself and his world directly addressed and described by Scripture. In his Wartburg interpretation of Psalm 37, he said, "No one should doubt that our opponents are the ones who are scolded in this psalm, and that we are the ones who are consoled therein."[40] He thus succinctly expressed his method of interpretation. The Word of God and his own period of time were contemporaneous. This was why the godless arrogance of the Jews, who were set apart as God's people through law and circumcision, was nothing but the haughtiness of the Roman church of his day when they believed that apart from papal laws and doctrine there can be only heresy deserving of the stake. "For the Jews could not tolerate the idea that a people of God should have and keep its own law rather than Moses' law, as in the case of the Ninevites who were held high in the Book of Jonah. And now how long will those have to wait who teach that there can be, indeed, are Christians who are not bound to keep either papal law or Roman church doctrines and customs? Heretics, heretics! Burn them!"[41] Thus Luther could also clear up questions on the correct behavior of Christians on the basis of specific events in the Old Testament. A few examples are sufficient. For instance, the sailors in the Book of Jonah drew lots to determine who among them had caused the tempest (Jonah 1:7 ff.). For Luther this was a good occasion to remark that drawing lots is an *adiaphoron.*

There are many similar things that may happen for both good and evil, such as Christ's prohibition against swearing in Matthew 5 [:33 ff.], although a divine oath may be made. Again, losing one's temper and killing are also prohibited, and yet it is godly to kill and punish evildoers through public trials.

Then he established his own criterion for this:

That is why, in works like these, one should look into the motive of the heart; he who does them out of his own passion sins. But he who does them out of obedience and the command of God, or out of duty and for the benefit of the neighbor, does well.[42]

[40] Preface to *Psalm 37 of David, to Teach and to Console the Christian Against the Mutiny of Evil and Blasphemous Hypocrites,* 1521 (*Der sechs {sieben} und dreyssigst Psalm David, eynen christlichen Menschen tzu leren und trösten wid- der die Mütterey der bösen unnd freveln Gleyssner*), *WA* 8, 213:11.
[41] *The Prophet Jonah,* 1526 (*Der Prophet Jona*), *WA* 19, 241:15.
[42] *Ibid.,* 212:1 ff.

Luther bared all the traits of human sinfulness he could find in the great pious figures of the Old Testament with a particular passion, sometimes even with gratification. He did not do it with vengeful satisfaction, to spoil the Old Testament for the believer, but, on the contrary, to endear it to him. He wanted to show that all these great men of God were worth something to God solely through the strength of their faith and God's free call, and not through their virtues. Thus he smashed the picture of the "painted" saints, of inhuman puppets of virtue, with which the Roman church seduced its believers into false human works and godless trust in men. Instead of making the pious men of antiquity into such false idols and worshiping them in false humility, he wanted, being proud in Christ, to place himself beside them. For the "dear saints" are no better than we are when God withdraws his hand from them; their salvation cost the same as ours.

This happens for our consolation, so that the saints do not become completely separated from us. We foolish preachers have placed the saints completely outside of sin and have accordingly been stricken by despair. Thus we have made the difference between the saints and ourselves the difference between heaven and earth, and so the mercy of God and Christ has been blasphemed. Peter has the same Lord I have; the blood that cleansed me has cleansed Peter, etc. If that is preached, we will have the hope of going where Peter went and we shall not make idols out of saints. But, you say, we should be humble; yet blasphemy occurs when you are unable to be elated enough through the blood of Christ, even though I may be a tenfold devil. This ought to be your humility: "It cost as much for Christ to redeem me as there are sins. Thus Jacob and Isaac are our brothers, although they may have had more gifts than we. The cost is the same. What the Lord gives us for consolation, we snatch in fear."[43]

Of course, if someone thought to find in Moses only stories of the unchastity of the Jews, Luther traced it back to the impure thoughts of the reader himself.

Thus I have heard all too often in school, not only from jurists but also from theologians, that the writings of Moses contain nothing but the lustful deeds of the Jews, since he devotes a great deal of attention to the recording of genealogies and marriages. Such opinions

[43] *Sermons on Genesis,* 1523–1524 (*Predigten über das erste Buch Mose*), *WA* 14, 371:9 ff. See also *ibid.,* 456:15, 29; 465:13; 472:9; and the edition of 1527 in *WA* 24, 484:20 ff.; 593:8 ff.; 607:24; 623:16 ff.

give proof of foul minds, which pass rash judgments on the deeds of the saints on the basis of their own character.[44]

Yet one must not forget that Luther, in principle and in his total judgments of the "saints," appeared more severe than his kind heart allowed him to be in the specific case. It was also part of his personality to be severe in his judgment of himself and to be able to excuse much in others. He still had an easier time unequivocally admitting the faults of the minor patriarchs, such as Lot,[45] Isaac,[46] and the sons of Jacob.[47] But he nevertheless tried to make the best of everything wherever he could, without recanting his strong words about the sins of the saints. Although he strongly emphasized even sins of holy men, he found an excuse in the concrete case most of the time.

What reason have we for exerting ourselves so diligently to excuse the sins of the saints? They were human. Therefore, when they were threatened by danger, they could be deceived at times and err. So far as the account before us is concerned, I excuse Lot and think that he adopted this plan without sinning.[48]

He wouldn't think of excusing Lot and his daughters, but he still wanted to understand what led to their action: not incest but the concern and shock that humanity was threatened with extinction.[49] Jacob's deceit of Laban obviously originated in inspiration from the Holy Spirit, who wanted to lead him away with his family and herds; besides, Jacob only attained the rights which had been fraudulently withheld from him.[50] "Even if it was fraud and deceit,

[44] *Lectures on Genesis,* 1537–1538, *WA* 42, 578:28; *LW* 3, 42.
[45] *Sermons on Genesis,* 1523–1524, *WA* 14, 288:3 (1527 edition: *WA* 24, 354:9).
[46] *Ibid., WA* 24, 461:16 ff.; *WA* 14, 347:6, 11. See also *Lectures on Genesis,* 1541–1542, *WA* 43, 446:14 ff.
[47] *Sermons on Genesis,* 1523–1524, *WA* 14, 456:15 (1527 edition: *WA* 24, 593:8).
[48] *Lectures on Genesis,* 1539, *WA* 43, 60:38; *LW* 3, 259. Luther was commenting on Lot's decision to deliver his daughters into the hands of the Sodomites (Gen. 19:8–9). But Luther does not excuse Lot's sin with the folklore explanation of the modern exegete, namely, that this demonstrates the high cost of hospitality. Rather, Luther means that Lot had not counted on the acceptance of his offer. But one should not conclude from this that smaller sins are permitted to prevent greater ones. "For what happens outside the law should not be taken as law but should be regarded as miracle, on the basis of which surely nobody should make a rule or law." *Ibid., WA* 43, 61:27; *LW* 3, 260.
[49] *Ibid., WA* 43, 97:26; *LW* 3, 310.
[50] *Sermons on Genesis,* 1523–1524, *WA* 14, 417:18 ff. (1527 edition: *WA* 24, 537:18 ff.). See also *Lectures on Genesis,* 1540, *WA* 43, 691:15.

Jacob still committed these acts by divine authority. . . . When God truly commands saints and faithful men to do something, it is without any doubt holy and permissible."[51] When Abraham presented his wife as his sister in Egypt to save his life, this was to Luther in his interpretation of Genesis 12 a praiseworthy sign of faith. For Abraham believed, even in this difficult situation, in God's promise that a great people would someday stem from him. That is why he was certain that God would preserve his life. And even if God could resurrect him from the dead to give him descendants, he, nevertheless, for the sake of the promise, did not want to neglect any means by which he could preserve his life. The lie must be an inspiration from the Holy Spirit, for it is the way in which God realized his promise. Thus Abraham's lie was really a sign of his faith and not a sign of his weakness; and so it is no sin.[52]

[51] *Lectures on Genesis,* 1540, *WA* 43, 694:22.

[52] *Lectures on Genesis,* 1537, *WA* 42, 470:15 ff.; 472:25 ff.; *LW* 2, 290, 294. I do not think it is feasible to put the blame for this interpretation on the editor, as Peter Meinhold does in *Die Genesisvorlesung Luthers und ihre Herausgeber* (*Veit Dietrich, Michael Roting, Hieronymus Besold*) (Stuttgart, 1936), p. 286, and to conclude from the remark recorded in the revision of 1539 (*WA,* DB 3, 179:30) that Luther assessed Abraham's lie more as a weakness of faith in his lectures two years earlier. All of Luther's interpretations of Genesis 12 agree with each other when they point up Abraham's behavior, unequivocally and without any deduction, as a model of true faith. Such an interpretation already appeared in the sermon of December 6, 1519 (*WA* 9, 431–32), and was even clearer in the sermon of August 23, 1523: Abraham trusts the promise and uses all available means to save his own life; not to do so would mean to tempt God. "Abraham endangered the honor of his wife because of his own life. For if there is something for one's own use, one should not seek anything else from God; if this is not the case, then it should be requested. Such faith is able to suffer want as well as to glory in riches, and vice versa" (*WA* 14, 227:13). "So much about faith. It follows then that God always responds to faith. Abraham . . . clings to the Word because it wants to bless him. The Lord deals with him in this way because he relies upon God's favor; just as the heart is affected by God, so he again is affected by man" (*ibid.,* 228:5 ff.). This was the same thing Luther taught in 1537, including the idea that Abraham may not tempt God. "Even though Abraham, full of faith, is aware of the various dangers, he still looks only at the promise. He knows that it has been given to him and to his seed and has, so to speak, been attached to his body. Hence, though he maintains that God will do what he has promised even if he should be killed in Egypt, he nevertheless feels that God must not be put to the test. Therefore he looks for every means to assure his safety or self-defense" (*Lectures on Genesis,* 1537, *WA* 42, 472:10 ff.; *LW* 2, 293–94). Moreover, the similarity of this interpretation appears most clearly in the comparison with Rörer's notes on the sermon of 1523, in which any literary use of the lectures on Genesis by the editors is out of the question (see Meinhold, *op. cit.,* pp. 295 ff.). Luther ranked Abraham's lie with the *mendacia officiosa,* the "obliging lies" (*Nutzlügen*), which are permitted for the sake of a higher value, of love, or, as is the case here, of the promise (see *Table Talk,* 1532, *WA,* TR 1, 179 [No. 412], 527 [No. 1044];

Luther's various themes are joined in this interpretation of Abraham's lie. Above all, he liked to use this and other opportunities to show that the path of faith can be a path opposed to the moral commandment and is subject to a higher justification. In connection with the lie he testified in other ways to the freedom that seeks only love and not a formal commandment. But his love for the great patriarch probably produced this (not to forget his opposition to the Jewish interpreters, the "sevenfold asses," who at this point charged Abraham with a mighty sin).[53] The fraud

---

3, 22–23 [No. 2842]; and *Lectures on Genesis,* 1537, *WA* 42, 470:30 ff.; 43, 109:33 ff.; *LW* 2, 291–92; 3, 32–33). Thus one will have to assume that Luther presented the interpretation in his lectures basically in the same manner in which it appeared in print. The editor could have added clarifications regarding details of formulations; in any case, we cannot use them as the norm for the lectures as a whole. The remark recorded in the revision of 1539 certainly does not represent sufficient evidence to ascribe the rather lengthy segment to the editor. In the face of it, one can only assume that Luther indeed put the accents somewhat differently two years later, or that Rörer's recorded remark is too scanty for a complete assessment of Luther's opinion expressed at that time. If such an explanation of the difference seems unsatisfactory, it is to be remembered that the difference between both interpretations appeared not at all very great to Luther himself. The printed lectures contain both, although they are clearly graduated. Even Abraham's weakness—as his lie could be interpreted—does not annul his unswerving faith in the promise. On the entire problem, see also Walther Köhler, *Luther und die Lüge* ("Schriften des Vereins für Reformationsgeschichte," 109–10 [Halle/Saale, 1912]), pp. 160 ff. Luther emphasized the sin of Abraham's lie much more strongly in his lectures on Genesis 20 than in the corresponding sermon of November 8, 1523 (*WA* 14, 289 ff.)—without any attempt on the part of the editor to erase the idea here, where not even a remark in the recorded revision stood in his way. But there, too, the right of Abraham to follow his reason in the matter, without any definite direction of the Holy Spirit, is strongly elaborated (*Lectures on Genesis,* 1539, *WA* 43, 104:37; 107:15; *LW* 3, 320, 323), besides naming very clearly Abraham's sin (*ibid., WA* 43, 114:3 ff.; *LW* 3, 333). He bravely kept his faith despite the fear that seized him (*ibid., WA* 43, 104:27; 114:12; *LW* 3, 319, 327, 328, 333). That is why God may have excused him of the sin (*ibid., WA* 43, 114:13; *LW* 3, 333). The entwining of motifs is already particularly evident in Roth's copy of the sermon of November 8, 1523: "Abraham's error is described as one which God forgives his own, not others. Abraham errs out of the Word of God, for as long as he obeys God, he is faced with such a necessity; thus his God cannot forget his works in Scripture" (*WA* 14, 290:33). Thus Luther already had put the accents differently in the lectures themselves. Even if he did not want to deny the lie of Abraham, it nevertheless was to him always simply a way in which Abraham proves his faith in God's promise.

53 *Sermons on Genesis,* 1523–1524, *WA* 14, 471:9. If Luther scolded the Jewish interpreters so severely, one can guess somewhat what he would do with the allegorist today who interprets Abraham and Sarah as symbols of ecclesiastical government and the church. See Hans Hellbardt, "Abrahams Lüge," *Theologische Existenz heute,* XLII (1936). For this allegorist not only accuses Abraham (the prototype of church governments in 1933) of the greatest sin—of lying, and of lacking confessional courage—but also destroys, through such an allegory, the example of faith and the assurance of the promise which Luther found in the text. How simple and full of evangelical truth is Luther's interpretation—

of Rebecca and Jacob (Genesis 27), which exacted Isaac's blessing for Jacob, was to Luther a similar example of faith. Here, too, everything was decided and excused beforehand through God's promise in which the elder should serve the younger (Gen. 25:23). Rebecca believed in it with all her might, even in the hour when everything was at stake. And so she found the exception to the rule, surely through the inspiration of the Holy Spirit, who carries out God's promise. Thus what should really be called the nastiest kind of fraud that exists in the world became obedience to God who himself provides the way out; and Rebecca is to be defended against the charge of lying, which the ancient interpreters, especially Lyra, made against her.[54] "This is why Rebecca handled the matter with skill, with cleverness, and with the most beautiful fraud, and handled it according to the will of God, who granted a happy ending in a matter so difficult and so filled with inherent dangers."[55] For whenever the first table of the law, obedience to God and his word, contradicts the commandments of the second, the second must give way.

Thus it happened according to God's pleasure, because parental obedience, the fellowship of brothers, and love were subjected to the first table of the law. The second table is weak and amounts to nothing when it impinges upon the first table. . . . In this case, God elevates the law so that I am not bound to obey only the second table. Yet, if the first and second tables do not clash, then law and obedience remain. . . . The first table should always be preferred to the second.[56]

---

which, of course, is no longer acceptable to us today—over against Hellbardt's "spiritual juggling" (*geistliches Gaukelspiel*), as Luther called these arbitrary allegorical tricks which are not directed to Christ as the center of Scripture. Against Hellbardt, see Adolf Schlatter, "Allegorien, klingende Schellen, tönendes Erz," *Evangelische Theologie,* III (1936), 422 ff., and Ernst Haenchen, "Zur Auslegung des Alten Testaments," *Deutsche Theologie,* IV (1937), 351 ff. It would be an attractive task to write a history of the Abraham interpretation. A preliminary segment of it is presented in Walther Völker, "Das Abrahamsbild bei Philo, Origines und Ambrosius," *Theologische Studien und Kritiken,* CIII (1931), 199 ff. In contrast to the Ambrosian Abraham, who is justified by works, Luther followed here too the path of St. Augustine.

[54] *Lectures on Genesis,* 1542, *WA* 43, 508:10; 504:17 ff.; 505:43 ff.

[55] *Ibid.,* 508:10.

[56] *Ibid.,* 507:4 ff., 27. Luther already had basically solved the problem in the same manner in his *Sermons on Genesis* of 1523–1524, as far as the copies indicate, even though he expressed his basic principle that he did not want the saints acquited of their sins. Yet he did not need this principle in this case, since God's promise placed it beyond the norm. *WA* 14, 370:7 ff. (1527 edition: *WA* 24, 482:7 ff.). See also the *Sermon on the Second Sunday after Epiphany on Rom. 12:6 ff., Lenten Postil,* 1525 (*Fastenpostille*), *WA* 17$^{II}$, 52:5 ff.

These excuses do not have the purpose of belittling sin as sin; but, morally speaking, they maintain its weight. They are historical examples, showing that faith may break the law and testifying how marvelously God leads his saints. This was so important for Luther that he elaborated on it again and again; he no longer asked himself whether this agreed with the simple facts of the story. Although these saints were given the divine right, or even command, to act against the law, we are seldom permitted to do so. Luther's meditation on these examples of faith stood outside any moral consideration, be it moral condemnation of these deeds or moral allusion to their model.

For you are not Lot, and because you depart from the rule, you are tempting God. It has not been given to you to depart from the rule and to imitate the examples and the wonderful deeds of others. Abraham killed four kings in Egypt, twice he exposed his wife to danger in regard to her honor, and Lot offered up his daughters to be defiled. Why they did it is none of your concern. God wanted to reveal his wisdom and power in this way.[57]

We can see how these saints attained their greatness in Luther's eyes only when we remember that they themselves had no models and had to come to faith without examples. And "it is hard to believe God without examples." It was Abraham's incomparable honor to have been able to do this. He was the single one, chosen

[57] *Lectures on Genesis,* 1539, *WA* 43, 62:6; *LW* 3, 261. See also above, p. 21, n. 48. It has been pointed out repeatedly that Luther, with this view, continued the interpretation of the sins of the patriarchs found in the Scotist-Nominalist tradition. See Alphons V. Müller, *Luthers theologische Quellen. Seine Verteidigung gegen Denifle und Grisar* (Giessen, 1912), p. 232, and Roland H. Bainton, "The Immoralities of the Patriarchs According to the Exegesis of the Late Middle Ages and the Reformation," *Harvard Theological Review,* XXIII (1930), 39–49. This is correct. And yet, there is a difference in the motifs. Whereas the medieval exegetes obviously tried to relieve the patriarchs and the Bible from these severe sins by assuming special divine commands concerning the violation of moral law, Luther elaborated the positive meaning of the patriarchs' behavior, namely, the test of faith. Bainton, in his essay—which was stimulated by the ideas in Karl Müller, *Luthers Äusserungen über das Recht des bewaffneten Widerstands gegen den Kaiser* ("Sitzungsberichte der königlichen bayrischen Akademie der Wissenschaften. Philosophisch-philologische Klasse," 8 [München, 1915]), p. 8—distinguishes, in an instructive manner, various solutions to the problem: 1) the assumption of a special divine command (scholasticism, Luther, Calvin); 2) the repetition of such a revelation (anabaptists, in part Ochino, the Libertines); 3) natural law (John of Salisbury, the Monarchomachs, who were a group of French authors who called for armed resistance against the emperor after Catherine of Medici instigated the famed Massacre of St. Bartholomew in 1572).

by God. He was forced to see the reluctance of all other nations toward the gospel.

To be alone in wisdom is difficult, for it is difficult to believe God without an example, to be led by God as he led Abraham, a solitary individual, to see all the other nations abhorring the religion you follow, to find that you alone believe and follow something different from all other men.[58]

Then man faces temptation *(Anfechtung)* after temptation. This means, according to Luther's wonderful word, God's embraces. "He offers the temptation of the world, of the flesh, and of the devil. These are his embraces, for in this manner he inhabits us; otherwise we shall never learn to hear, to see, and to forget."[59] And how much Noah, the greatest prophet the world has seen,[60] the "preacher of righteousness" (II Pet. 2:5), must have suffered when he stood alone and unsuccessful against a world ripe for destruction! Luther thought that he would have gone mad in a case like this in his ministry.

Noah was not only righteous and holy himself, but he was also a herald. He informed others of the promises and threats of God, and in that most wicked and depraved age he labored and suffered everything a person in a public position is obliged to suffer. If I had been aware that so many men in the generation of the wicked were opposing me, I surely would have given up the ministry in despair. No one believes how difficult it is for one man to oppose the common opinion of all other churches, to contend against the views of very good men and very good friends, to condemn them, and to teach, live, and do everything in opposition to them. . . . We observe and experience today how much wrath, hatred, and envy one sermon addressed to the people generates. To what, then, shall we suppose that Noah was subjected? He preached not a hundred, not two hundred, but even more years, up to the final hundred years, during which God did not want the ungodly to be instructed any longer because they would only become more infuriated and more wicked.[61]

The prophets experienced as a class what Noah and Abraham experienced as individuals. For it was precisely their example that made it clear to Luther that the most difficult thing is not for a

58 *Lecture on Psalm 45,* 1532, *WA* 40II, 595:11; *LW* 12, 289–90.
59 *Ibid., WA* 40II, 582:5; *LW* 12, 279.
60 *Lectures on Genesis,* 1536, *WA* 42, 280:5; *LW* 2, 26.
61 *Ibid., WA* 42, 301:26 ff.; 302:3 ff.; *LW* 2, 56–57.

man to be forced to stand alone in his struggle with faith. "But when he assumes his office and is obligated to console and support a whole people who are undergoing the same struggle as he is, then there is trouble, misery, and distress."[62] For prophets are never private persons.[63] Luther devoted himself to the prophets with a special love, probably precisely because the essence of their office, in its power to console as well as in its conflict *(Anfechtung),* made such a deep impression on his soul.[64] He saw a natural unity between them and the apostles. Both were committed to the same mission,[65] and yet the prophets are almost the greater ones because they had no example before them. His own struggles were depicted more strongly and more vigorously in the fate of the prophets than in the apostles. The same thing happened to him that happened to the Puritans later in their struggle against the Anglican church: the eventful history of the Old Testament occupied his imagination as the prototype of his life struggle more strongly than the more serene world of the New Testament. And yet he applied these transparent stories exactly opposite to the way the Puritans did. While they peopled the history of their own time with resurrected Jewish figures and circumstances, Luther projected his struggles into the events of the Old Testament and thus made them comprehensible to himself. Creative spirit and artificial reconstruction are well contrasted here, as are freedom in handling Scripture in Christ and biblicism. While the imagination of the Puritans was essentially historically oriented and their contemporary life completely overshadowed by the biblical background, Luther, as it were, sucked the historical events of the Bible into the here and now of his mission and fate. This difference is apparent in his attitude toward Calvin; the Puritans represent only a purer contrast.

[62] *The Prophet Habakkuk,* 1526, *WA* 19, 380:21.

[63] According to what is reported regarding the words and deeds of Moses, he is not "a private Moses, but the ordained prophet and head of the people of Israel, to whom he gives the law." See *On the Last Words of David,* 1543 (*Von den letzten Worten Davids*), *WA* 54, 78:27.

[64] Since Luther's rich concept of the prophets can only be indicated here in a few strokes, I refer the reader to the material in Hans Preuss, *Martin Luther, der Prophet* (Gütersloh, 1933), especially pp. 84 ff. However, essential viewpoints are missing there. The prophetic message concerning law and gospel will be treated below (pp. 120 ff.).

[65] *The Prophet Habakkuk,* 1526, *WA* 19, 396:29 ff.

How well Luther could imagine the clash between Amos and the Very Reverend Amaziah (Amos 7:10 ff.)! The priest of Bethel, just like the pope in Rome, led the dignity and awesome age of the royal sanctuary into the field against the prophet. He endowed Amos with the title of heretic and rebel, with which Christ and all the prophets were labeled. They had always received the same response to their cries of warning: "The church does not err, it is the people of God, Christ died for it, God's Spirit governs it," etc. Their threats of disaster were met with, "That cannot happen, for we are the church of God."

> The pope argues in precisely the same manner: on the basis of his dignity, his greatness, and the length of time he has ruled. They fill their bellies in the name of their rulership. Christ has to hear, "He stirs up the people" [Luke 23:5]. The prophets are called seditious. It is impossible to say, "The church does not err, it is the people of God, Christ died for it, the Holy Spirit rules it," etc. . . . All prophets are forced to hear, "This cannot happen, for we are the church of God."[66]

The sign of the unbelievers is that like the pope they always believe themselves saved by their own works. "God is in our midst," they say and so dispel the admonitions of the prophets. "Here you see the battles of the prophets. The godless have always claimed to have a gracious God because of their good works, just as the pope claims, 'God is in our midst.' "[67] It is this obduracy of those duly authorized, namely, the priests and rulers, which always makes the unauthorized into prophets like this Amos, the shepherd of Tekoa. That was why the contempt of the officials hit the unpretentious prophet and his ridiculous God—as Luther and his followers also experienced at the hands of universities and professors.[68] "The prophet as well as God himself appears foolish. What impression does that make?"[69] That is why Luther so well understood Jeremiah's sigh, "Oh, Lord, I am not worthy to preach" [Jer. 1:6]. "Therefore we say today, 'Oh, I am too insignificant to rise up against the universities.' "[70] That is also why he occasion-

[66] *Lectures on the Minor Prophets. The Prophet Amos,* 1524–1525 (*Praelectiones in prophetos minores. Amos propheta*), *WA* 13, 149:18 ff., 25 ff.
[67] *Ibid.,* 141:25.
[68] *Ibid.,* 124:22 ff.
[69] *Ibid.,* 125:5.
[70] *Lectures on Isaiah,* 1527–1530, *WA* 31$^{II}$, 270:26.

ally compared himself, in his office, to one of the major prophets. Once he compared himself to Isaiah, obviously because of his courageous language, for in the same Table Talk he called Melanchthon a Jeremiah, because Philip, like the prophet, was always afraid of scolding too much.[71] At other times he compared himself to Jeremiah; like Jeremiah he felt himself under attack *(Anfechtung)* because his pure proclamation was sure to bring about conflict.[72]

Most of all these comparisons apply to the mission of the prophets and the resulting situation. He did not want to put himself immodestly at their side; instead, he perceived a difference between then and now that filled him with astonishment at their prophetic courage. The prophets dared to fight *against Scripture.* When Isaiah (1:11), Micah (6:7), Jeremiah (7:21 ff.), and David (in Ps. 51:16) proclaimed, "You have no pleasure in sacrifice," they had the whole Mosaic law against them.

No one can fully explain this sermon, because the prophets belonged to a people among whom political rule was divinely instituted, and where sacrifice was accepted. And they dared to preach, against the established morality, against Mosaic law, and against the rites of the people, that there is no power in sacrifice. That was a terrible heresy. We are nothing compared with the prophets. What if the pope could use the authority of law and Scripture against us! We conquered the pope with the triumphant fact that he does not have Scripture on his side. Our victory, measured against their victory, is woeful and disgraceful. We rob the pope, willy-nilly, of all scriptural passages, and have left him with human tradition alone. He has nothing left but the church. He knows he has been robbed of Holy Scripture. Here the prophet truly speaks against Moses.[73]

The courage of the prophets was greater than Luther's proclamation that obedience to parents and authority is against God's will, although God himself commanded it in the law. "These are difficult articles, much more difficult than if I said, 'God commanded obedience to political authority, to parents, and to the second table

[71] *Table Talk,* 1531, *WA,* TR 2, 410 (No. 2296b). See also Holl, "Luthers Urteile über sich selbst," in *op. cit.,* I, 392; and Preuss, *Martin Luther, der Prophet,* pp. 113 ff.

[72] Letter to Wenceslaus Link of Nürnberg, July 10, 1518, *WA,* BR 1, 185:16; *LCS* 1, 97. See also *Table Talk,* 1540, *WA,* TR 5, 23–24 (No. 5242).

[73] *Lecture on Psalm 51,* 1532 (*Enarratio Psalm LI*), *WA* 40$^{II}$, 450:3 ff.

of the law,' and if I also said, 'This does not please God.' "[74] The prophets needed special gifts for this kind of defiance—an unbending faith and a deep knowledge of God's will, which perceives a different reality under the surface. An example of this is Elisha, who foresaw the abrupt end of the famine and was proven right despite the mockery from the king's court (II Kings 7). Luther saw this event as fitting well into his own time. Just as at that time the great thought themselves intelligent and superior, so in the year 1526, as Luther supposed, the emperor and princes sat at the Diet of Speyer and deliberated on how they could suppress the gospel. But God watches them and laughs at them. "These good people don't think that God knows their plan; they imagine he has gone to Calcutta or Ethiopia, and is having lunch with the Moors." But, in the middle of their deliberations, he "cuts off their spirit" [Ps. 76:12].[75] The prophets knew this, and Luther strengthened his own laughing defiance at their triumph. His heart expanded at the "wonderful proud pride" of the prophets who, like David (II Sam. 23:2), can say, "The Spirit of the Lord has spoken through me." However, it is precisely at this point that Luther again modestly raised the barrier between himself and the great patriarchs. He who can say this of himself "must of course be very sure of his ground." This is not born of human spirit; it is not David, Jesse's son, who speaks this way, but David the prophet, awakened by God through his promise. So we may not boast, unless we boast as their disciples, as "the prophets' children, who set up nothing of their own or anything new, as the prophets did, but instead claim to have everything from the prophets."[76]

He also began to understand, from the prophets, the immense prerogative of praying men to stand up for their people and to turn aside divine wrath with their prayer. The wrathful God himself certainly seeks someone who will erect a fence between him and the people (Ezek. 22:30); Moses had done it often. And Luther bravely knew himself as the one who still prevented God from striking out; but he feared that after his death God's judgment of punishment would come.

[74] *Ibid.*, 451:6.
[75] *Psalm 112 of David*, 1526 (*Der hundert und zwelffte psalm Davids*), *WA* 19, 314:30 ff.; *LW* 13, 404.
[76] *On the Last Words of David*, 1543, *WA* 54, 35:11 ff.

Ezekiel [22:30–31] says, "I sought for a man among them who would construct a hedge, and stand in the gap before me for the land, that I should not destroy it; but I found none. Therefore I have poured out my indignation upon them; I have consumed them with the fire of my wrath." With these words God indicates how he wants us to withstand him and turn away his anger from one another. It is frequently written of the prophet Moses that he restrained God, lest his anger should overwhelm the people of Israel.[77]

I am the block in God's road. If I die, he will strike out.[78]

It is most regrettable that Luther has not bequeathed to us any exegesis of one of the major prophets, in which he might have worked out his concept of prophecy. Although only student copies and other revisions remain from his brilliant and significant lectures on Isaiah in 1527–1530,[79] one becomes painfully aware of this gap. The profusion of literary and other commitments undoubtedly prevented Luther from completing an exegesis of a major biblical book after his commentary on Galatians in 1519. After that he managed only interpretations on a much smaller scale, and one must turn to the minor lights such as Jonah, Habakkuk, and Zechariah to peruse a complete book of a prophet in Luther's own handwriting and to find a complete personality fully portrayed. One gets an intimation of what one could have expected from an interpretation of Isaiah or Jeremiah from the way in which he breathed life into these minor prophets and understood how to fill their books with the breath of their battles fought with God.

Luther's work on Habakkuk in 1526 is the richest source for the office and method of the prophets. He depicted therein the prophet par excellence who, beyond all sense and reason, knew how to cling to the Word of God alone, by which the nation stands or falls.[80]

It is . . . highly needful, when the people flinch, that the prophet stands firmly on His Word, holds on tightly, neither retreating nor

[77] *Treatise on Good Works,* 1520 (*Von den guten wercken*), *WA* 6, 241:9; *LW* 44, 69.
[78] *Table Talk,* 1532, *WA,* TR 2, 191 (No. 1714). See also *Lectures on Genesis,* 1536, *WA* 42, 526:16; *LW* 2, 369; Hermann Dörries, *Luther und Deutschland* ("Sammlung gemeinverständlicher Vorträge," 169 [Tübingen, 1934]), pp. 10–11.
[79] *WA* 25 and 31$^{\text{II}}$.
[80] *The Prophet Habakkuk,* 1526, *WA* 19, 387:17.

wavering in the face of either misfortune or the people's unbelief, complaining, and blasphemy. For when he who should proclaim and preserve the Word and the consolation wavers and retreats, the cause is defeated; the banner falls, and the guard is dead. But when he stands firm, some will always cling to him and look up to him.[81]

Luther, in a totally unconscious and selfless self-confidence, described by the character of the strange prophet what he himself had experienced, but what to him was always only a confirmation of the proud prophetic language: "Here I stand on my guard, and station myself on the tower; and I watch and think of what will be said to me, and what I should answer him who scolds me" (Hab. 2:1).

But the apex of his interpretations of the minor prophets was his presentation of Jonah in 1526. Here he found a story and a prophecy combined; together they gave him the basis for a wonderfully rich psychology of faith and of temptation *(Anfechtung).* This prophet, who fled from his Lord, certainly did not owe his preservation in the stomach of the fish to his works, but only to the grace of God.[82] This is why he is one of the most powerful examples of saints who, much to our consolation, "so grossly sin against God."[83]

On the ship he slept in his sins and did not feel the raging of divine wrath.[84] But when he was awakened, the realization that the storm was meant for him overpowered him; now he saw no other sin but his own. "For this is what remorse does, when it comes and bites and frightens the conscience; then the whole world is pious and only he alone is a sinner."[85] Struck by conscience, he learned "sin's tender virtue," dumb shame.[86] Only the true confession of his sin let his tortured heart breathe again. Here was a lesson exemplifying all of pastoral care to those who are oppressed by their sin: "Quick, out with it, and freely confess."[87] But he first had to learn to feel, in fear of bodily death, the whole depth of the divine wrath[88] and, nevertheless, to save himself by

[81] *Ibid.*, 388:15.
[82] *The Prophet Jonah,* 1526, *WA* 19, 199:12.
[83] *Ibid.*, 199:22.
[84] *Ibid.*, 209:30.
[85] *Ibid.*, 210:11 ff.
[86] *Ibid.*, 211:1.
[87] *Ibid.*, 215:1.
[88] *Ibid.*, 217:26.

choosing the only path open to him: "Raise your hands, and quickly cry, 'Help, God my Lord!' Then you will soon feel that it gets better." Where one can still cry out and pray, hell is no longer hell.[89] His prayer showed how he slowly and laboriously mastered the art of praying, and succeeded in completely throwing off his despondent thoughts.[90] And he, whom God had finally extricated because of his faithful prayer, soon afterward again bickered with God on conferring his grace upon the city of the lawless and uncircumcised. "How can such faith and such vice stand side by side?"[91] To be sure, it was hard for him to understand God's will. "For to be a Jew and yet to preach that Judaism is unnecessary and that God's grace can be attained without it, this was as if a Jew wanted to make his own Jews worthless and unnecessary, and to elevate the pagans."[92] But in the end he nevertheless had to let himself "be mastered by God, and so return home humbled and in disgrace, yet with a sense of achievement and purpose."[93] It is wholly the story of Jonah that Luther here told and described, and wholly the story of Everyman, who through God experiences sin and death, faith and prayer, despair, grumbling, and shame. Luther combined both masterfully.

This model depiction of inner life and then the quite different description of the natural religion of the city of Nineveh and its encounter with the Word of God may be contrasted with Luther's exegesis of Zechariah in 1527, which does not yield much of an understanding of his view of the prophetic. He was continually forced into allegory by the plenitude of visions; only thus could a spiritual meaning be gained from the many details. And Zechariah himself gave enough indications about spiritual interpretation; for example, in the prophecy regarding the end of the old priesthood and the coming of a new one (Zech. 14:21).[94] The tiresome and unconnected variety of allegorical meanings precluded a view of the essense of prophecy and its exemplary image of faith. But it did serve *one* goal: to show the powerful and unified relation of the prophet to the Word and work of Christ. Zechariah was a "para-

[89] *Ibid.*, 222:12 ff.
[90] *Ibid.*, 229:19 ff.
[91] *Ibid.*, 239:30.
[92] *Ibid.*, 242:9.
[93] *Ibid.*, 243:30.
[94] *The Prophet Zechariah*, 1527, *WA* 23, 663:31.

gon" in the dual office of the prophet, a disciplinarian and a herald of Christ. He was the most illustrious of all prophets;[95] he was, therefore, "one of the most comforting prophets."[96]

Luther extracted specific *forms of prophetic proclamation* from all the prophetic books; they embraced the only message of the text: law and gospel. Prophetic prediction was seen as encompassing two things: prediction of future events and exposition of Scripture. The prophets of the Old Testament too won their reputation primarily because of their correct instruction and their leading to faith in the coming Christ. Predictions were not very frequent among them, and they often erred when they did predict, as Luther freely admitted. But they instructed daily, and never erred therein.[97] Thus Luther understood prophecy (in a New Testament sense) as proclamation rather than revelation. He observed keenly that much of what the prophet truly says of his own times could appear to be prediction, because the saints have similar experiences at all times. Thus much of what the prophets offered is not prediction but example.[98] But these examples, these truths valid for all times about man in the world and before God, constituted only one part of the prophetic proclamation. The prophets were more than teachers of a wisdom, even of a wisdom of faith they themselves had experienced. Their secret was that their proclamation was directed, often almost unnoticeably, toward a distant goal: toward Jesus Christ. A hidden tension, therefore, originated in their proclamation. It may appear as though it referred solely to their own time and their own people, and yet the souls of the people were at the same time led secretly toward the coming kingdom of Christ.

> Isaiah, therefore, says much about his people and about the existing political government, condemning sins on the one hand and praising justice on the other. And it seems as though almost the entire prophecy is directed to the people; yet, at the same time, he prepares and directs the souls of the people to Christ's future kingdom.[99]

95 *Ibid.,* 501:17 ff.; 502:15 ff.
96 *Preface to the Prophet Zechariah,* 1532 (*Vorrede auf den Propheten SacharJa*), *WA,* DB 11$^{II}$, 328:6; *LW* 35, 330.
97 *Lenten Postil,* 1525, *WA* 17$^{II}$, 38:26 ff.; 39:27 ff.
98 *Psalm 118, the Beautiful Confitemini* 1530, *WA* 31$^{I}$, 116:12; *LW* 14, 69.
99 *Lectures on Isaiah,* 1527–1530, *WA* 31$^{II}$, 2:4.

This was certainly a wonderful art, which the prophets did not possess of themselves. Only he who is taught by the Spirit may understand them. Only the Spirit could build the bridge which carried the thoughts of the prophets over to Christ. Their visions testified to their illumination through the Spirit. And glowing flames would leap out of their sayings toward him who knew how to glimpse the passions behind their words. "If anyone were able to describe every passion, he would see, in every single word, a furnace and vehement flames."[100] The external signs, which God imposed upon them, also witnessed to the fact that God's hand had reached out for them. For he is given to adding signs to his Word, like a seal to a letter. Nor were the sacraments of the new covenant basically anything else than the wooden yoke which Jeremiah wore to indicate the impending captivity [Jer. 27:12], or his purchase of land [Jer. 32:8 ff.], or the appearance of the naked Isaiah [Isa. 20:2 ff.].[101] As Luther knew from his own experiences, the Spirit also used the hours when the prophets played the zither or sang psalms. "Now and then the Spirit came when they played the zither or the psaltery, or sang some psalms and spiritual hymns."[102] "This is what Elisha confessed when he found the Spirit while playing the harp.[103]

## 3. THE OLD TESTAMENT AS A WORK OF ART

If prophetic inspiration and music could dwell so closely together for Luther, it was only one way that he saw the divine Word and the means of human artistic expression in secret, deep communion. Song and zither playing open man to receive God's Word and Spirit; and vice versa: the man grasped and moved by divine proclamation breaks out into jubilation and a wealth of speech and song, and for hours leaves his dust-bound everyday language far behind. That was why Luther did not consider it robbing God's Word at all when he observed quite clearly what artists and poets those men were who wrote the Bible. His heart opened at this,

[100] *Ibid.*, 3:12.
[101] *The Prophet Habakkuk,* 1526, *WA* 19, 390:3 ff. See also below, pp. 180–81.
[102] *Lectures on Genesis,* 1543, *WA* 44, 575:32; *LW* 7, 370.
[103] *A Preface for All Good Hymnals,* 1538 *(Vorrhede auff alle gute Gesangbücher), WA* 35, 484:9; *LW* 53, 320. See also Preuss, *Martin Luther, der Prophet,* p. 92, n. 2.

so that the seed of the Word could be received in double measure. As he liked to say, the communicative power of all the Old Testament stories and images of the external and internal world rested on the fact that they were "painted" so powerfully. Thus he himself poetically described the poetic greatness of the Old Testament —the prose as well as the poetry—a long time before Herder did.

Luther no longer made use of the categories and schemes taken from classical antiquity by the humanists in judging the poetry of the Old Testament. At most, he used them in making formal comparisons. He had no compunction about considering the Book of Job a real drama like the comedies of Terence. Job himself could not have talked like that. It must have been a sorely troubled theologian and poet, whose "vigorous and splendid" language Luther could not praise enough,[104] who took over the story and thoughts of Job, perhaps in the manner in which Virgil presented the personality of Aeneas. The author could not have been Moses, as some thought. Moses' style was simpler than the rhetoric of the Book of Job. More likely the author was Solomon or one of his contemporaries.[105] Luther took the differences in style among the Old Testament writers into consideration. Isaiah wrote more gaily and with more temperament than Jeremiah. The singer Asaph seemed to him to be very obscure; Solomon was skilful and rich in vocabulary; he had a tendency to invent new words. Luther, together with Jerome, perceived the joyful spirit of the Korah psalms. But his favorite poet was David, whose songs, compared to those of Asaph, were of an Attic delicacy; they were easy to pick out of all the others. David alone came close to the apex of Old Testament writers, namely, to the simple, magnificent style in the books of Moses.[106]

Luther repeatedly admired the apt terseness of Moses. "If you are pious, then you are pleasant; but if you are not pious, then sin crouches at the door. . . ."[107] "Cain rose up against his brother

[104] *Preface to the Book of Job,* 1545 (*Vorrede über das Buch Hiob*), *WA,* DB 10$^{I}$, 6:1 ff.; *LW* 35, 252.

[105] *Table Talk,* 1531, 1533; *WA,* TR 1, 67–68 (No. 142), 206–07 (No. 475); *LW* 54, 79–80 (No. 475).

[106] Psalm 122, *Lectures on the Fifteen Gradual Psalms,* 1532–1533, *WA* 40$^{III}$, 74:6. On Asaph and David, see also Psalm 73 in Luther's *German Bible,* 1531, *WA,* DB 3, 84:14; 87:33. On the sons of Korah, see *ibid.,* 105:6.

[107] Melanchthon made the following fitting remark at the session of the commission for the biblical revision of 1539: " 'Crouching' is just like an animal

Abel. . . ." "Should I be my brother's keeper?" (Gen. 4:7 ff.). What orator of classical antiquity could have expressed more tersely or appropriately the divine seriousness, the wild wrath against a brother, the treacherous defiance of the murderer, than these three sentences?[108]

> But what rhetorician could aptly describe what Moses expressed with one verb, that Cain "rose up" against his brother? Many denunciations of cruelty appear here and there. But how could shocking and detestable cruelty be better depicted than it is here? . . . What tragedies Cicero or Livy would have created out of these events![109]

Luther compared the art of Moses with that of the ancient artist who portrayed the father with his face covered as he sacrificed his daughter Iphigenia because such agony could not be depicted.[110] He noticed that not a single word was used to portray the sorrow of the parents in the story of Cain's fratricide. This was done purposely. Moses only aroused the imagination of the sympathetic reader; the reader must supply the imagination.

> Moses did not deal with all these matters; he merely suggested them, to stimulate the reader to reflect on this noteworthy story, which Moses presented in the smallest possible number of words, like a view through latticework.[111]

That was precisely why he did not elaborate on the brilliance and demonic greatness of the Cainite race or the Flood.[112] "Thus, although the Flood was a terrible event, Moses' description of it was very brief; for he wanted to leave it to men to ponder over events of such magnitude."[113] Luther was deeply touched by the

---

lies down. It seems to me to indicate this kind of great security. It puts itself down just like a dog does on his four paws. If you are not pious, you will lie in this manner for a little while; but [sin] will be revealed. . . . Sin is crouching, but in a dangerous place where it will be revealed. What a beautiful antithesis: horrible and clear!" See *ibid.,* 174:28.

108 *Lectures on Genesis,* 1536, *WA* 42, 206:25; 207:3; *LW* 1, 279, 280.

109 *Ibid., WA* 42, 194:30; 206:6; *LW* 1, 263, 279.

110 *Ibid., WA* 42, 206:39 ff.; *LW* 1, 279–80. Whether this reference is an addition of Veit Dietrich, as Meinhold (*op. cit.,* p. 338) assumes, can hardly be verified; it does not affect Luther's stylistic observations.

111 *Lectures on Genesis,* 1536, *WA* 42, 208:30; LW 1, 282. Luther saw something of a parental shock in Moses' taciturn hint that they obviously refrained from having more children for some time after the murder as well as after the Fall. *Table Talk,* 1542–1543, *WA,* TR 5, 199–200 (No. 5505); *LW* 54, 437–38; and *Lectures on Genesis,* 1536, *WA* 42, 239:3 ff.; 246:34; 261:18; 262:3; *LW* 1, 324, 336, 356.

112 *Lectures on Genesis,* 1536, *WA* 42, 246:15 ff.; *LW* 1, 336.

113 *Ibid., WA* 42, 246:34; *LW* 1, 335.

burdensome taciturnity of the story of Isaac's sacrifice. "'So the two of them went together.' The two were alone and wandered in solitude. The whole world did not know what was happening here. . . . Such a walk is described nowhere else in Holy Scripture."[114] Luther wondered why Moses did not allow father and son to exchange a single word at the beginning of the sacrifice, when the suspense had reached its climax. Moses was probably unable to go on writing because of his tears, and left it to the reader to imagine the conversation, which Luther then proceeded to do with a powerful witness to the victory of life over death.

> When the altar was built and the moment had arrived to go into action, he was silent; either he did not dare say anything—because the event was too great to be described with any eloquence—or he was unable to write because of his tears. And so he left wonder and amazement in the hearts of his hearers [readers]; he wished them to ponder the event themselves, since he could not reach them through words.[115]

But, on the other hand, Luther also observed that Moses often repeated his words. There must have been a reason for this. The complicated enumeration (supplemented by a pedantic glossologist)[116] of the animals Noah intended to take along in the ark (Gen. 7:2–3) caused Luther to remark that God repeatedly said the same things to Noah because he who is under spiritual stress needs comfort repeatedly.

> Reason considers this wordiness absurd, but for a heart battling desperation, nothing that gives instruction about God's will can ever seem sufficient or too much. God sees this attitude of the heart in its trial. He repeated the same words in close succession so that Noah, by that conversation and wordiness, could realize that he was not forsaken even though the entire world may have forsaken him. Rather, he had a friendly God who is kindly disposed toward him, a God who

114 *Lectures on Genesis,* 1539, *WA* 43, 215:10; *LW* 4, 111. See also the picturesque interpretation of the story in *Sermons on Genesis,* 1527, *WA* 24, 378 ff.

115 *Lectures on Genesis,* 1539, *WA* 43, 216:10; *LW* 4, 112. On Abraham's words to his son (Gen. 22:8), see the biblical revision recorded at the same time as the lectures on Genesis, *WA,* DB 3, 188:11.

116 See Hermann Gunkel, *Genesis, übersetzt und erklärt* ("Göttinger Handkommentar zum Alten Testament," I. Abteilung, 1. Band [4th ed.; Göttingen, 1917]), p. 61.

120 *Lectures on Genesis,* 1536, *WA* 42, 327:7; *LW* 2, 91.

loved him so much that he apparently could not converse enough with this pious man.[117]

In contrast to the rhetorical emotionalism of the classical authors, Moses used terse, factual repetition as part of his style to make an event seem urgent. The reader should experience his own emotions, not read them in a story. "Moses employs few words; but he repeats them several times so that the reader, thus reminded, may himself ponder the significance of the event and experience real emotions instead of merely reading about those of others."[118] Then he will be able to appreciate more realistically the feelings of the person who is portrayed. Luther, to be sure, admitted that much in the Old Testament is described so broadly and repeated so often that it could produce boredom. But it is nevertheless God's Word, which should be a joy for us to hear reverently no matter how often it says the same thing.

It is certainly an extensive and wordy exhortation. Here, just as elsewhere, he often repeats the same thing. If an ordinary reader who does not understand what it is about were present, he could not help being offended. It is for us to restrain the feeling of boredom, for we know that it is the Word of God we hear. To hear God is joy, even if he were to sound out the same syllable all the time; how much more so when he speaks such a variety of things and with such care! Therefore we must, with trembling, pay attention not only to the words, but most especially to the person of the speaker, namely, God.[119]

The Holy Spirit is not an empty chatterbox as those smug people think who read the Bible once or twice and then put it aside, claiming they could learn nothing more from it.[120]

But Luther would not have been the master of his own language if the task of interpreting and translating had not opened his eyes to the linguistic peculiarities and fine points of Hebrew. It is possible to give a comprehensive and satisfactory impression of this awareness only within the framework of a thorough examination of Luther's whole academic lifelong work as an Old Testament scholar. A few examples must suffice at this point. Luther

117 *Lectures on Genesis,* 1536, *WA* 42, 324:37 ff.; *LW* 2, 88.
118 *Ibid., WA* 42, 326:35; 330:19; *LW* 2, 91.
119 *The Deuteronomy of Moses, with Notes,* 1525, *WA* 14, 581:21 ff.; *LW* 9, 48.

observed a large number of Hebraisms in all his interpretations, for example, parallelism as an artifice of Hebrew poetry.[121] He made an effort to understand metaphorical terms, for example, "light" as an expression for happiness.[122] He took into consideration the use of abstract concepts instead of persons, for example, "imprisonment" instead of "prisoners,"[123] and, vice versa, the use of concrete things as symbols for abstract situations, for example, "whip" for political rule.[124] He saw the tendency of Hebrew to suggest the whole by reference to a part: "wall" for "house"; "soul" for "human being"; "to stand in the house of the Lord at night" for "to pray incessantly."[125] By using "soul" for "man" Hebrew attains a further intensification of expression. "My soul waits" intensifies and deepens the first half of verse 5 in Psalm 130.[126] It becomes clear from even this much that Luther regarded these similar expressions not as empty tautology but as intensification of impression. This, among other things, gave him the opportunity to glean objective distinctions from this passage when it was applied to the promise of Christ or to the individual's life of faith, according to Luther the "real" meaning of the Old Testament. For example, he understood "the yoke of their burden / and the rod of their shoulder / and the staff of their oppressor" in Isa. 9:4 to be the three great tyrants, Law, Sin, and Death.[127] But naturally he also knew the wordy convolution which the Hebrew language can have. "We found it in the field of the forest."[128] "Indeed, it is the intention of such a language to be as rich as possible in words as well as in sentences."[129] Many images of the Hebrew language,

[121] Ps. 127:3, *Exposition of Psalm 127, for the Christians at Riga in Livonia,* 1524 *(Der hundert und Sieben und zwentzigst psalm ausgelegt an die christen zu Rigen ynn Liffland), WA* 15, 375:3; *LW* 45, 333. See also Ps. 132:5, *Lectures on the Fifteen Gradual Psalms,* 1532–1533, *WA* 40$^{III}$, 398:3.

[122] Amos 8:8 ff., *Lectures on the Minor Prophets,* 1524–1525, *WA* 13, 152:11. Or he interpets the Hebrew *tamerurim* (*amaritudines* in the Vulgate) as "disobedience, rebellion" in the same lectures of 1524–1525 (*WA* 13, 60); the later biblical revision of 1539 renders it as "bitter idols," *WA,* DB 4, 224:7.

[123] Amos 1:6, *galut* in Hebrew (*captivitas* in the Vulgate), *Lectures on the Minor Prophets,* 1524–1525, *WA* 13, 128:1.

[124] Ps. 125:3, *shebet* in Hebrew (*virga* in the Vulgate), *Lectures on the Fifteen Gradual Psalms,* 1532–1533, *WA* 40$^{III}$, 166:9.

[125] Ps. 122:7, *ibid.,* 114:3; Ps. 120:2, Ps. 134:1, *ibid.,* 28:4; 472:6.

[126] *Ibid.,* 362:10.

[127] *Lectures on Isaiah,* 1527–1530, *WA* 31$^{II}$, 69:3 ff.

[128] Ps. 132:6, *Lectures on the Fifteen Gradual Psalms,* 1532–1533, *WA* 40$^{III}$, 402:4.

[129] *The Deuteronomy of Moses, with Notes,* 1525, *WA* 14, 606:33. See also Holl, "Luthers Bedeutung für den Fortschritt der Auslegekunst," in *op. cit.,* I, 571.

rich in distorted words and parables, seemed to him even stranger than these linguistic peculiarities.[130] Luther, with his great imagination, experienced the particularity and frequent strangeness of these Hebrew images countless times. Again, only a few examples: the "horn" as a symbol for strength and rule;[131] "to deal at the gate" as a designation for political negotiation;[132] the varied symbolic uses of "light," of which Luther collected a wealth of proof passages;[133] "to sprinkle" for cleansing or blessing.[134] Luther was frequently so taken with the vividness of the Old Testament images that he elaborated on them with wide variations and thus further marvelously disclosed their sense, sometimes even surpassing them. For example, one may read his descriptions of the Babylonian king: the fisherman who catches country after country in his nets (Hab. 1:15); the drunkard who, insatiable as death, drinks himself full with countries and peoples (Hab. 2:5); and the one who makes many others drunk with pain and misfortune (Hab. 2:15).[135] Luther occasionally stated openly that there was much about Old Testament images that was repulsive. Yet, this was not intended as a criticism of Holy Scripture. If Luther considered the images in Psalm 133 barbaric—the precious ointment which flows from Aaron's head into his beard and clothes, and the dew that flows from Hermon onto the mountains of Zion—it was not a criticism; it was, rather, the acknowledgment that they are truly Hebraic and strange to other peoples. Luther did not find fault with Scripture for reasons of taste; rather, he accepted the "barbarism" of the Holy Spirit and adhered to the sense of these parables.

Although this psalm is brief, it is straightforward and clear in content and meaning, with the exception of two barbaric or rather Hebraic and holy images which reflect conditions unknown to the Gentiles and so sound barbaric and absurd. On the other hand, the words of the Gentiles also sound barbaric to the Holy Spirit and the Holy Spirit sounds barbaric to the Gentiles. But I side with the Holy Spirit, who called the Egyptians "a barbaric people." . . . It is the barbarity

130 *The Prophet Habakkuk,* 1526, *WA* 19, 416:28.
131 Ps. 132:17, *Lectures on the Fifteen Gradual Psalms,* 1532–1533, *WA* 40III, 453:15.
132 Ps. 127:5, *ibid.,* 265:11.
133 Ps. 132:17, *ibid.,* 454:2 ff.
134 Isa. 52:15, *Lecture on Isaiah 53,* 1546, *WA* 40III, 697:27.
135 *The Prophet Habakkuk,* 1526, *WA* 19, 382:24 ff.; 397:5 ff.; 416:27 ff.; 418:8.

of the Holy Spirit, who speaks in this manner. He is barbaric to us and we are barbaric to him. Such was not the case among the Gentiles; that is why language and imagery are not very tender.[136]

Whenever it was possible to do so without damage, Luther eliminated such strange images in his translations of the Bible to make the text understandable to the German mind. Thus in his extensive Psalter revision of 1531 he changed his earlier literal translation of Ps. 63:5, "Let my soul fill up as with lard and fat," into, "That would be my heart's joy and ecstasy."[137]

It seemed quite natural to him that much of the Hebrew language and poetry should sound strange to us; it would surely have been the same the other way around. He thought that Habakkuk's book of consolation for the Jews consisted of "very crooked words, which are unusual to us Germans. But, we must get used to Hebrew poems. For if they should hear our songs, they should consider them as strange as their songs seem to us."[138]

He very easily made the Old Testament songs his own, particularly the psalms. In them, words and music had been melted into a unity. That was why they must have been the most effective of all the writings; the highest art, given to us against melancholy and spiritual stress *(Anfechtung),* was added therein to the sweet consolation of God's Word.

[David] [II Sam. 23:1] does not only mean the charm and sweetness of the psalms in grammar and music, because the words are arranged with delicacy and with art and the music sounds sweet and charming. This is usually called a beautiful text and beautiful music. He also means the charm and sweetness of the psalms in their theology, their spiritual understanding. Here, too, the psalms are charming and sweet, for they comfort all troubled and miserable consciences caught in the fear of sin, in the pain of death, in anxiety and in all kinds of misery and despair. To such hearts the Psalter is a sweet, comforting, and charming song because it praises and proclaims the Messiah, even

[136] *Lectures on the Fifteen Gradual Psalms,* 1532–1533, *WA* 40$^{III}$, 459:2 ff.; 463:8 ff. See also Holl, "Luthers Bedeutung für den Fortschritt der Auslegekunst," *op. cit.,* I, 570. These motifs emerge more strongly in the later edited copy of Luther's lecture on the psalm—Holl had not yet any access to it—than in the printed version, especially the equal evaluation of the two images, a fact which should be noted in regard to the understanding of the judgment "barbaric."

[137] *Defense of the Translation of the Psalms,* 1531–1533 *(Summarien über die Psalmen und ursachen des dolmetschens), WA* 38, 10:21 ff.; *LW* 35, 212.

[138] *The Prophet Habakkuk,* 1526, *WA* 19, 435:11.

> though it is the custom to read or to say only the words without the notes. But the music or the notes, a wonderful creation and gift of God, assist [the words] very well, especially when the whole crowd joins in the singing, and it is done properly. [Elisha and David made themselves happy by playing the harp, II Kings 3:15; I Sam. 16:17 ff.]. For the evil spirit does not feel well when the Word of God is sung or preached in true faith. He is a spirit of sadness and is unable to remain where there is a spiritual and joyful heart (that is, in God and in his Word).[139]

When Luther rewrote and arranged music for some of the psalms, he only re-established the effect which originally had been intended. But even when the psalms could only be read, they still moved Luther's heart because he sensed the musical rhythm in them. He felt the strange sobbing note in David's dirge for Absalom (II Sam. 18:33). "The structure of this song represents nothing but the passion of mourning. Its syncopation discloses sobbing."[140] But never does the sound or rhythm of the psalms work by itself; instead, it serves the truth which the psalm is intended to proclaim. Depending on the content, the language of the psalm sounds as consoling as a mother, heartrending and despairing, bold and believing, or threatening and eerie. This is how the psalms describe God's speaking with men. The power of divine speech was most marvelously heard and deeply experienced by Luther in Ps. 29:7: "The voice of the Lord flashes forth flames of fire." God speaks "carved, like stonemasons carve. . . . He breaks through like fire. . . . The voice of the Lord is like a stonemason and his chisel like flames of fire."

> "Flames." Break through like flames of fire; carved like stonemasons carve. He moves through flames, he speaks through flames. He wants to show his efficacy: he breaks through like fire. He moves in a single form with beauty and he exhibits his efficacy as if it were a burning instrument, a hammer, etc. The voice of the Lord lashes out with a fiery tongue; fire does not joke when it approaches a gate. The voice of the Lord is like a stonemason; it is harassing like a great flame.[141]

But Luther did not just take into account particular items of style or language in the Old Testament and set them against other

[139] *On the Last Words of David,* 1543, *WA* 54, 33:30 ff.
[140] *Table Talk,* 1532, *WA,* TR 2, 53 (No. 1333). See also Holl, "Luthers Bedeutung für den Fortschritt der Auslegekunst," in *op. cit.,* I, 571.
[141] Recorded biblical revision of Ps. 29:7, *WA,* DB 3, 20:19. Quoted in Hans Preuss, *Luther der Künstler* (Gütersloh, 1931), p. 216.

literature of classical antiquity. There are also Hebraic modes of expression that indicate an otherwise unknown *situation.* The most important example: no other people saw the Word of God as the means by which he created. He speaks and it happens. Nowhere else is this imperious speaking of God felt so powerfully and the unity of Word and deed in God so well recognized. Such a view could only have originated in the mind of a great poet. Even the prophets did not have it of themselves, but copied it from Moses, this "Virgil-like poet." Luther expressed his admiration for both with this comparison.

> Eloquence reigns, etc., and all goes well. If the Turk comes, then it is the Word, that is, the deed, of God. Now this is a Hebraic way of speaking, something the entire world does not understand. Such a manner of speech originates with Moses: "in the beginning," "let there be light," "stars," etc. All the prophets learned how to speak and how to use "by the Word of God," etc., from this Virgil-like poet. Christ spoke like a man and like us, but it was the Word and deed of majesty.[142]

[142] Ps. 2:5, *Lecture on Psalm 2,* 1532, *WA* $40^{II}$, 231:1.

# 3

# THE GOD OF THE OLD TESTAMENT

When Luther's mighty spirit encountered the vast riches of life in the Old Testament a many-sided picture of life developed. His inexhaustible imagination multiplied the riches he found. Yet, the Old Testament would have been but one formative element in Luther's life, just as it had been for many poets and painters, were it not for the fact that every word and phrase of the Old Testament bears testimony to the one God, *his* God. There are two observable characteristics of this description of God which distinguish the encounter with God in the Old Testament from the portrayal of God typical of the New Testament. Two areas of thought are involved: God and the gods and God and the world. Only when we have observed what is peculiar to these two realms can we approach the main area of Luther's interest in the Old Testament, the unity of the Word of God in both testaments.

## 1. GOD AND THE GODS

Luther's knowledge of non-Christian religions rested upon three sources: antiquity, Islam, and those features of pagan religion polemically described in the Bible. He was too far removed from Islam both in space and time to have a genuine picture of the life and nature of this religion, although he did know something about it. As for the ancient world, he knew some of its individual features, but not the vitality which is only vaguely revealed by the struggle of biblical faith against pagan piety. For he read the Bible with reference to contemporary questions and debates and not just as a historical document. Whatever significant traits of pagan antiquity he found in the Bible, he was much more interested in its wrestling with an alien faith. Moreover, he received a more comprehensive view of idolatry within and outside of Israel from the struggles against paganism in the books of law and in the prophetic writings than in the very short, general references to idolatry in the New Testament. It is only recent study of Hellenistic Near Eastern religions which has disclosed the meaning of New Testament references to them. Luther was not able to share this knowledge. Therefore, it was the world of the Old Testament which contributed significantly to his judgment of non-Christian religions and to his observations on paganism.[1]

Luther did not study paganism in the Old Testament from the viewpoint of the history of religions or the psychology of religions; he studied it in a more vital way, which also gave him more fundamental and more significant insights. He began his search for understanding from the viewpoint of faith. He always approached the questions where they concerned him and us. He observed four essential traits of the living power of true paganism, which his sensitive ear caught especially from the prophet's descriptions.

a) He recognized the unity within the complex and varied forms of polytheism. He did not do this for the purpose of seeking a unified, abstract idea of God or a universal religious need of man contained in all religions, animism, the worship of demons, the fertility cults, etc. More accurately, he completely penetrated the visible form of idol worship, which he showed to be a mirage, and he discovered behind it the hidden unity of all cults, *the idolization of man's own power.* "Even if you name God with your mouths and with your hands sacrifice and burn incense, it means only, in the depth of your hearts, that you think highly of yourselves and are pleased with yourselves, that you are able to do these things and think you are worthy of, and entitled to, merit."[2] Thus Luther genially translated the lamentation of Habakkuk into

[1] Here I have to limit myself to the contribution which the Old Testament view of paganism makes to an understanding of these questions. On the entire problem, see especially Herbert Vossberg, *Luthers Kritik aller Religion. Eine theologie-geschichtliche Untersuchung zu einem systematischen Hauptproblem* (Leipzig, 1922), and Holsten, *Christentum und nichtchristliche Religion nach der Auffassung Luthers.* However, I do not find an equal emphasis in both books upon those characteristics which, in my opinion, seem to be most significant for an understanding of what Luther learned from the Old Testament about pagan religion.

[2] *The Prophet Habakkuk,* 1526, *WA* 19, 384:14.

his own language. The prophet saw, with fear and trembling, how God awakened the Chaldean and let him snatch everything to himself, with his fishhooks and nets, his armies. "Therefore he sacrificed to his net and burned incense to his seine; for by them he lived in luxury, and his food was rich" (Hab. 1:16). The thank offerings men brought to the gods were praises to their own greatness. That is why reliance on one's own power and strength only seems to be different from idol worship.[3] The sacrifice only points to the sacrificer himself. This was how Luther uncovered the hidden background of idol worship and thus unmasked the secret idolatry of all times, which is always the same. "For he who boasts of something and is gay and happy about it . . . but does not thank the true God . . . makes an idol of himself, gives himself the honor, does not rejoice in God but in his own strength and work."[4] Luther thereby intensified his frequently repeated thought (especially expressed in the famous passage of the *Large Catechism*) that only the trust and faith of the heart make both God and idol.[5] Man's idol is not only that on which he relies; rather, he is again and again his own idol through the medium of all these idols' masks.

> For that which one cherishes, that on which one relies—that is one's God, because one should rely on no one but God alone, and cherish nothing but God. But the godless must console themselves with their own works and power, this is their God—they cannot do otherwise.[6]

Israel's false belief in election which relied on itself and which Luther found attacked in Deut. 7:7 ("It was not because you were more in number than any other people that the Lord set his love upon you and elected you")[7] is exactly the same kind of idol wor-

[3] Luther's observation is also important for an evaluation of the late forms of Germanic religiosity—now so frequently discussed, namely, the reliance upon one's own power and strength *(matt ok megin)*—in its structural relation to the polytheism which preceded it, and to their common opposition, despite all differences, to the Christian faith. See Hanns Rückert, *Die Christianisierung der Germanen; ein Beitrag zu ihrem Verständnis und ihrer Beurteilung* (rev. ed.; Tübingen, 1934), p. 17, and Walter Baetke, *Die Religion der Germanen in Quellenzeugnissen* (Frankfurt-am-Main, 1937), pp. 96 ff.

[4] *The Prophet Habakkuk,* 1526, *WA* 19, 384:10.

[5] *The Large Catechism (Deudsch Catechismus),* 1529, *WA* 30$^{I}$, 133:4; Theodore G. Tappert (ed.), *The Book of Concord* (Philadelphia: Fortress Press, 1959), p. 365.

[6] *The Prophet Habakkuk,* 1526, *WA* 19, 384:24.

[7] *Sermon of October 31, 1529, on Deut. 7:4 ff., Sermons on Deuteronomy, WA* 28, 679–80.

ship. Luther thus systematically reduced all idol worship—the proud self-reliance of the godless man and the false Jewish consciousness of election—to one common denominator and to one united front against the First Commandment. It was the front of natural man in all his disguises. This idolatry was basically nothing but the idol worship of the past.

b) Since the existence of the pagan gods not only presented Luther with a problem in the context of the history of religion but also in the quest for the reality of God, he was forced to expand his thinking on the subject. Whence do these idols, these "nothings" *(Nichtse)* of stone, wood, or iron get their enthralling power over man? Whereas modern philosophy of religion meagerly covers its perplexity on this question with animistic or magical pseudo interpretations, or resorts to threadbare psychological suggestion theories, Luther gave a very compact and courageous answer: *God's name is also hidden in the idols.* If idols have often revenged themselves upon mockers and desecraters, they have not done so without the will of the real, omnipotent God. "So jealously does God protect his name that he does not even allow it to be mocked by the idols."[8] Whoever mocks an idol also blasphemes the name of God hidden in every idol. The audacity of this answer is clear when it is compared to the essentially contradictory answer presented by early Christian apologetics to the same question: the accomplishments of the idols are due to the machinations of the demons.[9]

Luther found a reason for such thoughts in Hab. 2:8, where the king of Babylon was threatened with retribution for desecration, "that is, using force and injustice against divine and holy things,"[10] which he committed against Judah and Jerusalem. Luther thus expanded the concept of God's promised protection of his own sanctuary to include the sphere of the holy as such. "The histories also write that usually all desecration of holy things is immediately avenged."[11] And he added examples from ancient and modern times, of the revenge of idols and saints such as St. Anthony,

[8] *The Prophet Habakkuk,* 1526, *WA* 19, 404:16–17.
[9] Athenagoras (*ca.* 177), *A Plea for the Christians,* 23–27, *ANF* 2, 140 ff.; and *The Octavius of Minucius Felix* (*ca.* 210), 26, 27, *ANF* 4, 189–90.
[10] *The Prophet Habakkuk,* 1526, *WA* 19, 404:1.
[11] *Ibid.,* 404:6.

St. Valentine, and others. But one must at the same time carefully note that Luther did not develop a magical view of a saint surrounded by a protective aura, which could have appealed to a sixteenth-century man; nor did he fall into a modern psychological explanation of the effects of the holy upon the human psyche. On the contrary, even when he here spoke of the revenge that awaited desecraters of holy things, Luther held on to his functional concept of the holy. "For whatever one considers holy, even though it is not holy in itself, is holy to him who considers it such. For he takes God's name, which alone is holy, and misuses it, blasphemes against it, and desecrates it."[12] The holy receives its seriousness because it is born out of "trust and faith." Seen from God's viewpoint, the same situation means that God has lent his name to the gods and to the sanctuaries. He who blasphemes and mocks that which he has worshiped as God, even if it were a crass idol, blasphemes against the holy God himself.

Luther had no compunctions at all in applying his general conviction that God's name is hidden in the idols to particular idols in a concrete way. Thus he was convinced that the Moabites prayed to the real God under a false name *(Baal Peor)* and a false cult, as did the Israelites who worshiped Baal. "Hence, I believe that the true God was honored under this lying name and false worship by the Moabites; and by the children of Israel he was called *Baalim,* as the prophet Hosea testifies [Hos. 2:8]."[13] Luther did not realize that with such an understanding of idols he far surpassed the thinking of the Old Testament prophets, who rejected

[12] *Ibid.,* 405:2.

[13] *The Deuteronomy of Moses, with Notes,* 1525, *WA* 14, 589:22; *LW* 9, 55. It is probably this basic idea, developed here by Luther—that the name of God is contained in the idols—which is responsible for the somewhat different interpretation of the *Baal Peor* here compared with the one proposed earlier in *Against the Spiritual Estate of the Pope and the Bishops, Falsely So Called,* 1522 (*Wider den falsch genantte geystlichen stand des Bapst un den bischoffen*), *WA* 10II, 118:25 ff.; 121:1; 122:9. Luther did not change the translation of *Baal Peor,* "a man with his mouth open" (*vir hiatus, WA* 14, 589:22; *LW* 9, 55). Yet whereas he had described him earlier as an "unchaste gaper" (*unkeuscher mäulaffen, WA* 10II, 122:9)—interpreting him allegorically as spiritual unchastity and seduction of souls—he now suspected the "chief maw" (*primarius hiatus, WA* 14, 589:28; *LW* 9, 55) to be the god of revenge who will swallow the enemies of the people dedicated to him. See also *WA* 14, 761, and *LW* 9, 53. One can see how Luther rejected the allegorical method even with regard to details, and how he was willing to be led to clearer, more convincing explanations within the context of his growing theological insight. This is hermeneutically noteworthy, even though Luther missed the actual meaning. *Peor* is the name of a place (kind information from Albrecht Alt).

them as mere products of a corrupted imagination, who denied in them any reality at all, even the hidden meaning Luther envisioned in them. Nor could he have noticed it. His discernment of the reality of the divine name in the idols did not of course negate the prophets' conviction that idol worship was robbing God of the honor due him. Nevertheless, to Luther it was truly an actual robbery. The pagans had robbed God of his name. The godlessness of the pagans, of the idolatrous Jews, or of the papists was their acceptance of the true name of the true God and their dishonoring of him with rites not commanded by God but which they invented themselves.

> The Moabites and other nations did not worship demons because they knew that they were demons; they believed that they were serving the true God no less than do the idolatrous Jews, yes, all our papists, even the holiest and most religious. But their godlessness consisted in that they took over the true name of God and worshiped him with ceremonies not commanded by God but devised by themselves. . . . And so with their false imagination they indeed worship idols and demons in the name of the true God.[14]

Luther explained quite clearly that one should not think that the pagans deny the name of the true God; on the contrary, they passionately lay claim to it. He used the testimony of the prophets to substantiate this. And yet, because God's Word is missing in their cult, Satan rules among them under God's name and in his stead.

> Therefore, where there is no Word of God, there is no true knowledge of God; where there is no knowledge of God, there are godless ignorance, imagination, and opinions about the true God, which we choose strictly for ourselves, as though he were pleased by this. . . . For by all these ceremonies and teachings we think we please God, an opinion which is a deceitful idol of the heart, where, in the place and name of God, Satan sits and is worshiped.[15]

[14] *The Deuteronomy of Moses, with Notes,* 1525, *WA* 14, 587:19; 586:6; *LW* 9, 53. Thus it is incorrect to distinguish—as does Holsten (*op. cit.,* pp. 74–75)—between the Israelite folk religion, which was only infected by paganism, and true paganism. Both contain the same deceived knowledge about the name of God. Moreover, one should use Luther's lectures on Isaiah according to the copy of Lauterbach (*WA* 31^II^) and not according to the *scholia* of 1532–1534 (*WA* 25), as Holsten does. Otherwise much of the wealth of the lectures is lost.

[15] *The Deuteronomy of Moses, with Notes,* 1525, *WA* 14, 588:14, 23; *LW* 9, 53, 54.

The gods live by the name of God. This was, to Luther, the basic reality or, to speak with Hegel, the objective moment in religion.[16] The realization of these interrelations was never more strongly impressed upon Luther, as far as I can see, than in the battle of the prophets against the idols, even though and because for them the question of blasphemy was posed in exactly the opposite way. The prophets may mock as they do, for they practice their mockery in the name of God. They alone have a right to do so, although it would be blasphemy against the holy name of God as such for an unbelieving mocker to do so.

c) The name borrowed from the true God is the *content of truth in natural religion.* Natural religion is the foundation of all idol cults painted over with superstition and human lust.[17] For the relationship of God to the gods must correspond to its subjective appropriation by men. The veneration of the divine name belongs to the essence of man. True, there is only *one* "God by nature," as Luther said in agreement with Gal. 4:8, only *one* living God. The gods are products of human madness.

Paul indicates plainly that the term "God" is used in a twofold sense: of him who is God by nature, that is, the true, one, living, and eternal God; and of many other gods who are false and dead—that is, men, beasts, and birds. As we read in Romans 1 [:23], "and exchanged the glory of the immortal God for images resembling mortal man or birds or animals or reptiles." These, then, are gods, not by nature but in the opinion and mistaken notion of men who, contrary to the Second Commandment, assigned it to them, just as now, too, the name of the Lord renders service to countless superstitions. For since his name is holy and terrible and men are most powerfully swayed by the terror it inspires, it cannot be used as a pretext for any iniquities and deceptions whatever except with most harmful consequences. There is implanted in man, by nature, a veneration for the divine name; but it is very difficult to know when it is called upon in truth.[18]

But these idols live by his name, and the veneration of his name is the truth of natural religion. Thus truth and error are intimately

[16] See Walter Baetke, "Das objektive Moment in der germanischen Religion," *Zeitschrift für Theologie und Kirche,* Neue Folge, XVII (1936), 353 ff.

[17] Luther basically discovered this connection in pagan religion between the natural knowledge of God and the idols as images of human dreams in his lectures on Romans (1:20). *Lectures on Romans,* 1515–1516, *WA* 56, 176:26 ff.; *LCC* 15, 23; and below p. 56, n. 34.

[18] *Lectures on Galatians,* 1519 (*In Epistolam Pauli ad Galatas Commentarius*), *WA* 2, 537:22 ff.; *LW* 27, 291–92.

linked with each other, and only the power of the divine Word can separate the two. Luther expressed this interweaving relationship with masterly brevity when he called paganism "an opinion or false knowledge fabricated about the true God" *("opinio seu conscientia erronea de Deo vero ficta")*. Erring conscience thinks it has found the true God and yet it cannot find him without the light of the Word. Everything depends upon the true conscience; "for as the conscience is, so is God." He who in his conscience believes himself duty-bound to cowl and tonsure wears them in his heart as his God, and externally as idols with which he seduces others.

> We have often said and say again that strange gods are not only an external idol but much more an erring notion or conscience devised about the true God. For as the conscience is, so is God. If you believe that God is worshiped by a sacrifice of this or that kind, in this or that place, and that without a Word of God, then you have already lost the true God; and that notion concerning sacrifice to which you cling, under the name of the true God, is your God. If you believe that God is worshiped through cowl and tonsure, poverty, obedience, fasting, food, or drink (since here you do not have a Word of God), the cowl and tonsure is your God. Therefore, just as you have an inner assumption about the cowl in the place of God, so you extend this outwardly and erect, wear, honor, worship, and value the cowl as an external idol conforming to the likeness of the inner notion.[19]

Luther's fundamental understanding repeatedly broke through everywhere with great clarity, that paganism is not a phenomenon of the history of religion which can be separated from true religion by visible boundaries, but is an essential possibility of man. The veneration of God rooted in nature and the erring conscience are insolubly linked to it.

Luther gave as an example of this twofold aspect of pagan worship the ancient faith in Fortune, in which true perceptions can be contained in a hidden manner. The ancients knew that in case of war one should not depend solely upon the just cause or upon other human advantages. Instead, they sensed in the work of Fortune something of the boundless omnipotence of God, who

[19] *The Deuteronomy of Moses, with Notes,* 1525, *WA* 14, 648:13 ff.; *LW* 9, 130–31. See also Luther's *Table Talk* about idolatry, collected by Aurifaber, *WA,* TR 6, 56 ff. (Nos. 6584 ff.).

demands the complete and unconditional trust of man.[20] And yet the pagans' invocation of Fortune shows that they had no knowledge of God at all. They had the matter in hand but knew it not.

> Erudite theologians are those who not only have the matter in hand, like the pagans, but who also have understood the matter. Solomon says, "But the victory belongs to the Lord" (Prov. 21:31). The pagans accept the matter, but they know it not; they ascribe it to Fortune.[21]

This was how Luther explained Potiphar's testimony of God (Gen. 39:3).

> Here you see that there was not too much blindness in Egypt for God to be known in the same manner as before. And yet strong idolatry was committed there against the majesty of God's name . . . (just as is done today in the monastic orders). The idols testify that the pagans wanted to know God; but the pagans erred because everyone projected him for himself in some way or other, as he pleased. God's name was certainly present among the pagans, as long as it was invoked.[22]

That was why the boundaries between true worship of God and idolatry were constantly being crossed among peoples. "Under Moses there was also idolatry among the people," notes a Lower Saxon listener or copyist of Luther's lecture on Amos 5:26. "There was idolatry among the people under Moses, as Stephen testifies in Acts 7 [:42–43] on the basis of Amos 5 [:25 ff.]; they carried the God Rephan with them in the desert and the God Baal into the field of Moab. Thus secret idolatry always existed."[23] In reference to Jer. 2:11, Luther even drew from the prophet's complaint of the people's apostasy the premise, a false one from the viewpoint of the history of religion, "no people changes its God."[24] Only that people to whom God has given his revelation through the law betrays its Lord. On the other hand, the pagan sailors with whom Jonah sailed offered Luther an opportunity to give a short

[20] *Whether Soldiers, Too, Can Be Saved,* 1526 (*Ob kriegsleutte auch ynn seligem stande seyn künden), WA* 19, 650–51; *LW* 46, 124.
[21] Psalm 124, *Lectures on the Fifteen Gradual Psalms,* 1532–1533, *WA* 40$^{III}$, 137:14.
[22] *Sermons on Genesis,* 1523–1524, *WA* 14, 475:6 ff. This idea is obscured in the German revision of 1527 (*WA* 24, 640:10 ff.). In the lectures on Genesis of 1544 the passage is only explained as a Mosaic figure of speech (*WA* 44, 345:1). The degree of de-emphasis indicates how little understood was Luther's magnificent view by the editors of his lectures.
[23] *Lectures on the Minor Prophets. The Prophet Amos,* 1524–1525, *WA* 13, 143, n. 3. See also *ibid.,* 144:4 ff.
[24] *Lectures on the Minor Prophets. The Prophet Hosea, ibid.,* 41:24.

summary of natural religion. That God is a helper in all needs is "such a light and understanding in all men's hearts that it cannot be dimmed or extinguished."[25] He who denies this is refuted by his own conscience. But this great natural light of reason, "which regards God as good, gracious, merciful, and mild," lacks the knowledge that 1) God wants to help reason itself: "It knows and believes power, but doubts will, for it feels the contradiction in misfortune";[26] and 2) reason does not know who this God is. "That is why there is a great difference between knowing there is a God and knowing what or who God is. Nature knows the first, because it is written in all hearts. The latter is taught solely by the Holy Spirit."[27] Thus Jonah's sailors knew of God, although in their need they invoked the gods—each his own (Jonah 1:5). The city of Nineveh must have known and believed in the true God and creator of heaven and earth in the same way. And if one sees how quickly it repented, one would think "that sheer saints were in the city."[28] To be sure, it is called "a city of God" (Jonah 3:1–5), not because of its faith but because God had mercy on it and sent a prophet to it.[29]

Luther even made a variety of observations regarding the essence of God on the basis of this inner unity of religions, and on the basis of the natural religion which is secretly contained in them but is distorted into idolatry without knowledge of the true God. "A God," as he liked to say abstractly, "must be great in giving." The greater he is in giving, the greater is his honor and glory.[30] God's nature is based on giving.[31] "To have one's own

[25] *The Prophet Jonah,* 1526, *WA* 19, 205:35.
[26] *Ibid.,* 206:17.
[27] *Ibid.,* 207:11.
[28] *Ibid.,* 233:27 ff.; 234:29 ff.
[29] So also *Psalm 82,* 1530, *WA* 31<sup>I</sup>, 193:27; *LW* 13, 46.
[30] *Sermon of October 1, 1525, on Eph. 3:14 ff., Sermons of 1525, WA* 17<sup>I</sup>, 432:16.
[31] That this is the basis for Luther's doctrine of justification and of the rejection of all self-righteousness and works-righteousness is shown in the fine essay of Paul Althaus, "Gottes Gottheit als Sinn der Rechtfertigungslehre Luthers" (*Lutherjahrbuch,* XIII [1931]). This essay, to be sure, and also his second, more general treatment of the theme ("Gottes Gottheit bei Luther," *Lutherjahrbuch,* XVII [1935], 1 ff.) should be supplemented by a reference to this abstract character of God's divinity. This character, however, should not be understood as being isolated from the viewpoint of the philosophy of religion. The presupposed concept of God, from which Luther thought to gain the "divineness" (*das Gotthafte*) in a purely analytical way, stems from the observation of the historical reality of religion—not only from the words of Scripture, since Luther was free enough to combine his biblical view with a view of pagan gods, too.

people is part of being a true God."[32] This was the way Luther, in plain terms, formulated another insight he gained from the "owned people" of the Old Testament, as well as from national gods about whom he received much information in the Old Testament. He encountered this "property" relationship between God and people much more richly and more meaningfully in the Old Testament. It undoubtedly incited him to unfold the concept of God's people in a wonderful way, and to set the church born out of God's Word as the center and goal of history over against the covenant people and polytheistic nations.[33]

d) Luther was faced with the particularly tortuous problem of *how to distinguish real worship of God from false,* in the interweaving relationship of paganism with natural religion, of idols with the name of God, which is honored in them as much as it is misused. It is not just difference in content—which, of course, simply cannot be separated from Jesus Christ as the revelation and meaning of Scripture per se—which is at stake here, but our first concern is a phenomenological outline which has to be discovered empirically. We shall restrict ourselves to the thesis that a God must have his own people, or we could say that the people of God is unconditionally dedicated to its revealed God, who in turn is bound to his national sanctuary. A true people of God knows who its God is, where and how he is worshiped. It remains loyal to him, even if he appears weak and helpless to the world. "It is something great to know a particular God." It certainly is not enough to know only of the necessity of worshiping a God. Then one could easily exchange one's own God for another who seems to be stronger. It is prophetic faith to trust and to defy one's own apparently very weak God at the moment of such temptation. When the Assyrian messengers delivered Sennacherib's arrogant advice to King Hezekiah not to depend upon his own God and expect him to rescue Jerusalem, Hezekiah was able to pray in the spirit of the prophets, "Lord Sabaoth, God of Israel, who sits above cherubim, you alone are God over all kingdoms" (Isa. 37:16).

32 *Sermon on Christmas Day on John 1:1 ff., Church Postil,* 1522, *WA* $10^{I,1}$, 226:22.

33 Especially in Part III of *On the Councils and the Church,* 1539 *(Von den Conciliis und Kirchen), WA* 50, 624 ff.; *LW* 41, 143 ff. See also Pahls, *Luthers Auffassung von Staat und Volk,* pp. 109 ff.

It is certainly great to know God. For all idolatry has a God, saying, "God must be worshiped." But it errs in minor things, namely, that it creates many gods. Augustine and Francis made the cult itself a God. This cult is offered in the name of the true God, thus reason is deceived in the divine cult, just as the wisest pagans are deceived. The true God is he whose cult was divinely instituted above the cherubim in Israel. That was why this king was faithful, although his God seemed weak and confined, seated above the cherubim in a political community. The God of the Assyrians seemed strong and powerful. Yet this king was not ashamed of the infirmity of his God; he was not offended by the ridiculous situation of his God. He was not confounded by the Assyrian might. Instead, he said, "You are the only true God, I appeal to you who are sitting above the cherubim. . . ." True cult demanded that he remain faithful to his small and weak God, close to the Word, to his religion and to the place constituted by God. In the same manner, it is foolish for the flesh to ask for a glorious God, and yet we invent for him a form according to the foolishness of our flesh. We must not be offended by either his majesty (which we are unable to comprehend), or by his weakness. . . . The king starts with weakness and he apprehends his God in foolishness, until he ascends by faith to something higher, namely, to his God who alone rules over all kingdoms. This is the best example of prayer; in it we see true faith.[34]

In his lecture Luther emphatically showed what strong faith was necessary for this prayer, at a time when all the nations in the vicinity of Israel had already been conquered by the Assyrians. "Imagine that some tyrant had conquered all of Saxony and Meissen and had camped before our walls—then we would recognize the power of faith within us."[35] It was the prophets' great art,

[34] *Lectures on Isaiah,* 1527–1530, *WA* 31II, 235:15 ff.; 236:1 ff., 9 ff. The copy shows that Luther kept the concept of "practical syllogism" *(syllogismus practicus)* which he used during his early years, namely, that a "theological conscience" *(theologisches Gewissen)* forces everyone to accept a God. He interpreted, in connection with Rom. 1:20, this conclusion—adopted from the scholastic tradition—as the logical result of the natural knowledge of God (major premise: natural knowledge of God; minor premise: application to the actual worship of God). "This 'major' of the 'practical syllogism,' namely, this basic 'theological conscience' [*syntheresis theologica*] is in every mind and can never be obscured." *Lectures on Romans,* 1515–1516, *WA* 56, 177:14 and n. 14; *LCC* 15, 24, n. 46. On the difference between Luther and Melanchthon (judgment of conscience) and Calvin (conclusion a posteriori from good works to the state of grace), see Otto Ritschl, *Dogmengeschichte des Protestantismus: Grundlagen und Grundzüge der theologischen Gedanken-und Lehrbildung in der protestantischen Kirche* (4 vols.; Leipzig, 1908–1927), II, 282; III, 209. The difference between these interpretations reveals, just like the shimmering facets of a crystal, something of the structural difference in the theology of the three reformers.

[35] *Lectures on Isaiah,* 1527–1530, *WA* 30II, 227:27.

proven in need and in spiritual trial *(Anfechtung),* to call upon God as "their" God, to know him bound to his temple, his place of reconciliation, and nevertheless to believe in him as the almighty Lord of heaven and earth, whereas pagans and papists want to reach him only through fanciful speculation. Such prophetic faith is the Old Testament prefiguration of faith in the God of the new covenant, who can only be found in Christ, the Reconciler.

> You have often heard that the prophets, when they speak about God, speak of nothing but him alone. That is why I often attack the speculations of theologians, such as the Muhammadans, the Turks, and the papists, who hold that they can deal with God through their own knowledge. Then, when they find similar opinions in their reading of the prophets, they regard the prophets as speculators and thus draw their words into their own fantasies. This is the devil. Even the Jews had their God imprisoned, as I like to say, namely, in the sanctuary, the temple. They worshiped him, they talked about him; there was no knowledge of a God except that God who dwells in a finite place. He alone is the God in heaven and on earth, the creator of everything. Accordingly, the prophets did not speak about him outside the tabernacle and the sanctuary; rather, he said, "Here I shall dwell, here is my fire and furnace" [Isa. 31:9]. That is why there is no reference in this psalm to a tabernacle and sanctuary; instead, it simply speaks to God; it does not attack the pope or Muhammad. Therefore, apply the psalm to its own time—just as today we cannot speak about God unless we speak with God in our sanctuary, our temple, that is, Christ, who is our "place of propitiation." There is nothing to know, to hear, and to learn about God except through him.[36]

Recognition of the theme of God and the gods and understanding of proper worship of God in the prophets took Luther to the heart of prophetic theology, namely, to the proclamation of the coming Redeemer and the clear portrayal of him.

## 2. GOD AND THE WORLD—CREATION

Martin Luther, a truly aware man, was able to understand thoroughly and deeply the Old Testament descriptions of God as he works in creation. He had a profound understanding of nature as characterized by its creatures,[37] which made him feel more com-

[36] Psalm 130, *Lectures on the Fifteen Gradual Psalms,* 1533, *WA* 40$^{III}$, 335: 10 ff.

[37] On Luther's idea of nature, see my sketch, "The Picture of Nature," in *Luther's World of Thought,* trans. Martin H. Bertram (St. Louis: Concordia Publishing House, 1958), pp. 172 ff. I also refer the reader to the descriptions

fortable with that form of the biblical message where God's working in nature was seen in all its abundance. The New Testament by contrast does not deal with nature, except for a few passages. We are not here concerned with details of natural science or collecting descriptions of plants and animals, dew and rain, storm and sun. Nor do we record the majestic portrayals of nature which are found abundantly in Luther's exegetical writings. They will be mentioned here only as they afford a view of the basic structure of the world and show God's activity in the creation. Luther enjoyed the manner in which natural things were carefully described in the Old Testament while the rest of the world was so blind to the marvelous gifts of God. It was his deep, frequently expressed conviction that only through the eyes of faith can creation be seen. The jubilant Psalm 104 opened his heart. "It finds its pleasure and joy in God's creatures, so wonderfully created and so well ordered. But who pays attention and sees them like that? Only faith and the Spirit."[38] According to Luther, faith can always see another world behind the natural one; nature is full of signs and parables. He especially admired beautiful and meaningful comparisons in the Old Testament. Thus Luther had high praise for David's comparisons of snow and wool, hoarfrost and ashes, morsels and ice (Ps. 147:16–17). "How attentively this man has studied God's creation . . ." because these comparisons are based upon excellent observation, because with wool, ashes, and morsels David anticipates the "warmth and food" of the coming summer, a consolation even in the winter of suffering and inner conflict *(Anfechtung)*.[39] Thus an eye for the true unity of summer and winter teaches a regard for the unity of the Creator, while, if one were to look at both individually, one would be tempted to divide the world, as the Manicheans did, into the realms of two gods.[40] The problem of the world cannot be solved by a dualism of the gods; rather, there is an inseparable duality. It is simultaneously both a created and a corrupted world. God's means of creation is

in Werner Elert, *The Structure of Lutheranism,* trans. Walter A. Hansen (St. Louis: Concordia Publishing House, 1962), especially chaps. 31–32; and Preuss, *Luther der Künstler.*

38 *Defense of the Translation of the Psalms,* 1531–1533, *WA* 38, 53:22.

39 *Psalm 147,* 1532, *WA* 31$^{I}$, 448:36 ff.; *LW* 14, 127–28.

40 *Ibid., WA* 31$^{I}$, 447:12 ff.; *LW* 14, 125.

the "large plow, which is called 'HE SAID' [*DIXIT*]," of which Luther spoke to the students in his lectures on Genesis.[41] The Word makes everything possible, and all the questions we wish to ask about the creation of the world and of man are thus answered from the very beginning.[42] The Word goes on working ceaselessly in the world, and fills everything once created with life, that is, makes it ever new, even if no new creatures are produced. Thus God rested on the seventh day and yet he never rests; one must not attempt to outthink him with our time-bound concepts. "For with God there is nothing that is earlier or later, swifter or slower; in his eyes all things are present. He is simply outside the scope of time."[43] The angel in Zechariah 1 motivated Luther to propose God's inward way of sustaining life in the world over against the outward ways whereby he works through angels, apostles, and preachers through the worldly order. This inward order, which Luther described so powerfully, particularly in well-known passages of his writings on the Lord's Supper, is "one which he does alone by himself without co-operation from creatures; it functions entirely through his power alone, as, for example, when he creates and multiplies creatures, sustains them, and gives them strength and character—no one helps him in this."[44] God's sole and unmediated work is therefore the inward sustenance of life itself in its created form; for the particular government of the world, he makes use of his helpers. In fact, God sustains the world generally through the created means of nature: Noah had to store provisions obediently before he could enter the ark. One should not tempt God by demanding exceptions and miracles from him.[45]

The created world was corrupted by the fall of man. It did not fall of itself. Luther did not know, and did not read in the Old Testament, any speculations about a fallen creation. Instead, the creature is subjected to "vanity" "for our sake"; creation has been cursed to punish us for our sin. Luther explicitly refused to expand sin to the world itself, to the animals, for instance. "Creation and

41 According to the plausible conjecture of Ficker, *Luther als Professor,* pp. 17, 44, Luther even wrote the word on the blackboard. *Lectures on Genesis,* 1535, *WA* 42, 27:3.
42 *Ibid., WA* 42, 37:5; 97:21; *LW* 1, 49–50, 130.
43 *Ibid., WA* 42, 57:42 ff.; *LW* 1, 76.
44 *The Prophet Zechariah,* 1527, *WA* 23, 511:35 ff.; 513:36 ff.
45 *Lectures on Genesis,* 1536, *WA* 42, 316:18 ff.; *LW* 2, 76.

nature remain in the animals as it was created." Luther quite clearly established this line of thought: creation, too, has been struck by the punishment because God wants to punish man—and even destroy him, in the Flood—together with all of his dominion.

Among the beasts the creation, or nature, stayed the way it was created. They did not fall by sinning, as man did. . . . That even the animals bore the punishment of sin and perished by the Flood, together with mankind, happened because God simply wanted to destroy man, not only in body and soul but also with his possessions and the dominion with which he had been created.[46]

Nature innocently bears the curse of having to inflict suffering upon us in punishment for our guilt. The sun is by far not as bright and clear as it was at the beginning of creation; instead, it has become darker, and sootier. Useless trees and herbs, thorns and thistles, lice, bedbugs, flies, fleas, the destructive powers of water and fire are all punishment for our sin and are preachers of divine wrath.

And what of thorns, thistles, water, fire, caterpillars, flies, fleas, and bedbugs? Collectively and individually are not all of them messengers who preach to us about sin and God's wrath? . . . Not only in the churches, therefore, do we hear ourselves charged with sin. All the fields, yes, almost the entire creation is full of such sermons, reminding us of our sin and of God's wrath, which has been aroused by our sin.[47]

Indeed, Luther was certain that these plagues had gotten worse and worse as sin had swelled in the course of time. "As sins increase, penalties also increase."[48] Moses, in Gen. 3:18, certainly would not have spoken of just thorns and thistles, but also of storms, frost, and earthquakes if these powers of wrath, which are today inimically girded for our destruction, had already existed at that time.[49] When the heretofore unknown syphilis and "sweating sickness" appeared, Luther was sure that the plagues had increased in his own time and were a threatening sign of the end.[50]

[46] *Ibid.*, *WA* 42, 302:41 ff.; 303:5 ff.; *LW* 2, 58.
[47] *Lectures on Genesis*, 1536, *WA* 42, 156:1, 24; *LW* 1, 208–09. See also *ibid.*, *WA* 42, 29:8; 153:1; *LW* 1, 38, 204; and the *Sermon of June 20, 1535, on Rom. 8:18 ff.*, *Sermons of 1535*, *WA* 41, 309:10 ff.; 19 ff.
[48] *Lectures on Genesis*, 1535, *WA* 42, 154:34; *LW* 1, 207.
[49] *Ibid.*, *WA* 42, 153:38 ff.; 155:19; *LW* 1, 206.
[50] *Ibid.*, *WA* 42, 154:40 ff.; *LW* 1, 207.

Adam, after the Fall, was surely plagued less than we are in a world that has grown old.

> Thus today we experience more frequent disasters to crops than in former times. The world is deteriorating from day to day. . . . Hence, the misfortunes which were placed upon Adam were insignificant in comparison to ours. The more closely the world approaches its end, the more it is overwhelmed by penalties and catastrophes.[51]

And human procreative powers must have been greater, men must have been stronger and healthier, and the fruits must have been better and tastier before the Flood than today.

> The addition, "And Eve conceived and bore Cain," is a sure indication of a better physical condition than there is today; for at that time there were not so many ineffective cohabitations as there are in this declining world. But when Eve was known only once by Adam she immediately became pregnant. . . . I spoke earlier about the damages suffered by the products of the earth. I am also convinced that the human body was healthier then than it is now. Proof for this is the length of life among people before the Flood, which seems incredible to us. The Lord does not threaten Adam with apoplexy, leprosy, epilepsy, or other pernicious evils. . . . There were two results of the Flood: the powers of man were diminished; and his wealth, together with that of the earth, was reduced. The fruits produced by the trees are utterly unlike those they bore before the Flood. Before the Flood turnips were better than melons, oranges, or pomegranates were afterward. Pears were more delicious than spices are today. The strength in a man's finger was probably greater than it is in his entire arm today. In like manner, his reason and wisdom were far superior then. But God inflicted punishment for sin not only on man but also on his possessions and dominion, so that his wrath might also be a lesson to his descendants.[52]

Even if the sweeping strokes with which Luther painted these cosmic messengers of wrath, especially in his lectures on Genesis, seem strange to us, some of the lordly might with which the Old Testament prophets saw their God above locusts, sandstorms, and flooded lands was again brought to life therein.

God's wrath produces inner conflict *(Anfechtung)* for faith. When wrath and punishment become cosmic powers, it is no

[51] *Ibid.*, *WA* 42, 154:10; 155:30; *LW* 1, 206, 208.
[52] *Ibid.*, *WA* 42, 179:26; 154:35; 308:17 ff.; *LW* 2, 65–66.

wonder that this inner conflict too assumes cosmic dimensions.[53] Luther found the image of the rustling leaf, at which a soul in inner conflict with God can be frightened to death, in Lev. 26:36.

For there is nothing more insignificant and despised than a dry leaf lying on the ground; all the little worms crawl over it and it cannot even defend itself against a speck of dust. Even Job, when he wanted to evaluate his own utmost insignificance, could find nothing more insignificant to compare himself with before God than a dry leaf. But when the hour comes, its rustling must frighten horse, man, spear, harness, king, duke, the strength of a whole army, all political power, and those stubborn, greedy, and angry tyrants who usually cannot be frightened by either hell, wrath of God, or judgment, and who would instead only become more proud and obdurate. Aren't we great fellows—we are not frightened by God's wrath, but we stand petrified and afraid, and flee from the wrath of one helpless dry leaf! And such a leaf's rustling shall make our world too narrow and shall become our wrathful God, we who before could poke and defy heaven and earth.

If the rustling leaf can frighten a bad conscience that much, how much more will the surging sea or hellfire or the sight of godly majesty do so![54] Luther's monastic life had given him little understanding of these problems, so it was of utmost value to him that he came to understand them through the Bible. It was primarily in the Old Testament that he found powerful portrayals of conflict on the cosmic level. He observed and described particularly in Jonah how a man is trapped by his conscience: "There is then neither a corner nor a hole in all creation, not even in hell, into which he could crawl. Instead, he must allow himself to be

[53] It is to the great merit of Theodosius Harnack that he forced attention to these two sides in the midst of the nineteenth century, which did not favor such views, even though he did not connect them explicitly, and even though today —especially in view of a deeper knowledge of Luther's doctrine of *Anfechtung* —a much richer picture of these connections could be painted. Harnack, *Luthers Theologie mit besonderer Beziehung auf seine Versöhnungs- und Erlösungslehre,* eds. W. F. Schmidt and Oskar Grether (2nd ed.; 2 vols.; München, 1927), I, 253, 262 ff. See also the fine and thoughtful study of Lennart Pinomaa, *Der Zorn Gottes in der Theologie Luthers* ("Annales Academiae Scientiarum Fennicae," B, 42, 1 [Helsinki, 1938]), especially pp. 157 ff. Rich material on the experience of *Anfechtung* is found in Günter Jacob, *Der Gewissensbegriff in der Theologie Luthers* ("Beiträge zur historischen Theologie," 4 [Tübingen, 1929]). On the theology of *Anfechtung,* see also Karl F. Schumann, *Gottesglaube und Anfechtung bei Luther* ("Theologia Militans," Heft 18 [Leipzig, 1938]).

[54] *The Prophet Jonah,* 1526, *WA* 19, 226:16 ff. See also the Preface to *Sermons on Genesis,* 1527, *WA* 24, 23:14 ff.

looked at by all creatures, to stand there with all his shame, as bad consciences feel when they have been hit hard."[55] But there is more than the creatures—in them and through them there is God himself. Jonah no longer thought that the sailors threw him into the sea. No, "You [the Lord] threw me into the deep, into the heart of the sea" [Jonah 2:3].[56] And he did not say, " 'The sea's waves and billows rolled over me,' but rather, 'Your waves and your billows,' because he felt in his conscience that the sea with its waves and billows served God and his wrath, to punish sin." And he felt "as though all the water in heaven and earth flowed over him and as though there were no one but him that God's wrath was pressing—all creatures, together with God, were against him."[57] This is the inimically staring circle of cosmic forces through which the conscience-stricken man flees to and fro like Cain and many another murderer, for whom heaven and earth "have taken on another countenance."[58] Nowhere did Luther find a truer, more shocking expression for this desperate restlessness of sinful man who at every moment fears that "God stands behind him with a club" than in the Old Testament. "The Lord will give you a quaking heart, and failing eyes, and a languishing soul; so that your life will float before you; night and day you shall be frightened and unsure of your life" (Deut. 28:65–66). Or in the words of Proverbs, "The godless flee and no one pursues" (Prov. 28:1).[59] And Luther knew "no harsher saying in the Bible" expressing the reality of the wrathful God than the cosmic image in Deut. 4:24, "The Lord your God is a devouring fire, a jealous God."

Beware: you have a God who is fire and consumes; who devours you and is jealous; who swallows you up and has great pleasure in it. Yet it is unbelievable unless it becomes actual experience. . . . I know no harsher saying in the Bible than this, which gives voice to a devouring God, even though it may appear, for a certain period of time, as though it were not so, etc. But in His own time . . . Moses issued a serious warning like this before the time of the Ten Commandments so that people would not think they heard some kind of fable, but

[55] *The Prophet Jonah,* 1526, *WA* 19, 216:29.
[56] *Ibid.,* 226:9.
[57] *Ibid.,* 227:1 ff.
[58] *Lectures on Genesis,* 1536, *WA* 42, 211:38; *LW* 1, 286.
[59] *Sermon on the Fourth Sunday in Advent on Phil. 4:4 ff., Advent Postil,* 1522 (*Adventspostille*), *WA* $10^{I,2}$, 171:5.

rather something of utmost seriousness. When God is called fire, devouring and jealous, it means that he who does not keep the commandments has to be devoured. Fire is the most vehement of all elements. What can neither be forced nor changed is usually attacked by fire.[60]

## 3. GOD AND THE WORLD—HISTORY

Just as all cosmic life assumes its depth and mystery because God himself effects it and throughout all natural events continuously views man and speaks to him, so many-sided and ulterior is the mirror image of historical life which Luther found in the Old Testament and which we have sketched. Everything in it is God's work and will. Thus that which at first appears to be only a colorful picture of the lively world of human beings becomes, to the eye of the believer, a palimpsest recounting the hidden miracles and puzzles of God's work. It is as unnecessary to list all the particular traits and events here as it was in the depiction of nature to understand how important it was to Luther to find the Lord of history immediately and concretely at work everywhere in the Old Testament.[61] Luther, with an openness of faith which did not change in reflection or doubt, saw God intervene in the life of individuals of every vocation, from kings to shepherds, the same God who is at the same time the Lord of far-reaching world events, whom Jews and pagans must serve. In the Old Testament as nowhere else Luther found nourishment for his tremendous power to see the God he knew as the creating life force, in the leaf, the stone, and the animal, acting personally, with utmost clarity and determination. History, as God's field, is in none of its traits profane or irrelevant to either him or us. Rather, it is in its whole development judgment history and salvation history *(Heilsgeschichte)*, always full of decision, threat, and grace.

It is God's grace when a charismatic man is born to a people.[62]

[60] *Sermons of June 20 and August 1, 1529, Sermons on Deuteronomy, WA* 28, 559:5; 562:1; 581:12.

[61] See also the collection of glosses on "the kingdom of God and earthly kingdoms" in Knolle, *Luthers Glossen zum Alten Testament,* pp. 22 ff. On Luther's understanding of history, I refer the reader to Hans Lilje, *Luthers Geschichtsanschauung* ("Furche Studien," 2 [Berlin, 1932]); Johann Müller-Bardorff, *Geschichte und Kreuz bei Luther* (Stuttgart, 1938); Ernst Kohlmeyer, "Die Geschichtsbetrachtung Luthers," *Archiv für Reformationsgeschichte,* XXXVII (1940), 150 ff.; and my lecture, "God and History," in *Luther's World of Thought,* pp. 195 ff., upon which I have drawn in the subsequent section.

[62] See above, pp. 12–13.

When Luther praised these "healthy heroes" he did not forget to add that "it was God's work."[63] And the strongest biblical passages to substantiate his belief in the divine institution of political authority were those in which the judges were called gods (Exod. 21:6; 22:7–8; 22:27; Ps. 82:1). That was where the dignity, but also the limitation, of political authority was expressed. "They should not go above God's Word. For God's Word appoints them and makes them gods, and subjects everything to them. That is why they should not overrun that which has established them and appointed them; they should be subject to it and allow themselves to be judged, punished, created, and mastered by it."[64] God intends to remain the Supreme God, Judge over those people set by him in the divine office of judge.[65] Only when they know this can they preserve the "truly godly virtues" which they need to fulfil their superhumanly difficult office. "Yes, as Scripture says, 'They are called gods' [John 10:35]; for they certainly ought to shine with godly virtues far beyond human means, since they must successfully provide for that weak and diversified mass of people subject to Satan in a hostile land."[66] Luther also found the subjection of political authority under the divine will expressed most concisely and sharply in an Old Testament passage, in the speech by King Jehoshaphat to the judges he appointed: "See to it and judge rightly, for the judgment is God's" (II Chron. 19:6).[67] According to Luther, only he who executes his office with this knowledge can be a true judge at all; that means "a victor over all passions, fear, love, attraction, pity, greed, fame, life, and death. He must quite simply love the pure truth and a just verdict."[68] And, once again, Luther used a passage from the Psalter to exemplify a significant distinction between trust in God and confidence in political authority: in Ps. 118:8–9 he differentiated between "trust" and "use."

One should use and enjoy the princely office and temporal government as God instituted it, for food, protection, and peace on earth. But one

[63] *Psalm 101,* 1534–1535, *WA* 51, 244:19; *LW* 13, 200.
[64] *Psalm 82,* 1530, *WA* 31I, 195:36; *LW* 13, 48.
[65] *Ibid., WA* 31I, 191:31; *LW* 13, 44.
[66] *The Deuteronomy of Moses, with Notes,* 1525, *WA* 14, 551:18; *LW* 9, 17–18.
[67] This is Luther's original translation. *Psalm 82,* 1530, *WA* 31I, 191:35; *LW* 13, 44. See also *The Deuteronomy of Moses, with Notes,* 1525, *WA* 14, 555:10; 667:4; *LW* 9, 163.
[68] *The Deuteronomy of Moses, with Notes,* 1525, *WA* 14, 667:1; *LW* 9, 163.

should not rely, trust, hope, or boast in them. One must use other temporal goods—money, cattle, houses, homes—but one must not place one's trust, hope, and confidence in them. To trust and to use are two different matters. The former is appropriate to God; the latter is appropriate to creatures.[69]

But who knows this difference, who really depends solely upon God's care? That is why God's right alone to dispose over all means, ways, and goals of the course of history must by itself, without the intervention of the divine will or wrath, become the judgment and punishment of unbelievers. But God sends his messengers to their well-meaning council meetings from time to time so that they do not forget to take him into account in their advice.

Dear Gabriel, go down there and take Isaiah along with you, and read them a secret lesson through the window, and say, "You shall see nothing with seeing eyes; you shall hear nothing with hearing ears; you shall understand nothing with understanding hearts" [Isa. 6:10]. "Take counsel together, and it will came to naught; speak the Word and let it not stand. For mine is both proposing and disposing" [Isa. 8:10].[70]

This, of course, is only a hidden effect of divine wrath. But to Luther there were enough signs of it clearly visible to all eyes. Nowhere do we feel Luther's historical sense as strongly as in the trembling with which he gazed upon the fallen nations.[71] For they did not die a natural death. Luther did not know of a single natural death in history. The thought of a biological aging and dying of nations was still quite foreign to him and would have contradicted his whole view of historical life. To be sure, one of Luther's elementary feelings was that of living in a world grown old. As we have seen, he even thought he saw clearly the signs of this in the increase of inimical elements in nature and in the biological weakening of the human race.[72] But these were elicited by the growth of sin in the course of history. Nations do not die of themselves; rather, they are extinguished by God because of their sin. The history of nations is the history of the acting God who sends death as he wills. And he can, like a farmer, "scatter

[69] *Psalm 118, the Beautiful Confitemini,* 1530, *WA* 31^I^, 114:10; *LW* 14, 68–69.
[70] *Psalm 101,* 1534–1535, *WA* 51, 203:35; *LW* 13, 150.
[71] See above, pp. 15–16.
[72] See above, pp. 59–61.

cities like grain, indeed, throw kingdoms into the bag"—an image Luther coaxed from the literal translation of Zech. 1:17.

Our passage, "My cities shall again overflow with prosperity," means in Hebrew that "the cities will be scattered because of great prosperity. . . ." He indicates by this passage how easy it is for Him to restore a nation and to fill it with cities, as if he could scatter and sow cities like a farmer scatters and sows grain in the field. . . . Yes, who believes that? Should a man believe that God can scatter cities like grain, indeed, throw kingdoms into the bag, if we are unable even to believe that he would or could nourish us one day with a piece of bread?[73]

Because Psalm 2 paints so powerfully the contrast between the agitation of the kings and the God who inhabits heaven, laughing at them and mocking them, this "boor"[74] among the Psalms, who speaks with princes as though they were peasants, children, and slaves, is a song dear to Luther's heart. Rorer's excelent and somewhat hurried notes still convey to us the breathtaking seriousness with which Luther described how God swept away the peoples and kings. With verse 5, "Someday he will speak with them in his wrath, and terrify them with his fury," he could not get his fill of showing how Word and deed with God become one lightning unity.

When God speaks he throws one or four kingdoms away. When he speaks, the whole universe reverberates. As long as he speaks through the sunrise and sunset, through the growth of plants, and through the propagation of man, and through the beasts—this is the language of our Lord God. It is not a voice like the sound of instruments; rather, Word and deed are one. When a thing speaks, it stands right there. . . . It is a Word for the destruction of unbelievers and for our own consolation. When it comes, it has no end. . . . The man Christ speaks like us—it is the Word and deed of majesty.[75]

Therefore Luther very boldly named the people God sent out to overthrow other kingdoms which had become godless "God's Word," his "Word of wrath." Of course they did not escape their own fate. One nation was sent by God against the other, the Persians against the Babylonians, the Babylonians and the Romans against the Jews. Germanic tribes brought down the Romans.

What He says here against unbelievers is certainly terrible, because God speaks, does, says one Word and sends the Romans against the Jews

[73] *The Prophet Zechariah,* 1527, *WA* 23, 519:29 ff.
[74] *Lecture on Psalm 2,* 1532, *WA* 40$^{II}$, 276:10.
[75] *Ibid.,* 229:12; 231:5.

and devastates them through his Word, sending weapons and fire against the holy nation. Then the Goths and Vandals become the Word of God. Their weapons and fire become the Word of God against the Romans; the Persians against the Babylonians, the Babylonians against the Jews. This means speaking a strong language. When the Lord smashes twenty kingdoms at once, as he does through plagues and famine, it means that majesty itself opposes the unbelievers.[76]

And the Turk, as God's "Word of wrath" stood before Germany.[77] Luther had a twofold biblical prediction for the Turks and their atrocities. He believed that they were foretold in the small horn which grew out of the fourth animal in the vision of Daniel (Dan. 7:8, 24). For they appeared in the fourth world monarchy, the Roman, and they exterminated the three older horns, Egypt, Greece, and Asia.[78] Second, he found them described very accurately in the vision of Ezekiel about Gog (Ezekiel 38 and 39), the vision which seemed to him particularly confirmed because of its role in the eschatological drama (Rev. 20:8).[79] During his quiet days at Coburg Luther first started work on a small tract with the translation of Ezekiel 38 and 39 because he was impressed by the danger from the Turks[80] and wanted to direct the attention of the whole world to this danger. "Gog has tasted German blood; he intends to drink his fill of it." But at the same time he also wanted to uncover the true reason for the Turkish power: our sins, "which have awakened God's fury and have hidden his countenance from us, and allow Gog to rage so horribly."[81]

Germany, too, had its appointed part in the wild drama of the nations. In the *Confitemini* (Psalm 118), Luther painted the magnificent picture of the God who shoots at the nations and whose muskets are always loaded. He shot the Jews through the Romans, the Romans through the Goths and Vandals, the Chaldeans through

[76] *Ibid.*, 231:7. On the whole question, see *ibid.*, 232 ff., and *The Prophet Habakkuk*, 1526, *WA* 19, 360:12 ff.; *Psalm 118*, 1530, *WA* 31^I, 127:20; *LW* 14, 74; Dörries, *Luther und Deutschland*, p. 7, and the *Table Talk* cited there: *WA*, TR 2 (1531), 276 (No. 1953), 608 (No. 2709); 6 (from various years), 31–32 (No. 6543), 100–01 (No. 6656), 224–25 (No. 6839).

[77] *Lecture on Psalm 2*, 1532, *WA* 40^II, 230:8.

[78] *Army Sermon Against the Turk*, 1529 (*Eine Heerpredigt wider den Türken*), *WA* 30^II, 166:20 ff.

[79] *Ibid.*, 171:12.

[80] *Ezekiel 38 and 39 Concerning Gog. Translated into German by Martin Luther*, 1530 (*Das XXXVIII und XXXIX Capitel Hesechiel vom Gog. Verdeudscht durch Mart. Luther*), *WA* 30^II, 223 ff.

[81] *Ibid.*, 225:29 ff.

the Persians, the Greeks through the Turks. "He will probably find a bullet for us Germans too, which will hit us and not miss. For we have overdone things and still refuse to quit." Perhaps the Turkish bullet is meant for us,[82] for this contempt and coolness toward the divine Word cannot go unavenged. Isaiah's description (Isa. 41:23–24) of the calmness with which the ruler of the worlds, against whom it is senseless to fight, spoke to the arrogant peoples compelled Luther to cry with distress during his lecture, "If they take the gospel out of the German lands, then the nation will go also."[83] Luther, in his terrible concern, rose up to the full height of his prophetic office. He, like Moses or Jeremiah, wanted to step into the breach before God. He was, of course, constantly torn between the consoling examples—that God, for the sake of *one* man saved a people, or its church[84]—and the bottomless fear that it was already too late to do so. This worry overcame him not just at the end of his life, but as early as the outbreak of the Peasants' War, when he remembered the threats of Jer. 15:1 and Ezek. 14:14, that even Moses and Samuel, Noah, Daniel, and Job could no longer step into the path of the wrath of God.[85] But even if the Turks should topple Germany, the game would still not end, provided the world would still remain. They too would be overthrown."[86]

Thus the external course of the history of nations and the history of mankind's faith are inseparably woven together, indeed, they are one and the same. History is an indivisible whole. Its course is only the result of the innermost changes in the human race: of the preservation of the natural orders God wrote into the hearts of peoples, of the particular revelation and covenant he made with his own "owned people"; it is the history of obedience and rebellion, patience and trial, extermination of self-confident pride and

[82] *Psalm 118, the Beautiful Confitemini,* 1530, *WA* 31$^{I}$, 126:33 ff.; *LW* 14, 74. See also *Lecture on Psalm 2,* 1532, *WA* 40$^{II}$, 230:8 ff.; and Dörries, *op. cit.*, pp. 8 ff.
[83] *Lectures on Isaiah,* 1527–1530, *WA* 31$^{II}$, 303:30.
[84] *Table Talk,* 1540, *WA,* TR 5, 23–24 (No. 5242). See also Preuss, *Martin Luther, der Prophet,* pp. 116 ff.
[85] *Admonition to Peace, a Reply to the Twelve Articles of the Peasants in Swabia,* 1525 (*Ermanunge zum fride auff die Zwelff artikel der Bawrschafft ynn Schwaben*), *WA* 18, 334:20; *LW* 46, 43. See also *A Sermon on Keeping Children in School,* 1530 (*Eine Predigt das man kinder zur Schulen halten solle*), *WA* 30$^{II}$, 585:13–14; *LW* 46, 255–56.
[86] *The Prophet Habakkuk,* 1526, *WA* 19, 360:16.

the saving of the faithful remnant in the fulfilled time of salvation. All historical life is related to God and effected by him. That was why Luther called it God's "mummery." He found plentiful quotes in the Old Testament for just this idea of a divine masquerade. In his exposition of Psalm 127 he taught the Christians in Riga to regard all armaments as "our Lord God's mummery," exemplified by David's wars and the people of Israel.

> [We] should regard all such preparation and armament as the work of our Lord God under a mask, as it were, beneath which he himself alone effects and accomplishes what we desire. He commands us so to arm ourselves also for the reason that he might conceal his own work under this disguise, allow those who boast to go their way, and strengthen those who are worried, so that men will not tempt him. He conducted all the wars of King David and of the whole people of Israel in the Old Testament in this way. He does the same thing today, wherever there is a faithful political authority like this. In like manner, he made Abraham, Isaac, and Jacob wealthy, etc., through their own labor. Indeed, one could very well say that the course of the world and especially the work of his saints are God's mask, under which he conceals himself and so marvelously exercises dominion and introduces disorder into the world.[87]

And he depicted in verse 4 how God, like a giant, sends out the great and the young as his arrows.[88] He found the proof text for the game God plays with nations and individuals in the proverb, "I played on his earthly ground and delighted in the children of men" (Prov. 8:31).[89] Luther, of course, did not speak of this game in the manner of a Gnostic myth which, in timid awe, describes the view of a divine onlooker who is far removed from man. Rather, he understood it as a serious game and, therefore, always, whether it be in the large historical world or in the small personal world, as conflict *(Anfechtung)* and a test of faith by the God who disguises himself.

Luther found a particularly illustrative depiction of this divine game in Joseph's behavior in his meeting with his brothers; that

[87] *Exposition of Psalm 127, for the Christians at Riga in Livonia,* 1524, *WA* 15, 373:7 ff.; *LW* 45, 331. On the whole problem, see Fritz Blanke, *Der verborgene Gott bei Luther* ("Stimmen aus der deutschen christlichen Studentenbewegung," 60 [Berlin, 1928]).
[88] *Exposition of Psalm 127, for the Christians at Riga in Livonia,* 1524, *WA* 15, 376:23 ff.; *LW* 45, 335.
[89] *Lectures on Genesis,* 1544, *WA* 44, 466:22; *LW* 7, 225.

was why he interpreted Genesis 42 as an example and mirror of the divine world rule.

"Blessed is the man" said James [1:12], "who endures conflict, for after he has proven himself, he will receive the crown of life which God has promised to those who love him." That is why we should believe with certainty that our misfortune or trouble, our sighing and sorrowing, and even death itself are nothing else than a very joyful and beautiful game of divine goodness with us. But how many are there who understand or believe this? ... But when I think of what a poor sinner I am, and that I am being punished because of my sin, I judge this quite differently. For then I do not feel that God is my Father, that he is kind and merciful; rather, I feel that he is the devil himself. That is why you should know that God is almighty and that such a serious game is therefore befitting and rhymes very well with such a great majesty. . . . Therefore he gives you his promise, his Word and sacraments as the surest signs and evidence of his grace, namely, that he has adopted you to be his child and requires from you nothing more than that you bear and suffer his game, which is pleasing to him and wholesome for you.... Thus God now plays a fatherly game with us when he lets pestilence, famine, sickness, or sorrow overcome us; this is how he melts us and purges us. But who can bear all this? The Jews had not hoped for a Messiah like this; instead, they wanted to have one who would make them kings and lords of the whole world. No, said Malachi, they are going to fail in that: for it looks as if he will thoroughly sweep them away. And no matter how gruesome this purge may be, our Savior does not play with us so that we should be ruined, but rather so that we shall be improved.... But this wisdom and this game of God applies to those who sob and cry, to a broken and beaten heart, as a glowing wick. These are the ones who feel it; to these, one must offer such consolation so that they do not lose heart but remain strong and manly.[90]

If Luther summarized this almighty and all-creating work of God in the friendly image of a game and made its hidden meaning transparent, he also tried to put into words its merciless offensiveness and its crushing mystery, especially in *On the Bondage of the Will.* In fact, what he said there was not just a temporary or extreme form of his ideas; he emphatically subscribed to it

[90] *Ibid., WA* 44, 467:7 ff.; 470:38 ff.; 472:11 ff.; *LW* 7, 226, 230–31, 232–33. I quote for the sake of the old color tone from the translation of Johannes Gudenus in *St. L.* 2, 2131–32. On Luther's interpretation, see my remarks in "Luthers und Böhmes Auslegung von Gen. 42. Mit einer Erläuterung," *Vierteljahrsschrift der Luthergesellschaft,* IX (1927), 60 ff.

again many years later.[91] The scriptural passages which Luther in his fight against free will had earlier quoted singly and now pushed forward in a united front, stem for the most part from the Old Testament. To name only the most important evidence for his decisive theses: against free will he used Gen. 6:3, "My spirit shall not always remain in man, because he is flesh" (according to the Vulgate, not the Hebrew text);[92] Gen. 6:5 and 8:21, "Everything the human heart does is evil from childhood on";[93] Isa. 40:2, "Its warfare has an end" (that means that the law which turns to the will is abrogated as useless);[94] Isa. 40:6, "All flesh is grass";[95] Jer. 10:23, "The action of man is not within his power";[96] Prov. 16:1, "Man does make plans in his heart, but what the tongue shall say comes from the Lord";[97] Prov. 21:1, "The king's heart is a stream of water in the hand of the Lord; he directs it wherever he wills."[98] This is how God himself, in his revelation, judges the will power of man. At the same time, the Old Testament provided Luther with his belief in double predestination, the facts without which he would probably have avoided this terrible knowledge: Gen. 25:23 about Esau and Jacob, "The elder shall serve the younger";[99] Exod. 9:12, "The Lord hardened the heart of Pharaoh" (also Exod. 4:21);[100] Mal. 1:2–3, "I love Esau and hate Jacob."[101] Nowhere did he find universal omnipotence, inseparable from predestination and the power acting in both good and evil, so well proven as in the Old Testament. "The Lord creates everything for a definite goal, even the godless for the evil day" (Prov. 16:4),[102] which is once again illustrated in Pharaoh, whom God allows to live despite his raging to then punish him

[91] Letter to Capito, July 9, 1539, *WA*, BR 8, 99:7.
[92] *On the Bondage of the Will*, 1525 (*De servo arbitrio*), *WA* 18, 733:22 ff.; J. I. Packer and O. R. Johnston (trans.), *Martin Luther on the Bondage of the Will* (Westwood, N. J.: Fleming H. Revell Co., 1957), p. 239.
[93] *Ibid.*, *WA* 18, 736:6 ff.; Packer and Johnston, *op. cit.*, p. 242.
[94] *Ibid.*, *WA* 18, 736:40 ff.; Packer and Johnston, *op. cit.*, pp. 244–45.
[95] *Ibid.*, *WA* 18, 739:23 ff.; Packer and Johnston, *op. cit.*, pp. 247–48.
[96] *Ibid.*, *WA* 18, 745:20 ff.; Packer and Johnston, *op. cit.*, pp. 255 ff.
[97] *Ibid.*, *WA* 18, 746:30 ff.; Packer and Johnston, *op. cit.*, pp. 527–28.
[98] *Ibid.*, *WA* 18, 747:21 ff.; Packer and Johnston, *op. cit.*, pp. 258–59.
[99] *Ibid.*, *WA* 18, 722:30 ff.; Packer and Johnston, *op. cit.*, p. 225.
[100] *Ibid.*, *WA* 18, 713:1 ff.; Packer and Johnston, *op. cit.*, pp. 211–12.
[101] *Ibid.*, *WA* 18, 724:27 ff.; Packer and Johnston, *op. cit.*, pp. 225 ff.
[102] *Ibid.*, *WA* 18, 747:16; Packer and Johnston, *op. cit.*, pp. 258–59. So also as early as 1520 in *Defense of All the Articles of Martin Luther, Which Were Unjustly Condemned Through the Bull of Leo X* (*Assertio omnium Articulorum M. Lutheri, per Bullam Leonis X nouissima damnatoru*), *WA* 7, 144:34.

that much more terribly. "That is why I have preserved you, that my strength appear through you and my name be proclaimed in all lands" (Exod. 9:16).[103] In comparison to these passages, the New Testament passages Luther called upon lacked strength and originality. They were weaker, more negative, like the "giving up" of pagans to their evil passions (Rom. 1:28).[104] Or they were only an echo of the Old Testament pronouncements, like the obduracy in Rom. 9:18, or the parable of the potter and the clay in Isaiah 45 and Jeremiah 18.[105]

Does this mean that Luther's teachings in *On the Bondage of the Will* fell victim to the Old Testament conceptions? This would be the case if one took into account only *On the Bondage of the Will* and derived from it his doctrines of omnipotence, enslaved will and predestination, and true faith (but fortunately not necessary to salvation). Arno Deutelmoser was probably not aware that the homunculus he had artificially created, an un-Christian Luther cleansed of faith in justification and in Christ, as the proof texts of *On the Bondage of the Will* show, was a purely Old Testament Luther.[106] To understand *On the Bondage of the Will* correctly, it is necessary to know the unity of Luther's concept of God, as well as his concept of the unity of both testaments. Luther only formulated his viewpoint as strongly as he did from Old Testament material because of this unity. He found both most clearly joined together in Romans 9–11, where he certainly kept encountering Old Testament foundations. Moreover, the Old Testament gave him the vital demonstration of the actual course of these events, which he dared to name only with fear and trembling. One need only remember the arch image of the psychology of obduracy, namely, Pharaoh.

In Romans 9–11 Luther encountered divine guidance in history which was particularly moving for him, the *fate of the Jewish people.* He never doubted the election of Israel. He saw it not

103 *On the Bondage of the Will,* 1525, *WA* 18, 714:2; Packer and Johnston, *op. cit.,* p. 210.
104 *Defense of All the Articles,* 1520, *WA* 7, 144:36.
105 *On the Bondage of the Will,* 1525, *WA* 18, 714:38 ff.; 727:3 ff.; Packer and Johnston, *op. cit.,* pp. 212 ff., 229ff.
106 See Arno Deutelmoser, *Luther. Staat und Glaube* (Jena, 1937). How much "mixing" counts for him too was shown when his literary sources were revealed in Theodor Knolle, *Luthers Glaube. Eine Widerlegung* ("Schriftenreihe der Luthergesellschaft," 10 [Weimar, 1938]).

only in the revelation of God they had received, but also in their historical-political mission. They were the sword with which God in his wrath destroyed the Canaanites, as God is accustomed to do to the nations deserving death. Yet here there was already a difference between them and other peoples. If at times God's verdict remained hidden when he punished godless nations through equally godless ones, in this case the verdict he pronounced over an idolatrous people through his elected people was obvious. His command to the believing conscience was clear.

> But the swords of other nations are different from the sword of Israel because God uses their fury in a hidden judgment and crushes the ungodly through the ungodly; but the sword of Israel is sanctified by a clear and certain mandate from God so that the godly destroy the ungodly with a pure and holy conscience and shed blood in the holy act of religion.[107]

Nor did the Jews have the command to annihilate other nations beside the Canaanites.[108] However, their political mission is thus inseparably tied to their particular superiority: God gave his Word to them alone.

> God indeed gives everything to all; but to his own people he adds the promise that they should not only live by bread, as the rest of the nations do, but also by the Word. (That is why God gave them the land of Canaan.) He did not choose the nation because of the place, but the place because of the nation.[109]

God's election was not based on the superiority of the Jews over other peoples. It was his free choice. The Old Testament itself certainly said this clearly enough: "It was not because you were more in number than any other people that the Lord set his love upon you and chose you, for you were the fewest of all peoples; but it is because the Lord loves you and is keeping his oath" (Deut. 7:7–8). God did not let the Jews destroy the idolatry of the pagans so that instead they could erect the idol of presumptuous self-confidence; to protect them from this is the purpose of the First Commandment.

107 *The Deuteronomy of Moses, with Notes,* 1525, *WA* 14, 624:26; *LW* 9, 83.
108 *Ibid., WA* 14, 624:31 ff.; *LW* 9, 83.
109 *Ibid., WA* 14, 643:16 ff.; *LW* 9, 118.

It takes an even greater spirit not to glory in having destroyed such a cult, and not to set up the internal idol of a very empty trust in place of the external idol. Therefore it is a great thing to know the true and only God purely, and to fear, worship, have, and believe genuinely in him. Hence, Moses has to use many words to set forth the First Commandment.[110]

But... the law was given to the Jews . . . so that by its light they might better come to know their cursed state and more fervently and heartily desire the promised Seed; therein they had an advantage over all the pagan world. But they turned this advantage into a disadvantage; they undertook to keep the law by their own strength and failed to learn from it their needy and cursed state. They thus shut the door upon themselves so that the Seed was compelled to pass them by. They still continue in this state, but God grant not for long. Amen.[111]

But the Jews did not let themselves be protected and so fell victim to this self-idolatry. Nothing in the course of history disturbed Luther so much as the turning of election from a blessing to a curse. He found prophecies warning of this everywhere in the prophets and the psalms. With a consternation still to be felt today he interpreted the terrible maledictions of Psalm 109 as the curse of Christ on the Jews who rejected him.[112] Everything the psalm prophesied was frightfully fulfilled in this people.[113]

"Let there be none to extend kindness to him, nor any to pity his fatherless children!" [vs. 12]. My God, this is all too true! People regard the Jews as dogs, and anyone who can harm them or do them dirt supposes he is doing a good deed. Because they and all their children refuse to accept Christ, there is no mercy for these obdurate people. And yet they put up with it and cling to their vain hope for something better. So entrenched "stands Satan on their right"![114]

Verse 18, "He clothed himself with the curse as with his shirt; it flowed into his body like water and like oil into his bones," became

110 *Ibid., WA* 14, 626:33; *LW* 9, 85.
111 *The Magnificat,* 1521 (*Das Magnificat*), *WA* 7, 600:10 ff.; *LW* 21, 354.
112 Psalm 109, *The Four Psalms of Comfort,* 1526, *WA* 19, 595 ff.; *LW* 14, 257 ff.
113 *Ibid., WA* 19, 601:14 ff.; *LW* 14, 264. For example, "His children must become orphans, and his wife a widow [vs. 9]—at the destruction of Jerusalem." "His children must wander about and beg; they must look for a new place because his dwelling place is destroyed. The creditors must seize all that he has; strangers must plunder the fruits of his toil" [vss. 10–11]. I have quoted Luther's remark about this fulfilment above, p. 6.
114 *Ibid.*

for him the most compelling depiction of obstinacy that he wrote besides the description of the obdurate Pharaoh (in *On the Bondage of the Will*). Their obstinate defiance of the gospel is to them as close as a shirt to the body, indeed it is more, as unexpendable as it is if one does not want to go about shamelessly naked. As water into the body and oil into the skin, "so is the curse and the obstinacy of the Jews driven through their heart, mind, senses, through their marrow and bones, so that they are beyond help."[115] They can no longer help it, they are forced to reject Christ as a poison to his people. "There they are, the oil has entered their bones, and they go on soaking up the water. What a terrible judgment and example of divine wrath."[116] When Luther saw how the papacy condemned and suppressed the gospel in the same manner, he shuddered at the delusion of the world. "O Lord God, let us commit other sins than these, if we must sin!"[117] For God must avenge such contempt for the gospel; he cannot amicably forgive this as should be the case between man and man. "Where God and issues are involved, there is neither patience nor blessing—only sheer jealousy, wrath, vengeance, and malediction."[118]

If the elected people of God could allow their hearts to become so hardened, then Luther considered it a serious warning to other peoples as well as his own. He was convinced that the gospel falls on nations like a passing shower. He wanted to scream it, with a thrice cutting "what's gone is gone" into the ears of the responsible authorities of his time, namely, the "councilmen of all cities in Germany."[119] This conviction was based on prophecies such as Amos' about the famine of God's Word, "that they shall scurry from sea to sea, from midnight to morning, to search for the Lord's Word; but they shall not find it" (Amos 8:11–12). It was absolutely confirmed for him by the fate of Judaism, and had become threateningly certain for the Christian nations.

"Now I will do differently," that is, it will not be the Word of God. "Differently" means to withdraw grace, teachers, and to transform the

[115] *Ibid.*, *WA* 19, 607:24; *LW* 14, 269.
[116] *Ibid.*, *WA* 19, 608:18; *LW* 14, 270.
[117] *Ibid.*, *WA* 19, 606:16; *LW* 14, 268.
[118] *Ibid.*, *WA* 19, 595:30; *LW* 14, 258; see also below, p. 202.
[119] *To the Councilmen of All Cities in Germany that They Establish and Maintain Christian Schools*, 1524 (*An die Radherrn aller Stedte deutsches lands: das sie Christliche Schulen auffrichten und hallten sollen*), *WA* 15, 32:6 ff.; *LW* 45, 352.

Word of God into God's greatest blow.... This will happen to us because we have neglected the Word. The Jews have been punished in this way, and so the Christians will be punished because they preach for a long time without any effect at all. "Famine" means that the hearing of the Word of the Lord will be removed; that is, no one will say, preach, or teach the Word of the Lord. He who will not have the Word of God must have the word of Satan and of men, because nature cannot remain silent.[120]

Even in his severest writings about the Jews, Luther never forgot to drive the historical fate of this obdurate and punished people into the hearts of Christians. "Although I am not a Jew I really do not like to think of such horrible wrath of God upon this people. For it frightens me so much that I tremble in every limb. What will the eternal wrath in hell do to false Christians and all unbelievers?"[121] We should recall once again what we said at the beginning:[122] Luther did not let the apostasy of later Judaism confuse the fact of the election of the ancient people of Israel and the uniqueness of their history as recorded in the Old Testament. Election found its natural conclusion in the crucifixion of Jesus. Moreover, God visibly confirmed the fact that Israel was no longer his nation by the destruction of Jerusalem and the expulsion of the Jews from the Holy Land. Nor did they have any promise of a return to Palestine.

And if God had not permitted the destruction of Jerusalem and had not expelled them from the country, but had allowed them to possess it as usual, then no one could say to them that they are not God's people.... Even now they cannot give up their nonsensical and mad boasting that they are God's people, although they have remained expelled, destroyed, and truly condemned for fifteen hundred years. Nevertheless, they still hope to regain their status on the basis of their own merit. For they no longer have a promise for their own consolation, except the kind of smear they read in the Scripture out of their own erring darkness.[123]

Luther did not speculate at all about a particular status of the Jewish people at the end of time. His prophetic interpretation of the Old Testament prophecies, which he applied to Christ and the church, already precluded his doing so. Nor did Luther, as he had

[120] *Lectures on the Minor Prophets*, 1524–1525, *WA* 13, 153:3 ff.
[121] *On the Jews and Their Lies*, 1543, *WA* 53, 418:29.
[122] See above, p. 6.
[123] *On the Jews and Their Lies*, 1543, *WA* 53, 447:27 ff.

already expressed pointedly in his lectures on the psalms, ever believe in a conversion of the people of Israel to Christ before the Last Judgment. According to Isaiah's prophecy (10:21), only a small remnant would be saved.

> But I wonder how the total conversion of the Jews can be effected—as many say here—since Christ says clearly, "This generation will not pass away till all this takes place" [Luke 21:32]. And Malachi 1[:4], "And there will be a people with whom the Lord is angry for ever." And, according to Isaiah 10 [:21], only a remnant will be saved.[124]

Paul's statement in Rom. 11:25–26, to be sure, then gave him a lot of trouble in his lectures on that epistle. But one could only read into this a conversion of the whole nation, he thought, if one would accept unconditionally the exegesis of the fathers; the text itself was not convincing.

> This text is the basis of the common opinion that at the end of the world the Jews will return to their faith. However, it is so obscure that unless one is willing to accept the judgment of the fathers who expound the apostle in this way, no one can, so it would seem, obtain a clear conviction from this text.[125]

This was why he emphasized that Paul here speaks of a "mystery" to which nobody has access; and he finally explained it to himself in such a way that the mass of the people was here addressed as holy for the sake of the elect.[126] Thus he applied the same synecdoche according to which he also called the congregations "church," namely, for the sake of the true believers in these congregations. But the passage in Paul remained obscure to him,[127] and he also later sharply rejected appeals to it.[128] He clung to his conviction until his death: "Out of the whole mass, let him hope

[124] *Lectures on the Psalter,* 1513–1516, *WA* 3, 329:26. See also *ibid.,* 100:38; the revision of Psalm 1 in *ibid.,* 24:27, 39; and Theodor Pahls, *Luther und die Juden* (3 vols.; Bonn, 1939), I, 61 ff.

[125] *Lectures on Romans,* 1515–1516, *WA* 56, 436:25 ff.; *LCC* 15, 315. See also Johannes Ficker (ed.), *Luthers Vorlesung über den Römerbrief, 1515–1516* (2 vols.; Leipzig, 1925), II, 261:20 ff.; and Pahls, *Luther und die Juden,* I, 61 ff.

[126] *Lectures on Romans,* 1515–1516, *WA* 56, 438:27 ff.; Ficker, *Römerbrief,* II, 263:24 ff. Luther, therefore, interpreted "all of Israel" (*omnis Israel*) in the gloss as "all that are to be saved in Israel" (*omnes de Israel salvandi*). Ficker, *Römerbrief,* I, 106:9; *Lectures on Romans,* 1515–1516, *WA* 56, 113:15; *LCC* 15, 316–17.

[127] On Ps. 14:7, *Works on the Psalms,* 1519–1521 (*Operationes in Psalmos*), *WA* 5, 428:5.

[128] *Table Talk,* 1543, *WA,* TR 5, 247 (No. 5567). See also *On Shem hammephorash,* 1543, *WA* 53, 580:3.

who will. I do not have any hope there, and do not know any Scripture for it. Since we cannot convert the great mass of our Christians, and must be content with the small crowd, how much less possible it is to convert all these children of the devil."[129] From his reasoning one can see how impossible Luther considered a future conversion of the whole people of Israel to be. He emphatically resisted the undoubtedly natural interpretation of the Pauline passage to avoid contradicting the apostle.

But as abysmally deep as the fall of the later Israel was from the earlier Israel, there was nevertheless a unity in the history of the Jewish people: it was the encounter with the Word of God in grace and judgment. Election and condemnation grow from the same root: the claim of God, who called Israel to his mission, unique among the nations of the ancient world, and the punishment of the nation which hardened its heart, a punishment which has lasted longer than Israel's independence.

> For if one calculates carefully, then their misery under the Roman Empire lasted longer than their previous existence and rule in the land of Canaan. No matter how you calculate the years from their exodus from Egypt to the latest destruction of Jerusalem, which they experience now, the result is fifteen hundred years. They have now been in misery not many years less, and the misery will last even longer because they still have no prophets or prophecy concerning the end of this. But how can one believe that God permits his people to be without political rule longer than they were with political rule, to be without the law, temple, worship, Jerusalem, priesthood, principality, land longer than they were with these things?[130]

The unbelief of the Jews since the days of Jesus does not nullify the faith with which their fathers listened to the Christ already

[129] *Ibid., WA* 53, 580:3. In view of this entire—and, on the whole, rather unanimous—judgment of Luther throughout his life, the question needs to be asked whether Aurifaber, in his edition of the sermons on Matthew (1537–1540), did not somewhat shift the emphasis, although Luther's doubts become sufficiently clear even there. "Some hold that the Jews should be converted en masse to the Christian faith before the end of the world. This may well be possible. But that they should again come to Palestine and build the city [Jerusalem], the temple, and the priesthood is impossible. And we see with our own eyes how this prophecy [Matt. 24:15 ff.] is fulfilled in fifteen hundred years." *Sermon on the Twenty-fourth Sunday after Trinity on November 16, 1539, Sermons on Matthew 18–24,* 1537–1541, *WA* 47, 571:2. See also *WA* 47, 545:7 ff.

[130] *A Letter of Martin Luther Against the Sabbatarians, to a Good Friend,* 1538 (*Ein Brieff D. Mart. Luther wider die Sabbather, an einen guten Freunnd*), *WA* 50, 336:30 ff.

speaking to them secretly in the words of Moses and the prophets. To Luther, the later history of Israel became the reverse image of the New Testament. Just as God's promises of grace were fulfilled in Christ and his church, so did the Jewish people have to experience personally the truth of their prophets' prophecies of damnation and God's threats against any unbelief in his Word.

Luther's picture of God acting in history, since it was derived from the Old Testament, everywhere pressed home the point that this mighty God is simultaneously he who himself spoke through Moses and through the prophets. The Old Testament was not a picture book about the Creator and King of nations; instead, it was for Luther a part of God's dealing with mankind. That is why Luther's portrayal of the God of the Old Testament can only be understood in this manner: God here revealed himself and described himself. Thus we are faced with the central question, namely, why Luther considered the Old Testament the Word of God.

# 4

# THE OLD TESTAMENT AS WORD OF GOD

## 1. THE TWO TESTAMENTS: DISTINCTION AND UNITY

It would be well at the outset to remember that for Luther "Old Testament" and "New Testament" were not just the names of two books. He constantly distinguished between old and new covenants, a covenant or testament being the last will or final disposition of one about to die.[1] This is why he was able to speak of the two "testaments" in such a way that the chronological distinction between the two books was nullified. The new testament was promised from the beginning of the world and was fulfilled in Christ. God's old covenant with the people of Israel was promised through Moses and was fulfilled with the conquest of Canaan under Joshua. Moses was only a copy of the eternal testament.

Here Moses points out the difference between the New and the Old Testament. The New Testament is the older one, promised from the beginning of the world, yes, "before the times of the world" as St. Paul says to Titus [1:2], but fulfilled only under Christ. The Old Testament, promised under Moses, was fulfilled under Joshua. However, there is this difference between the two: the New Testament is founded wholly on the promise of the merciful and faithful God without our works; but the Old Testament is founded also on our works.... The promises of Moses, therefore, do not last longer than the statutes and judgments serve. For this reason the Old Testament finally had to become obsolete and had to be put aside; it had to serve as a prefiguration of that New and eternal Testament which began before the ages and will endure beyond the ages. The Old Testament, however, began in time and after a time came to an end.[2]

1 *The Babylonian Captivity of the Church*, 1520 (*De Captivitate Babylonica Ecclesiae*), *WA* 6, 513:24 ff.; *LW* 36, 38.
2 *The Deuteronomy of Moses, with Notes*, 1525, *WA* 14, 602:34 ff.; *LW* 9, 63.

For the Old Testament, which He gave through Moses, was a promise —not of remission of sins or of eternal things, but of temporal things, namely, of the land of Canaan; no man was thereby renewed in his spirit to lay hold of the heavenly inheritance.[3]

This distinction between the testaments is the equivalent of that between law and gospel. It is primary, and precedes the differentiation between the books; Luther carried it right through the Old Testament writings.

If we take this into account, then it is not very difficult to recognize the evidence—at first seemingly complex—in its simple basic feature. At first glance it does seem that Luther's statements about the two testaments fall apart in hopeless contradictions. For instance, put the following judgments side by side:

Luther lets Jeremiah prophesy:

"The Old Testament will no longer be preached, only the new one, so that this righteousness will be spread the width of the world."[4]

And against this:

There is no word in the New Testament that does not look back into the Old, in which it was proclaimed before. The New Testament is nothing more than a revelation of the Old; just as when someone first had a sealed letter and then opened it. In like manner, the Old Testament is a testamentary letter of Christ, which he opened after his death and had read and proclaimed everywhere through the gospel.[5]

Or:

Now if someone holds Moses up before you and wants to press you into holding to him, say, "Go to the Jews with your Moses. I am no Jew. Do not entangle us with Moses. If I accept one item of Moses (says Paul to the Galatians in chapter 5 [:3]), then I

And against this:

Just as the art of all the Greek poets flowed out of Homer as out of a fountain, so did all the prophets' books, indeed, the whole New Testament, which was promised in them, flow out of Moses. And everything which is taught and becomes good and divine among

[3] *The Babylonian Captivity of the Church,* 1520, *WA* 6, 515:8; *LW* 36, 40.
[4] *Sermon of November 25, 1526, on Jer. 23:5 ff., Sermons of 1526, WA* 20, 579:11.
[5] *Sermon on Christmas Day on John 1:1 ff., Church Postil,* 1522, *WA* $10^{I,1}$, 181:21 ff.

am bound to keep the entire law." But not a dot in Moses concerns us.[6]

the people of God or in the church originated with Moses.[7]

One could effortlessly continue this line of antitheses with many other examples from Luther's writings. Nevertheless, these few arbitrarily selected passages suffice to show how the contradictions are to be resolved. Law and gospel are to be found in the Old Testament too, just as law is contained along with the promises of the gospel in the New Testament. Therefore one must really know how to differentiate between the two in reading all of Scripture.

There is no book in the Bible that does not contain both. God has placed them side by side in every way—law and promise. For he teaches through the law what there is to do, through the promise whence it should be taken. But the New Testament is primarily called gospel above other books because it was written after the advent of Christ, who fulfilled God's promise and through oral preaching publicly disseminated that promise which was before hidden in the Scripture. Insist, therefore, upon this difference; and read whatever book is before you—be it Old or New Testament—with such a difference so that you may notice: where there are promises, that is a gospel book; where there are commandments, that is a law book. But because there are a heap of promises in the New Testament and a heap of commandments in the Old, we call one the gospel book and the other the law book.[8]

Thus Luther saw the Scripture as so unified that he could determine the amount and number of basic contradictions governing it in the individual books. We shall have to go into detail to show how he did this, how he unraveled the interwoven gospel and law in the Old Testament.

Luther's concept of the unity of Scripture becomes even more evident when we realize that Luther understood how the New

[6] *Sermon of August 27, 1525, on Exodus 19–20, How Christians Should Regard Moses* (*Ein Unterrichtung wie sich die Christen ynn Mose sollen schicken*), *WA* 16, 375:10; *LW* 35, 166.
[7] *Preface to the First Part of the Old Testament. The Five Books of Moses, with Notes by Wenceslaus Link of Colditz,* 1543 (*Das erst teyl des alten Testaments. Annotation in die fünff bücher Mosi, durch Doctor Wentzelslaum Link, von Cholditz*), *WA* 54, 2:6; see also above, p. 44.
[8] *Sermon on the Third Sunday in Advent on Matt. 11:2 ff., Advent Postil,* 1522, *WA* 10$^{I,2}$, 159:7; *LE* 10, 100.

Testament and the ancient church used the word "Scripture." In the New Testament, "Scripture" naturally meant only the Old Testament. That is why Luther contrasted "Scripture" with "proclamation," the Word of the gospel originally spread only by word of mouth. The gospel, the proclamation of Jesus and the apostles, intended to be nothing but a true introduction to "Scripture," that is, to the Old Testament according to its promises. If one does not see this and insists on taking only the New Testament as Holy Scripture, while rejecting the Old Testament, then the result is, according to Luther, that one makes a law book out of the New Testament. Luther complained:

Because we were not allowed to study the Scripture and learn about Christ therein, we hold the Old Testament of no more value than that it is finished and no longer valid; and we believe that the gospel should not really be Scripture but rather the spoken Word, which proclaims Scripture as Christ and the apostles did. That is why Christ himself wrote nothing; instead, he only spoke and his teaching is not Scripture but gospel, that is, he called it good news or proclamation, which should be propagated by mouth rather than by pen. Thus we go ahead and make a law book, a mockery, out of the gospel, a Moses out of Christ, and a mere teacher out of the Savior.[9]

Thus the books of Moses and the prophets are also gospel, since before Christ they proclaimed and described that which the apostles preached and wrote down after Christ. And yet there is a difference; for although both have been written on paper with letters, the gospel or New Testament should, in reality, not be written down, but should instead appear as the living voice which resounds and is heard everywhere in the world. It was superfluous to write it down. But the Old Testament is only recorded in letters and therefore is called "a letter of the alphabet"; the apostles call it "the Scripture," for it only pointed to the future Christ. The gospel, however, is a living sermon about the Christ who has come.[10]

At first this is a surprising and not an easily comprehended thought: the rejection of the Old Testament makes a law out of the gospel

[9] *A Brief Instruction on What to Look for and Expect in the Gospels,* 1522 (*Eyn kleyn unterricht, wie man ynn den Evangelijs suchen und gewarten soll*), *Church Postil,* 1522, *WA* 10$^{I}$,1, 17:4 ff.; *LW* 35, 123.

[10] *St. Peter's Epistles, Preached and Interpreted,* 1523 (*Epistel Sanct Petri gepredigt und ausgelegt*), *WA* 12, 275:5; *LE* 3, 53; Ernst Rietschel, *Das Problem der unsichtbar-sichtbaren Kirche bei Luther. Darstellung und Lösungsversuch* ("Schriften des Vereins für Reformationsgeschichte," 154 [Leipzig, 1932]), pp. 41 ff.; Bornkamm, *Das Wort Gottes bei Luther,* p. 32.

of the New Testament. It is an even stranger thought when this conclusion is brought into relation with the oral characteristic of the gospel. And yet this thought is precisely the key to at least a preliminary understanding of this striking concept of Luther. That the gospel is not a doctrine but a result of and witness to an act of God, namely, the incarnation in Christ, was evident to Luther precisely in the way that it stood in the context of divine action, that it was promised and expected. And God's present action remains since it is spread by word of mouth and always arouses new life. The oral message of the gospel stands in a context of events reaching backward and forward, and is thus truly historical—namely, God's action in time. Because "Scripture" pointed to something in the future, its testimony had to be written down and safeguarded until the hour of the coming event. In contrast to this, the gospel is the testimony of this event which always recurs through the preaching of the Word; or, as Luther liked to say, it is "distributed." This is why the gospel cannot be a law book.

> For it does not order us to do works to become pious; rather, it proclaims to us the grace of God, given freely without our merit, and tells how Christ stepped into our stead, rendered satisfaction for our sin, paid for it, and made us pious and blessed through his work.[11]

Whoever rejects the Old Testament dissolves this relationship of "Scripture" and oral Word, according to Luther, and makes the gospel, which alone was declared "Scripture," into a law.

Luther did not invent this relationship between Old and New Testament; rather, he read it out of the New Testament itself. He aptly observed how little Paul and Peter report the individual acts of Jesus in their letters: Paul wrote gospel by making mighty sermons out of a very few passages of the Old Testament, whose fulfilment in Christ he demonstrated; and yet everyone must say that they contained the truth. And Christ himself did it no other way. Therefore it is no wonder that Luther promised that if he were a prophet he would make a New Testament out of Moses.

> [Moses] was known among the prophets, and their books were spun out of his book. And I, if I were rich in the spirit, should like to make a New Testament out of it. Paul and Peter report little about Christ's

[11] *St. Peter's Epistles, Preached and Interpreted,* 1523, *WA* 12, 259:15; *LE* 3, 33–34.

individual acts. You can truly see what kind of gospel Paul creates because he certainly makes mighty sermons out of a very few passages of the Old Testament; and everyone is forced to say, "It is the truth." What did Christ do in Matthew 22 [:32]? He used the most common word the Jews had: "I am the God of Abraham." This they knew very well; this was the best-known text. What does Christ conclude from it? The Sadducees know nothing about either the Spirit or the angels. Here Christ lets Moses speak and be seen by those who are blind.[12]

So in reading Luther we must always keep the unity of the two testaments as much in mind as their differences. The unity consists in that the complete content of the divine Word, law and gospel, includes both and is contained in both. There are two main differences: in the Old Testament the laws and in the New Testament the promises are contained "in heaps"; and, on the other hand, God's act of salvation is promised in the Old Testament but certified as fulfilled in the New Testament. This is a difference of matter and time. This concern for unity and difference is combined in Luther with the inescapable double meaning of "testament" as "covenant" and as "book." One may not utilize Luther's judgments about the relationship of the Old Testament to the New Testament without taking these differences into consideration. I shall once more place two of Luther's statements side by side to show the application of the concepts more clearly.

Just as the Old Testament is a book in which are written God's laws and commandments, together with the history of those who kept them and those who did not keep them, so the New Testament is a book in which are written the gospel and the promises of God, together with the history of those who believe and those who do not believe them.[13]

Since the Gospels and Epistles of the apostles have been written to direct us to the writings of the prophets and of Moses in the Old Testament so that we might read and see for ourselves how Christ was wrapped in swaddling clothes and laid in the manger—that is, how he is contained in the writings of the prophets.[14]

Both statements are from two small tracts which not only

[12] *Easter Sermon of April 6, 1534, Sermons of 1534, WA* 37, 365:7.
[13] *Preface to the New Testament,* 1522 (*Vorrede auff das newe Testament*), *WA,* DB 6, 2:16; *LW* 35, 358.
[14] *A Brief Instruction on What to Look for and Expect in the Gospels, Church Postil,* 1522, *WA* 10I,1, 15:1; *LW* 35, 122.

belong together chronologically but are also closely related in thought:[15] the preface to the *September Testament* and the (chronologically preceding) introduction to the *Christmas Postil* of 1522, *A Brief Instruction on What to Look for and Expect in the Gospels.* The contrast of the formulations seen at such close quarters makes especially obvious how inseparable the two sides of his view of the Old and New Testaments were for Luther.[16]

But the striking feature of Luther's view is not the separation of the two books, but the assertion that Moses and the prophets also contained gospel, and that one must differentiate within the testaments rather than between the testaments. How did Luther arrive at this view? Was it perhaps the result of a particular method of exegesis which Luther inherited from the ancient church and from which he did not completely depart?

## 2. LUTHER'S EXEGETICAL METHOD

The question of whether Luther's discovery of the gospel in the Old Testament stemmed from a particular exegetical method suggests itself when one remembers the strange hermeneutical premises with which Luther began his work.[17] Medieval theology, by reaching back to its origins in Augustine and John Cassian, had united the various forms of the exegeses of the ancient church into a fixed scheme. The rule of the "four senses of Scripture" had developed out of earlier, less complex forms. 1) the literal; 2) the allegorical—the spiritual interpretation applied especially to the church and its progress and property; 3) the tropological, or moral sense, which applied the particular text to the life of the

[15] A fact which is pointed out correctly by Walther Köhler in his Introduction to the *Wartburg Postil,* 1522, *WA* $10^{I,2}$, LXXIV.

[16] The two brief writings mesh in other respects. Thus the preface enumerates the most important Old Testament promises of the Gospels, the *Instruction* a number of New Testament flashbacks to the Old Testament. *WA,* DB 6, 4:24 ff.; *LW* 35, 359 ff.; and *WA* $10^{I,1}$, 15:5 ff.; *LW* 35, 122 ff.

[17] See Karl A. Meissinger, *Luthers Exegese in der Frühzeit* (Leipzig, 1911); Holl, "Luthers Bedeutung für den Fortschritt der Auslegekunst," in *Gesammelte Aufsätze zur Kirchengeschichte,* I, 545 ff.; Heinrich Böhmer, *Luthers erste Vorlesung* ("Berichte über die Verhandlungen der Sächsischen Akademie der Wissenschaften in Leipzig. Philosophisch-historische Klasse," 75, 1 [Leipzig, 1924]), pp. 45 ff.; Vogelsang, *Die Anfänge von Luthers Christologie*, pp. 16 ff.; Fritz Hahn, "Luthers Auslegungsgrundsätze und ihre theologischen Voraussetzungen," *Zeitschrift für systematische Theologie,* XII (1935), 165 ff.; Ebeling, *Evangelische Evangelienauslegung.*

individual; and 4) the anagogical, or eschatological sense of Scripture.[18]

Luther had ventured into the land of the Old Testament with this famous four-horse chariot in his first lecture series on the Psalms in 1513–1515, and he had, understandably, brought back with him the rich fruits of an evangelical interpretation of the Psalms. Of course Luther gave his own personal accent to this exegesis. With Faber Stapulensis and the ancient church and in opposition to such a decisive interpreter as Lyra, he understood the "literal" sense not as historical-factual interpretation, but as "literal, prophetic sense," namely, as the interpretation speaking out of the spirit of the prophets which pointed to the coming Christ.[19] Each one of the exegetical methods is justified by this turning toward Christ; not just in the sense of a dogmatic presentation, but rather, in the sense that thereby Christ's call to decision in the life of the individual becomes, at the same time, visible tropologically. Thus Luther killed the four senses of Scripture at the moment he applied them. And out of the combination of prophetic and tropological interpretations[20] Luther's only exegeti-

[18] See Ernst von Dobschütz, "Vom vierfachen Schriftsinn," *Harnack Ehrung* (Leipzig, 1921), pp. 1 ff.; and Vogelsang, *Die Anfänge von Luthers Christologie,* pp. 20 ff. On the Catholic side, see A. Vaccari, "S. Tommasso e Lutero nella storia dell'esegesi," *La civiltà cattolica,* LXXXV/LXXXVI (1935), II, 561 ff., and III, 36 ff. While Luther's relation to the scholastic and humanistic exegesis has frequently been investigated, information concerning his relation to the Jewish exegesis is contained only in the rich collection of material in C. Siegfried, "Raschi's Einfluss auf Nicolaus von Lyra und Luther in der Auslegung der Genesis," *Archiv für wissenschaftliche Erforschung des Alten Testamentes,* I (1869), 428 ff., and II (1871), 39 ff.; and in Moritz Freier, *Luthers Busspsalmen und Psalter. Kritische Untersuchungen nach jüdischen und lateinischen Quellen* ("Beiträge zur Wissenschaft vom Alten Testament," ed. Rudolf Kittel, 24 [Leipzig, 1918]); however, it treats only the questions of translation and goes too far in its assumption of the influence of Jewish exegetes. See the critical review of Johannes Ficker in *Theologische Literaturzeitung,* XLIV (1919), 59, and Pahls, *Quellenstudien zu Luthers Psalmenübersetzung,* pp. 128–29. The lectures on Genesis, of course, have hitherto usually been exploited most for exegetical, dogmatic, and other material. See also, in addition to the work of Meinhold (*Die Genesisvorlesung Luthers und ihre Herausgeber*), Otto Zöckler, "Luther als Ausleger des Alten Testamentes," *Evangelische Kirchenzeitung,* IX–XIII (1881), and Erich Seeberg, *Studien zu Luthers Genesisvorlesung. Zugleich ein Beitrag zur Frage nach dem alten Luther* ("Beiträge zur Förderung christlicher Theologie," 36 [Gütersloh, 1932]).

[19] See F. Hahn, "Luthers Auslegungsgrundsätze," pp. 166 ff., and, by the same author, "Faber Stapulensis und Luther," *Zeitschrift für Kirchengeschichte,* LVII (1938), 356 ff.

[20] One should not be tempted by the frequent description of the tropological sense as "first sense" (*sensus primarius*) to isolate it from the others. See

cal goal soon rose above the formal differentiations: to make Christ, the content of Scripture, present for the individual in judgment and grace.

Luther further applied the traditional methods to this goal. He certainly did not give up *allegory* either when he turned away from the scheme of th efour senses of Scripture after his lectures on Romans in 1515–1516; he only pushed its importance further back and sought to free it from arbitrary interpretation through fixed norms. Karl Holl pointed out that Luther ended a centuries-old error when he removed the equation of spiritual understanding and allegorical explanation used heretofore.[21] Luther called the prophetic-tropological sense "spiritual," namely, Scripture's pointing toward Christ who is savior and judge. He used this "spiritual" criterion rather than false allegorizing. All of his various reasons for his countless complaints against the spiritual games of Origen, Jerome, and others can be traced ultimately to the one all-inclusive reason: the allegorists miss the sense of Christ in Scripture. This is evident where they read all sorts of arbitrary allusions into the text where it applies to Christ or to man under the Word.[22] If the Christological understanding is missing, one stands before the Old Testament in utter confusion, be it because one does not know how to interpret the promises correctly, or because one does not know how to interpret the law correctly. Luther sagaciously recognized that the allegorical methods with which Origen or Jerome sought to bring the Old Testament to the

Psalm 77, *Lectures on the Psalter,* 1513–1516, *WA* 3, 531:33; and Psalm 60, *ibid.,* 335:21. It presupposes the "literal prophetic sense" (*sensus literalis propheticus*) and breaks up the whole scheme of the four senses of Scripture.

21 See Holl, "Luthers Bedeutung für den Fortschritt der Auslegekunst," in *op. cit.,* I, 558. See also below, p. 249. On the question of allegory as such, one must now refer to Ebeling (*op. cit.*), who used Luther's relation to it almost as the methodic theme of his study of Luther's interpretation of the Gospels (see especially the Contents and the Index).

22 Thus monastic theologians, for example, related "Jerusalem" in Isaiah 37 to the humility of the monastic vocation, while Luther understood it as an image of the terrified conscience "as far as Word and faith are concerned." *Lectures on Isaiah,* 1527–1530, *WA* 31$^{II}$, 242:16—243:3. He frequently cited the unlimited interpretation of all feminine terms as references to Mary or the monasteries, etc.—the "house" (*castellum*) of Martha (Luke 10:38)—to show the meaninglessness of allegorical interpretations. *The Deuteronomy of Moses, with Notes,* 1525, *WA* 14, 560:29; *LW* 9, 24–25; *Lectures on Isaiah,* 1527–1530, *WA* 31$^{II}$, 242:20.

level of Christian taste and spirit in reality gave it the *coup de grace:* the allegorical interpretation killed the spiritual sense of the Old Testament.

> There are some who have little regard for the Old Testament; they think of it as a book that was given to the Jewish people only and is now out of date, containing only stories of the past. They think they have enough in the New Testament and assert that only a spiritual sense is to be sought in the Old Testament. Origen, Jerome, and many other distinguished people have held this view.[23]

While they sought something supposedly greater in it, they missed the examples of faith and the divine promises contained therein. Of course a greater message is often hidden in a situation such as the reconstruction of the temple. But the future kingdom of Christ is promised therein at the same time.[24] The allegorists in their spiritualization could recognize the correct sense of the law no better. Luther, in important basic explanations of the Old Testament in the preface of 1523 and in his instruction *How Christians Should Regard Moses* of 1525, indicated how he deduced the questions which he applied to Scripture from the failure of Origen, Jerome, and their followers.[25]

Luther usually contrasted false allegory with "history."

> One should think much, and magnificently, about history, but little about allegory. You should use allegory like a flower, for it illustrates the sermon rather than strengthens it.... In history you have complete as well as incomplete promises. Allegory does not establish doctrine, but, like color, can only add to it. The painter's colors do not build the house. The human body does not consist of a wreath of flowers, or a beautiful garment, etc. This proves that faith is not grounded in allegories.[26]

By this he meant the actual course of Israelite history. If one looks at the consoling picture of God's preservation of this people in the midst of powerful enemies and does not dissipate it allegorically, then one's hope for help in one's own need is strengthened.

[23] *Preface to the Old Testament,* 1523 (*Vorrede auf das Alte Testament*), *EA* 63, 7; *LW* 35, 235.
[24] *The Prophet Zechariah,* 1527, *WA* 23, 608:32.
[25] See above, p. 89, n. 21, and *How Christians Should Regard Moses,* 1525, *WA* 16, 393:11; *LW* 35, 174.
[26] *Lectures on Isaiah,* 1527–1530, *WA* 31^II^, 97:15 ff.

This is your consolation in every affliction. Do not despair; know that God is truthful and able to remain steadfast, as he promised, even if a hundred cities of Babel had to be destroyed. Israel had to endure bodily captivity; you have to endure spiritual captivity. If you believe, God will also liberate you and will not abandon you.[27]

Thus Luther's fundamental dictum, "Faith rests upon history,"[28] meant the actual course of history seen as God's work, as his guidance or as his judgment. There is no separation of public and private in this history of God; it is a unity. That is why past historical events can become a comfort and help in our spiritual history. "Therefore we suffer spiritually, according to our personal history, what our ancestors suffered physically, according to their public history."[29] One recognizes history when one follows the *literal sense* and refuses to be knocked off one's feet by allegories. Otherwise Scripture becomes a "torn net": "everyone poked a hole in it wherever his snout pointed, and followed his own opinions, interpreting and twisting it any way he pleased."[30] This literal sense, correctly understood Christologically, is solely "the whole basis of faith and Christian theology" and, in opposition to the forever uncertain allegory, the only secure footing in conflict *(Anfechtung).*

[The literal sense] alone holds the ground in trouble and trial, conquers the gates of hell [Matt. 16:18] along with sin and death, and triumphs for the praise and glory of God. Allegory, however, is too often uncertain, unreliable, and by no means safe for supporting faith. Too frequently it depends upon human guesswork and opinion; and if one leans on it, one will lean on a staff made of Egyptian reed [Ezek. 29:6].[31]

For Luther it was also the literal sense when he interpreted the Song of Songs as poetic imagery. In contrast to Erasmus (love song), the Jews (allegory about God and the synagogue), Christian allegorists (Christ and the church), and tropologists (Christ and the soul), he conceived of the Song of Songs as a hymn of praise for the felicitous order in the nation, for peace, for the

27 *Ibid.*, 97:26 ff.
28 *Ibid.*, 242:24.
29 *Ibid.*, 243:7.
30 *That These Words of Christ, "This Is My Body," etc., Still Stand Firm Against the Fanatics*, 1527 (*Das diese wort Christi [Das ist mein Leib etc.] noch feste stehen wider die Schwermgeister*), *WA* 23, 66:5 ff.; *LW* 37, 14.
31 *The Deuteronomy of Moses, with Notes*, 1525, *WA* 14, 560:14; *LW* 9, 24.

correct relationship between people and political authority and people and God.[32] It is the way of the poet to sing of such things in images: "You can see that speaking in images is the way of poetry";[33] and this is quite different from allegory, from which Luther particularly and decidedly departed in this connection.

I leave allegories alone. A young theologian should avoid them as much as he can. I think that in a thousand years there was no more economical allegorist than myself.... Become a text critic and learn about the grammatical sense, whatever grammar intends, which is about faith, patience, death, and life. The Word of God does not deal with frivolous things. Hence, we call it "Song of Songs," that is, a supreme song, because it writes about the highest things, which are political.[34]

Allegory carries an ulterior, spiritual sense into the text, whereas imagery is a natural poetic means to express figuratively the sole and unequivocal sense of the work of art. It is therefore the literal sense.

Now and then Luther contrasted allegory with *revelation,* which, next to knowledge, prophecy, and doctrine, Paul had elevated above speaking in tongues. Here once again his reason for rejecting allegory is made especially clear: "Revelation is, of course, something more than allegory—namely, to meet something special in Scripture that not everyone can meet."[35] This particularity, in contrast to allegorical confusion, is once again nothing else than the trademark of the whole Scripture: law and gospel.

Luther often used allegory in spite of his untiring warning, "Beware of allegories."[36] How is this possible? He considered allegory permissible if used according to the "analogy of faith" and directed to a goal which was clearly and unequivocally determined by the literal sense of other Scripture passages.

This is done when, according to the injunction of Romans 12 [:6], prophecy is according to the analogy of faith. You first take a definite statement in the Scriptures, explain it according to the literal sense,

[32] *A Brief, Yet Clear Exposition of the Song of Songs,* 1530–1531, *WA* 31^II^, 589:6 ff.; 591:10 ff.; 592:2 ff.; 639:25 ff. See also the Preface, *ibid.,* 587:24 ff.; and above, p. 16.

[33] *Ibid.,* 594:20.

[34] *Ibid.,* 592:16 ff. I therefore do not believe it is right to understand, as Holl does (*op. cit.,* I, 554), the meaning of allegory in Luther from the viewpoint of poetic imagery.

[35] *Psalm 117,* 1530 (*Der Hundert und siebenzehende Psalm*), *WA* 31^I^, 254:23; *LW* 14, 36.

[36] *Lectures on Isaiah,* 1527–1530, *WA* 31^II^, 243:20.

and then at the end connect an allegorical meaning which says the same thing, not as though the allegory proved or supported the statement of doctrine, for it is proved or supported by the statement, just as a house does not hold up the foundation but is held up by the foundation.[37]

By this is meant not only Christ, in the narrow sense of person, but also the whole broad extent of his kingdom.[38] This is demonstrated by a few examples from Luther's interpretation of Deuteronomy (1525), where, according to literal interpretation, the mystery in almost every chapter is explained allegorically. The names of places in Deuteronomy 1 were interpreted by deductions in terms of law and gospel, of the old and new man.[39] That Moses no longer crossed the Jordan (Deuteronomy 3) meant that law does not lead to the kingdom of God; Joshua represented Christ;[40] the golden calf (Deut. 9:16) referred to the doctrine of works-righteousness, which the priests invented to their advantage;[41] splitting hooves (Deut. 14:6) meant differentiating law and gospel;[42] killing the neighbor (Deuteronomy 19) meant ruining a soul through false doctrine; an eye for an eye meant false teachers are punished by God;[43] wars of nations (Deuteronomy 20) meant spiritual wars;[44] not to fell fruit trees (Deut. 20:19) meant not to deny the bit of truth contained in every heresy. "'The fruit trees are not to be cut down' means that if they have true pronouncements on Scripture, these should not be denied. For there never was any heresy which did not also speak some truth."[45] That betrothed men should not be sent into war (Deut. 20:7) meant newly baptized men should not be commissioned as preachers.[46] The heifer that has not yet borne a yoke (Deut. 21:3) meant Christ in his sinless human flesh.[47] That one should not plow with both an ox

[37] *The Deuteronomy of Moses, with Notes,* 1525, *WA* 14, 561:20; *LW* 9, 25. See also *Lectures on Genesis,* 1536, *WA* 42, 367:33; *LW* 2, 150–51.
[38] See the spiritual interpretation of Isaac's sacrifice in *Sermons on Genesis,* 1527, *WA* 24, 398:29.
[39] *The Deuteronomy of Moses, with Notes,* 1525, *WA* 14, 562:30 ff.; *LW* 9, 26–27.
[40] *Ibid., WA* 14, 579:34 ff.; *LW* 9, 42–43.
[41] *Ibid., WA* 14, 638:9; *LW* 9, 108.
[42] *Ibid., WA* 14, 650:20; *LW* 9, 136.
[43] *Ibid., WA* 14, 689:19 ff.; 690:30 ff.; *LW* 9, 197 ff.
[44] *Ibid., WA* 14, 693:24 ff.; *LW* 9, 205.
[45] *Ibid., WA* 14, 694:28; *LW* 9, 206.
[46] *Ibid., WA* 14, 694:35; *LW* 9, 206.
[47] *Ibid., WA* 14, 697:28; *LW* 9, 213. See also the *scholia* to Heb. 9:13, *WA* 57, 206:29; *LCC* 16, 170; and Emanuel Hirsch and Hanns Rückert (eds.),

and an ass together (Deut. 22:10) meant one should not teach both faith and works at the same time.[48] This list of allegorical equations could be continued at will and complemented with other interpretations of Luther: out of the postils,[49] the "spiritual" explanation of the Book of Exodus (1524–1527),[50] of Jonah (1526),[51] of Zechariah (1527), where, as Luther said himself, he "began allegorical interpretations";[52] out of the complete, even grotesque, allegorical interpretation of Psalm 68 (1521)[53] and Psalm 45 (1532),[54] of Isa. 1:2, 6; 14:2; 37:31, etc. (1527–1530),[55] and out of the allegorical interpretations of the lectures on Genesis (1535–1545).[56]

These dates show that Luther used allegory at all periods of his life. Of course he became more cautious in his use of it as time went on. There is a sharp and definite break after 1525.[57] In his lectures on Genesis, which have relatively few allegorical interpre-

---

*Luthers Vorlesung über den Hebräerbrief nach der Vatikanischen Handschrift herausgegeben* ("Arbeiten zur Kirchengeschichte," 13 [Berlin and Leipzig, 1929]), p. 222:22. Here Luther clearly appealed to the agreement with all church fathers.

48 *The Deuteronomy of Moses, with Notes,* 1525, *WA* 14, 705:11; *LW* 9, 225.

49 *Lenten Postil,* 1525, *WA* 17II, XXIII; *Sermon on the Feast of the Annunciation, on Luke 1:26 ff., ibid.,* 404 ff. When Luther interpreted the two wives of Elkanah [I Samuel 1] in this sermon, which is a revision of a sermon of 1523 (*WA* 12, 461:30 ff.), in terms of the righteousness of law and faith (*WA* 17II, 407:37 ff.), not only the connection with the medieval exegesis is disclosed in it (see the *glossaria ordinaria* cited by Arnold Schleiff in *Luther's German Bible, WA,* DB 9I, 522), but also the differentiation from it. For Luther sharply separated law and faith here, whereas the gloss connects them. One can always hear Luther's basic theme in his allegorical variations, namely, justification.

50 *Sermons on Exodus,* 1524–1527, *WA* 16.

51 *The Prophet Jonah,* 1526, *WA* 19, 245 ff.

52 *The Prophet Zechariah,* 1527, *WA* 23, 524 ff.; 522:8 ff.

53 *German Exposition of Psalm* 68, 1521 (*Deutsche Auslegung des sieben und sechzigsten [68] Psalms*), *WA* 8, 25:31 ff.; *LW* 13, 26–27.

54 *Lecture on Psalm 45,* 1532, *WA* 40II, 473:5; 598:6; *LW* 12, 198, 291.

55 *Lectures on Isaiah,* 1527–1530, *WA* 31II, 4:8; 53:8 ff.; 97:29 ff.; 243:1. In any event, Isaiah 6 is the only chapter which, in contrast to the interpretation of Deuteronomy, contains an elaborate allegory. See also below, p. 206, n. 459.

56 *Lectures on Genesis,* 1536, *WA* 42, 310:8 ff.; 368 ff.; 43, 490:14 ff.; 44, 766:6; *LW* 2, 67–68, 151 ff.

57 So also Ebeling (*op. cit.,* p. 87), who, in addition, refers to the clearer, but less significant break around 1529; after this date the use of allegory diminished even further. He is certainly right when he relates both turning points to the experiences which Luther gained in his struggle with the biblical interpretations of the enthusiasts (*Schwärmer*) and of Erasmus and those of the northern Germans (*ibid.,* p. 357). The rich allegorical interpretation in the exposition of Zechariah, whose visions otherwise do not yield any useful meaning, represents a special case all by itself; it throws light on Luther's basic position concerning allegory only from the opposite side. See above, pp. 33–34.

tations, he again more strongly than in many previous lectures kept the rule he had established after overcoming the four senses of Scripture: allegory is recommended when the text does not yield any other useful sense. In any case, using this rule he still interpreted Ps. 19:1 in *Works on the Psalms,* 1519–1521, "The heavens are telling the glory of God," to mean the apostles, while those passages he really could not understand he interpreted allegorically in his lectures on Genesis.

> But the clear circumstances and the logical connection of what is said here, as well as the authority of the New Testament, force us to grasp an allegory, which otherwise is to be avoided by the biblical interpreter as much as possible.... For we frequently say that one should not play around with allegory in Scripture (at least not in a debate), if allegory is not forced upon us by other biblical passages.[58]

So he applied the prediction that Judah would wash his garments in wine (Gen. 49:11) to the overflowing wealth of the Holy Spirit. "This is why absurdity forces us to move away from carnal understanding, as Augustine used to say, or from the washing of actual clothes, and to insist upon a spiritual or allegorical sense; for this never happened literally in the tribe of Judah, much less under Christ."[59]

Therefore it is not true that Luther depended upon allegory as the only interpretation. He used it only where a figurative meaning alone seemed possible.[60] Otherwise, he often used both methods of interpretation side by side. But one must also differentiate accurately: except in cases of obvious necessity, Luther never invalidated the literal sense for the allegorical; but he often added a spiritual interpretation of Christ and his kingdom to the literal interpretation. Once Luther departed from the methods of scholastic-humanistic exegesis, already characteristically modified by him, he was never again confused about the clear sense of Scripture. Luther was

58 *Works on the Psalms,* 1519–1521, *WA* 5, 541:12 ff. (differently interpreted in 1530–1531, *WA* 31$^{I}$, 339:21; 581:4; *LW* 12, 140). See also the other passages collected by Holl (*op. cit.,* I, 553, nn. 5–6) from the writings between 1519 and 1521: *Works on the Psalms,* 1519–1521, *WA* 5, 111:23; *The Babylonian Captivity of the Church,* 1520, *WA* 6, 509:10; *LW* 36, 95; *Against Latomus,* 1521 (*Rationis Latomia Confutatio*), *WA* 8, 63:27; *LW* 32, 167; *Against Henry, King of England,* 1522 (*Contra Henricum, Regem Angliae*), *WA* 10$^{II}$, 206:17 ff.

59 *Lectures on Genesis,* 1544, *WA* 44, 766:6 ff.

60 For an example, see below, p. 191.

strengthened in this regulated application of allegory because he recognized it as an artistic device frequently used in Scripture itself. He interpreted the sword and bow of the godless (Ps. 37:14) with Ps. 57:4 as their nasty tongues.[61] But above all Luther was encouraged by Paul's manifold use of allegory, such as the veil over Moses' face (II Cor. 3:13),[62] Sarah and Hagar (Gal. 4:22 ff.),[63] and that which was used in the Epistle to the Hebrews.

Luther's moderate use of allegory therefore does not offer any explanation for his own assertion that the Old Testament also included gospel besides law. Moreover, the method of allegorical interpretation is so infrequent in Luther that it only appeared as an exception to the comprehensive *prophetic application of the Old Testament to Christ.* Luther did not hold on to it for reasons of tradition; it was an inseparable part of his theology as a whole. The Christ, who is the eternal Word, awaits discovery in Scripture (John 5:39).[64] God's historical guidance by his promise of fulfilment, the wonderful divine veiling of the Spirit in the letter, the appointment of the law to be the disciplinarian for Christ were the unshakeable foundations of Luther's theology. He never faltered for even a moment in finding the Christ of the new covenant already promised and anticipated in overwhelming profusion in the old covenant. But yet he was not content to assume this axiomatically; rather, he thought he could also demonstrate it in the Old Testament. For example, Zech. 2:8, "He sent me to the pagans," must have been said about Christ. This can be demonstrated because it simply does not fit the prophet himself.[65]

Luther made such comprehensive use of the prophetic application, in his firm conviction that all of Scripture is filled with secret references to Christ, that it can in no way be sufficiently documented through single examples. The Old Testament idea of king-

[61] *Psalm 37 of David,* 1521, *WA* 8, 220:6 ff.
[62] *The Deuteronomy of Moses, with Notes,* 1525, *WA* 14, 561:26; *LW* 9, 26.
[63] *Lectures on Galatians,* 1519, *WA* 2, 549:27 ff.; *LW* 27, 310 ff.
[64] See Bornkamm, *Das Wort Gottes bei Luther;* Otto Scheel, *Luthers Stellung zur Heiligen Schrift. Vortrag* ("Sammlung gemeinverständlicher Vorträge," 29 [Tübingen and Leipzig, 1902]); Paul Schempp, *Luthers Stellung zur Heiligen Schrift* ("Forschungen zur Geschichte und Lehre des Protestantismus," II, 3 [München, 1929]); F. Hahn, "Luthers Auslegungsgrundsätze," pp. 165 ff.
[65] *The Prophet Zechariah,* 1527, *WA* 23, 532:37 ff.

ship,[66] priesthood, and sacrifice, the stories of the patriarchs[67] and the witness of the prophets, the spiritual ideas and images of nature in the Psalms[68] suggested an anticipation of the coming glory of Christ and his kingdom. The preponderance of this Christocentric sense of the text was so great that Luther even decided that debatable passages conformed to it. In the passage from Ps. 118:27, still debated today, Luther, in contradistinction to the translation of the rabbis, "bind the sacrificial lamb with ropes up to the horns of the altar," arrived at the German translation "adorn the festival with branches . . ." *(schmücket das Fest mit Maien)* through the prophetic sense of the whole psalm. He did not like "sacrificial animal" for the debatable Hebrew term *ḥag,* and therefore decided in favor of the other meaning, "festival."

The meaning is that at the time of Christ every festival will be a daily festival, in which one joyfully preaches in faith and thereby renders sacrifices of thanksgiving to God. This is what it means to "adorn the festival with branches up to the altar," to be joyful in word and faith and thus, in Christ who is our altar, to glorify and praise God.[69]

The case of the textual difficulty of Ps. 22:16 was much easier for him. For compared to the traditional translation he followed, "They will pierce *(karu)* my hands and feet," the literal translation of the Masoretic text by the rabbis, "like a lion" *(ka'ari),* was completely senseless. But on this occasion he expressed with particular clarity that the Christological orientation of the whole psalm completely eliminated any choice in this case.

66 On the law for the election of kings (Deut. 17:14 ff.): "The appointment of a king properly denotes Christ, who comes after the law, which is symbolized by the judge." Then follows an exact enumeration of the traits of Christ which agree with the regulations for the election. *The Deuteronomy of Moses, with Notes,* 1525, *WA* 14, 673:1 ff.; *LW* 9, 171.

67 There is rich evidence in Luther's sermons on Genesis and Exodus (1524–1527), *WA* 16 and 24. See also the convenient survey in Karl Eger, "Luthers Auslegung des Alten Testamentes, nach ihren Grundsätzen und ihrem Charakter an Hand seiner Predigten über das 1. und 2. Buch Mose untersucht," *Festgruss Bernhard Stade dargebracht* (Giessen, 1900), pp. 297 ff. See also the lectures on Genesis.

68 Only one example (Ps. 19:4): "He says that a tent has been set for the sun in heaven, that is, that Christ will reign and rule in all the lands that will believe in Christ, and that the holy Christian church will be as wide as the world." *A Very Brief Christian Exposition of Psalm 19,* 1531 (*Ein sehr Christliche kurtze Auslegung über den neuntzehenden Psalm*), *WA* 31$^{I}$, 582:18; *LW* 12, 141.

69 *Defense of the Translation of the Psalms,* 1531–1533, *WA* 38, 15:21 ff.; *LW* 35, 220.

It is very easy for us—who believe in Christ and think, on the basis of evangelical authority, that this whole psalm is spoken about Christ—to prove that "they have pierced" and not "like a lion" should be read. For we do not elucidate the text out of the mysteries of Scripture, but the mysteries of Scripture out of the text. That is, we illustrate the Scripture of the Old Testament through the gospel, and not vice versa; and we compare the sense of the former through the sense of the latter.... But since we are certain that the hands and feet of Christ were pierced on the cross and no less certain that this psalm fits Christ, then the sense agrees in an extraordinary manner and everything else compels the reading "they have pierced," especially since there is not even a grammatical reason against this; we read without contradiction and hesitation, "they have pierced."[70]

And he had the easiest time in the passages where, although he knew the textual problem, he found the Christological sense in the Masoretic text itself and thus could keep to the original wording, for example, in Ps. 2:12.[71]

With very little effort we could pile up examples of Luther's prophetic exegesis as high as a mountain. But it seems to me more important, and more characteristic of his method of interpretation, to illustrate it by studying one example closely. If one wishes to understand the sense of his interpretation one should not confine oneself to isolated surprising and tradition-bound clever examples. Instead one should seek an example of his prophetic-Christological method of exegesis. I chose his beautiful interpretation of *Psalm 117,* which he wrote at Coburg.[72] It is particularly suitable, not only because of its transparent simplicity but also because the psalm almost puts a New Testament interpretation into Luther's mouth without requiring exegetical tricks.

Praise the Lord all you pagans,
Praise the Lord all you peoples.
For his goodness and faithfulness
Reigns over us for ever. Hallelujah!

According to Luther, the psalm has four things to tell us:

[70] *Works on the Psalms,* 1519–1521, *WA* 5, 633:15 ff., 22 ff. (an elaborate discussion of the textual problem follows). I am grateful for the reference to this passage in Fritz Hahn, "Zur Verchristlichung der Psalmen durch Luthers Übersetzung," *Theologische Studien und Kritiken,* CVI (1934–1935), 187 ff.
[71] "Kiss the Son" (Vulgate: *apprehendite disciplinam*). *Lectures on the Psalter,* 1513–1516, *WA* 3, 34:1 ff.; *LW* 12, 82–83. See also F. Hahn, "Zur Verchristlichung der Psalmen," pp. 184 ff. Further examples below, pp. 227–28.
[72] *Psalm 117,* 1530, *WA* 31$^{I}$, 223 ff.; *LW* 14, 1 ff.

*1. A prediction:* the promise of the gospel and of the kingdom of Christ, for if the pagans are called to proclaim God's praise, he must first have become their God. He must first be preached to them, and all idolatry must have been overcome through God's Word for them to believe in him. "Now see what an uproar this little psalm caused in the whole world, how it raved and raged among the idols."[73] Thus the psalm became a witness to the almighty power of the divine Word. What a comfort and what a promise of victory for the church, which often seemed almost lost among the peoples!

*2. A revelation:* the kingdom of Christ will be a spiritual, heavenly one, and not a temporal, earthly kingdom, for the psalmist lets the pagans remain where they are, and does not call them to gather together in Jerusalem. He also lets them remain what they are, and does not demand that they quit their vocation and estate to accept new laws and customs, namely, Jewish ones. Thus the law of Moses is "mightily" nullified and something higher is commanded: to praise God in all nations. But then he must have let himself be heard in all the world. "And where is there a God whose Word has sounded so far into all the world . . . as the gospel of Christ?"[74] This commandment to all the pagans demonstrates that the gospel is above all worldly laws and that the spiritual and the secular may never be mixed—as happens in canon law and everywhere in the papacy. The whole Roman cult has thus also been annulled through this revelation, and the external legalism of the anabaptists has been condemned.[75]

*3. A doctrine:* we can stand before God only in faith, for his *goodness,* his free grace, reigns over us and thus nullifies all of our own holiness under Jewish law, mass, monastic life, and good works. The heaven of grace arches over and outlasts the clouds of our sins. "Reigns *over us*": this "over us," in the mouth of the royal psalmist, teaches how Jews and pagans become one single people of God in faith, and how the old law is completely annulled. And "*his faithfulness* reigns over us": thus God commits himself and calls us to hope, even if we only get to see the opposite of

[73] *Ibid., WA* 31<sup>I</sup>, 230:1; *LW* 14, 10.
[74] *Ibid., WA* 31$^{I}$, 237:10; *LW* 14, 18.
[75] *Ibid., WA* 31$^{I}$, 242:12 ff.; *LW* 14, 23–24.

his goodness and grace—the cross and wrath of God. Faith must "grant the devil one small hour of divinity, and let him ascribe to our God satanity. But that is not yet the end of it. The last word is: his goodness and faithfulness reign over us."[76]

*4. An admonition:* to praise and to thank. Thus the sacrifices of the old covenant are overcome as much as the sacrifices of the mass, and monastic vows, pilgrimages, and the cult of the saints, with which one wants to bargain and horse-trade with God.[77] That is why vows and pledges are not binding when the conscience realizes that they are against God. Whatever is not based solely on Christ the cornerstone but on one's own piety or pious work (such as the baptism of the anabaptists) does not endure in the severe conflict *(Anfechtung),* which Luther subsequently described so grippingly.[78]

With the hand of a master, Luther had polished the small psalm into a radiant gem reflecting the full brilliance of the gospel: its overcoming of the Mosaic law, the Roman church and all its ways of life, canon law, anabaptist legalism; its confirmation of estate and vocation, of the right relationship between the spiritual and the secular; and countless other features. But the brilliance flowed from a single source: the prophetic application of the psalm to the coming Christ. Yet it was not a messianic psalm which simply and directly presented the figure of the coming Messiah. Rather, it spoke indirectly about him: each word of the psalmist presupposed the future revelation which meant that it already was communicated in veiled form.

As much as this example of Luther's exegesis moves us, it also shows very clearly that every bit of his work was based on his prophetic-Christological view. This was not simply a collection of loose formulations full of faith and spirit; rather, it all followed directly from its root premise. But this means that we are not prepared to follow his textual procedure, since our modern exegesis is directed toward finding historicity, as it will continue to be, regardless of any seductive "signs of the times." But at the same

[76] *Ibid., WA* 31$^{I}$, 250:34; *LW* 14, 32.
[77] *Ibid., WA* 31$^{I}$, 252:26; *LW* 14, 34.
[78] *Ibid., WA* 31$^{I}$, 255:33 ff.; *LW* 14, 37–38.

time we shall discover that Luther's interpretation possesses a power to bring the text into our present experience and possesses a meaning which unfortunately we usually miss in our exegesis. The powerful timeliness of such interpretation is directly linked with his drawing his bow like an archer and aiming toward Christ as his goal. Therefore, just such an example better illustrates Luther's genuine position in his Old Testament interpretation than does some easily ignored strange allegorizing or typology of his.

It seems to me it would be helpful to distinguish more carefully between the interpretation of Old Testament Scripture as direct prediction of Christ and the more indirect way in which the New Testament gospel permeates the Old Testament interpretation. Certainly this cannot be done completely. Yet, there is no other way to get at the individual features of the problem.

## 3. PREDICTIONS OF CHRIST AND THE TRINITY

The direct application of the Old Testament texts to Jesus Christ, his words and deeds, his death and resurrection, his church and his work in the believer was by far the strongest and most comprehensive theme in Luther's interpretation of the Old Testament. In fact, countless events and sayings in the Old Testament became much clearer to him as he applied them to Christ and his work. Even if we consider only the varied situations and the testimonies of the pious in the psalms which Luther applied to Christ, we can see what a wealth of possibilities emerged for analyzing and describing the inner and outer life of Christ. For Luther the predictions included more than the customary "messianic" passages. He saw an unbroken chain of pronouncements, of prophetic prediction beginning from the first anticipation of the gospel *(Protevangelium)* in Gen. 3:15 (the promise of victory over the serpent)[79] and continuing throughout the whole Old Testament. Even if we ignore

[79] Luther had found, since the very beginning of his interpretation, a male victor prophesied in the Hebrew text. *Sermons of Luther Collected by John Poliander,* 1519–1521, *WA* 9, 336:21 ff. Consequently, he corrected the Vulgate text (*ipsa conteret caput tuum*) in his revision of 1529 (*ipsum conteret...*, *WA,* DB 5, 16:9) and quarreled, in his lectures on Genesis, with the traditional interpretation in Augustine, Gregory, and especially Lyra, among others, who related the promise to Mary. *Lectures on Genesis,* 1535, *WA* 42, 138:1 ff.; 143:9 ff.; *LW* 1, 184, 191. See also *On the Last Words of David,* 1543, *WA* 54, 70:28 ff.

the many allegorical "figures" among whom Luther saw allusions to the coming Christ, which he clearly distinguished from the true prophecies, an abundance of prophetic material remains.

Luther once[80] listed the messianic prophecies in the Books of Moses: the *Protevangelium,* the promise of the blessing on Abraham's seed (Gen. 22:18),[81] and the promise of a prophet like Moses whom God will send (Deut. 18:15 and 18).[82] At other points Luther added to the direct prophecies: Eve's cry of triumph (Gen. 4:1), which, after several attempts, Luther finally translated as "I have the man of the Lord" and so offered this as proof of the divine-human nature of Christ;[83] and the messianic prophecy about Judah (Gen. 49:10), about which he often quarreled sharply with the Jewish interpretation.[84]

Moreover, there were many passages in Moses which were not messianic prophecies, but which nevertheless contained Christological promises. The interpretations of Exodus 33 and 34 in the writing *On the Last Words of David* (1543) are particularly clear

[80] *How Christians Should Regard Moses,* 1525, *WA* 24, 11:1 ff.

[81] See also Gen. 12:3, "For this blessing is the gospel. He himself preaches this; thereby is clearly declared the promise to Adam. He himself shall strike at the serpent's head." *Sermon of August 16, 1523, Sermons on Genesis,* 1523–1524, *WA* 14, 223:18. See also Gen. 13:16; 15:5; 26:4; 18:14. This is the content of the promise, according to Luther: the human nature of the coming Christ (born of the tribe of Abraham); the justification by faith (blessing over all nations); the divinity of Christ and the difference of the persons (the promising Father and the promised Son). *Lectures on Genesis,* 1539, *WA* 43, 245:10 ff.; 251:21 ff.; 252:8 ff.; 259:25 ff.; *LW* 4, 151–52; 160 ff.; 171–72.

[82] See Luther's interpretation in *The Deuteronomy of Moses, with Notes,* 1525, *WA* 14, 675:11 ff.; 680:1 ff.; *LW* 9, 176 ff., 182.

[83] On the passage, see Heinrich E. Bindseil (ed.), *Verzeichnis der Original-Ausgaben der Lutherischen Übersetzung sowohl der ganzen Bibel als auch grösserer und kleinerer Teile und einzelner Stellen derselben, in systematischer Ordnung* (Halle, 1841). There is an elaborate exegesis in *Lectures on Genesis,* 1536, *WA* 42, 179:32 ff.; *LW* 1, 241 ff.; and in *On the Last Words of David,* 1543, *WA* 54, 71:28 ff. See also the biblical revision of 1529, *WA,* DB 3, 173:24; and *Table Talk* (from various years), *WA,* TR 6, 43:30 (No. 6563). Lyra saw in it the joy of Eve over her participation in the production of a man, whereas she had not participated in the creation of Adam. See Siegfried, *op. cit.,* p. 437. The translation "with the Lord" appears only in the revised Bible of 1893. According to Gunkel (*Genesis, übersetzt und erklärt,* p. 42), the passage is irrecoverably spoiled.

[84] *Sermons on Genesis,* 1523–1524, *WA* 14, 481:36 ff.; *On the Jews and Their Lies,* 1543, *WA* 53, 450:19 ff.; *Lectures on Genesis,* 1545, *WA* 44, 753:27 ff. Luther solved the age-old—and even today—controversial textual problem of the Hebrew *silo* (Gunkel, *op. cit.,* p. 481), which he understood as "Messiah" even as late as 1543 (*WA* 53, 459:6) in the lectures on Genesis, according to the proposition of Bernard Ziegler, through the derivation from *sileja* ("afterbirth," "son of the womb"); thus he added the passage to other messianic prophecies, such as Gen. 3:15; 4:14; Isa. 7:14. *Lectures on Genesis,* 1545, *WA* 44, 755:34 ff. See also below, p. 227.

examples of this: in Exod. 33:18–19 God answers Moses' plea to see his majesty: "I will let all my goodness pass before your eyes and I will preach in the Lord's name before you." Obviously the Father here speaks about his Son, "who is all of his possession, through whom he has created everything." And more plainly still, in the second part of the verse: "Don't they have to be two different persons? One Lord, who preaches there, and one Lord in whose name the Lord preaches. Only this preacher, who is a Lord, must surely become a man if he is to preach before Moses and Israel." And the content of the sermon is immediately and clearly stated: "But to whom I am gracious I am gracious." That certainly means, "I do not want to preach as you, Moses, have to preach. For you must preach the law, that is, 'I command you today to do and keep this and that; if not, it will not go well with you.' But I want to preach in this way, 'Before God the Lord no man is pious or righteous through the law.'" Thus Moses is in agreement with the New Testament in so far as "Jesus Christ Jehovah is God and man, and was the preacher of the people of Israel."[85] This one passage shows the approach Luther used countless times. He extrapolated the quality of the divine persons from the peculiarly Hebrew repetition of God's name, which he did not treat as a pronoun. He inferred the antithesis of law and gospel from the words of grace appearing in the Old Testament. Although this passage contained no messianic prophecy, Luther presupposed the promise of the coming of Christ, his person and work, in it. For this reason it was not allegory for him but a natural interpretation of the text when he related other aspects of the same narratives to Christ: the protection through the rock and the hand of God held above Moses, "You will see behind me," that is, you will see the inheritance of the crucified and resurrected one.[86] Luther then found exactly the same promise of Christ in the appearance of God (Exod. 34:5 ff.) and in the covenant of God with the people of Israel (Exod. 34:8 ff.).[87]

Next to the messianic passages in the Books of Moses, which had a primary significance for him, Luther particularly treasured

[85] *On the Last Words of David,* 1543, *WA* 54, 78:12 ff.; 79:1 ff., 29.
[86] *Ibid.,* 80:32 ff.
[87] *Ibid.,* 81:25 ff.; 83:17 ff.

the prophecies of David. Above all, David's last words (II Sam. 23:1 ff.), his "right of the soul" *(Seelrecht, Testament),*[88] seemed to Luther a marvelous prediction of the coming Christ. While the Jewish interpreters considered David himself the "righteous ruler" named in the text, Luther explained:

> No, it is another man, this ruler in righteousness and fear of God. David did not make a single human being fear God or make anyone righteous through his reign, not even himself, and Moses, with his law, did not either (Romans 3). Rather, all of them were made righteous and God-fearing by this Lord, Messiah, and Shepherd of Israel, Jesus Christ.[89]

Otherwise, the promise, which David "praises so reverently and heartily," would be turned into commandment and law.[90] This is an example of how Luther used the New Testament concept of righteousness as proof for his finding a Christological meaning in Old Testament passages. In his prediction David could lean upon the Word which God himself had addressed to him through the prophet Nathan (II Sam. 7:11 ff.; I Chron. 17:10 ff.). Luther, in sharp disagreement with the Jewish interpreters, here also argued, this time historically, not logically, for the messianic character of the passage. The promise, "Your house and your kingdom shall exist forever" (II Sam. 7:16), must apply to the king who will replace the earthly kingdom of the house of David.

> For it is obvious that at the time of Herod the scepter of Judah fell all the way; but it is even more obvious that the Romans destroyed Jerusalem and the scepter of Judah. Now if David's house is to be eternal and God is to be true, then the right king of Judah, the Messiah, must have come at the same time. No squabbling, interpreting, or glossing over will alter this. The text is too powerful and too clear.[91]

Since God himself had spoken a word of messianic meaning here, David was without a doubt justified in making "such endearing psalms" out of it.[92]

In the rich poetry he discovered in Davidic psalms, Luther found

88 *Ibid.,* 31:13.
89 *Ibid.,* 95:8.
90 *Ibid.,* 37:7 ff.
91 *On the Jews and Their Lies,* 1543, *WA* 53, 468:21. There is an elaborate discussion of II Samuel 7 and 23 in *ibid.,* 462:16 ff. In *On the Last Words of David,* 1543 (*WA* 54, 38 ff.), Luther especially emphasized that the entire Trinity speaks in II Sam. 7:11 ff.
92 *On the Last Words of David,* 1543, *WA* 53, 38:18.

many predictions of Christ. This is equally true of the non-Davidic psalms. Luther's *Defense of the Translation of the Psalms* (1531–1533), in which he divided the psalms into five categories and presented a brief argument for the placing of each one, offered the simplest survey of the Christological prophecy he found in the Psalms. He classified as psalms of prophecy: 2, 8, 9, 14, 16, 19, 21, 22, 24, 29, 45, 47, 67, 68, 72, 87, 89, 92, 93, 95–98, 100, 110, 113, 117. Many of these psalms were read as predictions about the person of Christ, his suffering, death, resurrection, and kingdom. Others point to the gospel, the kingdom of Christ, Christianity, or the church. But there was also a wealth of prediction in the other categories of psalms. A few were to be viewed as prayers of Christ per se. But it should be noted that Luther differentiated them from the predictions and regarded them, according to their literary form, as psalms of prayer.[93]

To Luther the apex of the predictions is naturally Psalm 110, in which he found a favorite nickname for Christ: "Sit-on-my-Right-Hand" *(Schefliminі).*[94] "Nothing in the whole Scripture

[93] *Defense of the Translation of the Psalms,* 1531–1533, *WA* 38, 17:21 ff.; *LW* 35, 222. The other four categories are: 1) psalms of doctrine (*Lehrpsalmen*): 14 (in part promise), 15, 32, 36, 49–51, 53, 62, 73, 77, 78, 90, 99, 101, 109, 127, 128, 131, 133, 134. The psalms of doctrine are the most important source for the relationship between law and gospel in the Psalter; 2) psalms of consolation (*Trostpsalmen*): 1, 4, 37, 39, 52, 58, 75, 82, 84, 91, 112, 121; 3) psalms of prayer (*Betpsalmen*): 5–7, 10–13, 17, 20, 25, 26, 28, 35, 38, 40–44, 54–57, 59, 61, 63, 64, 69–71, 74, 79, 80, 81, 83, 85, 86, 88, 94, 102, 119, 120, 123, 130, 132, 137, 140–143. Some of these are prayed "in the person of Christ": 40, 41, 59 (which, however, can also be understood as a prayer of David), 69, 88. Psalm 71 is a prayer of Christianity; 4) psalms of thanksgiving (*Dankpsalmen*): 18, 23, 27, 30, 31, 33, 34, 46, 48, 60, 65, 66, 76, 103–108, 111, 114–116, 118, 122, 124–126, 129, 135, 136, 138, 139, 144, 145 (thanksgiving for the kingdom of Christ), 146–150. Other groups which are determined by a different content are dissolved through these categories; for example, the psalms of penance. Formal characteristics, however, rather than emotions—as in the opinion of Emanuel Hirsch, *Luthers deutsche Bibel. Ein Beitrag zur Frage ihrer Durchsicht* (München, 1928), p. 23, n. 33—were decisive, it seems to me, in the process of detailed classification. Most of the psalms of penance, of course, belong to the category of psalms of prayer; Psalm 32, which is no psalm of prayer, belongs to the psalms of doctrine. It is striking that the prayer, Psalm 51, is classified among the psalms of doctrine. Yet this is the classic proof for original sin (*WA* 38, 36:25) and is also otherwise full of doctrine: "It contains the doctrine about the chief parts of our religion, about repentance, sin, grace, and justification, as well as about the worship we ought to render to God." *Lecture on Psalm 51,* 1532, *WA* $40^{II}$, 315:28 (printed in 1538); *LW* 12, 303. See also the copy, *WA* $40^{II}$, 315:10.

[94] *Table Talk,* 1533, *WA,* TR 1, 233:23 (No. 510); 397:6 (No. 817); 2 (1532), 175:15 (No. 1675); 3 (1533), 137:1 (No. 2999); 167:21, 23 (No. 3084a); 246:21 (No. 3281a); 4 (1540), 658:1 (No. 5096); *LW* 54, 387–90 (No. 5096); *WA,* TR 6 (from various years), 19:36 (No. 6528); 158:27 (No. 6740).

equals" this psalm, "and it is easily used as the noblest way to confirm Christian faith. For Christ is nowhere prophesied as a priest, and eternal priest, in such lucid and stark words which so annul the priesthood of Aaron."[95] Although it stands in relationship to earlier prophecies, it is much richer than they. It has woven a wonderful tapestry out of the basic promise to Abraham (Gen. 22:15 ff.). "The most beautiful tapestry he spun out of this promise."[96] Luther could not find the words to express the joy he heard ringing from this psalm about the resurrection and lordship of Christ. "Oh, if I could glorify the article of the resurrection in this way! It is as beautiful as the sun; and if my heart were filled with such faith, I, too, would create psalms and would sing and ring."[97] He found in it everything that the Christian heart must know about the main articles of faith: the divinity and humanity of Christ, his ascension to the right hand of the Father, his glorious reign, but also the hiddenness and weakness of his kingdom on earth, the ceaseless struggle in which Christianity must follow the example of its Lord in this world, the promise of consolation through the gospel and the Holy Spirit, the priesthood of Christ, the church, etc.[98] But at the same time the psalm is a beautiful model of faith: the comforting hope in the faraway, the coming Anointed One out of his own tribe, made David happy in composing the psalm.[99] Rörer reported that at the end of his sermon series Luther read the whole text out loud, which he did only in

[95] *Defense of the Translation of the Psalms,* 1531–1533, *WA* 38, 54:31 ff. Two illustrative preliminary studies, undertaken for the defense of the translation of Psalm 110 and elaborated, in part, according to Luther's well-known graphic catchword method, are printed in *Smaller Studies on the Psalms,* 1530–1532 (*Kleinere Arbeiten über Psalmen*), *WA* 31^I, 508–09. Further studies are in *ibid.,* pp. 531, 563. See also the contemporaneous *Table Talk, WA,* TR 3, 201:14 ff. (No. 3157b), and *Table Talk* (from various years), *WA,* TR 6, 221:23 ff. (No. 6835). In these studies Luther planned to interpret this significant psalm—he had already published an interpretation in 1518 (*WA* 1, 687 ff.; 9, 176 ff.)—once again according to its worth (*Table Talk,* 1532, *WA,* TR 2, 68:37 [No. 1356]). Only in 1535 did he manage to treat it in sermons; they were printed in 1539. *Psalm 110, Sermons of 1535, WA* 41, XIX, 79 ff.; *LW* 13, 227 ff.

[96] *Lectures on Genesis,* 1539, *WA* 43, 260:21; *LW* 4, 172.

[97] *Psalm 110, Sermons of 1535, WA* 41, 81:7; *LW* 13, 229.

[98] *Ibid., WA* 41, 89 ff.; *LW* 13, 234; *WA* 41, 95 ff.; *LW* 13, 240 ff.; *WA* 41, 110:31 ff.; *LW* 13, 253 ff.; *WA* 41, 116:20 ff.; *LW* 13, 259 ff.; *WA* 41, 117:26 ff.; *LW* 13, 290 ff., 309 ff.; *WA* 41, 139:11 ff., 149:6 ff.; *LW* 13, 324 ff.; *WA* 41, 174 ff., 195:26 ff.

[99] *Ibid., WA* 41, 92:2 ff.; 98:12 ff.; *LW* 13, 239, 243–44.

special cases. "Let us stay with the psalm and thank God for it and invoke him."[100]

As often as Luther elevated Psalm 110 above the others, he also named Psalm 2 in conjunction with it. "There is no prouder psalm in the whole Psalter than Psalm 110 and Psalm 2."[101] Luther loved the latter passionately and dedicated a lecture to it in 1532.[102] He could feel how majestically the divine promise of the victory, won through the Passion, distinguished itself from the rebellion of the worldly powers. That was why this psalm was to him an application of the fundamental fact of Christian faith which preceded all other realizations. "This psalm flows out of the First Commandment, in which God promises himself to be our God."[103]

> Thus the prophet points to the passion of Christ—they certainly may kill Christ, but they cannot take away his kingdom. Christ is the sign of contradiction, against which they rage, albeit ineffectively. They speak against him, but without effect; they gather together and plot, but nothing comes of it.[104]

> It is a prophecy about Christ; how he shall suffer and thus become a king and Lord over the whole world.[105]

Among the rest of the prophetic psalms, Psalm 24 was probably especially important to him, because he found Christ described as the king of glory, the Lord Sabaoth.[106]

But the other psalms which Luther did not include among the predicting psalms because of their literary form are of course also full of prophetic proclamation and the expectation of the coming Christ. Almost every one of Luther's interpretations of the psalms

[100] *Ibid., WA* 41, 238:16 ff.
[101] *Smaller Studies on the Psalms,* 1530–1532, *WA* 31$^{I}$, 563:5. See *Table Talk,* 1532 *WA,* TR 2, 139:21 (No. 1577), where he added Psalm 22 to these two.
[102] *Lecture on Psalm 2,* 1532, *WA* 40$^{II}$, 193 ff.; *LW* 12, 3 ff. See also above, p. 67, and *Sermon on Christmas Day on Heb. 1:1 ff., Church Postil,* 1522, *WA* 10$^{I.1}$, 164 ff.
[103] *Defense of the Translation of the Psalms,* 1531–1533, *WA* 38, 18:34.
[104] *Lectures on the First Twenty-five Psalms,* 1530 (*In Psalmos vigintiquinq Priores . . . enarrationes*), *WA* 31$^{I}$, 266:14.
[105] *Defense of the Translation of the Psalms,* 1531–1533, *WA* 38, 18:29. See also *Lecture on Psalm 2,* 1532, *WA* 40$^{II}$, 196:1 ff.; *LW* 12, 5–6.
[106] *Lectures on the First Twenty-five Psalms,* 1530, *WA* 31$^{I}$, 370 ff.; 373:26. See also *Table Talk* (from various years), *WA,* TR 6, 221:32 ff. (No. 6835).

documents this. Therefore it is enough to say that Psalm 132 was particularly important to him because, according to it, God "swore a true oath" to David, that he would place a bodily heir of his tribe on the throne (vs. 11). This promise of a particular person far surpassed the general promise to Abraham and Jacob.

"He swore to David." These are grand words, because he mentions the person. He does not allow the succession of the kingdom to spread to indefinite persons. Thus it is the highest promise. Abraham and Jacob also had a promise, but not of a specific person. But here the kingdom is limited to David and his successors.[107]

Luther understood this as a promise of the uninterrupted rule of the tribe of David, as Jeremiah prophesied it (Jer. 33:17). Christ took over the reign for all eternity when the worldly Jewish kingdom collapsed; the prophecy of the psalm thus leads us to this. Luther gained from it an important argument against the messianic expectation of the Jews of his day. If they compare their situation with the exile, they are in error. God gave three clear signs for this:

1. The conferring of royal honors upon Jehoiachin during the captivity (II Kings 25:27 ff.).

2. The presence of prophets and priests during the time of the exile.

3. The limitation of captivity to seventy years (Jer. 25:11).

The Jews no longer have these three important signs since the destruction of Jerusalem and their dispersion into all the world. Thus their promised kingdom has been taken away from them.[108] "Their captivity, therefore, represents the destruction and desolation of the corporeal kingdom; and this promise about the kingdom of Christ is fulfilled because the people of God must not remain without a kingdom."[109] The prophecy in Ps. 132:11 was all the more significant to Luther because it touched on God's oath in Ps. 110:4, "You are a priest forever in the manner of Melchizedek." For kingdom and priesthood, ruling and blessing, are indeed a unity in Christ.[110]

Luther carefully considered in each case whether the psalm

[107] *Lectures on the Fifteen Gradual Psalms,* 1532–1533, *WA* 40$^{III}$, 424:6 ff.
[108] *Ibid.,* 425:7 ff., where one should read *dicunt* (not *dicebant,* 425:8); otherwise the relation to the contemporary Jews remains unclear.
[109] *Ibid.,* 426:1.
[110] *Lectures on Genesis,* 1539, *WA* 43, 260:36 ff.; *LW* 4, 173.

should be applied to Christ. He decided that Psalm 18 should really be better put in David's mouth and applied only allegorically to Christ.[111] On the other hand, he was not content to understand the song of the released prisoners in Psalm 126 as applying only to the Babylonian or another captivity. Such sublime words could only be sung as thanksgiving for redemption through the coming Christ. They can be applied figuratively to the individual and to the captivity only by distortion.

The psalm is to be interpreted in terms of the redemption of mankind through Christ our Lord because these are grander and more majestic words than can be said about particular captivities.... Thus we can introduce this second meaning, namely, that it is a prophecy about the coming redemption through Christ, about the gospel which is to be spread, about the kingdom of Christ which is to be enlarged, and about death, sin, and all evil which are to be conquered. Once this general prophecy is maintained, it may be applied to individual or general [captivities].[112]

All the prophets speak of the coming Messiah and his kingdom exactly as David does. We have already observed, in the form of the prophetic sermon, that for Luther prophecy was not prediction but proclamation.[113] This proclamation was no different than at the time of the apostles or our own time; it still required only the form of prophecy. The prophets' task was "to hold the people in faith in the coming Christ; and so they clung to Christ with the Word, they believed in him as well as we now believe in and cling to him."[114] They carried the people through disappointments with the power of the Word. For just "when the people sat in the land and had kings and dukes and now waited and gaped for the Messiah and his new kingdom," the Assyrians came, and later the Babylonians. But the prophets maintained in faith that all this was not happening against God's will and that the arrival of the Messiah would not be held up because of it.[115] Moreover, the nature of the coming Messiah was disclosed precisely through the

111 *Lectures on the First Twenty-five Psalms,* 1530, *WA* 31$^{I}$, 325:1.
112 *Lectures on the Fifteen Gradual Psalms,* 1532–1533, *WA* 40$^{III}$, 174:10 ff. Luther, however, did not use this figurative interpretation in his impressive interpretation; instead, he only let cross, *Anfechtung,* and redemption resound in the crying, laughing, and boasting of this psalm.
113 See above, p. 34.
114 *The Prophet Habakkuk,* 1526, *WA* 19, 388:31 ff.
115 *Ibid.,* 351:28 ff.; 352:27 ff.

political collapse of the nation, and the faith in the paradoxical Word of God was proven true.

You see and feel the disorder in your kingdom; that is why you must, through faith, pass over the feelings and be sure, even in the midst of the disorders, that your kingdom will come and be established marvelously. Here we see how the prophets preached and propagated faith in Christ as well as we did in the New Testament.[116]

Thus the historical situation itself, in which the prophets continued their proclamation of the coming king, pointed to the spiritual sense of this kingdom. What must have appeared absurd to the Jews in their messianic hope was precisely the most sensible thing to the interpreter looking back.

The prophets themselves clearly expressed the expected Christ. Out of passages like Isa. 9:6, 51:4–5, 51:6, and Dan. 9:24 ff., it was irrefutable to Luther that the king, whose kingdom of peace shall have no end and who shall bring eternal justice, "must be God himself and yet David's son, an ordinary man." Thus this kingdom was generally foretold in harmony with the New Testament.[117] Luther found Christ promised in divinity and humanity everywhere in the prophets. Not only did the prophecy of Daniel about the Son of Man (Dan. 7:13–14) clearly demonstrate the difference between the Son and the Father, but also a passage such as Isa. 60:19–20, the Lord promised to us an "eternal light," must have meant God himself, and yet still a person other than the Father who makes the promise.[118]

On the whole the prophets offered Luther extensive documentation for the ecclesiastical doctrine of the two natures. The servant of God, above all, and "the arm of the Lord" in Isaiah 53, are the obvious images of this mystery which only very few in the old covenant have understood; only the Holy Spirit made it plain at Pentecost. Extreme lowliness and divine majesty are so inseparably fused therein that this chapter motivated Luther to a harsh critique of Nestorius.[119] But with correct understanding, the Jewish interpretations destroyed themselves. That the servant of God may not be understood collectively was made quite clear because one cer-

[116] *Ibid.*, 394:24.
[117] *On the Last Words of David,* 1543, *WA* 54, 46:6 ff., 26.
[118] *Ibid.*, 47:38 ff.; 46:53 ff.
[119] *Lecture on Isaiah 53,* 1544, *WA* 40$^{III}$, 702:10 ff.

tainly cannot call the people the "arm of the Lord" to whom lordship (Isa. 40:10) is promised. And if the Jews wanted to apply the passage to Moses and the law which was scorned by the pagans, it should be countered that the reference is to a person scorned and rejected. This fits neither Moses nor the law.

"The arm" is revealed through the prophets. And this is one of the passages, and a common manner of biblical speech, in which the Son of God is called the arm of the Lord. "The arm of the Lord will rule" (Isa. 40:10) cannot be understood collectively to mean the people of Israel. They are certainly not the arm of the Lord. "But," they say, "we do not speak about the Messiah, but about Moses. Who among the heathen believes our law? And to whom is 'the arm' revealed, whereby we have been led out of Egypt?" But we see that the prophet speaks of a person who is of low estate, despised and rejected. And yet he will water the nations, that is, those to whom nothing was told. Coherence and logic exist in all of this.[120]

So Luther not only bypassed the ancient and constantly recurring problem of interpretation[121] with his Christological meaning, but also showed the precariousness of the other solutions. Luther refused to consider the description of the servant of God in terms of bodily misery or ugliness of the Messiah; for Jesus was handsome and healthy. Only the lowliness and the unmajestic advent of this king is said to be expressed therein.

But in addition, the prophet does not speak about the personal form of Christ. He was uncorrupted and had a healthy body, the purest flesh; he was conceived without sin, and was born of an unblemished virgin.... But the prophet speaks of a political and royal figure of a regent who is to become an earthly king.... He walks as the lowest servant among servants, and there was not seen a man more despised in the whole world than he.[122]

Precisely the same God-man relationship is promised in Isa. 61:1 ff.: the humbled Christ is sent to the lowly, a powerful repul-

120 *Ibid.*, 700:27 ff. That Isaiah 53 was applied to the people of Israel by Jewish interpreters, an interpretation which Luther regarded as a sign of the deep spiritual decay of Judaism, was already mentioned above, p. 4.

121 See the recent renewal of the collectivistic interpretation in Otto Eissfeldt, *Der Gottesknecht bei Deuterojesaja (Jes. 40–55) im Lichte der israelitischen Anschauung von Gemeinschaft und Individuum* (Halle/Saale, 1933). The same problems, of course, present themselves formally in reality quite differently to the modern exegete, since Luther does not ask for the historical self-understanding of the prophet and his own time, but for that which may be true in view of the claim of the Word of God.

122 *Lecture on Isaiah 53*, 1544, *WA* 40$^{III}$, 696:16.

sion against the Jews, who wait for the glamorous Messiah, and against the pope, who pretends to be the vicar of the glorious Christ.[123] Zech. 2:8 offers an example of the differentiation of the divine persons (not of the natures of Christ): "Thus says the Lord Sabaoth, 'He has sent me to the pagans,'" which exposes, if taken literally, an absurdity. "He who speaks there is also sent; the Lord Sabaoth sends the Lord Sabaoth." This can only be understood if one knows how to differentiate the two persons of the deity.[124] Luther's interpretations of the prophets contain a number of similar examples.

Luther thoroughly disagreed with the Jewish interpreters over a number of prophetic pronouncements. An example of this is the prophecy of Jer. 33:17 ff., that a member of the house of David would always sit on the throne of Israel. To him it was a consolation to be able to prove the historical continuity of the Davidic dynasty. The kingdom and its future were assured in the young boy Jehoash, even when Athaliah had almost exterminated the royal house. Of course, this was a hard test of faith in God's promises. "Jehoash was an awful temptation to the house of David."[125] But one may believe in God's truthfulness with much more consolation precisely because he kept his word, which can be proven historically; that is, one must understand the prophetic passage messianically. In the same way he demonstrated how the prophecy of Hag. 2:6 ff. was realized historically: the Jews had peace for "only a little while," namely, until the time of Antiochus; since then they had had no rest in the world. On the other hand, the prediction of a marvelous temple did not materialize and must therefore be understood in a spiritual sense.[126] And Luther also calculated with historical accuracy the time at which the promised Messiah had to appear from the saying in Dan. 9:24 ff., "one of the noblest in the entire Scripture": as the Jews also admit, the seventy weeks in Daniel should be understood as "year-weeks" and these will end in four hundred ninety years with the destruction of Jerusalem. The Messiah must have appeared in the last "week"; the Jews also expected him at that time, the time of Jesus. This

[123] *Lectures on Isaiah,* 1527–1530, *WA* 31$^{II}$, 515:23 ff.
[124] *The Prophet Zechariah,* 1527, *WA* 23, 532:37 ff.
[125] *On the Jews and Their Lies,* 1543, *WA* 53, 469 ff.; 475:30.
[126] *Ibid.,* 476–92.

is evidenced by Herod, John the Baptist, the insurrections against the Romans, and Bar Kokhba.[127] As with the Psalms, we again see that Luther was not content with a fundamental faith in the fulfilment of the prophecies in the new covenant. Instead, he convinced himself of their true historicity by uncovering how many of them were already fulfilled in the surveyable and unambiguous course of time until the appearance of Jesus. He used every means to support faith in the prophecies with historical arguments.

The question arises whether Luther saw a progression and deepening of understanding from the earlier to the later predictions about Christ in the Old Testament. He certainly listed clearly enough a series of turning points in the salvation history *(Heilsgeschichte),* whereby God leads men. Each step toward a new knowledge of Christ canceled the previous one. If Adam and Noah had lived at the time of Abraham, their faith in the coming Redeemer would have been of no use to them if they had not expected him from Abraham's seed. Likewise, the same thing would have happened to Abraham and David if they had lived in the respectively subsequent epochs of revelation (in the time of David, or of John the Baptist).

If Adam, Noah, and other patriarchs had lived at the time of Abraham, who received the new promise, it would have been necessary for them to believe that Christ would be of the seed of Abraham, or they would have lost God, who promised the coming of the seed.

If Abraham had lived at the time of David, it would have been necessary for him to believe that the coming Christ would be of the lineage of David, or he would have believed in vain in the seed of a woman.

If David had lived at the time of John the Baptist, it would have been necessary for him to believe in Jesus, the seed of his descendant Mary, or he would have perished.

[127] *Ibid.,* 492–510. Luther, in this connection, again thoroughly disagreed with the Jewish interpreters. He also knew the Jewish tradition according to which Bar Kokhba ("son of the stars") was renamed Barkosiba ("son of lies"; actually, however, the name of a place or family) to express the disappointed messianic hope. Luther illustrated this process of renaming in a very fine manner: "Just as we Germans too would like to rhyme 'You are not a German but a cheater' [*nicht ein Deudscher, sondern ein Teuscher*]; 'You are not a Frenchman but a forger' [*nicht ein Welscher, sondern ein Felscher*]. And I might say about a usurer, 'You are not a burgher but a murderer' [*nicht ein Bürger, sondern ein Würger*]." *Ibid.,* 497:3 ff. That Luther found a significant difference between the messianic hope of the Jews then and in his own time, I have already mentioned above, pp. 2–3. See also the contemporaneous *Table Talk, WA,* TR 5, 237:27 ff. (No. 5554b).

If John the Baptist had lived after the resurrection of Christ—no, if he had believed, in his own time, that Christ would come or had not yet come—he would have been damned.[128]

God's hours of revelation are irrevocable. They render yesterday's truth today's error, by which salvation is gambled away. As we have already seen, Luther also applied this understanding especially to the faith of the Jews: "The Jews still believe in vain in a God who promises a Messiah, although their fathers once correctly believed this."[129] Nevertheless, one cannot consider this spiritual evolution. This idea was far from Luther's mind. Instead, God makes use of all these forms of the promise to accomplish the same thing, to have Christ according to his divinity and humanity foretold at each step. He simply expresses himself ever more clearly through new allusions to the promised person. The appearance of Christ then brings the decisive turning point from the shadow of all promises to clarity and fulfilment, and thus distinguishes itself fundamentally from the earlier steps, which it completes once and for all.

The prediction of the *Trinity in the Old Testament* requires a special word. It is no surprise, in view of Luther's prophetic interpretation as a whole, that he found the Trinity there in many places. But it is worth noting how severely he held to his exegetical premises. He renounced as proof texts those favorite passages of the allegorists, especially their classical reference to the appearance of God in the three men who visited Abraham in Mamre (Genesis 18). Luther openly agreed with the judgment of the Jewish interpreters, that the true, historical sense of this text knows nothing of the Trinity. He conceded to the allegorical interpretation of the fathers not as proof, but only as adornment and symbolic confirmation of the matter which was otherwise abundantly proven.[130]

As far as this passage [Gen. 18:2 ff.] is concerned, let us concede that its historical sense is of no use against the Jews; but sometimes misinterpretations [see *LW* 12, 346, n. 16] also have their place. . . . But

[128] Theses 12–15 of *The Licentiate Examination of Heinrich Schmedenstede,* 1542, *WA* 39$^{II}$, 188:7 ff.; *LW* 34, 304.
[129] Thesis 16 of *idid., WA* 39$^{II}$, 188:17; *LW* 34, 304. See also above, p. 1.
[130] *Lectures on Genesis,* 1538–1539, *WA* 43, 11:18 ff.; *LW* 3, 190 ff.

if there were no other proof of the Trinity than these three forms, I certainly would not believe in it. But we have other solid and sure foundations. . . . Hence the fathers were right in making use of this passage, for it is one thing to prove something and another thing to adorn it. Rhetorical arguments do not always present proof; but they provide strong adornment and contribute persuasiveness to the things which dialectics has proven.[131]

Other passages in which Luther used Genesis 18 directly as proof for the Trinity have to be interpreted according to this rule.[132] Nor did Luther want any part of the idea that the Trinity is pictured in Adam, the image of God, according to the three Augustinian capabilities of the soul—memory, intelligence, and will. He warned against such uncertain speculations as often as he spoke about the image of God (Gen. 1:26).[133]

But where he did find evidence for the divine Trinity he seldom neglected to emphasize its still obscure and doubtful meaning over against the clarity of the New Testament texts.[134] He nevertheless referred often enough to a series of passages in which the Trinity was quite clearly presupposed or expressed for him who wished to see it. But Luther preferred to begin with linguistic observations, which he considered especially convincing. He found several persons within the one divinity irrefutably and clearly expressed, according to ancient ecclesiastical interpretation,[135] in the passages

131 *Ibid., WA* 43, 12:12; 13:34; 14:1; *LW* 3, 190, 192, 194. Luther was already equally reserved in his judgment in the sermons on Genesis of 1523–1524.

132 *The Three Symbols or Creeds of the Christian Faith,* 1538 (*Die drey Symbola oder Bekenntnis des glaubens Christi*), *WA* 50, 280:14 ff.; *LW* 34, 225.

133 *Sermons on Genesis,* 1523–1524, *WA* 14, 110:7 ff., 35 ff. (1527 edition: *WA* 24, 49:6 ff.); *Lectures on Genesis,* 1535, *WA* 42, 45:1 ff.; *LW* 1, 60.

134 *Trinity Sermon of May 31, 1523, Sermons of 1523, WA* 12, 587:28; *The Three Symbols,* 1538, *WA* 50, 278:28; *LW* 34, 223; *Lectures on Genesis,* 1543, *WA* 44, 186:1; *Trinity Sermon on John 3:10 ff., House Postil,* 1544 (*Hauspostille*), *WA* 52, 338:30. See also *The Licentiate Examination of Erasmus Alberus,* 1543 (*Die Promitionsdisputation von Erasmus Alberus*), *WA* 39$^{II}$, 256:11 ff.

135 Since Justin Martyr (*Dialogue with Trypho,* 61–62, 129, ed. G. Archambault in 2 vols. ["Textes et Documents," 8, 11 (Paris, 1909)]; *ANF* 1, 227–28, 264) and Irenaeus (*Against Heresies,* IV, Pref. 2, ed. W. W. Harvey [2 vols.; Cambridge, 1857]; *ANF* 1, 463–64; and *The Demonstration of the Apostolic Preaching,* 43; Armenian version in ed. K. Ter-Mekerttschian and E. Ter-Minassiantz ["Texte und Untersuchungen," 31 (Leipzig, 1907)]; English translation available by J. A. Robinson [New York: Macmillan, 1920]). The material about it and the evidence of the pre-existent Christ elsewhere in the Old Testament, according to the exegesis of the early church, has been col-

wherein God speaks of himself in the plural. "Let us make man" (Gen. 1:26); "Behold, Adam has become like one of us" (Gen. 3:22); "Come let us go down" (Gen. 11:7).[136]

That God had spoken of himself in the *majestic plural,* as the Jews interpreted it, was to Luther a highly amusing thought; the Holy Spirit does not write in any courtly style.

It is utterly ridiculous for the Jews to say that God is following the custom of the princes who, to indicate respect, speak of themselves in the plural. The Holy Spirit is not imitating this courtly style (to give it this name); nor does Holy Scripture sanction this manner of speech. Consequently, this is a sure indication of the Trinity.[137]

The plural in God's name *Elohim* should also give them pause; it strikingly proves the plurality of persons.[138] This plurality can first of all be easily recognized as the duality which Luther also pointed up everywhere else in the Old Testament, as we saw with regard to Moses, David, the Psalms, and the prophets. The second person must be fully divine, for God does not share his glory with anyone else (Isa. 48:11).[139] But the introduction of the third person always requires a particular reason. Luther, first of all, insisted that the Spirit in the Old Testament appears as an independent divine effect and, according to the law of the indivisible glory of God, must therefore be fully God, too.[140] If this is recognized, then the existence of the Spirit as a particular person is both confirmed and

---

lected in J. L. Koole, "De overname van het Oude Testament door de christlijke Kerk" (Dissertation, Free University of Amsterdam, Hilversum, 1938). See below, p. 247, n. 1.

[136] Assembled in the manner in *Lectures on Genesis,* 1543, *WA* 44, 185:32 ff. For details, see the treatment of the following passages in the sermons and lectures on Genesis: Gen. 1:26 (*WA* 14, 110:5, 35; 24, 49:6 ff.; 42, 43:1, 12; *LW* 1, 57–58); Gen. 3:22 (*WA* 42, 166:32 ff.; *LW* 1, 222 ff.); Gen. 11:7 (*WA* 14, 212:28 ff.; 213:22 ff.; 24, 229:33 ff.; 42, 422:20 ff.; *LW* 2, 226 ff.). See also *The Three Symbols,* 1538, *WA* 50, 279:7 ff.; *LW* 34, 223–24.

[137] *Lectures on Genesis,* 1535, *WA* 42, 43:35 ff.; *LW* 1, 58. See also *WA* 42, 10:23 ff.; *LW* 1, 12; and *The Three Symbols,* 1538, *WA* 50, 279:31 ff.; *LW* 34, 223–24.

[138] *Lectures on Genesis,* 1535, 1543, *WA* 42, 10:11; 44, 186:20; *LW* 1, 11–12, 59; and *The Three Symbols,* 1538, *WA* 50, 278:32; *LW* 34, 223. Further examples: *WA* 50, 280:14 ff.; *LW* 34, 225–26.

[139] See also Isa. 46:9; Hos. 13:4; I Kings 18:36 ff., *Sermons of 1523, WA* 12, 586:9 ff.

[140] Ps. 33:6, 139:7, *ibid.,* 587:31 ff.; Joel 3:1 ff., *House Postil,* 1544, *WA* 52, 341:20. Luther understood *ruah* in Gen. 1:2 first of all as "wind," later as "spirit"; "wind": *Sermons on Genesis,* 1523, *WA* 14, 200:2, 29; 24, 27:4, 16; and doubtfully, a little later, in the *Trinity Sermon of May 31, 1523, WA* 12, 587:28; "spirit": *Lectures on Genesis,* 1535, *WA* 42, 8:21; *LW* 1, 9.

made apparent. One can now find the Spirit quite easily in those places where the duality of persons is mentioned: "Wherever Scripture speaks of the two persons, of the Father and the Son, the Holy Spirit, the third person who speaks these things through the prophets, is also present."[141] Thus the Holy Spirit is undoubtedly contained in all Christological predictions, so that Luther, when he wanted to discuss them in the writing *On the Last Words of David,* was pushed into a corner. "Where shall we seat these favored guests? This little book is too narrow; I cannot seat them all herein, since not enough of Moses can get into it." He therefore listed only the passages he thought of most often: Ps. 2:7–8; Exod. 33:19; Gen. 19:24; Hos. 1:7; Zeph. 3:9; Ps. 45:7, 11; Jer. 23:5–6; Isa. 50:1, 6–7; Ps. 97:7 (Heb. 1:6); Ps. 102:2–3 (Heb. 1:10–11); I Chron. 17:12; Gen. 22:18; Gen. 49:10.[142] There are undoubtedly also single passages, such as in the last words of David (II Sam. 23:2), in which the Holy Spirit is specifically mentioned and the Trinity alluded to.[143] But much more important is the fact that the differentiation between Father and Son can only be revealed through the Spirit; for example, on Dan. 7:13, "Thus the Holy Spirit, who says it through Daniel, is there. For no one can know such a highly secret thing if the Holy Spirit does not reveal it through the prophets—as was often said before, Holy Scripture is spoken through the Holy Spirit."[144] "And how could flesh and blood, reason and human wisdom speak of such high, incomprehensible things?"[145] Therefore, that Scripture is filled with the Spirit, which is attested to by the ancient prophets themselves and experienced by the believing heart, is the factual proof for the existence of the Holy Spirit.

In this way Luther's exegesis of the Trinity over against the allegorical exegeses preceding him once again becomes quite obvious.

141 *On the Last Words of David,* 1543, *WA* 54, 41:3. See also *ibid.,* 39:8; 86:4.

142 *Ibid.,* 85:24 ff. A similar enumeration is given in *The Three Symbols,* 1538, *WA* 50, 281:7 ff.; *LW* 34, 226. Several passages are discussed above. As an illustrative example we add only Gen. 19:24: " 'The Lord rained on Sodom and Gomorrah brimstone and fire from the Lord.' Here you can see very easily that the Lord who lets it rain is the Son; 'from the Lord,' that is, from the Father, for the Son is from the Father, not vice versa." *On the Last Words of David,* 1543, *WA* 54, 86:7 ff.

143 *Ibid.,* 34:32 ff.; 35:31 ff. See also above, pp. 102–03.

144 *Ibid.,* 48:19. On Isaiah, see *ibid.,* 47:6.

145 *Ibid.,* 38:13.

Whereas allegory aimed at discovering the three hypostases in the Old Testament, Luther concerned himself with showing how the threefold manner of God's work, in its unity and distinctiveness, was felt everywhere. That was why he did not limit himself to formal proofs of three divine persons; rather, he emphasized the division of divine functions. He approached this task from various angles: the special significance of the Holy Spirit, just mentioned —"Thus one now gives to the Holy Spirit the whole Holy Scripture and the external Word and sacrament, which touch and move our external ears and senses"[146]—but also the mission of the Son in the world. The trinitarian sense of Gen. 48:15–16 ("The God before whom my fathers Abraham and Isaac walked; the God who has nourished me all my life[147] long to this day; the angel who has delivered me from all evil") becomes so clear precisely because the same rescuer *(go'el)* is called upon here as in Job 19:25, "I know that my Savior lives." He must be differentiated from the other two persons, God the Father and the caring Shepherd.[148]

Finally Luther found this division of functions also in Genesis 1, which was his favorite among all the predictions of the Trinity. The most important witnesses in Scripture, Moses, David (Ps. 33: 6), John (1:1 ff.), and Paul (Col. 1:15 ff.), agreed about the triunity of the Creator, the Word, and the Spirit. All of his life Luther expressed what it meant to have the whole of Scripture and his "true, principal gospel" agree so solemnly in their beginnings. In the *Church Postil* he wanted "to run behind us into the Old Testament, to the foundation on which this gospel bases itself," to understand John 1 correctly; and he found Christ clearly proven in Genesis 1.

Who is so smart, who would contradict here? He must let the Word be something else than God, its speaker, and yet he must confess that it was there before all creatures and made the creatures through itself; so he must certainly let it be God also, for besides the creatures there is nothing but God.[149]

[146] *Ibid.,* 35:2. See also *ibid.,* 35:34.
[147] So Luther's German Bible text until 1883; only thereafter: "... the Lord who was my shepherd. . . ."
[148] *Lectures on Genesis,* 1545, *WA* 44, 697:8 ff.; 698:32 ff.
[149] *Sermon on Christmas Day on John 1:1 ff., Church Postil,* 1522, *WA* 10^I,1, 182:6; 184:8. See also the *Trinity Sermon on John 3:10 ff., House Postil,* 1544, *WA* 52, 338:30 ff.

And at this point he made the acid test, whether Moses "would let himself be made a Christian," and whether John could awaken him from the dead. And indeed, "Moses hears quite well, freely approaches, and says, 'Here I am, for just as you, John, speak of the Word, so did I too speak and still speak, and you take the words right out of my mouth.'" So they agreed "without being forced to, and without being directed, but all by themselves."[150] Ps. 33:6 especially witnesses to the tri-unity: "Heaven was made through the Word of the Lord, and all their hosts were made through the Spirit of his mouth."[151] But Word and Spirit are also distinguished in Genesis 1: the Spirit is suggested by God's pleasure with his creation as he saw and blessed it. "This is the third person: the eternal will and pleasure whereby everything was approved and preserved. And it is the Holy Spirit who vivifies everything, keeping and preserving it."[152]

The Old Testament made no essential independent contribution to Luther's doctrine of the Trinity. It only offered him a series of welcome documentary passages; it did not, however, form for him the doctrine taken from the New Testament and ecclesiastical tradition. He received the majority of Christological-trinitarian evidence in the Old Testament through misunderstood peculiarities of the Hebrew language, particularly the repetition of God's name in place of a pronoun[153] and the parallelisms of expression. However, these things were of special importance to Luther since they held the certainty of grammatical proof. The rest of the material was mini-

[150] *On the Last Words of David,* 1543, *WA* 54, 55:1 ff., 23 ff.; 56:7. See also *Sermons on Genesis,* 1523–1524, *WA* 14, 100:19 ff. (1527 edition: *WA* 24, 32:3 ff.), and *Lectures on Genesis,* 1535, *WA* 42, 13:34 ff.; *LW* 1, 15–16.

[151] Here too the relation to the Trinity is, according to Luther, grammatically urged: "Only once does He say 'made.' . . . He mentions three persons independently—namely, the Lord, the Word, and his Spirit; and yet he proposes not more than one maker, without any difference. Everything is made. By whom? By a maker who is the Lord, Word, Spirit. . . . All three are different persons; there is one maker of each work, and each work is the work of all three persons as the work of one maker or master." *On the Last Words of David,* 1543, *WA* 54, 57:9. Thus this passage of the psalm became a strong proof to Luther of his principal clause, which agrees with Augustine: "The works of the Trinity are indivisible externally." *Ibid.,* 57:35 ff.

[152] *Sermons on Genesis,* 1527, *WA* 24, 30:1 (1523–1524 edition: *WA* 14, 101:6 ff.; 23 ff.); *Sermon on Christmas Day on John 1:1 ff., Church Postil,* 1522, *WA* 10^I,1^, 185:20 ff.; *Lectures on Genesis,* 1535, *WA* 42, 37:25 ff.; 38:7 ff.; *LW* 1, 50.

[153] See above, p. 103, and almost all the examples enumerated above, p. 117, n. 142.

mal. Indeed, his functional doctrine of the Trinity, together with his exegetical principles, protected him against letting the Old Testament texts rage allegorically. He was satisfied with rediscovering, in decisive passages, the arch-forms of divine work—creation, Word, and Spirit, which he knew from the New Testament. And he concluded the existence of the Spirit, usually, from the revelatory and convincing force of the biblical Word itself. Thus the trinitarian prophecy of the Old Testament is firmly within the circle of Luther's theology: law-gospel-faith.

## 4. LAW AND GOSPEL

The prophecy of Christ found in profusion everywhere in the Old Testament was Luther's unique reason for talking about gospel in the Old Testament. For Luther the testimonies of divine grace, mercy, and the forgiveness of sins, often emphasized in more recent theological scholarship and also testified to in the Old Testament, would not have been enough to elicit the gospel. The gospel was not a new image of God to him, but evidence of God's historical entrance into the world through Jesus Christ. And, therefore, it can be encountered in the Old Testament only because it stands on the rock of the prophecies of the coming Christ. However, even if prophecy is the basis of gospel in the Old Testament, gospel still is not limited to individual prophetic passages. Rather, for Luther, the gospel now floods the whole Old Testament land out of these sources.

Having first dealt with the prophecies about Christ and the Trinity, which obviously represent an insoluble part of the problem of law and gospel, we are now free to see the inconspicuous, but all the more inclusive, permeation of the Old Testament with the gospel, which Luther showed in his exegesis. To him the text was obscure until seen with the eyes of one redeemed by Christ. The meaning of the entire Old Testament was concealed until clarified by the gospel. Everything he read, therefore, assumed a transformed meaning. The struggle of faith—such as Jacob's wrestling with God, or the struggle of the prophets—was to him temptation *(Anfechtung)*. The law no longer bore its own meaning and goal; rather, it became the disciplinarian that could only drive one either toward death or toward Christ. The promise of the prophets was measured by fulfilment; it was either confirmed as God's Word or condemned as the word of man.

From the viewpoint of Luther modern theological study has this problem: how can the Old Testament be understood in a Christocentric sense, how can the Old Testament be substantially directed toward Christ, if historical exegesis no longer understands Christological prophecy in the sense of Luther's interpretation? For scholarly exegesis investigates the concrete historical direction of prophetic prophecies. Such study can only disclose the wide gap between the historical direction of prophecy and Luther's explanation. Particularly at this point it will also emphasize Luther's connection with the early interpreters, especially with Augustine and Faber Stapulensis, whom Luther frequently consulted in his early years[154] and in whom Luther encountered the interpretation of Scripture as a "spiritual letter" *(litera spiritualis)* pointing to Christ.

The basic problem in the relationship of both testaments, namely, the relationship of law and gospel, is filled with a dialectic tension which we now have to unfold in its various aspects.

### *a. The Books of Moses as Jewish Customary Law*[155]

Anyone seeking clarity on law and gospel in the Old Testament is grateful for Luther's approach to the problem in his famous sermon of 1525, *How Christians Should Regard Moses.*[156] His basic viewpoint is clearly unfolded here. Law and gospel are the content of the only two sermons God publicly let resound from heaven: on Sinai and at Pentecost.[157] To whom did God speak in the law

154 See F. Hahn, "Luthers Auslegungsgrundsätze," pp. 165 ff., and "Faber Stapulensis und Luther," pp. 356 ff.
155 *LW* 40, 98, n. 20.
156 *How Christians Should Regard Moses,* 1525, *WA* 16, 363 ff.; *LW* 35, 161 ff. In this connection, one may tolerate the fact that the text was not written by Luther himself, but was prepared on the basis of copies of sermons. But everything essential is so excellently evidenced through the extant copy of Rörer that one may have no hesitation citing the edited wording of the sermon, which was printed several times after 1526 as Luther's own opinion. A similar brief survey of the problem is found in the second part of *A Letter of Martin Luther Against the Sabbatarians,* 1538, *WA* 50, 323 ff. A good collection of passages concerning the problem of law is offered in Beyer, *Luther und das Recht.* See also his description in "Glaube und Recht im Denken Luthers," *Lutherjahrbuch,* XVII (1935), 56 ff.
157 *How Christians Should Regard Moses,* 1525, *WA* 16, 363:16 ff.; *LW* 35, 161.

of Sinai? Only to the Jews. "The Mosaic law does not bind the pagans, but only the Jews."[158] One must "gag" especially the enthusiasts *(Schwärmer)* and anabaptists, who appeal to Old Testament regulations.

Moses was an intermediary solely for the Jewish people, to whom God gave the law. . . . Moses does not concern us. If I accept Moses in *one* commandment, I must accept all of Moses. Thus it would follow that if I accept Moses as master, then I must let myself be circumcised according to Jewish custom, eat, drink, and dress thus and so, and observe all that stuff.... Now if anyone confronts you with Moses and his commandments and wants to press you to keep them, say, "Go on to the Jews with your Moses; I am no Jew, don't entangle me with Moses."[159]

Therefore, let Moses be the folk law [*Sachsenspiegel*] of the Jews and leave us pagans unconfused by it.[160]

The Old Testament clearly shows that the pagans were not required to obey the law. There was no circumcision before the time of Abraham. Nor was any other item of the law imposed upon the pagans who were converted through one of the patriarchs or prophets: Pharaoh through Joseph, the city of Nineveh through Jonah, Nebuchadnezzar through Daniel, Darius and Cyrus also through Daniel and other Jews. Neither were Job, King Hiram of Tyre, and many others who learned to believe in the true God, circumcised. Luther quite correctly observed that Moses did not speak of circumcision after the exodus from Egypt, and that although Exod. 12:43 ff. demanded circumcision for the enjoyment of the Paschal Lamb, it did not force strangers in the land either to eat the Passover meal or to be circumcised. Thus it was an unjustified exaggeration when the Jews began to require circumcision from the proselytes.[161]

The reference of the enthusiasts *(Schwärmer)* to the point that

[158] *Ibid., WA* 16, 371:13; *LW* 35, 165.
[159] *Ibid., WA* 16, 373:4 ff.; 375:10; *LW* 35, 164–65, 166; *Against the Heavenly Prophets in the Matter of Images and Sacraments,* 1525 *(Widder die hymelischen propheten, von den bildern und Sacrament)*, *WA* 18, 77:28 ff.; *LW* 40, 94; letter to George Spalatin, March 14, 1524, *WA,* BR 3, 254:21 ff.; *LCS* 2, 223; letter to the City Council of Danzig, March 5(?), 1525, *WA,* BR 3, 484:2 ff.; *LCS* 2, 311.
[160] *Against the Heavenly Prophets,* 1525, *WA* 18, 81:14; *LW* 40, 98. See also *How Christians Should Regard Moses,* 1525, *WA* 16, 378:11; *LW* 35, 167.
[161] *A Letter of Martin Luther Against the Sabbatarians,* 1538, *WA* 50, 327:16 ff.; 328:38 ff. See also *The Prophet Jonah,* 1526, *WA* 19, 193:24 ff.

the Mosaic law was nevertheless God's Word was sharply refuted by Luther.

But let God's Word be what it may, I must know and pay attention to whom the Word of God is addressed.... One should not only see whether it is God's Word, whether God has said it, but rather one must see to whom it is said, whether it strikes you.... There are two kinds of Word in Scripture: the first does not concern me; it does not apply to me. The second does. And I can boldly dare and depend on the Word that concerns me as upon a strong rock. If it does not apply to me, then I should stand still.[162]

But one must not be led astray by Luther's extremely selective examples (the building of an ark, of a temple, the sacrifice of the son, the promise of the Messiah out of one's own tribe, etc.).[163] By that which does not apply to us Luther meant the Mosaic folk law, including those items he considered right and worthy of being copied, such as the tithe (Deut. 14:22), the jubilee year, in which properties and lands that have been sold can be bought back (Lev. 25:8 ff.), the sabbatical year (Lev. 25:1 ff.), and the law of divorce (Deut. 24:1 ff.).[164] As highly as Luther valued these and other points of Israelite law, particularly its social codes, protection of the poor, etc., and as much as he would have liked to see them instituted, it was still not demanded by God but rather left to choice, "just as when one nation follows examples from laws of other nations, as the Romans took the Twelve Tables from the Greeks."[165] "And would that all the other inequitable taxes were removed which today devour lands and people, and that tithes were instituted instead!"[166] Then the spirit of usury and greed raging in Germany would be curbed. "The tithe, therefore, is the best of all fixed charges, and it has been in use since the beginning of the world, and in the old law it is praised and established as the fairest of all arrangements according to divine and natural law."[167] But

[162] *How Christians Should Regard Moses,* 1525, *WA* 16, 384:13 ff.; 385:7 ff.; *LW* 35, 170. See also *WA* 16, 388:10 ff.; 389:18 ff.; *LW* 35, 170.
[163] *Ibid., WA* 16, 384:10 ff.; 385:10; *LW* 35, 170–71; *The Prophet Jonah,* 1526, *WA* 19, 195:5 ff.
[164] *How Christians Should Regard Moses,* 1525, *WA* 16, 376:16 ff.; 377:14 ff.; *LW* 35, 166–67.
[165] *Against the Heavenly Prophets,* 1525, *WA* 18, 81:24; *LW* 40, 98.
[166] *The Deuteronomy of Moses, with Notes,* 1525, *WA* 14, 652:15 ff.; *LW* 9, 138–39.
[167] *Trade and Usury,* 1524, *WA* 15, 321:25; *LW* 45, 308–09. Luther valued in the tithe the fact that it was measured according to produce; thus "the creditor

Luther especially explained about a provision of Mosaic law which he also rejected for other reasons, the stoning of adulterers, "Such a law is certainly not given to the Jews."[168]

Mosaic law was that much more tied to Judaism since it was, as Luther recognized with noteworthy historical keenness, only in its smallest part a creation of Moses; it was, rather, an ancient Jewish folk law, "which Moses took, wrote down, and codified for the most part from ancient tradition already in use among the people." By this observation Luther gained an insight into the development of real and lasting law, and thus he used this as an example by which he advised Landgrave Philip of Hesse against instituting a universal church order like the one in Hesse *(Reformatio ecclesiarum Hassiae),* and recommended a slow, step-by-step progressing regulation of imperative practical issues.[169]

### *b. Decalogue and Natural Law*

"Moses is dead." "Not one iota of Moses concerns us."[170] This complete and unambiguous conclusion has one reservation: in so far as the law of Moses "rhymes with natural law,"[171] that is, in so far as it agrees with the moral law also known to the pagans, it is also obligatory to us. For Luther, natural law encompasses the two customary basic traits: first, the duty of worshiping God, known to all men. He was impressed by the effect of idolatry in the Old Testament. "Nature provides that one should call upon God; the pagans attest to this, too. For there has never been a pagan who did not call upon his idols."[172] Second, consideration for one another, ac-

---

would bear the risk as well as the debtor, and both would have to look to God." *WA* 15, 321:14 ff.; *LW* 45, 309. See also *Against the Heavenly Prophets,* 1525, *WA* 18, 81:20 ff.; *LW* 40, 98; *Psalm 117,* 1530, *WA* $31^{I}$, 238:26 ff.; *LW* 14, 20.

168 Letter to the Mayor and Council of Zerbst, October 8, 1524, *WA,* BR 3, 355:6. On Luther as marital judge, see Walther Köhler, "Luthers als Eherichter," *Beiträge zur sächsischen Kirchengeschichte,* XLVII (1942), 18 ff.

169 Letter to Philip, Landgrave of Hesse, January 7, 1527, *WA,* BR 4, 157–58; *LCS* 2, 391–92. "These are views which modern Old Testament study arrived at with difficulty; significant discoveries have enabled us now to document them historically to a considerable extent." Hermann Guthe, *Luther und die Bibelforschung der Gegenwart* ("Sammlung gemeinverständlicher Vorträge," 83 [Tübingen, 1917]), p. 22.

170 *How Christians Should Regard Moses,* 1525, *WA* 16, 373:12; 375:14; *LW* 35, 165, 167.

171 *Sermons on Exodus,* 1524–1527, *WA* 16, 394:5.

172 *How Christians Should Regard Moses,* 1525, *WA* 16, 379:10 ff.; *LW* 35, 168; *Against the Heavenly Prophets,* 1525, *WA* 18, 80:18 ff.; *LW* 40, 96–97;

cording to Matt. 7:12, which Luther explicitly equated with the love of neighbor; the particular commandments and prohibitions naturally proceed from it. "Nature teaches, as does love, that I should do as I would have done to me" (Luke 6:31).[173]

> This is as much as to say, "Love your neighbor as yourself" [Luke 10:27], and, "Whatever you wish to have done to you ..." [Matt. 7:12]. For everyone feels that he wants to be loved and not hated; thus he also feels and sees that he owes just the same to the next man. But this means to love the neighbor as oneself.[174]

But Luther stressed sharply that we obey this natural law for its own sake and not for the sake of Moses. "Thus I keep the commandments which Moses has given, not because Moses commanded it, but because they have been implanted in me by nature, and Moses agrees exactly with nature."[175] Thus Moses is not a legislator whose laws are binding upon non-Jews. Where he agrees with natural law, he is only one more accidental voice; in reality, we all stand directly, together with all the world, before another master.

This double differentiation applies particularly to the Decalogue: in so far as it is the national law of Moses it no longer concerns us; and in so far as it binds us in conscience as an expression of natural law, it does not derive from Moses. The introduction already makes it emphatically clear how little the Decalogue as such and the revelatory event on Sinai concern us. "I am the Lord your God, who brought you out of the land of Egypt, out of the house of bondage" (Exod. 20:1)—God has not led us Germans out of Egypt.[176]

> If I came before God and said, "O Lord God, who has led me out of Egypt, out of misery," etc., I would look just like a sow in a Jewish school. For God did not do such work for me. This is why God would

---

"The First Commandment," *The Large Catechism,* 1529, *WA* $30^{I}$, 134:35; Tappert (ed.), *The Book of Concord,* p. 367. See also below, pp. 128–29.

173 *Temporal Authority: To What Extent It Should Be Obeyed,* 1523 (*Von weltlicher oberkeyt, wie weytt man yhr gehorsam schuldig sey*), *WA* 11, 279:19; *LW* 45, 128.

174 *Lenten Postil,* 1525, *WA* $17^{II}$, 102:15. See also *The Lord's Prayer Explained to Simple Laymen,* 1519 (*Auslegung deudsch des Vater unnser, für dye eynfaltigen leyen*), *WA* 2, 120:22; *LE* 24, 299; *Against the Heavenly Prophets,* 1525, *WA* 18, 80:30; *LW* 40, 97. The demands of natural law are to be distinguished from these two items of natural moral law. See below, p. 131.

175 *How Christians Should Regard Moses,* 1525, *WA* 16, 380:9; *LW* 35, 168.

176 *Ibid., WA* 16, 373:14 ff.; *LW* 35, 165.

call me a liar, or I would have to make an invented God out of him. And yet I still have to say and to keep everything in the First Commandment. I also could say, "You are my God, the God of us all and, at the same time, Creator, who, to be sure, led the children of Israel out of Egypt, but not me; rather, you led me out of my own Egypt and misery." Thus the First Commandment remains valid for both Jews and pagans.[177]

Luther usually explained that the Decalogue also contains ceremonial law bound by national customs, the prohibition of images and the commandment to sanctify the Sabbath. Luther even secured himself doubly against the iconoclasts and Carlstadt: on the one hand he tried to prove that "making no image or likeness" means only, according to the context of this text and other passages (Lev. 26:1; Deut. 4:15 ff.; and others), not to worship them.[178] But if one still insists on understanding it literally, then it falls, like the Sabbath, into the category of ceremonial laws, which according to Paul (Col. 2:16–17; Gal. 4:10–11; 5:3) have been abrogated through the coming of Christ.[179]

But sometimes Luther explained even more explicitly why the Decalogue, in the formulation of Moses, did not bind us to a large extent, but was instead Jewish folk law. Moses did it exactly like a good prince who builds his own national and domestic order, applying only to his own people, upon the general human law, particularly the fear of God.[180]

Thus Moses, too, when he was to bring order to his people, who had been led out of Egypt, first let God issue his Ten Commandments, which belong to the whole world. Then he gave his people a special national order, still based upon God's command, which had nothing in common with other nations. And just as the people of Moses were obliged to obey his order, because God commanded him, so also was each nation and family obliged to keep the order of its prince and head of the family; for it also was the command of God, who instituted all political rule in the world.[181]

Luther demonstrated this interrelationship of natural law and Jewish national order in a whole series of commandments, in *Letter of Martin Luther Against the Sabbatarians* (1538): the First is ex-

177 *A Letter of Martin Luther Against the Sabbatarians,* 1538, *WA* 50, 331:24.
178 *Against the Heavenly Prophets,* 1525, *WA* 18, 69 ff.; *LW* 40, 86–87.
179 *Ibid., WA* 18, 77:3 ff., 28 ff.; *LW* 40, 93–94.
180 *A Letter of Martin Luther Against the Sabbatarians,* 1538, *WA* 50, 331: 37 ff.
181 *Ibid.,* 332:13 ff.

plained by the rescue out of Egypt.[182] Although the Third is a general and natural commandment, its choice of particularly the seventh day is only a "timely adornment" with which Moses embellishes it; the patriarchs knew nothing of this either, so it is equally immaterial to us.[183] The promise of the Fourth Commandment assures well-being and long life to the Jewish people in the land of Canaan. We, in contrast, can apply it only to individual life.

We pagans can neither say nor believe (nor can God tolerate it) that he led us out of Egypt or into the land of Canaan, where we are to fare well if we honor father and mother; rather, we have to let it be generally understood that God wants to bring happiness and well-being to each in his own country, to anyone who honors father and mother, just as we, to be sure, can observe that nations and principalities, indeed, even families and inherited goods, change so marvelously or remain intact, according to one's obedience or disobedience. Moreover, it has always been found true that he who does not honor father and mother, does not experience well-being or die a happy death.[184]

The Jewish divorce law is presupposed in the Ninth and Tenth Commandments.[185]

This is why the most careful differentiation must be made within the Ten Commandments: whatever goes beyond natural law is removed; only the "common natural laws" appear throughout all the nations, "just as France does not accept the Saxon common law *(Sachsenspiegel)* and yet certainly agrees with it in natural law."[186] But this natural law does not come from Moses; he is not the author but "the interpreter and illustrator of the biblical commandments in the minds of all men."[187] God had to impress it on humanity

182 *Ibid.*, 331:20 ff.
183 *Ibid.*, 332:21 ff.
184 *Ibid.*, 334:37 ff. If, therefore, the folkish sense of the Decalogue, and with it that of the Fourth Commandment according to the Old Testament, has again been emphasized—for example, in Karl Cramer, "Das alttestamentliche Gesetz," *Schule und Evangelium,* X (1936), 228—one should not overlook the fact that Luther himself became the criterion for the individualistic interpretation of the "Thou shalt" in the Protestant church. This emphasis is also disclosed in "The Fourth Commandment," *The Large Catechism,* 1529, *WA* 30$^{I}$, 147–48; Tappert (ed.), *op. cit.,* pp. 379–80. Luther, of course, always recognized and clearly and forcefully expressed the effects of the Fourth Commandment, in particular, upon the stability of national life.
185 *A Letter of Martin Luther Against the Sabbatarians,* 1538, *WA* 50, 335:15.
186 *Against the Heavenly Prophets,* 1525, *WA* 18, 81:15; *LW* 40, 98.
187 *Second Disputation Against the Antinomians,* 1538 (*Secunda disputatio contra Antinomos*), *WA* 39$^{I}$, 454:3, 15. In this connection, Luther did not at all disregard the fact that Moses, according to Exodus 20, was not only the originator but also the receiver of the Decalogue (Herntrich, "Luther und das

again through Moses, since it had largely been forgotten. Luther here developed a view of the history of the soul in humanity directly opposite to that of the Enlightenment. While for the Enlightenment (for Locke or Lessing) God's revelations anticipated goals at which humanity would arrive by itself even if by longer roads, Luther saw human history not as natural progress, but as a progressive separation from purer beginnings. That was why God had to communicate once again with particular clarity his natural law through Moses.

> Then, because men had reached the point where they cared for neither God nor man, God was compelled to renew these laws and to put them on tables before our own eyes, written with his own fingers, so that we are reminded of what we were before Adam and what we shall be sometime in Christ.[188]

The Decalogue receives its convincing and overpowering force not from itself, but from our conscience—even today, in so far as it does not consist of time-bound cultic commandments.

> Circumcision and other ceremonies belonged to a certain people and to a certain time; then they came completely to an end. The Decalogue is indeed now attached to conscience. For if God had never established the law through Moses, the natural human mind would still have this notion to worship God and to esteem him highly.[189]

The universality of God's wrath rests upon this universality of natural law. Wrath is nothing else than "the feeling of the law's sermon in the conscience," and falls upon both Jews and pagans.

> The law is written in the depth of the heart; it cannot be removed, as one can see quite well in the psalms of lamentation where the dear

Alte Testament," *Lutherjahrbuch,* XX [1938], 103–04). Although Luther could say, "The Decalogue is not the law of Moses and he himself was not the first to give it" (*Second Disputation Against the Antinomians,* 1538, *WA* 39$^{I}$, 478:16), he did not forget the pre-eminence of the Decalogue over against the rest of Mosaic law, because it was proclaimed from heaven "in a public sermon" by God himself (*How Christians Should Regard Moses,* 1525, *WA* 16, 364:12; 367:17 ff.; *LW* 35, 161, 162). But this Decalogue, in its Sinaitic form, is only intended for the Jews and applies to us only when it is in accord with the natural law in the conscience. The question of Moses' authorship does not even for a moment overlook the divine originator; rather, it only states that the generally obligatory, principal meaning of the Decalogue has been inscribed in the hearts of men long before Moses.

188 *Second Disputation Against the Antinomians,* 1538, *WA* 39$^{I}$, 454:10. See also n. 189 below.

189 *Ibid.,* 374:1 ff.

saints cannot bear the wrath of God; this cannot be anything else but the feeling of the law's sermon in the conscience. And the devil, too, knows very well that it is impossible to remove the law from the heart; St. Paul attests in Romans 2 [:14–15] that the pagans who have not received the law through Moses, and thus have no law, still are a law to themselves. They have to admit that it is the work of the law written in their hearts.[190]

This voice of conscience differentiates the human being from the animal. One could preach the law to it for a hundred thousand years—it would be in vain. For

the soul is not made or formed in such a way that such things could fall into it. But a man, when the law is held up before him, will soon say, "Yes, it is so, I cannot deny it." One could not convince him of this so quickly if it had not been written in his heart beforehand. Now, because it is in the heart beforehand, no matter how obscurely and completely faded, it is reawakened with the Word so that the heart must confess that it is like the sound of the commandments.[191]

When Herntrich concludes from this passage that "only from Scripture does one know about natural law; only through the Holy Spirit is the fulfilment of natural law possible, as certain as Luther was that pagans too can do works of natural law,"[192] it contradicts the function of natural law for Luther. For one thing, knowledge and fulfilment are two different things; for another, knowledge comes not alone from Scripture but precisely, as the pagans show, primarily from the innate conscience and, to the extent it is awakened by the Decalogue, from the harmony of both. One must not argue a false scriptural absolutism here; for then one would tear salvation history *(Heilsgeschichte)* and creation apart.[193] Natural law belongs, if one insists on formulating it like Herntrich,[194] absolutely on the side of biological life *(bios)*. And it is, in fact, "positively a human possession." Luther said often enough that the

[190] *Against the Antinomians,* 1539 (*Wider die Antinomer*), *WA* 50, 471: 23 ff.
[191] *Sermons on Exodus,* 1525, *WA* 16, 447:27 ff.
[192] "Luther und das Alte Testament," pp. 105–06.
[193] If one calls, according to Herntrich's doubtful formulation, natural law "an open door of the knowledge of God" (*ibid.,* p. 105), then it can never be denied that it stands "beside and outside of Christ." He himself cannot deny it, even though he deduces the knowledge about natural law from Scripture and not from conscience; for then it is derived from the Decalogue, from Moses, whom one cannot at all mistake for Christ.
[194] *Ibid.,* p. 104.

Decalogue, in contrast to faith, is written in the hearts of all men. "Moreover, the Ten Commandments are inscribed in the hearts of all men anyway [Rom. 2:15]. No human wisdom can comprehend the faith; it must be taught by the Holy Spirit alone."[195]

The Decalogue belongs to the whole world; it is inscribed and engraved in the hearts of all men from the foundation of the world.[196]

For there is no one who does not feel, and is forced to confess, that natural law is right and true when it says, "What you wish to have done and not done to you, that do and do not do to another." The light lives and glows in the reason of all men, and if they wanted to look at it, what need would they have of books, teachers, or any law? They carry a living book in the depth of their hearts, which would tell them abundantly enough what they should do, not do, condemn, accept, and reject.[197]

And when this law, actually in all men, though more in one and less in another, has been obscured by the devil, it must be rekindled not only with the commandment of political authority, but also with the law of Scripture.

Evil lust and love obscure such light and blind a human being so that he does not look at such a book in his heart and does not obey such a clear command of reason; that is why one must drive him back and force him, with external commandments, books, sword and force, and remind him of his own natural light and hold his own heart up for him to see.[198]

And finally, if this does not help either, sword and penal law must prevent the evil deed. Luther did not thereby consider all men to be of the same stamp. Crude methods were necessary for those whom he called "the world." But there were also people to whom the natural law could be addressed more easily. But it was common to all that it was inscribed in the human heart, namely, from the very beginning of creation. It was therefore also incorrect to see in the instituting of the blood-law (Gen. 9:6) the date on which

[195] "The Creed," *The Large Catechism,* 1529, *WA* 30$^{I}$, 192:19; Tappert (ed.), *op. cit.,* pp. 419–20.
[196] *Second Disputation Against the Antinomians,* 1538, *WA* 39$^{I}$, 478:17; 454:4; *A Letter of Martin Luther Against the Sabbatarians,* 1538, *WA* 50, 331:1 ff.
[197] *Sermon on the Fourth Sunday after Epiphany on Rom. 13:8 ff., Lenten Postil,* 1525, *WA* 17$^{II}$, 102:8.
[198] *Ibid.,* 102:19.

God gave the natural law. The blood-law, according to Luther, was the basis of the system of law among nations, but not the origin of the natural law of conscience. "Here is the source from which stems all civil law and the law of nations. For if God grants to man the power over life and death, surely he also grants power over what is less, such as property, the home, wife, children, servants, and fields."[199]

One sees Luther distinguish between the law of nature, or "the rights of man" and natural law. Natural law *(natürliches Gesetz)* for him means worship of God and love of neighbor. The law of nature *(natürliches Recht)* is, for Luther, not a system of simple rules like the law of nature *(Naturrecht)* in classical antiquity, but the sum total of the naturally developing rules of social and community life. To be competent in the operation of these "rights of man" *(natürliche Rechte),* which can neither be defined nor codified, is the fine art of great statesmen and charismatic leaders.

> One now starts to praise the law of nature *(natürliches Recht)* and natural reason as though all written law had come from and flowed from them. And this is certainly true and praiseworthy. But the trouble is that everyone likes to think the law of nature *(natürliches Recht)* is encased in his own head.... The precious gem called the law of nature and natural reason is a rare thing among the children of men.[200]

The natural demands of life, which require legal regulations, also belong to the law of nature *(Naturrecht).* They are also reflected in part in the Decalogue, for example, the requirement of rest for man and animal, out of which the Sabbath and the Sunday have originated. Since such a natural regulation may conform to need, Luther was certainly not, aside from the hearing of the Word of God, a defender of a Puritan Sunday rest.

> It is not necessary to observe the Sabbath or Sunday because of Moses' commandment. Nature also shows and teaches that one must now and then rest a day, so that man and beast may be refreshed. Moses also recognized this natural reason in his Sabbath law, for he places the

199 *Lectures on Genesis,* 1536, *WA* 42, 360:30; *LW* 2, 140. Against Herntrich, "Luther und das Alte Testament," p. 106.

200 *Psalm 101,* 1534–1535, *WA* 51, 211:36; 212:24; *LW* 13, 160–61. Herntrich, who confuses law of nature with natural law in the covenant of Noah as elsewhere, did not observe that according to his description ("Luther und das Alte Testament," p. 104) only genial politicians know the natural law, that is, have a conscience.

Sabbath under man, as Christ also does (Matthew 12 [:1 ff.] and Mark 3 [:2 ff.]). For where it is kept for the sake of rest alone, it is clear that he who does not need rest may break the Sabbath and rest on some other day, as nature allows. The Sabbath is also to be kept for the purpose of preaching and hearing the Word of God.[201]

If Luther rendered the Decalogue transparent to the power of natural law *(natürliches Gesetz)* which was behind it, it was definitely not to declare it superfluous. Quite the contrary: the Ten Commandments are the inescapable pertinent formulation of the law written in our hearts, and therefore the law per se. As long as one finds the content of the proclamation in the social and religious imperative, the Decalogue is not to be surpassed.

What can be a better proclamation than the Ten Commandments? Nothing can be said that is higher than the First Commandment. It is impossible to invent a more excellent doctrine after Moses; to worship, to praise, and to give thanks to God is the highest and most excellent doctrine that can be handed on. The Decalogue, therefore, is the highest doctrine! ... This is the ancient [doctrine]: believe in God, love him as much as you love yourself. No more perfect law can be handed on.[202]

Luther even concluded from this how senseless it is to see Christ as a new lawgiver; he could not surpass the Decalogue. "It is ridiculous to make Christ the giver of the law and to see in him the promise of another law. Since nothing can be higher in heaven and on earth than the law of Moses for man to understand, to do so is hardly possible."[203] One repeatedly reaches for the law tables of Moses because the natural laws "are nowhere so well and so methodically drawn up as in Moses."[204] The reason for this is not only the striking formulation and the inclusive arrangement, but above all the inner logic which deduces all commandments from

[201] *Against the Heavenly Prophets,* 1525, *WA* 18, 81:26 ff.; *LW* 40, 98. To sanctify is more important than to observe holy days; but to observe holy days would be necessary only for the time one needs to hear the Word of God. *A Letter of Martin Luther Against the Sabbatarians,* 1538, *WA* 50, 332:21 ff.; "The Third Commandment," *The Large Catechism,* 1529, *WA* 30$^{I}$, 144; Tappert (ed.), *op. cit.,* p. 376.

[202] *Lecture on Psalm 2,* 1532 (copy), *WA* 40$^{II}$, 246:8; 247:12; *LW* 12, 44. See also "Conclusion of the Ten Commandments," *The Large Catechism,* 1529, *WA* 30$^{I}$, 178:22; 179:24; 182:8; Tappert (ed.), *op. cit.,* pp. 407, 410. Deut. 6:5 and Lev. 19:18 are for Luther the commentary on the Decalogue. *The Deuteronomy of Moses, with Notes,* 1525, *WA* 14, 607:24; *LW* 9, 67.

[203] *Preparations to Lectures on Galatians,* 1531, *WA* 40$^{I}$, 15:25.

[204] *Against the Heavenly Prophets,* 1525, *WA* 18, 81:18; *LW* 40, 98.

the First Commandment, something Luther pointed out untiringly. Like the rim holds the wreath—this is the beautiful way Luther described it in the *Large Catechism*—so does the First Commandment hold all the others together. The commandments of the first, as well as of the second, table are, if understood correctly, really all contained in the First Commandment and receive their goal and their meaning from it. "Thus you see how the First Commandment is the chief source and the fountainhead from which all the others proceed; again, to it all the others return and cling, so that end and beginning are linked and bound together."[205] "For if the First Commandment is missing and does not give light, then none of the others will give proper light, and the understanding will be entirely faulty."[206]

Yes, the First Commandment is so much the criterion and judge of the others that if faith or love require it, it even invalidates them. Killing is sometimes God's commandment, as the examples of Abraham (Gen. 14:13 ff.) and Ahab (I Kings 20:31 ff.) attest. So also with the other commandments. The First Commandment thus contains the inner meaning, speaking with Aristotle, the "fairness" *(epieikeia),* of the whole law. There is a "legitimate" use of the law only where this is preserved.

> He wants you to know that the First Commandment is the measure or yardstick of all others, to which they are to yield and give obedience. Therefore, you may kill, in violation of the Fifth Commandment, for the sake of faith and charity.... Similar is the case of theft, ambush, and trickery against the enemies of God; you may take spoils, goods, wives, daughters, sons, and servants of enemies. You should hate father and mother so that you may love the Lord (Luke 14:26). In short, where anything will be against faith and love, there you shall not know that anything else is commanded by either God or man. Where it is for faith and love, however, you shall know that everything is commanded in all cases and everywhere. For the statement remains, "These words shall be in your heart"; there they shall rule. Furthermore, unless they are also in the heart, certainly no one will understand or fol-

205 "Conclusion of the Ten Commandments," *The Large Catechism,* 1529, *WA* 30I, 181:1, 21; Tappert (ed.), *op. cit.,* p. 410.

206 *Psalm 101,* 1534–1535, *WA* 51, 204:16; *LW* 13, 151; *Treatise on Good Works,* 1520, *WA* 6, 209:24 ff.; 212:23 ff.; *LW* 44, 30, 32; *The Ten Commandments, Preached to the People of Wittenberg,* 1518 (*Decem Praecepta Wittebergesi predicata populo*), *WA* 1, 430:6; "The First Commandment," *The Large Catechism,* 1529, *WA* 30I, 139:11; Tappert (ed.), *op. cit.,* p. 371.

low this graciousness [*epieikeia*], or ever employ laws successfully, safely, and legally. Therefore, Paul says in I Timothy 1 [:9] that "the law is not set up for the righteous," for the reason that the fulfilling of the law is love from a good heart and from faith that is not feigned [I Tim. 1:5], which uses the law lawfully when it has no laws and has all laws—no laws, because none bind unless through faith and love; all, because all bind when they serve faith and love.[207]

This does not contradict the natural character of the law. For it did not come out of nature's own powers; nature itself is not creative. Instead, it is implanted by the Creator himself and therefore demands, as the noblest commandment, faith in him. "To have a God is not just a law of Moses, but also a natural law."[208] Under no circumstances must one let this realization be obscured by the fact that Luther naturally declared the pagans' belief in God to be false, since they do not depend on the true God who revealed himself only in the revelations and promises of the old and new covenants.

The demand contained in the First Commandment, "to have a God," to love him and to trust him, was to Luther a natural law written in the hearts of all men.[209] And the inner logic of the Decalogue in the First Commandment means, first of all, that without love and trust in God every other commandment is thrown off course and out of order, and becomes senseless. Nor is the natural character of the Decalogue altered through the First Commandment, in so far as it is commandment. That it also contains an affirmation, "I am the Lord thy God," and that it enters into the service of such affirmations as a whole commandment—of which more will be said in the proper place—is not thereby invalidated;

[207] *The Deuteronomy of Moses, with Notes,* 1525, *WA* 14, 611:29 ff.; *LW* 9, 70. These are the words Moses adds to the First Commandment that one should take these words to heart (Deut. 6:16).

[208] *Against the Heavenly Prophets,* 1525, *WA* 18, 80:18; *LW* 40, 97.

[209] Against Herntrich ("Luther und das Alte Testament," p. 115), who, once again, does not distinguish clearly enough and thus, through the obscuring and reawakening of the law, annuls its natural character in a false dialectic. The First Commandment is indeed "to be assigned to natural law." Herntrich is everywhere in danger of losing the proper balance between the function of the Old Testament as *Heilsgeschichte* and natural law, as argued by Luther. That is why he proposes a number of slanted formulations: God spoke at Sinai not "to the congregation" (*Gemeinde*) but to Israel (*ibid.,* p. 109). And that the history of the *Gemeinde* "begins at Sinai," and that there is no history of the *Gemeinde* of Jesus Christ "which does not remain within the context of Sinai" (*ibid.,* p. 109) is only a half-truth.

nor does it invalidate the meaning of the First Commandment as a demand written in the heart. Luther considered the naturalness of the Ten Commandments so important because they are then not, like the law of Moses, bound to the sphere of influence of the Sinai revelation, but are rather the inexorable law of God by which all of mankind becomes guilty.

### *c. The End of the Law*

But Christ is the end of the law (Rom. 10:4). Of which law? Of the Mosaic law or also of natural law? On the basis of what was said above, the obvious answer is: of natural law, since the national law of Moses does not obligate us anyway; it was not proclaimed to us. "Christ rescued us from the curse of the law" (Gal. 3:13).

But the pagans were never under the curse of the ceremonial law. All the redeemed, therefore, were under the curse of the law, for, as I have also said before, Christ would have achieved too little if he had freed us only from circumcision, Sabbath, clothing, foods, and washings, and not to a far greater extent from the more grievous sins against the law, lust, greed, wrath, godlessness. Then he would really not have been a savior of souls; he would have been a savior of bodies, because all these things concerned the body. Accordingly, the work of any law whatsoever is really sin and a curse, if it is done outside of faith, that is, outside purity of heart, innocence, and righteousness.[210]

But Luther nevertheless declared the Antinomians disciples of Satan when they thought that the law was something finite which ended under Christ, like circumcision. "These true disciples of Satan seem to consider the law as something finite, which ended under Christ, just like circumcision."[211] It would be simple to set up a series of

210 *Lectures on Galatians,* 1519, *WA* 2, 514:16 ff.; *LW* 27, 257. See also *ibid., WA* 2, 468:33 ff.; *LW* 27, 188; *Preparations to Lectures on Galatians,* 1531, *WA* 40$^{I}$, 450:4 ff.; *LW* 26, 289. Luther also converted the simple translation of the law in Heb. 7:12 into this annulment of the whole law, appealing to the abrogation of the law in Paul, "where under the term 'law' he understands simply whatever has been commanded from a divine or human standpoint, whether it be a matter of ceremonial, or a judicial and moral issue. The meaning of the words, then, 'the law is changed' is this: it is fulfilled in Christ." *Lectures on the Epistle to the Hebrews,* 1517–1518, *WA* 57, 192:16 ff.; *LCC* 16, 139. See also Hirsch and Rückert (eds.), *op. cit.,* p. 203:3 ff., and Holsten, *Christentum und nichtchristliche Religion nach der Auffassung Luthers,* pp. 26 ff.

211 Thesis 48 in the second set of *Theses Against the Antinomians,* 1537–1540 (*Die Thesen gegen die Antinomer*), *WA* 39$^{I}$, 350:5.

antitheses again, which would prove the annulment of the law on the one hand and its continuance on the other. And this series would not be just a reflection of the antitheses on the validity and the end of the Old Testament,[212] since there the law's continuance in the New Testament was not based upon its remaining significance but upon the promises contained in it. But it suffices here to show the simple differentiations which Luther combined in his pronouncements on the continuance and end of the law. The law is annulled in so far as it concerns justification. It continues to be valid until the end of the world in so far as we have to struggle with sin until our death.

8. As far as heaven is removed from earth, so far must the law be removed from justification.
9. And nothing is to be taught, said, and considered in the matter of justification, unless it is exhibited solely in the word of grace in Christ.
10. Hence, however, it does not follow that the law is to be abolished and removed from the assemblies of the church.[213]

Therefore the commandments are necessary only for sinners. However, the righteous are also sinners because of their flesh.... Consequently, the commandments are necessary, not so that we may be justified by doing the works they enjoin, but so that as persons who are already righteous we may know how our spirit should crucify the flesh and direct us in the affairs of this life, lest the flesh become haughty, break its bridle, and shake off its rider, the spirit of faith. One must have a bridle for the horse, not for the rider.[214]

The forgiveness of sin abrogates the law and yet at the same time irrevocably presupposes it. Otherwise man would never know what sin is.

20. The law, the indication of sin, and the revelation of wrath are synonymous terms, just as man, a creature, is able to laugh and to be rational.
21. To abrogate the law and yet retain the revelation of wrath is as much as to deny that Peter is a man, and yet to argue that he is a creature able to laugh and think.

212 See above, pp. 82–83.
213 Theses of the second set of *Theses Against the Antinomians,* 1537–1540, *WA* 39$^{I}$, 348:5 ff.
214 *Lectures on Galatians,* 1519, *WA* 2, 497:36; 498:10; *LW* 27, 232. For example, there is also a fine, simple formulation of the contrast in *The Deuteronomy of Moses, with Notes,* 1525, *WA* 14, 677:23 ff.; 678:4 ff.; *LW* 9, 178–79.

22. To annul the law, and yet to teach that sin is to be forgiven, is the same kind of wisdom.[215]

A false doctrine, insisting that the law no longer obligates us, is therefore a work of Satan which destroys everything—Christ, Scripture, and God himself.

28. Thus it becomes evident that Satan literally teaches sin, penance, and Christ through these his instruments.
29. Yet in reality he annuls Christ, penance, sin, and all of Scripture; moreover, he annuls even its author, God himself.[216]

Even though the thorn of accusation has been removed from the law here on earth through the forgiveness in Christ, the law still keeps its existence unto eternity: an eternal task for the damned, fulfilled in the saved.

45. For when the law existed before Christ, it certainly accused us; but under Christ, it is pacified through the remission of sins, and is now to be fulfilled through the Spirit.
46. Thus it will remain fulfilled after Christ in future life, because then the new creature the law demanded will be a reality.
47. Thus the law will be abrogated in eternity but it will remain and will have to be fulfilled by the damned, as it has been fulfilled by the saved.[217]

The fulfilment of the law here on earth is the deed of Christ. He brought into the world the justification which is the only goal of the whole moral law, albeit differently than the man under the law thinks. That is why we participate in the fulfilment of the law only in faith. For faith receives the forgiveness and awakens the love for free and joyous works.

35. Faith in Christ alone justifies (Rom. 3:28); it alone fulfils the law; it alone does good works without the law.
36. For it alone receives the forgiveness of sins and does good works voluntarily through love.[218]

And so the question concerning the end (that is, fulfilment) and continuance (that is, not-yet-being-fulfilled) of the law must finally

215 Theses of the second set of *Theses Against the Antinomians,* 1537–1540, *WA* 39^I^, 348:29 ff.
216 *Ibid.*, 349:5 ff.
217 *Ibid.*, 349:39 ff.
218 Theses of the fourth set of *Theses Against the Antinomians,* 1537–1540, *WA* 39^I^, 354:1 ff.

be judged according to whether the law is put in Christ or outside Christ.

9. We receive the law outside of Christ, that is, the letter [of the law] which is not yet fulfilled; and yet it must of necessity be fulfilled by us. 10. The law, to be sure, is fulfilled in Christ; sin is deleted, death is destroyed.[219]

Luther regularly expressed himself on this distinction about the end of the law. The presupposition is always that the Mosaic law is no longer valid for us. On the other hand, the question of the validity of the natural law can be answered briefly only in the way Luther did so against Carlstadt and the iconoclasts. "Now where the law of Moses and natural laws are one and the same, the law remains and is not abrogated externally, except spiritually through faith, which is nothing else than fulfilling the law" (Rom. 3:31).[220] Luther's use of language, therefore, also shows a certain discrimination, certainly not slavishly kept, in view of his linguistic elasticity. "To fulfil" or "the end of the law" is something other than "to abolish." Because Luther always had to protect himself against both the Nomians and the Antinomians, his pronouncements on the law acquired a diversity, in which he placed the accent differently every time. This becomes especially evident in the *First and Second Disputation Against the Antinomians* (1538), in which even the two copies still extant occasionally change accent, although they end up with the same meaning.

A. The Decalogue had its appointed time, in which Christ, of course, appeared in the flesh and subjected himself to the law; he took away its claim and curbed its verdict so that it could not create despair or condemn.[221]

B. Consider that the universal law is to be annulled; but [consider] as many parts of it as you please [as valid] in their own time. The ceremonial part is already abrogated. For these ceremonies were given to last until the time of Christ; but the Decalogue [was given] because it is inscribed in nature. It even remains valid now, but in such

[219] Theses of the fifth set of *Theses Against the Antinomians,* 1537–1540, *WA* 39$^{I}$, 354:27 ff. On the question of the annulment of the law, see the significant remarks in Friedrich K. Schumann, "Bemerkungen zur Lehre vom Gesetz, *Zeitschrift für systematische Theologie,* XVI (1940), 600 ff.
[220] *Against the Heavenly Prophets,* 1525, *WA* 18, 81:4; *LW* 40, 97.
[221] *First Disputation Against the Antinomians,* 1538, *WA* 39$^{I}$, 374:5.

a way that it does not accuse or condemn us who believe in Christ. It remains valid up to his time, that is, all the way to the time of Christ and into future life, when it will no longer be important to consider and obey it.[222]

A. Christ fulfilled the whole law. For he himself is the end of the law, not only of ceremonial and judicial law, but also of the Decalogue itself. He is the remission of sins, which the gospel offers all those who believe in him, not only in eternal life, but also formally.[223]

B. If this argument about Mosaic law is understood, then all this is true. For Christ ended the Mosaic law because it was temporal; and although he even ended the Decalogue for those who believe, it is nevertheless not abrogated in us, because it is not yet completed in us. But when we have been resurrected from the dead, even the Decalogue will be abrogated in us.[224]

All these accents show an insoluble unity, if one looks at the core of the matter. Christ is the end of the whole law, of the Mosaic ethnic law in any case, of natural law if it concerns justification before God. That is why Luther applied the ancient prophecy in which Moses prophesies his own succession ("The Lord your God will raise up for you a prophet like me," Deut. 18:15 ff.) to this double end of the law as a whole.[225] The words of Jesus, "All prophets and the law prophesied until John" (Matt. 11:13), intends to say the same thing: there is the lamb of God, who carries the sin of the world; therefore, away with all law! "When this occurs, and is known as well as received, I no longer have to say that all laws accuse and condemn me, even the Decalogue itself. For when I have Christ through faith, I have that which the law requires and demands of me." And yet, aside from this, the fact remains that "the law cannot be abrogated in the universe."[226]

If Christ put an end to the accusation of the law by fulfilling it, then it also means the end of obligation to the law *for the believer.* As severely as Luther maintained the binding power of

222 *Ibid.,* 374:27 ff.
223 *Second Disputation Against the Antinomians,* 1538, *WA* 39^I, 453:9.
224 *Ibid.,* 453:22–23.
225 *Preface to the Old Testament,* 1523, *EA* 63, 20; *LW* 35, 246; *The Deuteronomy of Moses, with Notes,* 1525, *WA* 14, 675:11 ff.; 680:1 ff.; *LW* 9, 176, 182–83; *A Letter of Martin Luther Against the Sabbatarians,* 1538, *WA* 50, 323:12.
226 *Second Disputation Against the Antinomians,* 1538, *WA* 39^I, 455:5; 456:18.

the law for obdurate souls, and that is to a very large extent each Christian soul, he also concretely depicted how much freedom from a particular commandment is given to the believer through the conquering of the law. Instead of many examples,[227] the one courageous word, "We shall make new Decalogues," demonstrates how seriously Luther meant that the believer is entirely freed from the imprisonment of the law. If the pagans, with their obscured knowledge, could be "a law unto themselves" (Rom. 2:14), could not the true Christian do so immeasurably better?

53. We shall make new Decalogues, just as Paul does in all the epistles, and as Peter does; but above all, as Christ does in the gospel.
54. And these Decalogues are clearer than the Decalogue of Moses, just as the countenance of Christ is brighter than the countenance of Moses [II Cor. 3:7 ff.].
55. For if the pagans in their corrupt natures were able to know God and be a law unto themselves, Romans 2 [:14],
56. How much more is Paul, or the true Christian, full of the Spirit, able to institute a certain Decalogue and judge most correctly about all things.[228]

Thus the freedom which the First Commandment introduces into the law is fulfilled in him, because obedience and love toward God annul the commandments and fulfil them in a higher sense.[229] The sovereignty with which the Christian, in the assurance of faith and with the sure instinct of love, rules over all the relationships of life and changes and sanctifies all other works out of the only "good work," namely, faith (as Luther demonstrated marvelously in *Treatise on Good Works* in 1520), presupposes the end, the fulfilment, of the law in Christ. Only in this way does that wonderful connection of receiving and giving, of faith and love originate, which Luther saw as the essence of righteousness. The Christian receives the inner unity and wholeness, which is that of God himself, in this "free, joyous servitude to God," which does not originate from human striving and doing, but from God's creative action.

[227] See especially Holl, "Der Neubau der Sittlichkeit," in *op. cit.*, I, 221–22.
[228] *Theses Concerning Faith and Law for the Doctoral Examination of Jerome Weller and Nicholas Medler,* 1535 (*Propositiones Disputatae Vuittembergae, pro Doctoratu Eximiorum uirorum D. Hieronymi Vueller & M. Nicolai Medler*), *WA* 39I, 47:27 ff.; *LW* 34, 112–13.
[229] See above, p. 133.

When Moses says, "The Lord your God is one God," he takes away all human confidence. When he says, "You shall love the Lord," he arouses joyous and free servitude to God. For when I love God truly, I want everything God wants; nor is there anything sweeter than hearing and doing what God wants; carnal love also does this with its beloved. Thus through oneness with God in faith we receive everything freely from God; through love we do everything freely toward God.[230]

Man cannot achieve this any other way than through faith in Christ, who has fulfilled the law and made him free. This is the reason for the paradoxical statement Luther strikingly formulated, "No one may fulfil the law unless he is freed of the law and no longer under it."[231] "It is not works that fulfil the law, but the fulfilment of the law produces works."[232] Paul shows the Galatians "that through their observance of the law the opposite had turned out to be the result for them, namely, no observance at all; in fact, it was an actual and greater transgression."[233]

Now it was certainly not easy for Luther to transform his strong fervor for the new freedom into specific assertions on which of the commandments could be annulled through love. He usually limited himself to biblical examples, for example, those that cancel the Fifth Commandment, and to summary listings.[234] To show the conflict in the Fourth Commandment was still the easiest. And it impressed Luther deeply to find the direction in the Bible itself, "Forget your people and your father's house" (Ps 45:11). He was deeply affected by this kind of monstrous command to rebel and its opposition to the holy commandment in the law of God that was expressed herewith. But if God's will and honor, the first table of the commandments, require it, then one must free oneself from the requirements of the second table.

This means to encourage rebellion. He could not put it more monstrously than "your father's house." This means the highest obedience to God, and he himself commands the end [of the commandments]. This

230 *The Deuteronomy of Moses, with Notes,* 1525, *WA* 14, 609:24 ff.; *LW* 9, 68.
231 *Sermon on the First Sunday after Christmas on Gal. 4:1 ff., Church Postil,* 1522, *WA* 10I,1, 359:21. See also *ibid.,* 365:8; *LE* 1, 251–52, 255; *Sermon on New Year's Day on Gal. 3:23 ff., Church Postil,* 1522, *WA* 10I,1, 453:17; *LE* 1, 270.
232 *Lectures on Galatians,* 1519, *WA* 2, 492:20; *LW* 27, 223–24.
233 *Ibid., WA* 2, 564:5; *LW* 27, 331.
234 See above, pp. 133–34, and below, p. 142.

is a mandate against divine commandments! You shall honor your father, and your parents, but you shall prefer God to them. When this happens and it appears that God, as well as father, are to be forsaken in this world, one must say, 'Goodbye, father, with your commandment and with your entire second table. I know nothing about you, I have forgotten you." For the first table, not the Fourth Commandment, is at stake, whether God be true or whether the Son of God is to be heard....[235]

Thus the Spirit can and is used to doing works which look as though they were opposed to all of God's commandments. But they are opposed only to the commandments of the second table, which directs us to our neighbor and to God according to the first three commandments.[236]

These are, however, exceptions, which demand a specific commission from God and heroic strength. One really must be a Peter, Paul, Jacob, David, or Elisha; then "you too may curse in the name of God, with high and great merit before God."[237]

But the abrogation of the law also means that the Christian nevertheless has the freedom to fulfil it whenever he considers it right. Thus Luther rejected the objection that one should not cite the examples of the use of the sword in the Old Testament as justification for the right of political authorities to wield the sword. "It is thus that [the Old Testament] is abrogated, so that there is the freedom to keep it or not to keep it, and it is no longer necessary to keep it on penalty of losing one's soul, as was the case at that time."[238]

Now and then Luther even carried the abrogation of the law through to the grandiose conclusion that it was even abrogated bodily through the destruction of Jerusalem and the dispersion of the Jews, and no longer had any place of its own in the world. He usually called the actual ending of the law the result of these destructions and regarded them as God's punishment for the crucifixion of Jesus.

[235] *Lecture on Psalm 45,* 1532, *WA* 40$^{II}$, 578:3 ff.; *LW* 12, 276.
[236] *Sermon on the Second Sunday after the Epiphany on Rom. 12:6 ff., Lenten Postil,* 1525, *WA* 17$^{II}$, 54:5; *LE* 2, 46.
[237] *Ibid., WA* 17$^{II}$, 54:10; *LE* 2, 46. According to the biblical examples, Acts 8:20; Gal. 5:12; I Cor. 16:22; Gen. 49:7; Psalm 108; II Sam. 3:29; II Kings 2:24. See also Holl, "Der Neubau der Sittlichkeit," in *op. cit.,* I, 227. Thus there is a "curse against curse, God's curse against the curse of the devil." *Lenten Postil,* 1525, *WA* 17$^{II}$, 53:10; *LE* 2, 45.
[238] *Temporal Authority: To What Extent It Should Be Obeyed,* 1523, *WA* 11, 255:31 ff.; *LW* 45, 97.

How can it be explained [as the Jews explain] that the law is to remain unto eternity, since it has now been destroyed for one thousand and five hundred years, with its priesthood, temple, principality, and worship? I certainly think this means the end of the law! For they cannot maintain Moses' anointment or law outside the country and Jerusalem; this they cannot deny, and this they know very well. And God would not have permitted the setting aside of these laws for such a long time if he had wanted them to be kept for ever and ever, unto eternity.[239]

But occasionally he described this material abrogation of the law as the real intention of God in the annihilation of Jerusalem.

The Mosaic law was abrogated because of the conscience of faith. If the conscience were not violated by the opinion of justice, it would be good to have something external. But since in this section we are dealing with what is said about Christ our head, it is not only human tradition which is to be abrogated here, but universal law, even divine law itself; and Christ is to be retained in the purest faith. If law does not stop troubling faith—before I tolerate that I'd rather annul the law bodily. But if it grumbles too much, and if the flesh is seduced by the law and the righteousness of works is erected, then He disperses the Jews throughout the world and devastates Jerusalem.[240]

This development conforms to the historical task of the law, namely, to maintain the people to whom God has given his Word and his promise, through its discipline, until Christ.

God, therefore, gave the law and these ceremonies of the Levites to maintain the ministry of the Word and to have a discipline whereby you are maintained through such discipline, and whereby you learn the Word of God; also, to have a specific people that has the promise of God, and is its guardian and witness until the time of Christ. You were given the exercise of discipline, but you do not please the Father through this discipline.[241]

If the law had still maintained its place of honor undisturbed after Christ, it would have been a constant danger to faith. Therefore not only the "Mosaic law," but the law as a whole is meant. This audacious thought suggests that Luther regarded the event of salvation as the only historical redemptive reality. The fate of

239 *A Letter of Martin Luther Against the Sabbatarians,* 1538, *WA* 50, 323:20. See also *ibid.,* 313:12 ff.
240 *Lecture on Psalm 45,* 1532, *WA* $40^{\text{II}}$, 576:9 ff.; *LW* 12, 275.
241 *Lecture on Isaiah 53,* 1544, 1550, *WA* $40^{\text{III}}$, 706:37.

Judaism is more than a pedagogical example of how the cross produced a turning point in the life of peoples. The fate of Judaism is the indissoluble counterpart to the cross itself, to the spiritual overcoming of the law, and is therefore the externally visible factor of this unique turning point in the history of mankind. It is not just a consequence of it or a symbol for it; rather, it is, to speak with Luther, its "effective sign," in which the external event and the meaning of salvation are just as inseparably locked together as Word and sign in the sacrament.

This historical dimension of the termination of the law is another reminder that the issue is not a peaceful division of two periods, but a life and death struggle. That is why the lawgiver Moses is not the harmless proclaimer of an outdated concept of God. Rather, he is the deadly enemy of Christ; and he will remain so until the end of time, since the natural law, preached by him with particular clarity, also remains. Thus the severest judgment of the prison warden, slave-holder, executioner, and torturer Moses is justified; his harsh tongue already demonstrates allegorically that his rule of law is an oppressive slavery.[242]

> These are signs that the rule of law should not be delight, but a prison. Moses was unable to sing well because he has a harsh tongue and a heavy hand. He is a slow and stumbling writer; he has a bad voice, which neither sounds good nor is swift (unlike the poet of Psalm 45). I, however, have a joyful and good heart, which teaches promises and the joyful doctrines of peace, certainty in conscience, and consolation. All these things are allegorical. You can set up an antithesis between Moses and the gospel; then the psalm will become quite clear.[243]

Luther liked to call the lawgiver Moses an officer of sin and death, in comparison with Paul (II Cor. 3:6–7), because only in this connection does the horrible destiny which is linked to the law disclose itself in its full dimensions. Whoever wants to become righteous before God according to the law not only is shaken in his conscience and driven to despair because he never attains his goal, but he also remains prey to death, the metaphysical punishment for sin.

[242] *Lecture on Psalm 45,* 1532, *WA* 40II, 482:10; 486:2; *LW* 12, 205–06.
[243] *Ibid., WA* 40II, 483:4; *LW* 12, 205–06. See also *Lectures on Galatians,* 1531, *WA* 40I, 91:7; *LW* 26, 37; *Table Talk, WA,* TR 2 (1531), 364:21 (No. 2207A); 6 (from various years), 141:30 (No. 6714).

> So when we are stuck in sin, death soon presses upon us, as revenge and punishment for sin. This is the reason St. Paul calls sin "the sting of death" [I Cor. 15:56], because death, through sin, has all its rights and power over us. But if there were no law, there would be no sin. Therefore it is all Moses' fault. He incites and stirs up sin through the law; thus death follows upon sin with vengeance.[244]

The terrible effect of the law is that through it death becomes death. Through the resurrection the night of death becomes the daylight of faith, whereas the law subjects us to death and, before our desperate eyes, paints a death "which seeks to devour such a sinner and swallow him up into hell."[245] For this night is brightened like the day [Ps. 139:12], since the light of beginning life is brighter than departing death. These things are assured only to those who believe in Christ, but not to the unbelievers."[246] Thus the difference between law and gospel is like that between two choirs facing each other, which Luther spoke about in a timeless formulation: the law sings its "In the midst of life we are in death" and, on the other hand, the gospel sings its comforting "In the midst of death we are in life."[247] It is significant that the lawgiver Moses composed Psalm 90, which so majestically proclaims the seriousness of death. He herewith did his "essential work," as Luther liked to say, also applying the thought of Isa. 28:21 to him, too. No one else was so skilled in the "new rhetoric" which disclosed death as the agent of divine wrath.

> In this psalm our Moses treats death in a very different way. He proceeds, to begin with, to magnify to the greatest possible degree the meaning of death and all other miseries of this life. Here he is, in keeping with his calling, a lawgiver, Moses at his most Mosaic [*Mosissimus Moses*], that is, a stern minister of death, God's wrath, and sin. He therefore performs the ministry of the law in a magnificent manner; he depicts death in the most repulsive colors and thus demonstrates that God's wrath is the cause of our death. Yes, he shows that even

[244] *Preface to the Old Testament*, 1523, *WA*, DB 8, 21:23 ff.; *LW* 35, 242.
[245] *Ibid.*, *WA*, DB 8, 23:16–17; *LW* 35, 243.
[246] *The Fourteen of Consolation, for Such as Labor and Are Heavy-laden*, 1520 (*Tessaradecas Consolatoria pro laboratoribus et oneratis*), *WA* 6, 118:35; *PE* 1, 139.
[247] *Lecture on Psalm 90*, 1534–1535 (*Enarratio psalmi XC.*), *WA* 40$^{III}$, 496:4; *LW* 13, 83. The reversal of a famous medieval hymn which Luther published in German translation in 1524. *WA* 35, 126 ff., 453, 454; *LW* 53, 274 ff.

before we die physically, we have been put to death and are overwhelmed with dreadful miseries. And here a new rhetoric is used, when he calls death "God's wrath." In his own manner and reasoning he thus adds the efficient and final cause of death and of all miseries of this life. He reminds us that God is a God of wrath. He says, "Who realizes the power of your wrath?" [Ps. 90:11]. The fact that we die is the result of God's indescribable wrath against sin.... So Moses treats death as a lawgiver who addresses himself to hardened and insensitive sinners.... Therefore Psalm 90 is an exceedingly precious psalm. In it we hear Moses perform his essential office of terrifying sinners and directing attention to divine redemption, albeit in an obscure way. He does this to humble the proud and to console those who have been humbled.[248]

See, this is what it means that sin brings death upon us and kills us. This is what it means for the law to stir up sin and set it before our eyes, driving all our presumption into despondency, trembling, and despair.[249]

Both our bold spirit and our earnest conscience, aware of this Mosaic chain of sin and death, are driven into temptation *(Anfechtung)* and misery by the stern eyes of the lawgiver Moses. In this mortal danger any weapon is permitted in self-defense. "If someone is thus being tempted or involved with others thus under stress, then he should beat Moses to death and throw many stones at him."[250] "When I debate the law with Satan, he wins. That is why I want to help in the stoning of Moses; otherwise, he will remain with despairing and broken men rather than with the faithful and trembling consciences."[251] Indeed, the ultimate must be dared here: even when the lawgiver and judge takes on the mask of Christ, and "Christ comes and speaks to you (when you rue your sin) as Moses, 'What have you done?' then beat him to death. But if he talks to you like God and your Savior, then listen with both ears."[252]

Since temptation *(Anfechtung)* constitutes the crisis of faith, this death blow to Mosaic law in any of its forms is the intensification of the gospel's demands on the believer. To discard the command-

248 *Lecture on Psalm 90,* 1534–1535, *WA* 40III, 486:23; 487:13, 23; 489:17; *LW* 13, 77–78, 79.
249 *Preface to the Old Testament,* 1523, *WA,* DB 8, 23:18 ff.; *LW* 35, 243.
250 *Table Talk,* 1532, *WA,* TR 2, 75:25 (No. 1371).
251 *Ibid.,* 583:8 (No. 2655a).
252 *Ibid.,* 583:16.

ments is the only commandment of the gospel. But now the first Table Talk quoted above continues, ". . . and throw many stones at him. But if he recovers, one should preach the law to him."[253] We would misinterpret Luther's doctrine of temptation completely if we were to conclude from this that one who is undergoing such temptation needs only a pacifying deception. What he is here told is the whole truth for faith. But what remains is the insoluble joining of law and gospel, which is like the meeting and mingling of light and darkness at dawn. Thus the old and new man merge.[254] And that is why every description, no matter how forceful, of Moses the officer of death must take the same direction as Luther's preface to the Old Testament: "Nevertheless, this office of sin and death is good and very necessary."[255] For the disciplinarian of the law is indispensable to us until the end of our lives for the radical self-realization, the knowledge of our aversion and impotence to do good, which is the condition for the fruitful hearing of the gospel.[256] Luther even advanced this thought of the whip-master's office of Moses to the point that he explained thereby the endless number of laws and rules. They were given

> so that sins might become numerous and be heaped up beyond measure. The purpose is to burden the conscience so that obdurate blindness would have to recognize itself and feel its own impotence and nothingness in the achieving of the good. Thus it would be compelled and forced by the law to seek something more than the law and its ability, namely, God's grace promised in the Christ who was to come.[257]

But in this way the law destroys itself. That is the deeper meaning of the proclamation of the law; that is why it remains eternally necessary, precisely for the sake of the gospel. Luther here again proved his masterful ability to think through a contradiction in all

[253] *Ibid.*, 75:27 (No. 1371).
[254] *Lectures on Galatians,* 1519, *WA* 2, 586:9; *LW* 27, 363. On this figure of speech, see also my essay, "Äusserer und innerer Mensch bei Luther und den Spiritualisten," *Imago Dei* ("Beiträge zur theologischen Anthropologie. Festgabe für Gustav Krüger," 1932), pp. 90–91.
[255] *Preface to the Old Testament,* 1523, *WA,* DB 8, 21:31; *LW* 35, 242.
[256] See Luther's interpretations of Gal. 3:23 ff.: *Lectures on Galatians,* 1519, 1531, *WA* 2, 527 ff.; 40I, 517 ff.; *LW* 27, 276–77; 26, 335 ff.; *Sermon on New Year's Day on Gal. 3:23 ff., Church Postil,* 1522, *WA* 10I,1, 449 ff.; *LE* 1, 267 ff.; and the important series of sermons with which Luther opened the New Year on the Day of Jesus' Circumcision, interpreting this Epistle, *WA* 36 (1532), 8 ff.; 41 (1536), 497 ff.; 46 (1538), 113 ff.; 49 (1540), 1 ff.; 49 (1545), 652 ff.
[257] *Preface to the Old Testament,* 1523, *WA,* DB 8, 25:8 ff.; *LW* 35, 244.

its possibilities to its very conclusion. He turned a thought around and then pursued it upstream to its source. His talent for systematic thinking shows its chief method of procedure here. The secret goal, the "essential work" of the law, as he described it, is that only through it does death become death, the hopeless end. That is why he was now deeply satisfied because for Christians, who can hope for eternal life through Christ, death itself makes an end of sin and of the law in life and clears man's path to eternal perfection. Here Goliath is beheaded with his own sword, and sin is destroyed through its own work, death.

> [Death] not only concludes the pain and evils of this life, but (which is more excellent) makes an end to sins and to vice.... It is one of the most beautiful spectacles to see how sin is destroyed, not by another's work, but by its own; it is stabbed with its own weapon and, like Goliath, is beheaded with its own sword [I Sam. 17:51]. For Goliath also was a figure of sin, a terrible giant to all except the young boy David, that is Christ, who single-handedly laid him low and having cut off his head with his own sword said afterward that there was no better sword than the sword of Goliath (I Samuel 21 [:9]).[258]

The "essential" work of Moses thus always secretly serves, if understood in faith, its "alien" work, leading men to Christ. "You have heard Moses perform his essential office, that is, to terrify sinners and, though in an obscure way, to indicate redemption. He does this to humble the proud and to console the humble."[259] This is the exact opposite of God or Christ, who needs the *alien* righteousness of wrath in accomplishing his *own* work, grace. Thus the "office" of Moses has a secret Christocentric meaning. It means that by driving man to the end of all his own possibilities, Moses' office proves to him the impossibility of reaching God in this way and thus abrogates itself. The question of validity or abrogation of the general divine law, as contained above all in the Decalogue, can thus be reduced to the precise formula, "The Ten Commandments also cease, not in the sense that one should not keep them or fulfil them, but in the sense that Moses' office in them ceases; it no longer strengthens sin [Rom. 5:20] through the Ten Com-

[258] This is Luther's description of one of death's goods in *The Fourteen of Consolation,* 1520, *WA* 6, 123:21; 124:31; *PE* 1, 150–51.
[259] *Lecture on Psalm 90,* 1534–1535, *WA* 40$^{III}$, 489:6; *LW* 13, 79.

mandments, and sin is no longer the sting of death" 15:56].[260]

What the end of the Mosaic office means was nowhere expressed by Luther than in a Table Talk in which he depicted a scene in the Last Judgment: if he should enter the court and Moses should wish to accuse him before God in the name of the law, "then I shall repulse him in the name of the devil and say, 'Here stands Christ,'" And then "Moses will look at me and say, 'You have understood and judged me correctly,' and he will be in my favor."[261]

"You have understood me correctly." This includes the fact that Moses himself knows the end of his office; he knows of the gospel. Luther would say that this word is spoken by Moses the Christian.

### *d. Moses the Christian*

Luther in his *On the Last Words of David* (1543) asked the same Moses from whose office of executioner mankind was freed through Christ, "whether he would agree to become a Christian."[262] This segment, indeed, the whole extensive excursus about the question of whether the Old Testament harmonizes with the New Testament,[263] is the indissoluble counterpart to the above-mentioned instruction, *How Christians Should Regard Moses,* which had differentiated two sides of Moses. One sees Moses and the Old Testament with Luther's eyes only if one views both together. On the one hand there is the code of the Jews, with the folk law and the officer of death through the natural law of conscience; on the other there is a "main fountainhead, source, father, and master of all prophets" and "a good Christian."[264]

> For it is certain that our Moses is the fountainhead and father of all the prophets and sacred books, that is, of heavenly wisdom and eloquence, just as the wise men of this world say that Homer is the father

260 *Preface to the Old Testament,* 1523, *WA,* DB 8, 25:22 ff.; *LW* 35, 244.
261 *Table Talk,* 1532, *WA,* TR 2, 6:35 ff. (No. 1242); *LW* 54, 128 (No. 1242).
262 *WA* 54, 55:2.
263 *Ibid.,* 44:30; 47:14; 55:13; 70:27. The excursus is more extensive than the treatment of the last words of David as such, to which Luther returned only at the end. "I want to tie together again this little wreath at its end, for I have digressed enough." *Ibid.,* 93:26.
264 *Ibid.,* 55:1; 77:24.

of all poets, the fountainhead and even ocean of all learning and wisdom and eloquence. But since in this age everything begins to be restored, as if that day of restoration of all things [Acts 3:21] were near, I got the idea to try to find out whether Moses could be restored and I might return the brooklets to the fountainhead.[265]

Various lines of thought run together into a unified theme "Moses the Christian." The decisive factor and the whole content of the segment just mentioned is the sum total of the Christ prophecies which are found in the Books of Moses. To uncover them, Luther sent the "two loyal, conscientious legates" John and Paul after the buried Moses, "who are to search for him, find him, awaken him, and bring him here."[266] Since their pronouncements about the Logos, Christ as creator of the world, his humanity-divinity, the Trinity, etc., agree so well with him, it is proven that Moses is also a preacher of the gospel.[267]

And the apostles only do what they have learned from their Lord Christ, who "above all the other apostles was the best preacher."[268] When Christ interprets the elevating of the snake in the desert, in John 3:14, as prefiguration for the ascension of the Son of Man, "he unlocks Moses like a treasure chest and shows them the nugget concealed there. He explains what Moses intends with all of his illustrations and stories, namely, he points solely to Christ." Luther was convinced that Christ taught his disciples, especially in the forty days between his resurrection and ascension, "this proper method of interpreting Moses and all the prophets."[269]

One has to remember this rich prophecy of Christ in Moses and the whole Old Testament, which we have already discussed, to understand Luther's hymn of triumph opposed to the Jewish interpreters.

If now the ravens [rabbis] and Jews interpret all this differently and scorn our reason, it is right. God's enemy should not see God's Word. But what they spit out here about this text is not worthy of being read

[265] *The Deuteronomy of Moses, with Notes,* 1525, *WA* 14, 499:16 ff.; *LW* 9, 6. With these words in the dedicatory letter to George of Polenz, Luther placed his interpretation of Deuteronomy within the humanist revival of classical antiquity.
[266] *On the Last Words of David,* 1543, *WA* 54, 55:9.
[267] See above, pp. 118–19.
[268] *Sermons on John 3 and 4,* 1538–1540 (*Auslegung des 3. und 4. Capitels Johannis in Predigten*), *WA* 47, 60:18; *LW* 22, 332.
[269] *Ibid., WA* 47, 66:18 ff.; *LW* 22, 339, 340.

by a sow or a donkey, even if these could read. Moses' face has horns and shines so brightly that they cannot look at it. But we have Moses, whose unconstrained word, whose natural way of speaking, is in such hearty and good accord with the New Testament. And even if he must rule the obstinate evil people of his time in the Old Testament, he nevertheless also strongly prophesies Jesus Christ our Lord.... I believe and know for certain that I and all Christians have Moses on our side and that he is a true Christian, indeed, a teacher of Christians.

Just as a pious monk who, though still walking around in the cowl, nevertheless puts his trust in God, not because of the cowl but because of the grace of Christ, "so does Moses allow the other masses to boast of the law and circumcision and always walks around with this kind of cap—but his heart, faith, and confession is Jesus Christ, the Son of God."[270] This is the same Moses who, according to Luther's advice, should be beaten to death in the hour of temptation (*Anfechtung*)!

Luther found gospel in the Old Testament and called Moses a Christian. Here he had in mind the clear messianic prophecies, as well as the allusions which can be drawn from the context, and finally the allegorical "figures" which become recognizable on the basis of these presuppositions. This is also the meaning of the frequently quoted and much misused words in the *Preface to the Epistles of St. James and St. Jude* (1546, 1522): "All the genuine books agree in this, that they all preach and inculcate Christ. This is also the true test by which to judge all the books, when one sees whether or not they inculcate Christ."[271] It is necessary to remember that these words, which are often used as an excuse for personal arbitrariness and a pruning according to individual taste and individual criterion by which one decides what is considered "Christian," mean, first of all, nothing else than that all truly evangelical books speak thematically and emphatically about Christ, his person and his work. Luther indeed charged the Epistle of St. James with not once thinking of the suffering, the resurrection, or the Spirit of Christ. "He names Christ several times, but teaches nothing

270 *On the Last Words of David,* 1543, *WA* 54, 84:31 ff.; 85:11 ff.
271 *Preface to the Epistles of St. James and St. Jude,* 1546, 1522 (*Vorrede auf die Epistel S. Jacobi und Jude*), *WA,* DB 7, 385:25; *LW* 35, 396. Luther also spoke in other places about the fact that "the prophets preached and inculcated faith in Christ just as well as we [did] in the New Testament." *The Prophet Habakkuk,* 1526, *WA* 19, 394:26.

about him; instead, he speaks of general faith in God."[272] It is absurd that precisely these words, which would require exceedingly accurate and concrete pronouncements about Christ if the book is to be called Christian, are often used as a means of differentiation to abstract very general and indefinite Christian truths from the texts and to construct an effortless unity within the whole Scripture out of them. Luther here thought, as usual, quite realistically and historically. He meant the promise or witness of the historical Christ, of his essential being and his work of salvation. One wishes that the jaded talk of "inculcating Christ" would disappear again, and that we would make an effort to see again Luther's separation of law and the promise of Christ in its original clarity and fulness of content.

But as emphatically as one expresses that these prophecies make Moses a Christian for Luther, one must, at the same time, now see how the entire proclamation of Moses and the Old Testament is transformed on the basis of this promise. This power of the promise radiates in three directions into the Old Testament proclamation.

1. From it alone does the *law receive its deeper meaning.* If the ultimate goal of the law's sermon is the abrogation of the law, if an "alien" sense which everyone must serve elevates itself above its "essential" sense, then it is only because there is a way to God outside the law, by faith in the promise. Thus the law secretly aims at Christ. That is why both law and gospel are inseparably interwoven. And their relationship, which Luther could present as a war of life and death, must just as often be described as an inseparable dual work of God.

The two preaching offices, law and gospel, must be together, although their business is not the same. For Moses preaches about sins and thereby kills; Christ preaches about grace and thereby creates life. Yet grace can do nothing if sin has not first been revealed and recognized through law. The Lord himself says, Matthew 11 [:5; 10:6], that he preaches the gospel to the poor and to the lost sheep of Israel, that is, those who feel lost because of the law.[273]

[272] *Preface to the Epistles of St. James and St. Jude,* 1546, 1522, *WA,* DB 7, 385:20; *LW* 35, 396.

[273] *On the Last Words of David,* 1543, *WA* 54, 82:18. Luther did not present this interpretation of the "lost sheep" (Matt. 10:6; 15:24)—which represents a very significant example of the strict direction of his exegesis toward law and gospel—elsewhere in his numerous sermons about the Canaanite woman

Both sides of the issue are indivisibly meshed and constitute one paradoxical unity.

But Luther was not satisfied only to think through the inner logic of the law, which necessarily leads man to failure and results only in arrogance or despair.[274] Instead, he thought he also found this "alien" sense, the servitude of the law under the promise, directly expressed in the words of the lawgiver Moses. The most audacious example of this is his interpretation of Deut. 30:11 ff., that is, the passage which according to the literal translation well known to Luther[275] ("This commandment, which I give you today, does not exceed your strength") seems to indicate the possibility of fulfilling the commandment; that is, it seems to annihilate Luther's understanding of the law. It is also important because the difference between his exegesis and Paul's, who also used this passage Christologically (Rom. 10:6 ff.), becomes visible. Paul exegetes typologically; he lifts the passage with all its roots out of its native soil and without hesitation puts that which is expressed about the commandment into the mouth of the righteousness of faith.[276] Luther in no way considered this Pauline exegesis an interpretation of the text itself, but rather a free variation on a theme taken from it.

> Here we say first: Paul intentionally did not want to quote Moses word for word, at least in the first part; but with overflowing spirit he took occasion from Moses to compose a new and fitting text against works-righteousness.[277] Moses wrote these words in Deuteronomy 30 [:12], and he did not have the meaning in mind they have here; but the apostle's abundant spiritual insight enables him to bring out their inner significance. It is as if he wanted to give us impressive proof that the whole Scripture, if one interprets it inwardly, deals everywhere with

---

(Matt. 15:21 ff.; there is no sermon extant on Matt. 10:6.) There, in the dramatic context, he was much too strongly impressed by the harsh rejection of Jesus. Indeed, the woman became to him almost an example of misery and lostness, something Moses, too, produced through the law. *Sermon on the Second Sunday in Lent on Matt. 15:21 ff., Lenten Postil,* 1525, *WA* $17^{\mathrm{II}}$, 201:11; *LE* 11, 149.

274 *Sermon on the Third Sunday in Advent on Matt. 11:2 ff., Advent Postil,* 1522, *WA* $10^{\mathrm{I}},^{2}$, 155:23 ff.; 156:11 ff.; *LE* 10, 96, 97.

275 See below, p. 154, n. 279.

276 *The Deuteronomy of Moses, with Notes,* 1525, *WA* 14, 729 ff.; *LW* 9, 277 ff. On Rom. 10:6, see Hans Lietzmann, *An die Römer* ("Handbuch zum Neuen Testament," 8 [3rd ed.; Tübingen, 1928]), p. 96.

277 *The Deuteronomy of Moses, with Notes,* 1525, *WA* 14, 730:17, *LW* 9, 278.

Christ, even though, in so far as it is a sign and a shadow, it may outwardly sound different.[278]

Luther exegeted literally, albeit also with the goal of the prophetic interpretation of the Old Testament. That is why he was not interested here in climbing up to heaven and diving down into the depths, but in the interweaving of commandment and promise which he found in the passage. Moreover, he was obliged to wrest the text from the scholastics, who saw in Deut. 30:11 ("The commandment is not beyond you") a proof for the possibility of fulfilling the law. It is a good thing that they did not know Hebrew, for in that language it is even more plainly expressed, at first glance, than in the Vulgate.[279] "For the Hebrew says it thus, 'This commandment which I command you this day is not miraculous or difficult for you.' For *niphlaoth* meant 'miraculous' and 'difficult,' that which goes beyond our powers and which we are unable to attain."[280] And yet, according to Luther, it was precisely this text that was a plain prophecy of the gospel. For why does it say, "The Word is very close to you, in your mouth and in your heart"? Should not the word order be reversed? For here it is obviously clearly presupposed that, first of all, a sermon (a word "in the mouth") must come first to endear the law to man (for it says, "to have in the heart"). When this sermon, the gospel, has come, the commandment will no longer be either difficult for us or far from us. We can see in this artificial, imaginative way how Luther clung to the safe grammatical proof and how he was strengthened in his basic understanding of the law by the fact that he was able to coax the secret from even such an unruly passage as this one by means of keen interpretation. It is the secret of the gospel hidden everywhere in the Old Testament—the secret Christian in Moses.

2. Out of this deep inner direction of the law to Christ, Luther claimed the right to interpret those passages of the Old Testament in which reference is made to law in a prophetic context in terms of the "new law," the gospel. The words of Isaiah (2:3), "For out of you shall go forth the law, and the Word of the Lord from Jerusalem," certainly demonstrated plainly that he was concerned

[278] *Lectures on Romans,* 1515–1516, *WA* 56, 414:13; *LCC* 15, 288.
[279] *The Deuteronomy of Moses, with Notes,* 1525, *WA* 14, 729:7; *LW* 9, 277.
[280] *Ibid., WA* 14, 729:1 ff.; *LW* 9, 277.

with a new, a universal Word, in contrast to the revelation on Sinai; it is a prophecy about the dissemination of the gospel through the apostles.

See, here is truly the promise of a new Word, of a new law. This is indeed different from the one given at Sinai in the cloud, different from the place designated here as Sinai. The "law" means proclamation. The prophecy remains, out of Jerusalem shall go forth the proclamation, disseminated among all nations; this has happened through the apostles; it will be the strength of our faith against the Jews.[281]

Even "to magnify the law" from Isa. 42:21 ("to magnify the law and make it glorious"), which Luther could easily have placed next to "to magnify sin" and which he could have applied to the noble law of conscience which as disciplinarian leads to Christ, he still without hesitation decided to apply to the gospel. The context and the New Testament use of language led him to do so.

For faith is the new law whereby we die to the old law. I leave it to the judgment of the hearers whether it [Isa. 42:21] speaks of the law of Moses or of faith. I agree with the latter, namely, that faith is the new law whereby the righteousness of God is established. Thus it seems that something is said here about the new law which abrogates the old; this means that the Lord makes a new and admirable law, because it has pleased the Lord, in his justice, to magnify and to extol such law. He derogates the old [law], about which there is nothing admirable or grand. Thus the Christian life is a wonderful life, because it joins together the sanctity of the entire law.[282]

And this is how it is with a large number of other passages about the law, for example, Isa. 8:16, "Seal the law among my disciples," that is, until my disciples;[283] and naturally with prophetic promises like Isa. 42:4, "The islands wait for his law," or Isa. 51:4, "A law shall go forth from me."[284]

Here he prescribes the manner and form for the enlargement of the church, certainly through the law and the judgment of God; but it cannot be understood through the law of Moses which the Jews have. And yet God himself brought an end to the law; that means the sending forth of the gospel whereby the old law is abrogated.[285]

281 *Lectures on Isaiah,* 1527–1530, *WA* 31$^{II}$, 22:29.
282 *Ibid.,* 325:1 ff.; 324:25 ff.
283 *Ibid.,* 64:36.
284 *Ibid.,* 313:20.
285 *Ibid.,* 415:25 (Isa. 51:4). See also the interpretation of Mal. 2:7 in *Lectures on the Minor Prophets. The Prophet Malachi,* 1526, *WA* 13, 686: 15 ff.

Luther also liked to apply descriptions of the law's perfection to "the new law"; thus the entire second half of Psalm 19 (:7 ff.) is a great hymn of praise of the gospel and, word for word, an attack on the law of Moses.[286] But he still did not put all the Old Testament pronouncements about the law into one basket. When the sense indicated it, he still allowed the old understanding of the law to stand, even in those places where it was not obvious by clear references to the law of Moses or the people of Israel, especially if a particular view toward the gospel could be combined with just this understanding. This is what he did in Psalm 1, where he understood the law literally from the very beginning (although it would have been possible, without any great effort, to transfer the meaning), because he could thus show that the "passion for law" could only be a fruit of the gospel.[287] In addition, but more rarely, law was used in a general sense as an expression for "word" or "will of God" per se.[288] But most often the law was either the office of death in the service of grace, or prophetic expression for the new order of God in the gospel.

Luther was not aware that he overstepped the concepts of the New Testament with his transformation of many pronouncements about the law into gospel, even though the "new law" is indeed the formulation with which the church, since the Apostolic Fathers,[289] has made Christianity a new, higher law on the side of Judaism, thus destroying the Pauline proclamation of justification. The bridge to this distortion was built, unwillingly, by the formulations of Paul when he spoke about "the law of faith" (Rom. 3:27),

[286] Psalm 19, *Lectures on the First Twenty-five Psalms,* 1530, *WA* 31^I^, 341:35 ff.; *LW* 12, 142 ff.

[287] *Lectures on the Psalter,* 1513–1516, *WA* 3, 17:1 ff.; Vogelsang, *Der junge Luther,* pp. 208 ff.; Böhmer, *op. cit.,* pp. 34 ff.; *Works on the Psalms,* 1519–1521, *WA* 5, 32 ff.; *LW* 14, 293 ff.; Psalm 1, *Lectures on the First Twenty-five Psalms,* 1530, *WA* 31^I^, 264:18 ff.

[288] For example, in the interpretation of Psalm 119. *Psalm 119,* 1529 (*Der Hundert und neuntzehendt Psalm*), *WA* 31^I^, 1 ff. Luther did not always adhere to the definition given in the beginning. *Ibid.,* 2:26.

[289] *The Epistle of Barnabas,* II, 6, K. Lake (ed. and trans.), *The Apostolic Fathers* ("The Loeb Classical Library" [2 vols.; London, 1913], I, 345; *Ignatius to the Magnesians,* II, Lake, *op. cit.,* I, 199; *The Shepherd of Hermas,* Parable 5, VI:3; Parable 8, III:2, Lake, *op. cit.,* II, 167, 197. See also Neil Buchanan (trans.), *History of Dogma by Adolf v. Harnack* (7 vols.; New York: Dover, 1961), I, 172 ff.; Reinhold Seeberg, *Lehrbuch der Dogmengeschichte* (4th ed.; 4 vols.; Basel, 1953–1954), I, 181 ff.; Hans Windisch, *Der Barnabasbrief* ("Handbuch zum Neuen Testament," 19 [rev. ed.; Tübingen, 1923]), p. 311.

"the law of the Spirit of life in Christ" (Rom. 8:2), "the law of Christ" (Gal. 6:2). With the help of formulations like these the Old Testament concept of law found expression in ecclesiastical proclamation. Now Luther, in a counterattack, went across this same bridge back into the Old Testament and, wherever it seemed possible to him within the framework of the promise, gained ground for the "new law," the gospel. Luther naturally broadened the concept of law; he gave it the same meaning it had in the Pauline passages mentioned above: relationship to God. For the essence of this "law" is that it is indeed no law, but rather a life in freedom. "In the new law everything is free and nothing is necessary for those who believe in Christ."[290] Looked at formally, albeit with quite different content, Luther again brought the concept closer to the meaning of the order founded by God—be it of the life of men among themselves, or of their association with himself—the *nomos,* in the religious terminology of classical antiquity, or corresponding terms in other cultures such as the Persian *daena* and the Germanic *lag,* which mean both law and religion. But one should not overlook the fact that Luther could conceive of the "new law" as commandment also, in the sense of the Sermon on the Mount or of the commandment of neighborly love.

> I am saying this to prevent anyone from thinking that the apostle is teaching that in this way the old law is fulfilled through the new law, on the ground that the latter represents a spiritual understanding and consists of spiritual words; for grace alone is the fulfilment of the law, and words do not fulfil words, but reality fulfils words, and mighty deeds confirm speech. Besides, is not this thoroughly spiritual commandment to love one's neighbor written in Leviticus 19 [:18]? The whole law, therefore, is summed up in this one sentence, but it is fulfilled by grace.[291]

The necessary counterpart to the new law is the *new righteousness*; it cannot be disengaged from the understanding of law. For we know from Luther's own famous words with which he described,

[290] *Lectures on Romans,* 1515–1516, *WA* 56, 493:15; *LCC* 15, 380.
[291] *Lectures on Galatians,* 1519, *WA* 2, 575:37 ff.; *LW* 27, 348–49. This is the way in which Luther defended himself against a misunderstanding which could arise through the Vulgate translation of Gal. 5:14: "For the whole law is fulfilled in this one word, 'You shall love your neighbor as yourself' " (*Omnis enim lex uno sermone hoc impletur: Diliges proximum tuum sicut teipsum*).

in retrospect, the years of his great breakthrough, what indescribable suffering and effort it had cost him to find a meaning in the concept of "righteousness of God" which did not contradict the message of grace but rather included it.[292] Luther did not imagine the result of this wrestling to be a concern to overcome the Old Testament understanding of *iustitia dei* as legal justice—an understanding he had hitherto shared with the Catholic interpreters—through a genuinely New Testament evangelical one. How easily such a differentiation could have been made! For it dawned on Luther in this context (Rom. 1:17; 3:21) that the righteousness of God in Rom. 1:17 was only an expression for the justice given by God, namely, grace, according to the Table Talk, which is so important to the interpretation of this exegetical insight.

> The righteous live by faith; the righteousness of God is revealed without the law [Hab. 2:4; Rom. 1:17]. Thereupon I reflected: if we have to live out of faith, and if the righteousness of God must be for the salvation of all who believe [Rom. 3:21–22].... Thereupon my soul was excited: because it is the righteousness of God that justifies and saves us. And so these words became more joyful for me.[293]

It was decisively due to his conviction of the unity of Scripture, conditioned by his prophetic method of interpretation, that Luther did not, with this knowledge, critically refute the Old Testament use of the term; instead, he Christianized it wherever possible. But aside from this, he also stood in the Western tradition, especially deriving from Augustine, which applied the *iustitia* of the Vulgate to the relationship of the individual to God wherever it was not expressly applied differently. Actually, *ṣedhaqah* of Ps. 31:2 and 71:2, translated literally, need not have caused Luther the agony that the "in thy righteousness deliver me" caused him, which he read in the Vulgate psalm and sang in the breviary. For in the Hebrew psalm the oppressed calls for the protection of divine justice against his enemies. This passage that so excited Luther is a

[292] *Preface to the Complete Edition of Luther's Latin Writings,* 1545 (*M. Luther, Tomus Primum omnisum operum*), *WA* 54, 185:12 ff.; *LW* 34, 336 ff.
[293] *Table Talk,* 1532, *WA,* TR 2, 177:4 (No. 1681). See also Otto Scheel (ed.), *Dokumente zu Luthers Entwicklung bis 1519* ("Sammlung ausgewählter kirchen- und dogmengeschichtlicher Quellenschriften," II, 9 [2nd ed.; Tübingen, 1929]), p. 94; *Table Talk,* 1542–1543, *WA,* TR 5, 210:9 (No. 5518); *LW* 54, 442–43 (No. 5518); *WA,* TR 5, 235:3 (No. 5553); Scheel (ed.), *Dokumente,* pp. 172 ff.

classic example of what thinking in terms formed by the Vulgate and the exegetical tradition meant to him. It was therefore also important to him to find, besides the New Testament passages which had given him his understanding of *institia dei, ṣedhaqah* even translated as "mercy" *(misericordia)* in the Vulgate (Ps. 24:5).[294] Thus the way to his interpretation was once again pointed out to him in a particular manner.

Seen grammatically the issue was even quite the opposite for Luther than it would appear to us today: he believed he did not introduce New Testament concepts into the Old Testament; instead, he interpreted *iustitia dei* as a Hebraism often occurring in Paul, as a double-meaning Hebrew genitive, which could designate both righteousness as a divine attribute and righteousness granted to us by God.

> Thus the righteousness of God, as well as the work of God and the power of God, can be explained in both ways: according to Latin and Greek grammar, the righteousness of God is understood as the righteousness by which God himself is righteous. But this explanation is obscure and brings darkness into the whole text of Scripture. But if it is understood passively, then it is our salvation and consolation; for it means the righteousness of God by which I am justified by God's mercy.... I say this not only because of the present passage [Ps. 31:1], but so that this ambiguity of expression may be observed in many other passages. For formerly it caused me much trouble when I came to such expressions as "the righteousness of God," "the work of God," "your work," "your righteousness," which, if understood actively, are death; but if understood passively, are life and salvation.[295]

[294] On Ps. 5:8, *Works on the Psalms,* 1519, *WA* 5, 144:13. Here is a collection of passages upon which Luther also drew in his later reviews of the struggle for the *iustitia dei.* The Septuagint already had translated *ṣedhaqah* several times as *eleomosyne* ("mercy"). See Edward Robinson *et al.* (eds.), *William Gesenius, a Hebrew and English Lexicon of the Old Testament* (Boston and New York: Houghton and Mifflin, 1906). Luther on occasion even used "grace" as a translation of *ṣedhaqah* ("righteousness"). See below, p. 233.

[295] *Lectures on Genesis,* 1544, *WA* 44, 485:30; 486:22; *LW* 7, 251, 252. This is the passage discussed between Friedrich Loofs, "Der articulus stantis et cadentis ecclesiae," *Theologische Studien und Kritiken,* XC (1917), 335 ff., and Emanuel Hirsch, "Initium theologiae Lutheri," in *Festgabe für Julius Kaftan,* pp. 155 ff. Here Luther had come to speak about the double meaning of the Hebrew genitive (passive or active)—on the basis of a difficulty in the Hebrew text irrelevant to our context—and showed its application to the examples so important to him. Earlier interpreters interpreted such passages as Ps. 31:2, 71:2, and 25:10 incorrectly, "because they did not grasp the construction of the genitive correctly." *Lectures on Genesis,* 1544, *WA* 44, 486:34; *LW* 7, 253. See also *Table Talk,* 1542–1543, *WA,* TR 5, 210:7 ff. (No. 5518); *LW* 54, 442–43 (No. 5518).

But this was nevertheless only a later confirmation, and a more accurate insight; he acquired the insight itself by observing the New Testament textual logic rather than by this grammatical observation.[296]

He interpreted Ps. 5:8 and 22:30–31 several times according to this understanding of *instítia dei,* although in both cases righteousness once again means protection against enemies.[297]

And this manner of speaking about the righteousness of God [Ps. 5:8] caused many difficulties to many people, since it is quite different from the usual human manner of speech. But it should not be completely rejected when the righteousness of God is, even in the manner of speech mentioned, that righteousness by which God is just. Therefore God and we ourselves are righteous by the same righteousness—just as God creates by the same Word; and we are what he himself is, so that we are in him and his being is our being.[298]

He occasionally understood these enemies to be false teachers who wished to seduce the psalmist away from his realization of grace.[299] Indeed, even where the judgmental character of a passage in the Psalms could not be overlooked, Luther differentiated between "judgment" *(iudicium)* and "righteousness" *(iustitia):* "for judgment [*iudicium*] represents the death of sin; righteousness [*iustitia*], eternal life in Christ. . . . Although this psalm does not speak particularly about the Last Judgment, it is still frightening in its judgment."[300]

Luther's interpretations of the prophets showed the same kind of discrimination and the same understanding of *ṣedhaqah* as a whole. "The judgment [*iudicium*] is part of the law of damnation; righteousness [*iustitia*] is part of the law of absolution. The godless are condemned in the kingdom of Christ; the faithful are justified,

[296] See my essay, "Die iustitia Dei in der Scholastik und bei Luther," *Archiv für Reformationsgeschichte,* XXXIX (1942), especially pp. 26 ff.
[297] On Ps. 5:8, *Works on the Psalms,* 1519, *WA* 5, 144:1 ff.
[298] *Ibid.,* 144:17 ff. Luther, in this connection, also hinted at the possibility of the possessive understanding of the *iustitia dei* (that is, "whereby God is just" [*qua deus iustus est*])—without intending to elaborate it—so that God and we (according to the analogy of the creative Word) are linked together in the same *iustitia.* See also this new understanding of *iustitia dei* in the interpretations of 1530, *Lectures on the First Twenty-five Psalms,* 1530, *WA* 31I, 278:32 ff.; 497:4 ff.; see also Ps. 22:31, *Works on the Psalms,* 1521, *WA* 5, 671:18 ff.; and in *Lectures on the First Twenty-five Psalms,* 1530, *WA* 31I, 367:1; *LE* 1, 232–33.
[299] Study of Ps. 5:8 in *Smaller Studies on the Psalms,* 1531, *WA* 31I, 497:9.
[300] On Ps. 9:5, *Works on the Psalms,* 1519, *WA* 5, 292:29; 294:11.

saved, and liberated from sin and death."[301] In Isa. 10:22 Luther illustrated the goodness of God exhibited in punishment, although he had to reject the relationship of "overflowing righteousness" to the proclamation of grace by the apostles. "It is the description of God's goodness, which is exercised in the punishment of men and directed against the rule of the demonic and the world and which does not cease since not everyone has attained perfection. God, however, will save the remnant."[302]

He certainly found a number of passages in the prophets, especially in Isaiah as well as in the Psalms, in which the righteousness of God was a definite expression of a promise of salvation. For example, "He creates fine government through his Word; he cleanses us through his Word before he defends us. We become pious again" [Isa. 33:5].[303] "Righteousness is grace itself, a gift without merits. The Lord has pleasure in such righteousness" [Isa. 42:21].[304] "Word-righteousness [*verbum iustitia*], that is, *euangelion* in Greek, *ṣedhaqah* in Hebrew, is Word-righteousness-faith, grace, and the manner in which justification should be taught" [Isa. 45:23].[305] Even where this promise clearly means the return of the captive people of Israel, it was, for Luther, insoluble from the forgiveness God grants his people precisely in this way; and righteousness was an expression of divine grace to him.

Righteousness is the grace of remission of sins, whereby we are justified. As is said, "I will soon bring back, through righteousness, my people who are oppressed and penitent. For Cyrus will liberate them from captivity through my command," because in every calamity righteousness is absent among the oppressed, as far as time and emotion are concerned, but not in promise. Thus when someone is tempted, righteousness is missing; but when he comes to the promise, righteousness is truly present.[306]

He carried his new understanding of *iustitia dei* to its logical conclusion; there is no passage in the Old Testament where he left to the formula its usual meaning of legal justice. And he undoubt-

301 On Isa. 9:7, *Lectures on Isaiah,* 1527–1530, *WA* 31II, 72:5.
302 *Ibid.,* 80:9 ff.
303 *Ibid.,* 208:29. On Isa. 54:17, see also *ibid.,* 453:4 ff.
304 *Ibid.,* 324:21.
305 *Ibid.,* 368:6.
306 On Isa. 46:13, see *ibid.,* 375:25 ff.

edly had the right to tell his students, as he once did in a lecture, "I think you really should know what *iustitia dei* is!"[307]

With the application of "the new law" *(nova lex)* and "righteousness of God" *(iustitia dei)* to gospel and grace, he of necessity introduced extensive linguistic alterations of Old Testament terms and concepts to fit the spirit of the new covenant; this had to follow comprehensively but almost unnoticeably. It was inevitable that many other Christian meanings of Old Testament words and thoughts would result from the application of the prophetic method to these two new concepts proceeding from the law. However, it must suffice here to point out this result; it will occupy us only when we have come one step closer to Luther's understanding of the unity of Scripture.[308]

3. But Luther was not just concerned with new concepts; he was concerned with reality. Even *nova lex* and *iustitia dei* were not just new images to him; they were the expression of a new reality. That is what his classic sentence meant, "Words do not fulfil words, but reality fulfils words."[309] But even when understood in this way, these concepts would have remained empty to him, if the Old Testament itself had not corroborated this viewpoint. That is why it was so essential to him that he find not only an understanding of faith in Moses and the entire Old Testament, whereby the office of the law is discredited, but also *living examples of faith.* It was, as we discovered,[310] Luther's decisive argument against the allegorists that they did not understand the "examples of faith and the divine promise in the old stories." According to Luther's conviction of the true historicity of the Word, neither can be separated from the other. Wherever God gives his promise he also arouses faith. "And such faith is a great and powerful example to strengthen our faith."[311] That is why Luther did not content himself with the natural laws and promises, clearly formulated by him, when in his basic *How Christians Should Regard Moses* (1525) he listed the points by which one "should keep Moses and not sweep him under the rug"; he added explicitly "the beautiful examples of faith, love,

307 *Ibid.,* 324:23.
308 See below, pp. 219–46.
309 See above, p. 157, n. 291.
310 See above, pp. 89–91.
311 *The Prophet Zechariah,* 1527, *WA* 23, 608:32 ff.

and cross in the fathers Adam, Abel, Noah, Abraham, Isaac, Jacob, Moses, and all the rest. We should learn to trust and love God from them." But he also added, as counterparts, the examples of godlessness.[312] The homogeneity of the human situation before God becomes clear through examples like these; in faith and unbelief men are equally together. That is why in these examples Luther showed, in exact parallel, the same distinction he did in the question of the validity of the divine commandments. Just as I have to ask regarding the commandment whether it is said to *me,* so do I also have to ask the same question regarding the images of faith in Scripture. That applies to the New as well as to the Old Testament; for example, in the case of the ten lepers, "it does not concern me that he tells them to go to the priest and make their sacrifice [Luke 17:14]; but the example of their faith does concern me, that I should believe Christ, as they did."[313] We have already discussed exhaustively[314] how many examples of faith Luther uncovered, and how he found the essential aspect of the inner world of the Old Testament in the contrasts of faith and unbelief, temptation *(Anfechtung)* and certainty; further examples are therefore unnecessary. We would only like to recall, since we are dealing in this section with Moses the Christian, that he too, as a historical figure, belongs among the examples of faith. Moreover, he was to Luther a particularly valuable example of the wonderful combination of human frailty and divine power within the believer. How he fought against his call, although God girded him with miraculous power and the strongest promises![315] He lived from one despondency to another,[316] and lived as an example of faith, especially through the dangerous exodus out of Egypt. He bravely spoke the words he was commissioned to speak to the outside world and yet feared and trembled in his heart, so that God, who listens closely, addressed himself to his unexpressed cries. (Luther noticed the abrupt contrast between Exod. 14:13 and 14:15).[317]

312 *How Christians Should Regard Moses,* 1525, *WA* 16, 391:7 ff.; 376:6; *LW* 35, 173, 166.
313 *Ibid., WA* 16, 392:21; *LW* 35, 174.
314 See above, pp. 18–35.
315 *Sermons on Exodus,* 1524–1527, *WA* 16, 59:2, 16 (Exod. 4:13).
316 *Ibid.,* 94:11 (Exod. 5:22–23); 102:35 (Exod. 6:28 ff.).
317 *Ibid.,* 182:1 ff.; 184:4.

And there certainly was terror in his heart. And God said to him, "Why do you cry?" He did not cry, but his heart was full of despair and God heard it. Here you see the nature of faith.[318]

When people grumbled against him, and he knew no escape, he trembled in all his limbs, almost despairing. And yet he heard God say to him, "Why do you cry?" Oh, how he wanted to cry! Yet he could not lift his voice! Still, he reached the mighty ears of God.[319]

If Moses had not dared to go into the fog and darkness in which God had made his dwelling place and tent (I Kings 8:12; Ps. 18:11), if he had wanted to be sure of the result of his undertaking, the Israelites would probably still be sitting in Egypt today.[320] Moses repeatedly dared with a faith that one would be forced to call "tempting God" in others.[321] The most glorious expression of this faith can be found in the songs of Moses: the defiant, joyful victory song, Exodus 15;[322] the bitter song of wrath, Deuteronomy 32, in which Moses exercised his "essential office" against his people;[323] and above all, Psalm 90, in which all the parts of Moses' proclamation combine—the sermon of the Creator, which makes the beginning of the psalm a "copy of Genesis"; fleeting life and hope of eternal life; law (vss. 1–12) and the promise of Christ (vss. 13–17).[324] This psalm, which seemed very "Mosaic" to Luther, was an essential part of Luther's picture of Moses. "Moses is the author of this prayer; the subject matter, the theology, the language combine in the person of Moses."[325] The testimonies of faith gathered together in his great work are harmonized to the one theme of the certainty of the coming salvation. These speak a mightier language than all of Moses' personal testimonies of faith. This strong hymn with its promises of Christ and examples of faith triumphs over the antiphonal voices of the message of the law. It is this which makes Moses a Christian.

318 *Ibid.*, 183:3 ff.; 184:4.
319 *Table Talk*, 1532, *WA*, TR 2, 587:24 (No. 2658a). See also *Lectures on Genesis*, 1542, *WA* 43, 519:11 ff.
320 Letter to Melanchthon, June 29, 1530, *WA*, BR 5, 406:62 ff.
321 For example, in the Manna miracle (Exod. 16:15), *Sermons on Exodus*, 1524–1527, *WA* 16, 300:1 ff.
322 *Ibid.*, 190–91.
323 *The Deuteronomy of Moses, with Notes*, 1525, *WA* 14, 732:5 ff.; *LW* 9, 290 ff.
324 *Lecture on Psalm 90*, 1534–1535, *WA* 40III, 508:7; 484:5 ff.; 486:12 ff.; 489:6; 576:1 ff.; *LW* 13, 77, 79, 130.
325 *Ibid.*, *WA* 40III, 490:2; *LW* 13, 77.

## *e. The First Commandment*

No matter how much Luther's interpretation found a place for the gospel within the law of the old covenant, it still does not change the basic distinction between the old and the new covenant. Moses, the father of Jewish customs and man of the law, and Moses, the Christian and prophet of Christ, are deadly enemies in one and the same figure. Nor is this conflict negated in that the executioner's office of the law is forced to pay homage to the miraculous goodness of God, which brings life through death. But the unified work of the judging, creating, and saving God does become visible therein, encompassing his *own* and his *alien* work. The whole Bible, in both testaments or covenants, contains the totality of God in both its aspects.

Luther found this unity of God's working in a passage that meant more to him than any other in the Old Testament: the First Commandment. We have hitherto regarded this commandment, like the entire Decalogue, as simply the clear expression of a natural law. To have a God is a requirement inscribed in the heart of every man,[326] a requirement whereby the Creator shows himself even to the pagans. But the First Commandment is more than this. It is affirmation and commandment in one: an affirmation which demands, and a command which promises. The peculiar question has been asked concerning the First Commandment: What is really "commanded" in it? Some have answered that, besides the prologue ("I am the Lord your God"), it contains only a prohibition of idolatry ("Thou shalt have no other gods beside me").[327] To answer with one of Luther's best-known pronouncements on the First Commandment, "This is the work of the First Commandment, which commands, 'You shall have no other gods,' which is as much as to say, 'Since I alone am God you shall put in me alone all your trust, loyalty, and faith and in no one else.' "[328] The "command-

326 See above, pp. 134–35.

327 See Karl Thieme, "Das Evangelium in der Form des Gebotes," *Christentum und Wissenschaft,* VIII (1932), 334 ff. Against this, Otto Gühloff, "Gebieten und Schaffen in Luthers Auslegung des ersten Gebotes" (Dissertation, University of Göttingen, 1939), pp. 1 ff., is correct. For literature, see below, p. 176, n. 357

328 *Treatise on Good Works,* 1520, *WA* 6, 209:24; *LW* 44, 30; see also *The Large Catechism,* 1529, *WA* $30^{I}$, 132:35 ff.; Tappert (ed.), *op. cit.,* p. 365.

ment" is thus wrapped in both parts of the First Commandment, in the promise and in the prohibition. That is where the unity of the First Commandment lies. It requires me to believe God's affirmation and to recognize him alone as my God. Thus the promise is the reason for the commandment.

The commandment, based on an affirmation and aimed at this promise alone, is so different from all the rest of the law that Luther, to express the *sense of promise* of the First Commandment, could deny its character as a command altogether. It is the promise of all promises; it is a commandment in which nothing is commanded. "It is the promise of all promises, the fountain and head of all religion and wisdom, embracing the promise of the gospel of Christ. This is properly the First Commandment because it prescribes nothing when it says, 'I am the Lord your God.' "[329] Thus the purpose of this commandment is that we learn from it to despair of our works and to depend only on God's mercy. "This is the pure and honest meaning of the First Commandment: we should deem ourselves nothing regarding our own merit; but have, receive, and find power to do everything only by his mercy and to his glory."[330] The psalms which teach us this are therefore nothing but "syllogisms stemming from the First Commandment," which Luther showed in his love for logical games.

> David ... became a prophet and orator through Moses and thus is able to create the loveliest little psalms. For the entire Psalter is nothing but a series of syllogisms stemming from the First Commandment: the minor premise is called "faith," the major is called "Word of God," the conclusion is "deed" and "performance." [Or:] major premise: God cares for those who are miserable; minor premise: I am miserable. Conclusion: therefore God will care also for me. Man doubts the minor premise.[331]

We do not need to develop this understanding of the First Commandment any further; all of the scholarship dealing with these relationships agrees that to Luther it had the consolation of highest promise.

But Luther drew still one more conclusion from it deserving our attention: the First Commandment is the classic proof that the Old

329 *Glosses to the Decalogue*, 1530 (*Glossen Zum Dekalog*), *WA* 30II, 358:1.
330 *The Deuteronomy of Moses, with Notes*, 1525, *WA* 14, 626:22; *LW* 9, 85.
331 *Table Talk*, 1532, *WA*, TR 1, 160:4 ff. (No. 369).

Testament too knows about eternal life.[332] Luther, in his interpretation of the powerful Moses Psalm 90 on death and finiteness, frequently raised the question of whether the Old Testament really says as little about eternal life as was often asserted. He not only cited passages in opposition, in which one can today find the faith in resurrection and continuance of life evidenced or presupposed in later Judaism (Isa. 25:8; Dan. 12:2–3; Job 19:25 ff.; Ps. 49:17; Ps. 73:23 ff.). That would have seemed much too little to him. Rather, to him the faith in eternal life was secretly included in Moses' and the prophets' entire view of God. For the God to whom they turned in their prayers is an invisible God, and his kingdom is not of this world.

Although too little is said in the Old Testament about eternal life and immortality, we can, if we look at the Decalogue and all the prophets, see them call upon a God, king, or prince who dwells beyond all the things we see, far, far greater even than any prince. Accordingly, they all admit in their invocation that there is a life after this life, a second life more powerful than life or death. You have heard in the beginning of this section that Moses shows us a judging God beyond this age, [and] that there is another life, another kingdom than that of this world. Thus you can draw the safe conclusion from the First Commandment and from all that followed, that is, the entire first table, that there is another life, because he mentions another emperor who is beyond this world and who is capable of being merciful and angry.[333]

And yet he is real and a God of life. If, in the First Commandment, he himself claims to be God, then we may, according to the safe rule, interpret with the words of Christ, "God is not a God of the dead but of the living" (Matt. 22:32).

This is the rule and certain principle: wherever Scripture refers to the First Commandment, it is to be applied to Christ, who says in Matthew 22 [:32], "God is not a God of the dead." Wherever there is a reference to the First Commandment, you should know for certain that eternal life and the resurrection of the dead is referred to in veiled language. Thus there are other passages in this psalm [indicating] that the lawgiver teaches and shows, in veiled but unmistakable language, a remedy against death.[334]

332 See Althaus, "Gottes Gottheit als Sinn der Rechtfertigungslehre Luthers," *Lutherjahrbuch,* XIII (1931), 3–4.
333 *Lecture on Psalm 90,* 1534–1535, *WA* 40$^{III}$, 569:7 ff.; *LW* 13, 126–27.
334 *Ibid., WA* 40$^{III}$, 492:11 ff.; *LW* 13, 81, 83.

> Wherever, therefore, there is a reference to the use of the First Commandment, you find faith and hope in the resurrection of the dead included. Christ taught us to deduce and to arrive at this from the passages, "I am the God . . . ," etc., and "Therefore Abraham lives" [Matt. 22:32]. The following argument stems from the First Commandment: God is not a God of the dead. Accordingly, whoever worships God, believes, prays, hears God, even though he has been dead, etc., because he does not believe, pray, and hear the God of the dead, but . . . , etc. In short, such faith, prayer, and hearing of the Word include the article of the resurrection of the dead and that of eternal life. It is not for the human brain to know the first table in such a manner, but for Christ the teacher. It means: the first table is not given to brutes, dead unto eternity, but to men; that is why they will live in eternity. Thus, to put it simply, the first table gives life and resurrection from the dead.[335]

Therefore he is the God of a life beyond the life of this world, of an eternal life, compared to which our life really deserves to be called death. Wherever judgment or grace is proclaimed, eternal life is at the same time spoken of. Indeed, we have need of God only for the sake of this eternal life. Here on earth we need only the service of political and economic order, which is carried out for us by political authority. We do not need God for this. If *he* exists, then there is at the same time an eternal fate for us. Faith and prayer to this invisible God, therefore, always include a secret faith in or a sensing of eternal life. No doubt only a very few in the old covenant ever understood this. But those filled with the Spirit sensed it and waited for the full revelation of the incarnation.

> That is what "eternal life" means: to have a king in our favor because He is beyond this life. There should be an eternal life, because if there were no other life beyond this, we would not be in need of God. The immortality and eternity of life flow out of the First Commandment. . . . Kings and princes rule here where we need nothing but political and economic authority. But he himself interferes, he who is not political [or] economical, but invisible beyond this world, etc. Just as he himself is eternal and invisible, so also are grace and salvation. . . . Accordingly,

335 *Ibid., WA* 40$^{III}$, 494:10 ff.; 497:1 ff.; *LW* 13, 82–83. In the similar passage from Psalm 118 (*WA* 31$^{I}$, 154:8 ff.; *LW* 14, 87), where Luther deduced the resurrection from the First Commandment according to the same rule, he cited two reasons: 1) God himself, to whom the First Commandment points, cannot die; 2) he is, according to Matt. 22:32, a God of the living. "That is why [the Christians] must live forever; otherwise he would not be their God, nor could they depend upon him unless they lived. For this little group, therefore, death remains no more than a sleep."

it is clearly witnessed in the forum of conscience which the prophets saw, namely, that eternal life is to be expected from the God who was with them, the God become flesh. Although not all the Jews know this, some, the saints and those filled with the Holy Spirit, knew it.[336]

This kind of thinking led Luther to a compelling conclusion. The faithful Rörer gleaned a satisfied, "That is how it ends," from Luther.[337]

Even if the dedication with which God gives himself in the prologue of the First Commandment includes the whole promise up to and including eternal life, the First Commandment in its entirety does not cease to be a *commandment.* One in content with the command to love God and neighbor, it is indeed the purest and highest expression the law can find anywhere.[338] What follows from this is, first of all, a double effect of law and promise aiming in various directions: as promise, it aims at faith; as commandment and its related threat of judgment, it aims at unbelief. Thus Luther answered the question of how one could, as a preacher, reach both the pious and the godless: "With the First Commandment." It means judgment for the one, grace for the other.[339] That is why he also called the First Commandment the ocean out of which the prophets scooped their sermon of consolation as well as their sermon of punishment: consolation for the poor, those under temptation *(Anfechtung),* the sinners; and threat against the rich, the mighty, and the proud, that is, against those who depend on other things than God as their God, and therefore have other gods. In this double effect the two functions of the First Commandment are as separated in content, even though they are related to each other in one sentence, as law and gospel always are for Luther.

Thus he [Moses] teaches what it means that there is God, what it means to fulfil the First Commandment. Oh, what great fountains just

336 *Lecture on Psalm 90,* 1534–1535, *WA* 40$^{III}$, 578:6 ff.; *LW* 13, 131–32.
337 See the remark in *WA* 40$^{III}$, 495:3; *LW* 13, 82–83. The passage mentioned above (p. 168, n. 335; *WA* 31$^{I}$, 154:8 ff.; *LW* 14, 87) indicates the same kind of conclusion. It also includes the forgiveness of sins in the argument (*WA* 31$^{I}$, 155:10 ff.; *LW* 14, 87 ff.). Similarly, Luther also concluded from God's own Word (Exod. 3:6), "I am the God of Abraham, Isaac and Jacob," that the patriarchs are only removed from your eyes as far as body and soul are concerned, but are living with God forever. *Sermons on Exodus,* 1524–1527, *WA* 16, 44:10 ff.
338 See above, p. 132.
339 *Table Talk,* early 1530's, *WA,* TR 1, 432:19 ff. (No. 868). See also *ibid.,* 159:23 ff. (No. 369).

these words must have been for the prophets! From this source they have drawn whatever they proclaimed about the concern of God for the weak, the lowly, the poor, the sinners, the widows, the orphans, the judged, the condemned, the afflicted, and the wretched; also whatever they thunder about the wrath and vengeance of God against the wealthy, the tyrannical, the mighty, the critical, the violent, the hard, and the proud. For all these flow from the great ocean of the First Commandment and flow back into it, so that no richer consolation or voice is more plainly heard, yet none harder or more severe, than the voice of the First Commandment, "I am the Lord your God."[340]

The prophets have "explicated in masterful fashion" both aspects of the First Commandment,

how God threatens and consoles: how he threatens the godless who feel secure and proud; and if threats do not help, he backs it up with penalties, pestilence, famine, war, until they are destroyed; and thus he makes good his threat in the First Commandment. But he comforts those who fear him, who are in all kinds of need, and also backs it up with aid and counsel through all kinds of miracles and signs, against all the might of the devil and the world; thus he also makes good his consolation in the First Commandment [Exod. 20:6].[341]

But Luther's use of the First Commandment goes beyond this juxtaposition of command and promise. He had also seen both *within each other*, and this is the strange and at the same time debatable aspect of his use of the First Commandment. Here God made his commandment serve the promise; he demands that we accept his affirmation. The divine offer is simultaneously commandment. Luther saw clearly that God thereby even surpasses the simple word of promise, although his commandment naturally aims at nothing

[340] *The Deuteronomy of Moses, with Notes,* 1525, *WA* 14, 640:24 ff.; *LW* 9, 112. I should not have spoken in connection with this passage about a "being in one another" *(Ineinander),* but only of a "being side-by-side" *(Nebeneinander).* See "Christus und das erste Gebot in der Anfechtung bei Luther," *Zeitschrift für systematische Theologie,* V (1928), 474. Thieme, who raises a justified objection ("Das Evangelium in der Form des Gebotes," p. 336) against my use of the passage, again only isolates the prologue, according to his mistaken basic principle, and does not see that the proclamation of punishment is not only the reverse side of the promise, but also the threat of the commanding God against those who do not want to let him be God. One should not be confused by the fact that Luther cited the prologue only literally; rather, one must, in his use of the First Commandment, always take the part for the whole and maintain the unity. Luther always heard the promise at the same time as the command for unbelievers. Thieme himself recognized this correctly (*ibid.,* p. 346) in a similar situation.

[341] *Preface to the Prophets,* 1532 *(Vorrede auf die Propheten), EA* 63, 43–44; *LW* 35, 266.

but faith in the promise. God not only exerts his loving, coaxing, and wooing to move us to trust; he also places the commanding majesty of the Creator in the service of this overcoming of our unbelief. That is why he not only admonishes and begs us, but also commands us to let go of our doubts and to regard him as our God, as our dear Father. In distress when the conscience in temptation *(Anfechtung)* sees no way out and "must, against hope, hope for hope," the First Commandment will prove itself a strong rod and staff.

Bear all delays with patience, but do not doubt that you shall receive; that which will come, will surely come and will not delay [Hab. 2:3]. In the meantime, there must be the hoping for hope against hope. But to this end you will have the rod and staff of God to sustain and comfort you, namely, the first and greatest of all commandments of God, "You shall have no other God before me." We are not only reminded, admonished, and persuaded to this commandment to hope in him and to love him, but it is commanded to us on penalty of the greatest punishment and obligation (which is to have a God). You are not absolved from any sin by this commandment; indeed, it outweighs any sin, whenever the opportunity is at hand to keep and to fulfil the commandment. For if you had sinned against all other commandments, and had done so in various ways, you would not have sinned as much as when in this very moment you doubt this First Commandment. For this would be the same as to deny God, which is horrible even to think about. For who can tell God to his face, "You are not God"? Indeed, who can hear this? Yet he who doubts says this with the full and everlasting fervor of his heart. To him who is tempted, it does not seem he says it; indeed, he does not say anything like this at all. Instead, and this is nearer the truth, he suffers Satan to say it in him.[342]

Therefore see what a gracious God and Father we have. He not only promises us forgiveness of sins, but also commands us, on pain of committing the most grievous sin, to believe they are all forgiven. With this same commandment he constrains us to have a joyous conscience and, while using the terrible sin [against the Holy Spirit], drives us away from sin and bad conscience.[343]

342 On Ps. 5:11, *Works on the Psalms,* 1519–1521, *WA* 5, 171:9 ff.; *LE* 1, 280. See also *WA* 5, 172:14, 35, *LE* 1, 211. The segment appears within the larger context of a comforting address to the conscience threatened by despair (*WA* 5, 170:10 ff.; *LE* 1, 280). Thieme deals with Luther's treatment of the First Commandment in far too limited a way. He thinks ("Das Evangelium in der Form des Gebotes," p. 335) Luther had only the commandment against idolatry in mind here. But how should that alone be a consolation?

343 *The Sacrament of Penance,* 1519 *(Eyn Sermon von dem Sacrament der pusz), WA* 2, 717:36; *LW* 35, 14.

That a joyous conscience is not only permitted to us but even commanded was Luther's strongest consolation for him who is being tempted and does not have a joyous conscience.

But the just, who knows that God not only promised and anticipated Him but also commanded that one should believe and hope in him before all works, neither stands up, once again, because he trusts in works, nor remains flat on his face because he fell; but, remembering the promise and command of God, he has the mercy of God before his eyes, which he commanded should be the only thing before one's eyes when he said, "I am the Lord your God."[344]

He must learn that he insults God more with his unbelief, when he does not dare to accept his forgiveness, than with any other sin. "It is more rigidly commanded that we should believe in God than that we should not live in adultery and should not kill. That is why the omission of the faith commanded in the first table outweighs by far the committing of sins prohibited in the second."[345] Just as faith is simply the life of God, the only and all-encompassing "good work," so is unbelief simply the sin which opposes the First Commandment, *the* commandment per se. But he who trusts the commandment and grasps its promise will be cured of all guilt and saved from all temptation *(Anfechtung).*

Accordingly, just as unbelief, the source of all evil, does not permit any good work to occur, or, if it occurs, pollutes it and makes it susceptible to all sins, so, on the other hand, faith, the source of all good, permits no evil to occur, or, if it does occur, nullifies and purges it immediately and makes it susceptible to all good works.... That is why we should bravely hold that the First Commandment is the head and beginning of all commandments, and that its work is the head and beginning of all works.[346]

All monstrosities follow from the First Commandment, when a false doctrine about God is conceived in the heart. But if a man walks rightly in the First [Commandment], even if he should fall with regard to the rest of the commandments, he will rise again because his eyes are strong and not blind.[347]

344 *Works on the Psalms,* 1519–1521, *WA* 5, 400:1 ff.
345 *Ibid.,* 398:27. That is why God judges David more severely, because his sin, namely, adultery and the murder of Uriah (II Sam. 12:7 ff.), caused pagans to commit blasphemy. *Lecture on Psalm 51,* 1532, *WA* $40^{II}$, 320:6.
346 *Works on the Psalms,* 1519–1521, *WA* 5, 398:30 ff.
347 *The Deuteronomy of Moses, with Notes,* 1525, *WA* 14, 604:13; *LW* 9, 63.

He obtains the glorious freedom in which he is released from all calculation of his own thoughts and works and is consoled by the assurance of divine forgiveness.[348] Man becomes a believer by obeying the First Commandment. "The righteous one is made [righteous] through faith, which believes that God is gracious. He commanded the believer to believe this, saying, 'I am the Lord your God. You shall have no other gods beside me.' "[349]

Luther naturally did not attach all of this slavishly to the First Commandment. He only found the purest expression of it therein. But he could often broaden the First Commandment into the "first table," since the first three commandments are only variations of the same theme, the correct attitude toward God. That is why the other two commandments take precedence over those of the second table.[350] The positive interpretation of the Second Commandment in particular, namely, the correct usage of the name of God in prayer, is insolubly linked to the First Commandment. How often Luther told tempted souls that God commanded them to pray and to believe in the answer to prayer, that is, to know him as their gracious God, just as in the First Commandment, because of his "command and promise"![351]

> [God] not only promised but he also commanded most strongly, on pain of his eternal displeasure and wrath, that we should pray, trust, and receive.... Thus one must drive out the devil's temptation with God's command; then he will stop, and this is the only way.[352]

Does such a commandment, which only serves to strengthen the promise of grace, still have anything to do with the law? Or isn't the transition made here into another sphere, which allows only a metaphoric use of the term "commandment"? It is a commandment of consolation and a law in one; the behavior of a man deter-

348 *Treatise on Good Works,* 1520, *WA* 6, 207:15 ff.; *LW* 44, 26–27.
349 *Works on the Psalms,* 1519–1521, *WA* 5, 399:2.
350 *Ibid.,* 398:27 (see above, p. 172, and the summary of the three commandments in *ibid.,* 346:7).
351 "The Lord's Prayer," *The Large Catechism,* 1529, *WA* 30^I^, 196:4; Tappert (ed.), *op. cit.,* p. 423; *A Sermon on the Preparation for Dying,* 1519 *(Eyn Sermon von der Bereytung zum Sterben), WA* 2, 697:1.
352 *Treatise on Good Works,* 1520, *WA* 6, 235:35 ff.; *LW* 44, 62. Thieme, in his polemics against me and Vogelsang, here again takes apart that which belongs together. How can one separate faith in the answer of prayer and faith in salvation? The affirmation is here strengthened in the same manner through the commandment as in the explanations of the First Commandment in a narrower sense.

mines what it is to him. If one wishes to clarify it with Luther's concepts, one could say: the *essential* work *(opus proprium)* of the First Commandment in its unity of command and promise is the affirmation of grace; the *alien* work *(opus alienum)* is the judgment upon him who does not accept the promise. That is exactly the reverse of the law. The *essential* work of Moses is, as we saw, the office of executioner of the law.[353] Thus the place of the First Commandment is completely on the side of the gospel. It is simply the most powerful form of it. But then it simultaneously becomes the most powerful form of the threat of judgment, which is incurred if we do not take God's proffered hand. This is true not only when we place the command and promise side by side, but also when we see both "within each other" in the First Commandment. In it, just as in any other form of the commandment asking for faith, prayer, and hope, blessing and curse dwell ominously close to each other. "This is the voice which is heard for consolation [Ps. 51:8]; I know that God, according to his will, has ordered me to undergo eternal punishment unless I hope."[354] God also stands behind the command of promise in the dual figure in which he appears, depending upon the vision of faith or unbelief. He strikes both with his commandment, with judgment or consolation. He prods conscience or, with a consoling command, closes its mouth when it struggles suspiciously against the promise; he puts down the self-confident or gives him who is sorely tested the courage to believe. But both occur in the form of the commandment, which therefore encompasses a double meaning and requires belief in both God's punitive and forgiving Word. Whoever rejects such belief sins against the First Commandment.

For the will of God encompasses a twofold mandate: to believe what you should hold on pain of eternal damnation, according to divine law; and to believe what he wills so that you do not doubt the divine works of mercy, but instead learn in fear and trembling to flee to the promised mercy offered in Christ, even though you see nothing but sin and nothing but death.... Thus it seems as if God hates me, is hidden to me, and does not want me. Yet in reality he wants you and tells you through my mouth and that of St. Paul that you should hope in

[353] See above, pp. 145–46.
[354] *Lecture on Psalm 51,* 1532, *WA* 40$^{II}$, 415:12; *LW* 12, 373.

him and believe Christ who died and was raised again for you; through his death the wrath of God the Father was soothed and you were reconciled with the Father. If you would have doubted and despaired here, you would have sinned against the First Commandment, which wants you to believe in him who is your God, and not in the enemy, the devil, death, and sin.[355]

The terrifying and the comforting commandments both come out of the mouth of the same God. It is faith's difficult art to accept the Word of grace from that God whose judgment man feels so deeply in his heart. Precisely the commanding character of the promise in the First Commandment helps man the most to jump over this ditch. A man learns that he truly honors God, whom he would like to honor by obeying the law, only by trusting his word of forgiveness.[356] The same transformation thus takes place in the commandment of God as Luther had experienced in the "righteousness of God" *(iustitia dei)*. That which could cause only fear outside the gospel now became the greatest comfort. God's commanding voice does not, if understood correctly, drive one to fear, but rather to trust in him. Thus the service rendered by the First Commandment to the gospel far surpasses the law's service as disciplinarian *(Zuchtmeister)*. While the latter can only drive man to exhaust his own resources, and therefore prepare him for the gospel, the First Commandment is God's strongest appeal pointing to the rescue of him who is being tempted.

Luther did not say how this crossing of the ditch from temptation *(Anfechtung)* to faith is accomplished. Therein lies the difference from his understanding of the justice of God which we have used as comparison. There the issue was the clarification of a concept Luther attained as a sure result of his exegetical work, after a long search; here, in the "yes" to the offered and commanded promise, the issue is the decisive way of life, the total act of justification. A closer dissection of this process would only show how the divine

[355] *Second Disputation Against the Antinomians,* 1538, *WA* 39$^{I}$, 428:1 ff. See also the other edition, "divine majesty simply tells you not to despair." *Ibid.,* 429:25. Thieme helps himself with regard to this passage through the interpretation that the divine commanding should not be thought of here as emphasized ("Das Evangelium in der Form des Gebotes," pp. 357–58). But this is not necessary; the fact that it appears here suffices.

[356] See Holl, "Was verstand Luther unter Religion?" in *op. cit.,* I, 27 ff.

action is reflected in the human consciousness.[357] For here God works through the Creator Spirit. But Luther did not describe how this is done either; instead, he left everything to personal adaptation to life. His only concern was that a man should experience the creative God in his *unity* in the First Commandment. The servitude of the law under the gospel here becomes completely transparent. Commandment and promise have the same goal. The First Commandment shows the Creator who gives himself in it with all his might, so that we could not live without the First Commandment. We only really understand it when we have gotten into such distress that we no longer know what to do.

> Then the First Commandment comes along and cries to you and to all men, "I am the Lord your God"; this housefather will give you something to eat and drink. It must be baked and woven out of the First Commandment. If you are to have a shirt on your back and a slice of bread in your mouth, the First Commandment must give it to you....

[357] This is the only way in which Holl's attempt (*ibid.*, pp. 73 ff.) to show the inner intertwining of the experience of justification wants to be understood. There is, in this regard, always the danger that such an explanation can be misunderstood in terms of a reasonable, logically conclusive process, as was indeed the fate of Holl's descriptions. But there is even a greater reason why one should be aware that Holl wanted to avoid just that (*ibid.*, p. 77, and III, 247 ff.). His first description was, of course, not sufficiently safeguarded against the objection—raised against him in Friedrich Gogarten, "Theologie und Wissenschaft. Grundsätzliche Bemerkungen zu Karl Holl's 'Luther,' " *Die christliche Welt*, XXXVIII (1924), 34 ff., and now again by Gühloff (*op. cit.*, p. 29; see above, p. 165, n. 327)—that faith in grace cannot originate from the experience of the never ceasing divine demand. Holl's response (*op. cit.*, III, 244 ff.) to Gogarten shows more clearly that he did not mean it that way. If he emphasized so strongly there the sense of promise in the First Commandment, he did not do it to identify the First Commandment with the law as such. Holl's short statement only hinted at the contrast between the First Commandment and the law rather than clearly elaborating it. If in his description Holl had more sharply underlined the struggle "of God against God," he would have overcome completely a certain imbalance in his description. For the commandment to trust the promise indeed abrogates the law; and thus the door is wide open to the wide field of Christology itself. Holl was decisively concerned with an insight which was again taken up in Paul Althaus, "Gottes Gottheit als Sinn der Rechtfertigungslehre," especially p. 10. Both observe that for Luther the commandment underlying the promise helped to keep faith in forgiveness from becoming a wishful dream, a help, not a proof against it; for there does not appear to be logical force in this line of reasoning. As much as one may explain here, the moment of the decisive transition, in which a man tears himself loose and grasps the promise and commandment to believe in God's grace, grasps it from the same God whose law destroys him in the depth of his heart—this moment is indescribable. But in it the unity of God or, to speak with Althaus, "God's divinity," is experienced; in it the Lord of conscience and the Creator is understood as the God of grace, and vice versa. Temptation and help are not far apart, as I should like to remark against Gühloff (*op. cit.*, p. 30). What has to be initially deepest temptation becomes deepest help in obedience to the First Commandment. Again, it is especially

The word, "I am your God, I have sworn to do good to you," gives bread to the hungry.[358]

And the First Commandment directs us to Christ in just the same way, and that in a double sense. Like the sermons of the Psalms and prophets, the proclamation of Jesus is nothing but the application of the First Commandment; he "draws" the First Commandment to himself and thus becomes equal with the Father. "So we can also see Christ as the one who can do nothing but the First Commandment. Yet the fact that he applies it to himself is a great thing."[359] And on the other hand only he encourages us to trust

---

the work of Gühloff which shows how valuable it is to let the grass grow over such an embattled field as the controversy—begun by H. M. Müller ("Der christliche Glaube und das erste Gebot. Ein Beitrag zum Verständnis von Luthers Rechtfertigungslehre in Auseinandersetzung mit Karl Holls Lutherdarstellung," *Theologische Blätter,* VI [1927], 269 ff.) and concluded with neither a sound nor a convincing position by Thieme ("Das Evangelium in der Form des Gebotes")—about the First Commandment, and then to enter it once again so ingenuously. Gühloff is right when he declares that Müller and Thieme still owe an answer to the question of what the real character of the First Commandment is (*op. cit.,* p. 32). He offers extensive evidence for the demanding character of the First Commandment (*ibid.,* pp. 6 ff.), and places this character in the larger context of God's commanding and creating as such. Thieme tore apart the unity of the First Commandment (and with it other forms of the commandment to believe, identical to it) through a series of already mentioned unjustified distinctions in the controversy with Holl, with myself ("Christus und das erste Gebot in der Anfechtung bei Luther"), Althaus ("Gottes Gottheit als Sinn der Rechtfertigungslehre Luthers"), and, in part, Vogelsang ("Über das Buch von Privat-Dozent Dr. Hans M. Müller, *Erfahrung und Glaube bei Luther* [Leipzig, 1929]," *Theologische Literaturzeitung,* LVI [1931], 186); he finally admitted the emphasis of the form of commandment only as a "subsidiary secondary idea," turning the quote—cited by himself—"not only promised . . . but also commanded" (*WA* 5, 400:2) exactly upside down. But in the end he himself raised the question of whether the form of the commandment should not be more highly valued. Thus he left his original strongly expressed position open at the most decisive point. Consequently his work as a whole remained sterile, even though details, as always with him, deserve attention and should not be forgotten even today when, given our distance from the earlier formulations and Gühloff's later more comprehensive discussion about the sense of promise in the First Commandment as well as about its significance regarding its characteristic as a commandment, an agreement might be more easily reached. For a survey of the entire literature, see Gühloff, *op. cit.,* pp. 98 ff.

[358] *Sermon of November 28, 1529, on Deut. 8:1, Sermons on Deuteronomy,* 1529, *WA* 28, 721:35 ff. (I am quoting Aurifaber's edition here which is sufficiently safeguarded through Rörer's copy.) See also Friedrich Gogarten, "Die Bedeutung des ersten Gebotes für Kirche und Volk," *Deutsche Theologie,* I (1934), 291; Gühloff, *op. cit.,* p. 88.

[359] *Table Talk,* 1532, *WA,* TR 1, 160:21 ff. (No. 369). In answer to the question of how one can apply the First Commandment to Christ, Luther here drew a beautiful distinction which is also typical of his love for logical images: Christ applies it either to himself a priori, "that is, out of the Word," as in John 5:23—"'He who honors me also honors the father,' etc. He takes the Second Commandment and applies it to himself. 'All the glory of God,' he

God's Word and to serve him by recognizing him as our gracious God. "Thus the First Commandment is fulfilled by us through Christ's blood and God is quite thoroughly served."

> Now the worship of God consists in this: that you know, honor, and love God with your whole heart; put all your confidence and trust in him; never doubt his goodness, neither in life nor in death, neither in sin nor in doing good, as the First Commandment teaches. All this we can attain only through the merit and blood of Christ, who has gained for us and given us such a heart if we hear and believe his Word; for nature cannot have such a heart of itself. See, this is the highest expression of worship and the greatest thing, which we call upright Christian faith and love for God through Christ. Thus the First Commandment is fulfilled by us through Christ's blood and God is quite thoroughly served.[360]

Thus Luther found in the First Commandment the unity of command and promise, judgment and salvation, Fatherly care and grace of Christ, the complete self-disclosure of the one God to the world.

In short, a fourfold meaning of the First Commandment can be discerned in Luther: 1) as commandment to have a God, it is a part of natural law; 2) the prologue, taken by itself, is the sum total of all promises; 3) as a unity it contains, depending on whether it turns toward belief or toward unbelief, law and gospel side by side; 4) as commandment of promise for those being tempted, it intertwines command and affirmation—command comes to them as gospel, gospel comes to them as command.[361] But these four applications of the First Commandment do not contradict each other. They are rather, depending upon one's view—determined by the human situation—expressions of the unity of the creative God

---

says, 'I apply to myself. . . .' Thus he takes himself out of the Second and into the First Commandment." Or he argued a posteriori when confronting the Jews, on the basis of his works—"He says that he does as much and as many works as God himself" [John 10:37–38]. *Ibid.*, 160:24.

360 *Epiphany Sermon on Matt. 2:1 ff., Church Postil,* 1522, *WA* $10^{I,1}$, 675:6; *LE* 10, 413. See also Gühloff, *op. cit.*, p. 97.

361 The relationship is one of mutual definition. Holl (*op. cit.*, III, 248) and Althaus ("Gottes Gottheit als Sinn der Rechtfertigungslehre Luthers," p. 10) defined the First Commandment, in this case, as the form of the gospel. But Althaus himself already saw that the form is more than a mere form, "it has significance as far as content is concerned" (*ibid.*, p. 11). It is, therefore, unwise to use only these categories; instead, it is better to spell out the mutual representation. If, however, one wants to use the concept of form, one cannot, in any event, turn it around, as Gühloff (*op. cit.*, p. 11, n. 49) wants to do, and make the gospel a form of the commandment.

who demands in order to give, kills to bring to life, commands to promise, forgives to renew. The majestic love of God manifested itself to Luther from the First Commandment as from no other passage of the Old Testament. It encompasses all the stages of the history of God, from law to fulfilment in eternity, and will thus survive in eternal life when all other commandments have come to an end.

The First Commandment remains: it is our God. The commandment is not fulfilled in this life, but in the future life; there it will appear to be our God. On the other hand, the Second Commandment remains in this life and will cease in the future life; for here remains the name, that is, the kingdom of faith.... In the future life all commandments will cease, except the first.[362]

## 5. THE UNITY OF SCRIPTURE

The unity of the revelation of God in Scripture corresponds to the unity of God which is proclaimed by the entire Old Testament, from the First Commandment on. This unity does not erase the contrast between law and gospel. Rather, as demonstrated above, this contrast is made to serve the unity of God, who works creatively through what is "alien" to his nature as well as through what is essential to him. The Old Testament is indirectly and directly God's Word through both law and promise. In this it is one with the New Testament. But now we still have to show in what way the given unity of Scripture is evidenced, on what it is based, and what its effect is.

### *a. The Formal, Distinguishing Marks of Scriptural Unity*

#### Word and Sign
#### (The Old Testament Sacraments)

The necessary things have been said about the objective unity of the two testaments, namely, the contrast of law and gospel, going clear through both of them. How completely Luther accepts the Old Testament as the Word of God is clearly demonstrated in the fact that he regards the Old Testament as partaking fully of

362 From the valuable Table Talk frequently quoted above. *Table Talk,* 1532, *WA,* TR 1, 159:26 (No. 369).

the distinguishing marks of that Word. In our context no detailed description of the Word of God according to its essence, its form, and its effect is necessary.[363] I begin with the most important formal distinguishing mark of the Word: it is hidden. It is not "a manifestation of things already present, but a testimony of things not yet seen; a hidden wisdom."[364] The promise hidden in the law in the Old Testament and the secret Christian in Moses show this type of Word most distinctly.

But God has helped man to find the hidden Word and to understand its meaning. For he has always added signs to direct us to his promise. "As I have often said: the signs or visions God gives besides the Word are necessary to weak and troubled souls to strengthen their faith, for they cannot cling to the mere Word as well as they can to an image and a sign."[365] The Old Testament offered him a plenitude of examples for this. As in the passage just mentioned, from his interpretation of Zechariah, he meant the prophetic visions as well as the actions and miracles of the prophets. However, Luther knew that visions and miracles alone are a very dangerous basis for assurance. He did not believe a word of the enthusiasts *(Schwärmer)* based on their visions, and he knew very well that the devil, too, can perform miracles. "Satan, to destroy faith, did many signs through visitations from saints, apparitions from spirits, and the like."[366] All this is of no use without or against the Word. "I want the Word, but I do not want the miracle."[367] Nevertheless, signs and miracles have great value. Thus Luther, motivated by those instructions in Deut. 13:1 ff. and 18:21 ff., which appear contradictory to a superficial reader, differentiated more precisely: when new doctrines appear which are directed against the Word accepted since ancient times and fortified by God

[363] I may refer instead to my study, *Das Wort Gottes bei Luther.* In addition see Helmut Echternach, *Studien zur Ontologie des Wortes,* I (1931); and the studies of Hans Preuss, *Die Entwicklung des Schriftprinzips bei Luther bis zur Leipziger Disputation. Im Zusammenhang mit der Stellung Luthers zu den anderen theologischen Autoritäten seiner Zeit dargestellt* (Leipzig, 1901); Scheel, *Luthers Stellung zur Heiligen Schrift;* Schempp, *op. cit.;* Althaus, "Der Geist der Lutherbibel," *Lutherjahrbuch,* VI (1934), 1 ff.

[364] *Lectures on the Epistle to the Hebrews,* 1517–1518, *WA* 57, 139:1, 9; *LCC* 16, 70–71; Hirsch and Rückert (eds.), *op. cit.,* pp. 139:19; 140:5.

[365] *The Prophet Zechariah,* 1527, *WA* 23, 558:13.

[366] *The Deuteronomy of Moses, with Notes,* 1525, *WA* 14, 684:29; 685:6 ff.; *LW* 9, 188.

[367] *Table Talk,* 1531, *WA,* TR 2, 334:11 (No. 2138).

with signs, one should not believe them, even if they are confirmed by miracles and visions. On the other hand, one must demand confirmation, through signs and miracles, from prophets who, without contradicting the ancient Word of God, proclaim something new. For this is how the true Word of God has always authenticated itself.[368]

God never spoke a new Word which he did not confirm through signs. Thus he confirmed the law of Moses through very great signs; the gospel also, when it was first received, through very great and almost continual signs. When therefore a new doctrine appears, its acceptance is to be suspected until signs occur.[369]

Therefore he waited for the often-promised miraculous acts of the enthusiasts, being of course certain that "his" God would make it impossible for "their" God to perform such acts.[370] But as necessary as the strengthening of the Word through signs is, the essential and basic factor is still the Word. That is why we could, if it were necessary, sooner do without the miracles than the words of Jesus. "For even if the miracles of Christ did not exist and if we knew nothing about them, we would still have enough with the Word, without which we could not have life."[371]

If there is a line connecting the visions and miracles of the prophets with the visions and miracles in the New Testament, then there is also a line connecting the prophetic actions and signs of a particular kind with the signs of the new covenant, the New Testament sacraments. The many strange actions of the prophets—for example, the carrying of a wooden yoke and the buying of a field by Jeremiah (Jer. 27:2; 32:8 ff.), the appearance of the naked Isaiah (Isa. 20:2), and the writing down of the vision by Habakkuk (Hab. 2:2)—belong to this great line of external "manners or signs" which God usually presents as confirmation, "just as one adds a seal to a letter."[372] Luther also confirmed his refutation of Zwingli with such prefigurations of ecclesiastical sacraments: all these signs

368 *The Deuteronomy of Moses, with Notes,* 1525, *WA* 14, 647:21 ff.; *LW* 9, 129, 188.
369 *Ibid., WA* 14, 684:32 ff.; *LW* 9, 188.
370 *Ibid., WA* 14, 685:3; *LW* 9, 189.
371 *St. Peter's Epistles, Preached and Interpreted,* 1523, *WA* 12, 260:19; *LE* 3, 34.
372 *The Prophet Habakkuk,* 1526, *WA* 19, 390:5 ff.

are not marks of identification of Christians among themselves but God's confirmations of his Word, "the real Word, as it were."

Thus God is accustomed to add a sign to his Word, not for the sake of love or mutual recognition, since love itself is better and there are other fruits of faith and of the Spirit. And so it is possible that even treacherous people are baptized and share the table of the Lord. Moreover, the miracles of Christ are signs, not so that Christians can thus recognize each other, but so that faith is strengthened. God, however, adds signs to the Word so that faith and reverence are encouraged, and because he does not want to give his Spirit, except through some external means. That is why he instituted the ministry of the Word and signs whereby the Spirit is given.... Thus the sign is added as the real Word, as it were, before one's own eyes, so that this sign may teach the same as the Word teaches.[373]

These symbolic actions of the prophets are only a copy of signs which God himself adds to his Word. The most important ones which Luther frequently named are: the sign of sacrifice for Abel (Gen. 4:4), the rainbow for Noah (Gen. 9:13 ff.), circumcision as a mark of the justification of faith for Abraham (Gen. 17:10 ff.), the dewy pelt for Gideon (Judg. 6:36 ff.), the sacrifice of Manoah (Judg. 13:19–20), the birth of Immanuel predicted to King Ahaz (Isa. 7:10 ff.). On the strength of these examples Luther demonstrated in *The Babylonian Captivity of the Church* (1520) the constitutive significance of the sign for the sacrament.[374]

God made it a practice to give signs, or miracles, along with the Word. For God's Word is never revealed without accompanying signs: in the case of Abraham the circumcision [was added] to the Word; in the case of Moses the command to lead the people was added as a sign. Thus Christ filled the world with miracles; and so we Christians have the eucharists and baptisms.[375]

Luther, especially in these years, occupied himself repeatedly with the question of Old Testament sacraments. He therefore had to confront two problems posed by scholasticism, and experienced a change of viewpoint in the process.

1. He knew, from Gabriel Biel's commentary on the Sentences,

373 On Isa. 20:2, *Lectures on Isaiah*, 1527–1530, *WA* 31II, 118:30 ff.
374 *The Babylonian Captivity of the Church*, 1520, *WA* 6, 517:38 ff.; 532:6 ff.; *LW* 36, 43–44, 45.
375 On Ps. 45:11, *Lecture on Psalm 45*, 1532, *WA* 40II, 569:2; *LW* 12, 269. See also *Lectures on Genesis*, 1536, *WA* 42, 184:4 ff.; *LW* 1, 247.

that the scholastic theologians of all persuasions[376] rejected the doctrine of Peter Lombard that the Old Testament sacraments possessed no power of justification. Luther sided with Peter Lombard, albeit in a different sense than the latter had meant it. He found therein the basic premise that became increasingly significant to him: the sacrament as such does not justify at all, but faith in the sacrament does, more accurately, faith in the promise enclosed in the sacrament. But this is also true for the New Testament sacraments.

From this text the legitimate difference between the old and the new law is clearly established: the sins, righteousnesses, sacrifices, holy things, promises, doctrines, and priests of the old law all pertained to the flesh; they did not sanctify "as far as conscience is concerned" [Heb. 9:9], but only as far as the body is concerned. But now [under the dispensation of the gospel] our sins, righteousnesses, sacrifices, holy things, promises, doctrines, and priests pertain to the Spirit and sanctify as far as conscience is concerned. Nevertheless, both [dispensations] were given by God, but the old one [was given] (as it says here [Heb. 9:10]), "until the time of the reformation." Hence what the Master of Sentences [Peter Lombard] writes is to some extent true, although he used to be reproved by everybody. He says that the sacraments of the old law, "even though they were performed in faith and love," did not justify [*Sententiarum* IV, Dist. I, C. 5, *MPL* 192, 840]. This is absolutely true; for a man is not justified because of the sacraments and sacrifices he has performed [? something is missing here in the text], even if they are done in love, but only love and faith do. No wonder it says in the New Testament that it is not the sacrament, but faith in the sacrament which justifies.[377]

To this extent Luther placed both forms of the sacrament under the same presupposition. At that time (1517–1518) he still understood the sacraments to be manifestations of the Jewish cult, just as the ancient church and scholasticism had understood them.[378] Seen thus,

376 Even within the contemporary Wittenberg school of theology, "the Master [of Sentences, that is, Peter Lombard] does not hold it," according to Carlstadt's marginal note in his personal copy of the Sentences. *Lectures on the Epistle to the Hebrews,* 1517–1518, *WA* 57, 205, n. 26; *LCC* 16, 166, n. 1.

377 *Ibid., WA* 57, 205:18 ff.; *LCC* 16, 166. See also the edition and commentary of Hirsch and Rückert (eds.), *op. cit.,* pp. 220–21. They alone noticed the textual break in the sentence before the last, whereas Ficker prints the spoiled sentence without any hesitation *(WA* 57, 206:3 *sua).* The simplest correction, it seems to me—instead of the somewhat complicated suggestion of Hirsch and Rückert—would be the following word sequence, closely related to the passage in Peter Lombard (Franciscan edition of the Sentences [2 vols.; Quaracchi, 1916], p. 747:1): *aliquis iustificatus est, quia. . . .*

378 See G. L. Hahn, *Die Lehre von den Sakramenten in ihrer geschichtlichen Entwicklung innerhalb der abendländischen Kirche bis zum Konzil von Trient* (Breslau, 1864), pp. 41 ff.

the presupposition for the justifying action, namely faith, can never be fulfilled in the Old Testament. For the Old Testament sacrifices, rites, circumcision, etc., belong under the law; the New Testament ones, on the other hand, belong to the kingdom of Christ, where everything is spiritual. Wherever Luther still thought within the scholastic framework, it appears as if he rejected the Old Testament sacraments as works of law. This is still the case in the lectures on Hebrews and in the contemporary theses.

44. The sacraments of the old and new law differ in such fashion that those of the old pertained to the flesh, whereas those of the new truly pertain to the spirit of justification.
45. In the new [law] the Word of promise is present, whereas in the old it was absent; and the same is true concerning the faith which receives remission [of sin].[379]

The position changed as soon as he understood them as signs *of God* for the confirmation of his promise.

2. Two years later, while concerning himself with the question of sacraments for his tract *The Babylonian Captivity of the Church,* Luther had to deal with another problem posed by scholasticism. The scholastics generally agreed that the contrast between the old and new sacraments was that those in the Old Testament were mere signs, pointers to those of the new covenant, whereas the New Testament sacraments were efficacious "of themselves."[380] This doctrine Luther passionately repudiated. But his concept of sacrament

[379] *Theses for the Truth Which Is to Be Sought and for the Consolation of Timid Consciences,* 1518 *(Pro veritate inquirenda et timoratis conscientijis consolendis), WA* 1, 632. Compare this quotation with the one above, p. 183.
[380] Most simply in the formula of Alexander Hales, cited by Friedrich Kattenbusch in *RE* 17, 364:14, "The sacraments of the new law are signs and causes of invisible grace, by virtue of [that grace] itself, whereas those [of the old law] are signs and not causes." See also the *Decretum pro Armenis* of 1439 in Karl Mirbt (ed.), *Quellen zur Geschichte des Papsttums und des römischen Katholizismus* (4th ed. rev.; Tübingen, 1924), p. 235:1. Had Luther known Thomas of Aquinas even more exactly, he would have found formulations which he could have used to a great extent, because Thomas emphasized the significance of faith *(fides)* especially in the Old Testament sacraments. See the quoted passages in *RE* 17, 364 (*Summa theologica* P. III, Q. 62, a. 6, and *Sent.* IV, d. 2, q. 1, a. 4), "They did not have a different efficacy in the function itself [*ex opere operato*] but only in faith [*ex fide*]." His substitution of *opus operatum* for *fides* in the New Testament sacraments naturally separates him, like the rest of the scholastics, from Luther. Moreover, *fides* also is understood as *opus operantis* as even today Catholic dogmatics distinguishes the sacraments of the old covenant from those of the new. See Franz Diekamp, *Katholische Dogmatik nach den Grundsätzen des heiligen Thomas* (3 vols.; 11th and 12th eds.; Münster, 1937), III, 62 ff. The exceptional position of circumcision, assumed by the scholastics—which is said to have extinguished original sin—disappears again in Catholic teaching after the Council of Trent. See G. L. Hahn, *op. cit.,* pp. 69 ff.

had changed in the meantime. After his sermons of 1519 he no longer understood it from the standpoint of cult but rather from the meaning of the sign itself. The Old and New Testament sacraments are essentially identical: indeed, are nothing but signs.

Still, they are *God's* signs which accompany the Word of promise. God has given these signs from the beginning of earthly human history (Abel's sacrifice). Luther now sharply distinguished them from the rites of Jewish worship which Moses prescribed through his law.[381]

For it is an error to hold that the sacraments of the new law differ from those of the old law in the efficacy of their signs: they are both identical in this respect. The same God who now saves us through baptism and the bread saved Abel through his sacrifice, Noah through the rainbow, Abraham through circumcision, and all the others through their respective signs. So far as the signs are concerned, there is no difference between a sacrament of the old law and one of the new, provided that by the old law you mean that which God did among the patriarchs and other fathers in the days of the law. For those signs which were given to the patriarchs and fathers must be clearly distinguished from the legal symbols which Moses instituted in his law, such as the priestly usage concerning vestments, vessels, food, houses, and the like; these are vastly different, not only from the sacraments of the new law but also from those signs which God sometimes gave to the fathers living under the law.... In each of these alike some promise was given which required faith in God.[382]

Not the Old Testament cultic forms but the great messages of God which bring promise begin the uninterrupted series of signs,

381 *The Babylonian Captivity of the Church,* 1520, *WA* 6, 531:35 ff.; *LW* 36, 64.

382 *Ibid., WA* 6, 531:4 ff.; *LW* 36, 65. Everything depends upon this link between sign *(signum)* and the Word of promise *(verbum promissionis). Ibid., WA* 6, 532:19 ff.; *LW* 36, 65. See also the paragraph which erroneously appears in this tract (*LW* 36, 95, n. 165; *WA* 6, 552:28 ff.) and the theses—closely related to it and preceding this tract in time—in which Luther very clearly expressed the origin of the sacrament in the death of Christ, and at the same time, its distribution from the beginning of mankind: "1. We admit that the sacraments of the grace of Christ are defined by virtue of his passion and death. 2. Yet they exist only in the new covenant, and we firmly deny their existence after the fall of Adam. 3. Accordingly, the same Christ and faith reigned in the elect from Abel on to the end of this world through various centuries. 4. But there existed various signs of the same Christ and faith, which are truly called sacraments of grace." *Theses on the Signs of Grace,* 1520 *(Quaestio circularis signis gratiae), WA* 6, 471:3 ff. Luther here also still used the earlier concept of the Old Testament sacraments, but only to uncover the difference between true and false sacraments, the signs of God. "The sacraments of the old law, not given by God through grace, existed only as ceremonies of Aaron's priesthood." *Ibid.,* 471:17.

continued in the miracles of Jesus and in the sacraments of the new covenant. And even where Luther named cultic actions, particularly circumcision and sacrifice, as divine signs, he only did so because God expressly instituted them as marks of his grace. In this sense circumcision was to Luther the baptism of the Old Testament; this is the way in which children became God's children. For they thus received

> the Word with the sign, and these not separated from each other. For God is there, speaking to them, "I want to be their God," which circumcision has supplemented within them. Just as with us, the children receive the whole, right, complete baptism, the Word with the sign, and do not separate one from the other but get the seed in the pod.[383]

Luther did not think of sacrifice as a cultic act, even when he called sacrifice a "symbol" of Christ's sacrifice and thus of the eucharist; rather, he considered it a sign of the promise. He meant, like Paul, first of all the passover (or the sacrifice of Abel). And at the same time he also emphasized the profound difference beside the shadowy copy of the future finished sacrifice. The contrast of the dumb sacrificial animal to the Son of God defines the contrast between the two covenants: between the old one, through which the land of Canaan was promised to the people of Israel, and the new one, through which mankind obtains citizenship in the kingdom of God. "And so it was necessary that, as a symbol of Christ, a dumb beast should be slain, in whose blood the same testament might be confirmed and in such a way that the blood corresponded to the testament and the sacrifice to the promise."[384] He was careful not to make a direct connection between the temple sacrifice and the eucharist, if only for the reason that he had to destroy the concept of the sacrifice of the mass, and because he tenaciously clung to the thesis: "There is no other sacrifice in the New Testament than the sacrifice of glory."[385]

By substituting the divine signs for the cultic actions, and thus changing the point of comparison with the New Testament sacraments from worship to God's action, Luther completed his transformation, which conformed exactly to his decisive exegetical ac-

383 *On the Jews and Their Lies,* 1543, *WA* 53, 437:33 ff.
384 *The Babylonian Captivity of the Church,* 1520, *WA* 6, 515:11; *LW* 36, 40. This passage immediately follows the one quoted above, p. 81.
385 *Lectures on the Minor Prophets. The Prophet Hosea,* 1524, *WA* 13, 19:1.

complishment: the overcoming of allegory as the real, the spiritual interpretation.[386] He sought no allegorical, shadowy anticipation of the Christian cult in the Jewish one; rather, he searched for the great deeds of God and signs of grace in the old covenant, which, like those in the New Testament, provide a sense of the God who gives his promise to faith. To Luther God showed himself in the Old Testament through an event, not through figurative hints. Luther looked for the sign, not the cultic "sacrament."[387] Thus he severed the relationship of the Jewish worship to the Christian worship. Later Lutheran theology, as in so many things, did not remain true to its master in this liberation from a scheme of thought handed down by tradition. It once again limited the Old Testament sacraments to circumcision and paschal sacrifice as parallels to baptism and eucharist.[388]

386 See above, pp. 88–91.

387 The segment entitled "On the Signs" *(De signis)* in the first edition of Philip Melanchthon's *Loci Communes,* 1521, still contains an echo of this essential intention of Luther. See G. L. Plitt and Theodor Kolde (eds.), *Die Loci Communes Philipp Melanchthons in ihrer Urgestalt* (4th ed.; Erlangen and Leipzig, 1860), pp. 224 ff. Beginning with the second edition in 1533, the segment is entitled "On the Sacraments" *(De sacramentis).* The definitions show a shifting of the tone from edition to edition—1533: the sacrament is a "note" *(nota)* or a "sign" *(signum)* (*CR* 21, 467); 1553: "The ceremonies are instituted in the gospel because it is the testimony of promise" (*ibid.,* p. 847). In the *Examination of Ordinands,* 1554 *(Examen ordinandorum)*: "An instituted divine rite, added to the promise handed down in the gospel." "Sign" now is to Melanchthon an antiquated expression. "In the old days it was said that the sacrament is a sign of grace." *CR* 23, 39. See also *The Confession of the Saxon Churches,* 1551 *(Confessio doctrinae Saxonicarum Ecclesiarum), CR* 28, 413–14. In the first edition of the *Loci Communes* the same Old Testament signs are enumerated as in Luther's *Babylonian Captivity of the Church;* beginning with the second edition they are left out. The question of Old Testament sacraments in general is no longer considered in the context at all; instead, circumcision and sacrifices are mentioned within the context of their New Testament models. *CR* 21, 854, 871 ff. See the section on the sacraments in Clyde L. Manschreck (trans.), *Melanchthon on Christian Doctrine. Loci Communes, 1555* (New York: Oxford University Press, 1965), chap. 19.

388 See John Brenz, *Pericope of the Apology of the Württemberg Confession,* 1556 *(Apologiae confessionis Wirtembergicae pericopas)*: "Although circumcision and baptism, the paschal lamb and the Lord's Supper, are different sacraments, the reality signified by them, and the merits offered and distributed by them, are not different." Quoted in Heinrich L. Heppe, *Die Dogmatik des deutschen Protestantismus im 16. Jahrhundert* (3 vols.; Gotha, 1857), III, 267. See also Heinrich Schmid, *The Doctrinal Theology of the Evangelical Lutheran Church,* trans. Charles A. Hay and Henry E. Jacobs (3rd ed. rev.; reprint; Minneapolis: Augsburg Publishing House, 1961), p. 536. Orthodox teaching is especially well represented in the study of Aegidius Hunnius, *On the Sacraments of the Old and New Testament,* 1590 *(De sacramentis veteris et novi testamenti), Opera Latina,* ed. Helvicus Garthicus (5 vols.; Wittenberg, 1607–1669), I, 961 ff. He treats both Old Testament sacraments in terms of many detailed casuistic questions (*ibid.,* 984 ff., 993 ff.). Two trends of thought

## Canon and Critique

The formal unity of Scripture finds its expression in the concept of the canon common to both testaments. Luther did not fundamentally destroy this concept, despite all his freedom in the evaluation of individual books.[389] He deviated from the traditional selection of canonical writings even less in the Old Testament than in the New Testament. Solely with regard to the Book of Esther, which had already been rejected in the Greek church,[390] did he unequivocally state that it really did not belong in the canon.[391] It Judaized too much for his taste.

---

cross each other in his view. On the one hand, Luther's view of the concrete mediation of grace in the sacramental sign is not forgotten, especially in the sacrament of circumcision. "In it God was efficacious through the removal of the foreskin in children on the eighth day, or in adults circumcision took place at the time of maturity; and he preserved them in the covenant of his grace through faith in the Messiah, who was to be born out of the circumcised people and whose merits were legitimately conferred upon the circumcised at one time and sealed at another time." *Ibid.,* 984–85. But this view is outweighed by the old typological interpretation that the Old Testament sacraments are only shadowy figures of those in the New Testament. Thus the paschal meal means, besides the remembrance of the liberation from Egypt, "that Christ, the lamb of God, is prefigured from a distance with all his universal merits, and faith in him is confirmed in receiving hearts." *Ibid.,* 994. This typological interpretation is expanded through the enumeration of other Old Testament "types" *(typi)* in the treatment of the New Testament sacraments (for baptism: the ark of Noah, circumcision, passage through the Red Sea, the healing of Naaman; for the Lord's Supper: manna and the water flowing from the rock). *Ibid.,* 1013–14, 1078–79. These "types," however, are not sacraments, since no promise is added to them. One can see how Lutheran and early Christian ideas are mixed. The cultic definition of the sacrament preponderates and thus crowds the essential idea of Luther, namely, the definition of the sacraments as signs of God's deed.

389 See in general Julius Köstlin, *The Theology of Luther in Its Historical Development and Inner Harmony,* trans. Charles A. Hay (2 vols.; Philadelphia, 1897), II, 223 ff.; Otto Ritschl, *Dogmengeschichte des Protestantismus; Grundlagen und Grundzüge der theologischen Gedanken-und Lehrbildung in der Protestantischen Kirche,* I, 61 ff. (where older literature also is cited); the works mentioned above, p. 180, n. 363; and Paul Althaus, Gehorsam und Freiheit in Luthers Stellung zur Bibel," *Vierteljahrsschrift der Luthergesellschaft,* IX (1927), 74 ff.; and in Althaus (ed.), *Theologische Aufsätze* (Gütersloh, 1929), pp. 140 ff.; and Ebeling, *op. cit.,* pp. 402 ff.

390 It is missing in the canonical lists of Melito, Athanasius, Gregory of Nazianz, Leontius of Byzanz, Amphilochius, and in the "list of sixty canonical books" well known in the Greek church since the sixth century. On the other hand, Origen, Cyril of Jerusalem, Epiphanius, the Apostolic Canons, and others include it in their lists. The Latin church always included Esther in its canon. See H. L. Strack in *RE* 9, 760–61, and the literature mentioned there.

391 Luther said, against Erasmus, who inadvertently did not include Esther in the Jewish canon: "Although they have it in the canon, it is, in my opinion, less worthy of being held canonical than all the others." *On the Bondage of the Will,* 1525, *WA* 18, 666:23, Packer and Johnston (trans.), *Martin Luther*

> I dislike the Book of Esther and that of II Maccabees, for they Judaize too much and contain much pagan naughtiness. Yet by this time the horrible thing has happened that the Book of Esther has a greater reputation among the Jews than Isaiah or Daniel; for Isaiah most clearly announces Christ, and Daniel clearly describes the rule and kingdom of Christ.[392]

And the Jews' preference for this book seemed to him only too well founded: "Oh, how much they love the Book of Esther which so well fits their bloodthirsty, vengeful, murderous greed and hope!"[393] And yet he did not remove the book from the canon. He did not even make his distaste evident through his arrangement for printing, although he characterized the last four writings of the New Testament (Hebrews, James, Jude, Revelation) as inferior by not numbering them in the Table of Contents, just as the Old Testament Apocrypha, and by separating them from the main writings of the New Testament by a clear space.[394] That Luther did not at least place the Book of Esther among the Apocrypha, and on the other hand did not take I Maccabees, which (in contrast to II Maccabees) he valued highly, into the canon,[395] shows his hesitation to disturb

---

*on the Bondage of the Will,* p. 143. See the passage in Erasmus, *On the Freedom of the Will (De libero arbitrio),* ed. Johannes von Walter (Leipzig, 1910), p. 20:3; *Discourse on Free Will,* ed. and trans. Ernst Winter (New York: Ungar Publishing Co., 1961), p. 21.

392 *Table Talk,* 1534, *WA,* TR 3, 302:12 (No. 3391a).

393 *On the Jews and Their Lies,* 1543, *WA* 53, 433:17. Luther also expressed himself very powerfully several times in the biblical revision of August 11, 1540, "It Judaizes immeasurably. They love this book very much. Like Haman [Esther 6:1 ff.], they really wanted to be exalted." Regarding the permission to murder (Esther 8:11), "Well, this really soothed him; and these rascals would like to do it even today." *The German Bible, WA,* DB 3, 471:2, 21.

394 From the New Testament of September, 1522, to the last edition of the Bible in 1546. *Ibid.,* 6, 12–13. See also the critical revisions of the Vulgate in 1529, *ibid.,* 5, 479; the Old Testament Apocrypha, *ibid.,* 2, 217; *Preface to the Epistle to the Hebrews (Vorrede auf die Epistel an die Hebräer), WA,* DB 7, 345; *LW* 35, 394. See also Wilhelm Bousset, *Die Offenbarung des Johannes* (6th ed.; Göttingen, 1906), p. 317; Johannes Leipoldt, "Die Kritik des Reformationszeitalters am neutestamentlichen Kanon," *Deutsch-evangelische Blätter,* XXXI (1906), 785; Karl Thieme, *Die Augsburgische Konfession und Luthers Katechismen auf theologische Gegenwartswerte untersucht* (Giessen, 1930), pp. 21–22.

395 *Preface to the First Book of Maccabees,* 1530 *(Vorrede auf das erste Buch Maccabäorum), WA,* DB 12, 315–16; *LW* 35, 350. "Just as it is proper for the first book to be included among the sacred Scriptures, so it is proper that this second book should be thrown out, even though it contains some good things." *Preface to the Second Book of Maccabees,* 1530 *(Vorrede auf das ander Buch Maccabäorum), WA,* DB 12, 315–16; *LW* 35, 350. "Just as it is proper for the bate Luther permitted an appeal of John Eck to II Maccabees only with reservations. See Otto Seitz (ed.), *Der authentische Text der Leipziger Disputation, 1519* (Berlin, 1903), pp. 145, 147; *WA* 2, 324:8; 325:16.

the essential biblical materials. This hesitation was not based on unthinking loyalty to tradition, but on the basic restraint of human, reasonable considerations in matters of God's Word.[396] He found it much easier to refuse to remove individual books from the Old Testament because he was in any case forced to leave untouched much of the content of the canonical writings which had no connection at all to the core of the Bible, namely, to commandment and promise. In any case, he knew nothing of a "savior attested to in the Book of Esther," who was said to have been confessed, according to Wilhelm Vischer, by the churches of the Reformation.[397] On the contrary, he was horrified at the Jews because they valued the Book of Esther, which glorified their national triumph, so much more highly than the prophets, who really proclaimed Christ.[398]

Even though Luther respected the bounds of the canon of Scripture, he did express quite a few noteworthy critical judgments about individual passages of the Bible. His faith in God's Word did not need the crutch of the dogma of inspiration.[399] But one must have a somewhat clearer view of the *criteria for this critique* than is usually the case. Miracles and unexplainable assertions do not fall into this category. Even if Luther made astonishing observations about amazingly high numbers and inconsistencies in Old and New Testament accounts,[400] these nevertheless only heightened his admiration for the authority of the Bible. For he doubted these assertions as little as he doubted Jonah's stay in the stomach of the whale. "And who would believe it and not consider it a lie and fairy tale, if it were not written in Scripture?"[401] He did, when possible, attempt

396 See Althaus, "Gehorsam und Freiheit in Luthers Stellung zur Bibel."

397 "Esther," *Theologische Existenz heute,* XLVIII (1937), 13. The difference in this kind of exegesis from Luther's interpretation of the Old Testament becomes very evident in this example. Vischer's attempted solution is a combination of allegory (the gallows erected by Haman [Esther 7:9] and the cross of Jesus "greet each other across lands and centuries," *ibid.,* p. 20) and an indirect Christocentric exegesis. It compares, without the bridge of a direct Christological prophecy, both situations in their distance from each other and places the problem of Judaism, which breaks wide open in the Book of Esther, into the light of its solution on the cross. But thereby one reaches only the point of the necessity of salvation for such vengeful nationalism, and not the point of the proclamation of the Savior.

398 See above, p. 189.

399 Ebeling (*op. cit.,* p. 402) strikingly formulates, "Luther's theological starting point in the doctrine about Scripture is not the doctrine of inspiration but that of incarnation."

400 Further examples in Köstlin, *op. cit.,* II, 255 ff.; Holl, "Luthers Bedeutung für den Fortschritt der Auslegekunst," in *op. cit.,* I, 574–75.

401 *The Prophet Jonah,* 1526, *WA* 19, 219:26; *Table Talk,* 1538, *WA,* TR 3, 550:8 (No. 3705).

an explanation, even though he reconciled himself to inconceivable numerical assertions such as the ages of the patriarchs. The high number of those killed, according to the accounts of battles, were not to be taken literally: they signify the extermination of the whole might of the conquered nation.

> If one reads that great numbers were slain, for example, eighty thousand, etc., then I believe not even a thousand may have been slain. The whole people is meant here. He who beats a king in battle, beats everything [the king] owns. Just as is the case with the king of France: if ten thousand of his troops were slain, it is said eighty thousand were slain because he has so much power, etc. Otherwise, I cannot reconcile myself [to such figures].[402]

He left insoluble contradictions alone, especially those in the Synoptic Gospels, and often added the comment that these are not important—the decisive thing is the proclamation of the text.[403] The spiritual interpretation occasionally helped him in the Old Testament when he got into difficulties with the literal interpretation. Thus it seemed to him that the promised return of Ephraim to Gilead and Lebanon (Zech. 10:10) is contradictory to the ordinance of Moses and Joshua that the tribes should not be mixed. However, the problem is solved for Luther by explaining that Gilead and Lebanon really means Holy Scripture and Christendom.

> If this contradicts Moses, then Moses also contradicts Zechariah. One has to give way to the other. But it is proper that Moses submits to Zechariah and lets him speak of the spiritual Gilead and Lebanon. But Gilead means "mound of witness" and Lebanon means "brilliant" or "white," that is, Holy Scripture or Christendom, where witness is piled up when Christ is preached; in addition, it is brilliant and white because of sheer innocence and holiness. Ephraim comes to such a mound of testimony and whiteness, that is, to the Word of God and to faith. That is the way in which hearts become pure, white, and pious.[404]

He felt justified in explaining this passage only by using allegory, especially since he could substantiate it linguistically.[405]

Nor did it constitute a criticism of the Bible when Luther fre-

[402] *Table Talk,* 1542–1543, *WA,* TR 5, 241:13 ff. (No. 5560); *LW* 54, 452 (No. 5560).
[403] See the examples mentioned above, p. 190, n. 400. He discussed some "scruples" *(scrupuli)* in the appendix to his *Computation of World Years,* 1541 *(Supputatio Annorum Mundi), WA* 53, 177 ff.
[404] *The Prophet Zechariah,* 1527, *WA* 23, 630:27 ff.
[405] See above, pp. 94–96.

quently observed obscurities, indeed, obvious corruptions of the Old Testament text.[406] He realized quite well the errors that had entered through the process of transmission in many ways, including vowel pointing or vocalizing the Hebrew text. That is why he now and then attempted to correct errors in the text through conjectures.[407]

Luther's real *critical expressions* pertain primarily to two areas:

1. *Questions of authorship.* In his prefaces to the Bible translations of individual prophets he openly expressed his doubts regarding the writing of the books by these prophets themselves. His prefaces have disappeared from later editions of the Bible probably partly because of this. It was an open issue with him whether the arrangement of the sayings of Isaiah stemmed from the prophet himself or from someone "who collected and wrote down these prophecies, as is thought to have happened also with the Psalter."[408] Regarding Jeremiah, he emphasized even more strongly "that it looks as though Jeremiah did not compose these books himself, but that the parts were taken piecemeal from his utterances and written into a book."[409] Likewise with Hosea: "But it looks as though this prophecy of Hosea was not fully and entirely written down, but that several pieces and sayings were collected from his sermons and made into a book."[410] Of the writings of Solomon, the Preacher seemed to him to have been collected from sayings of the king,[411] while the "Wisdom" did not

[406] Especially often in Hosea: *WA* 13, 30:5, 9; 37:10; 43:16: 47:10, 15 (where he did not know the intransitive meaning of the Hebrew *baqaq*). "It is corrupted." *Ibid.*, 39:4; 56:23.

[407] They are, of course, still modest. For example, Isa. 9:5: *wayyiqqre'* for *weyyiqra'* (already in the Septuagint and Lyra). "It seems that the text was corrupted by those who inserted the vowels." *Lecture on Isaiah 9*, 1543–1544, *WA* 40$^{III}$, 664:3; Ps. 54:5: *zadim* for *zarim.* Biblical revision, *The German Bible,* 1531, *WA,* DB 3, 56:12; further examples, *ibid.*, 9$^{I}$, XXXI. In Hosea he frequently escaped the difficulties through insight into proper names, which he did not find in the Septuagint and the Vulgate. For example, Hos. 5:1, *Mizpah:* "It must be the proper name of a place; no one sees this interpretation. Is this not a temptation?" *Lectures on the Minor Prophets,* 1524–1525, *WA* 13, 22:13. Also Hos. 10:14, where again he suspected, in contrast to the Vulgate, proper names and places and a hint to an event not well known (as is also the case in Luke 13:1), *ibid.*, 52:1.

[408] *Preface to the Prophet Isaiah,* 1528 *(Vorrede auff den Propheten Jesaiam), WA.* DB 11$^{I}$, 23:1–2; *LW* 35, 277.

[409] *Preface to the Prophet Jeremiah,* 1532 *(Vorrede über den Propheten Jeremiah), WA,* DB 11$^{I}$, 193:14–15; *LW* 35, 280–81.

[410] *Preface to the Prophet Hosea,* 1532 *(Vorrede über den Propheten Hosea), WA,* DB 11$^{II}$, 183:14 ff.; *LW* 35, 317.

[411] *Preface to Solomon's "The Preacher,"* 1524, *WA,* DB 10$^{II}$, 104:4 ff.; *LW* 35, 263.

seem genuine to him. He shared with the older fathers the idea that Philo was the author. He knew Philo through Jerome.[412] Thus in making critical judgments in his prefaces Luther made little distinction between canonical and apocryphal writings,[413] just as he made little distinction between Old and New Testament writings. For he also expressed his doubts unhesitatingly about the New Testament—for instance, about the authorship of the Epistle to the Hebrews,[414] of the epistles of James and Jude, and of Revelation. In both the critical preface of 1522 to Revelation and in the one of 1545 he denied the authorship of the apostle John.[415]

All in all, Luther expected the same response from the simple Bible reader that his lectures or other critical observations required of his students in the classroom. Whether he drew general conclusions regarding the origin of the prophets from individual observations,[416] hinted at further critical possibilities,[417] or expressed positive conjectures regarding the authorship of doubtful writings,[418] there was never any basic difference from what he communicated in his editions of the Bible. He always disclosed with complete frankness the spuriousness of some biblical writings; and if there seemed to him to be reason to do so, he affirmed it. When John Forster

412 *Preface to the Wisdom of Solomon,* 1529 *(Vorrede auf die Weisheit Salomonis), WA,* DB 12, 50:1 ff.; *LW* 35, 340 ff. See also *RE* 1, 653.

413 The judgment that the Book of Judith is not historical (*WA,* DB 12, 5; *LW* 35, 337) was also not based upon dogmatic but upon historical reasons.

414 The Epistle to the Hebrews stems neither from Paul nor from any other apostle. In view of the discrepant impression caused by the "real fine" epistle, which however is hindered by such "hard knots" as the denial of penance after baptism (6:4 ff.; 12:17), he helped himself out with the explanation that it is "composed of many pieces and does not deal systematically with any one subject." *Preface to the Epistle to the Hebrews,* 1546, 1522, *WA,* DB 7, 344 ff.; *LW* 35, 394–95.

415 *WA,* DB 7, 385:6; 387:21; 409:15; 404; *LW* 35, 398, 399–400.

416 The Table Talk quoted by Hirsch (*Luthers deutsche Bibel,* p. 9) goes further than any of the others. "No sermon of any prophet was completely written down; instead, they occasionally composed a saying. Afterward they put some of these sayings together and thus the Bible was maintained with great toil." *Table Talk,* 1532, *WA,* TR 2, 234:15 ff. (No. 1839). More detailed in the *scholia* to *Lectures on Isaiah,* 1527–1529, *WA* 25, 138:29 ff. Since this explanation is missing in Lauterbach's copy (*WA* $31^{\text{II}}$, 93), it may represent one of the additions made by the editors on the basis of Luther's own pronouncements as well as on the basis of the Table Talk quoted above and the prefaces to Isaiah and Jeremiah. See *WA* 25, 82–83; $31^{\text{II}}$, IX.

417 For example, that II Peter is not genuine; Luther, however, denied it despite his doubts. *II Peter and Jude, Preached and Interpreted,* 1523–1524 *(Die ander Epistel Sanct Petri, und eine S. Judas gepredigt und ausgelegt), WA* 14, 73:22 ff.; *LE* 3, 366.

418 For example, Apollos as the author of Hebrews. *Lectures on Genesis,* 1545, *WA* 44, 709:19. Otherwise Luther only spoke of the "author" *(auctor)* or "master" *(Meister)* of the epistle.

told him that some people did not consider the Pentateuch to be Mosaic, he simply replied, "So what?" He undoubtedly meant that even if Moses did not write it, it was still a book of Moses; obviously because the proclamation of creation, for him, belonged inseparably to the sermon of Moses. "What has that to do with the matter? If Moses did not write it, it is still a book of Moses; for there is the only book which describes best the constitution of the world."[419] At another time he hinted at the possibility, on the basis of suggestions in the Bible itself, of pre-Mosaic sources for Genesis: Adam, Noah, and others had undoubtedly already taken notes.

> It [Genesis] is, in my opinion, not from Moses. For there were also books before his time and books are cited—the Book of Wars [Num. 21:14] and the Book of the Just of the Lord [Josh. 10:13]. I believe that Adam wrote about several generations, then Noah and the rest; they wrote about how they fared. For the Jews are the oldest writers; the Greeks began later, and the Germans wrote for hardly more than a thousand years.[420]

Naturally he always treated the Pentateuch as Mosaic anyway. That the death of Moses is recounted at the end gave him no difficulty. This was added by Joshua or Eleazar, if one refuses to accept the thought that Moses foresaw his end and described it himself.[421]

2. Much more significant than this great freedom regarding questions of authorship and composition is Luther's *criticism of subject matter,* which evaluated individual passages or books on the basis of the "Word," namely, the gospel. This criticism need not occupy us here for it is better treated in the realm of the New Testament. As far as the Old Testament is concerned, this freedom of treatment is seen in tension with the New Testament, that is, in the wrestling between law and gospel. But the unusual factor is that the truth of justification also receives critical significance in the New Testament. The most obvious expression of this is the above-mentioned separation of the last four books from the other writings, particularly the repudiation of the Epistle of James and, almost more extreme, the selection of a canon of "the true and noblest

[419] *Table Talk,* 1532–1533, *WA,* TR 3, 23:14 (No. 2844).
[420] *Table Talk,* 1540, *WA,* TR 4, 594:7 ff. (No. 4964); *LW* 54, 373 (No. 4964).
[421] *The Deuteronomy of Moses, with Notes,* 1525, *WA* 14, 743:23; *LW* 9, 310.

books of the New Testament" (Gospel of John, Pauline letters, and I Peter).[422] The "doing of the law" still breaks through in the New Testament, namely in James,[423] which calls for praise and condemnation at the same time. It is similar to sinful man whom God justifies. In the New Testament, too, "the subject matter" of the Bible, justification by faith, is also presented. Again and again in his struggle for the correct interpretation of Scripture, especially with the rabbis, Luther presented this interpretation by subject matter as decisive.

> It is necessary from the very outset ... that we have in mind the matter involved. But the basic matter which cannot escape notice is this: nothing is pleasing to God unless it is done in faith.... The second basic issue is that sin is something so enormous that it cannot be blotted out by sacrifices and other works, but only through mercy, which must be accepted by faith.... The rabbis lack this foundation. For this knowledge comes only from the Spirit of Christ, who, like the noonday sun, brings light into our darkness. Therefore, let us reject as wicked and false whatever is at variance with these basic facts.[424]

Although this critique of New Testament material is only briefly dealt with here, it is important to note that the unity of the entire Scripture is most clearly seen here.

### *b. The Father of Jesus Christ as God of the Entire Scripture*

The sole basis of Luther's entire exegetical work was the conviction of the unity of Scripture arching above the tension of law and gospel, as demonstrated in the above-mentioned characteristics. This conviction is based upon presuppositions which we must now examine more closely: 1) the God of the entire Scripture is the Father of Jesus Christ; 2) Christ is the Word of God making itself known in the entire Scripture; he is indeed the Lord Sabaoth himself.

In all his biblical translation Luther substituted God or Lord for Yahweh and other divine names in the Hebrew text. Not even

[422] *Preface to the New Testament,* 1522, *WA*, DB 6, 10; *LW* 35, 361. I Peter is missing in the repetition of the Vulgate edition of 1529. *WA,* DB 5, 478:34.
[423] *Preface to the Epistles of St. James and St. Jude,* 1546, *WA,* DB 7, 387:14; *LW* 35, 397.
[424] *Lectures on Genesis,* 1536, *WA* 42, 195:38 ff.; *LW* 1, 264–65.

the sum total of his prophetic-Christological, allegorical, or existential exegesis, the analogies and illustrative fantasy with which he Christianized and made the Old Testament contemporary, alters this fact. The God of the Old Testament is for him not a God named and therefore owned and controlled; rather, he is the unnamed, eternally present God. He is his God. Luther prayed the same psalms to him as the pious Jew once did, not to the God of that day, but to this God, to God. Luther made accessible and preserved the Old Testament for German Christianity in the same way it was preserved for the Greek and Roman Christian world—the Septuagint rendered the Hebrew words for God as *theos* or *kyrios*; the Latin translations, whether from the Greek or the Hebrew text, as *deus* and *dominus.* One need only compare more recent translations which leave the name Yahweh with the Luther Bible to feel the completely transformed effect.

This distinctive trait of Luther's translation and theology of the Old Testament is not the means of an artist whereby he brings the subject communicated closer to the sensitivities of his contemporaries; instead, it is the most earnest truth. Like the translators before him, Luther was fully convinced that the Jewish people had experienced and known this God, the Lord of heaven and earth, the Father of Christ. They had encountered not a Jewish folk God, but God—in a way not to be compared with other peoples. That was the meaning of the people's election. "For no other people under the sun had or knew the true God except the Jewish people; that is why they could say, 'My God.' "[425] To illustrate this Luther did not need to detour via the same way by which he found a hidden worship of the name in paganism. No, the encounter was quite direct. The ancient fathers consoled themselves with this God and built upon his promise, even when they did not yet know his full revelation; their consciences were steeled by his commandments. And yet they too became guilty, precisely because of this law. Inspired by this pure demand, they played for mankind, in classic manner, the role of a man who depends upon himself. Both sides correspond to each other. The reality of their encounter with God corresponds to the fact that they exemplified the most extreme possibilities of human existence before God: daring faith and mo-

[425] On Hab. 1:12, *The Prophet Habakkuk,* 1526, *WA* 19, 376:27.

rality which tries to secure itself before God. Abraham and the Pharisees belong among them; Moses encompassed both for Luther.

The most horrible consequence of this encounter with God himself is that their election became their snare. What was once true faith in the revelation graciously given to them alone later became the arrogant boasting of this people and their cult. They boast that God rejected all other peoples and desired to be revered only in circumcision.[426] They should have known better. For God repeatedly sent them pious pagans as a warning and reproof: Abimelech (Genesis 20), Jethro (Exodus 18), the pharaoh advised by Joseph (Ps. 105:22), Naaman (II Kings 5), Nebuchadnezzar, Darius and Cyrus, to whom Daniel proclaimed the true God, and others.

> One should not deny that there were also truly pious Christians among the heathen, as we read about King Nebuchadnezzar and Naaman the Syrian, who were also pious people; and there were many others like them among the heathen. That is why it is quite credible that Abimelech was also a believer.[427]

> This is a clear example that even before the birth of Christ, yes, even before the law was given, many who were not circumcised were joined to the church of the circumcised and were saved . . . , and the dream of the Jews that God cast away all the Gentiles and wanted to be known and worshiped only by those who are circumcised is a rash fabrication.[428]

Luther even recommended that a religious conversation with a Jew should begin not with the divinity of Christ, but with the sentence, "You alone should not be the people of God."

> This argument they cannot bear. . . . Such a debate with a Jew is like beating an anvil with a straw. If they do not admit that uncircumcised people are people of God, then they still have against themselves these examples from Scripture: the pharaoh of Egypt, Jethro—from Moses himself—Nineveh, the kings of Egypt whose daughters were given to

426 *The Prophet Jonah,* 1526, *WA* 19, 241:6 ff.

427 On Gen. 20:9, *Sermons on Genesis,* 1527, *WA* 24, 364:21; *WA* 14, 292: 7 ff.; 31 ff.; 293:20.

428 *Lectures on Genesis,* 1539, *WA* 43, 125:11; *LW* 3, 347–48. Luther here said about Abimelech, who assembled his servants in the morning and told them about the vision of God in his dream, "The heathen king Abimelech becomes a bishop and teaches the Word of God in his court." *WA* 43, 122:21; *LW* 3, 344. See also *On the Jews and Their Lies,* 1543, *WA* 53, 433:27 ff.; *Table Talk* (from various years), *WA,* TR 6, 173:31 (No. 6764).

Solomon, the kings of Tyre, etc., also Naaman the Syrian—what then should they do with the other argument? If they do not admit, "I am the God of people without circumcision," how can they believe the other truth that Christ is God, born of a virgin, etc.? This is called blindness, because they do not admit these small matters proven by so many examples.[429]

And was not Job from the land of Uz (thus, according to Gen. 36:28 and Lam. 4:21, an Edomite), an uncircumcised descendant of Abraham? He is therefore a particularly important example of the fact that God did not desert the pagans either.

They neglected the Word of God. It sounds very comforting that God did not condemn the miserable Gentiles Job, Naaman the Syrian, the Ethiopian, the queen of Sheba, Nineveh. He wants all of them in his kingdom, as he says, "Salvation will come out of Judah, and yet it will not only pertain to the Jews. You see, I seek the Holy Spirit in Job the Gentile. . . ." Is this [Job 19:25-26] not a glorious word about an uncircumcised Gentile? I know of no clearer way to say it. Thus God gave even the Gentiles their prophets, just like Babylon and the Persians had their own prophets; and yet, he gave no prophets to Alexander and to the Romans.[430]

However, one must not misunderstand these examples. Luther was not at all of the opinion that such pious pagans had of themselves almost correctly recognized God. All these cases show that they found the way to God only in their encounter with the Jewish people. To Luther the advantage of Israel was the Word of God, not the law of Moses with its circumcision. That is why law and circumcision alone did not protect them from God's punishment. "For where God's Word is gone, circumcision is no good anymore."[431] Although the pagans sometimes have a very excellent natural law of conscience within themselves, to find God such a law still requires the impetus of divine revelation. And such revelation had been given only to the Jews. From them it then went forth here and there through messengers and prophets and reached individual pious people or whole cities like Nineveh, which God preserved to the understandable sorrow of Jonah.[432] And, grasped by individuals, the message was handed on to others; finally whole

[429] *Table Talk,* 1532, *WA,* TR 1, 161:2 ff. (No. 369).
[430] *Table Talk,* 1538, *WA,* TR 4, 94:29 ff. (No. 4039).
[431] *On the Jews and Their Lies,* 1543, *WA* 53, 439:30.
[432] See above, pp. 32–33, and pp. 53–54.

regions were saved for the sake of one pious man. "The promises of the Jews went forth into all the world. Therefore not only were Job and Naaman alone faithful among the pagans, but also many others; and when Abraham died, he left behind all religions filled with knowledge of God."[433] "Salvation was given because of Naaman the Syrian."[434]

The conversion of these individual pagans was at the same time a preview of the great turn of world history which Luther found already sensed in the Old Testament. "I shall be found by those who did not seek me; and I say to the pagans who did not call my name, 'Here I am, here I am'" (Isa. 65:1; Rom. 10:20). The pagans to whom God was merciful without being obligated to them through his Word were thus a striking refutation of free will.

> These pagans did not have a particular God who would have involved himself with them through a definite word, as was the case with the Jews; instead, strange persons roamed about, and yet these pagans still found God, whereas the Jews do not find the God who has made himself known.[435]

But the Jewish perversion of election does not nullify election itself. The God of the Old Testament is the eternal God himself. He separated, forgave, and punished the people of Israel, spoke to and worked through the patriarchs, kings, and prophets. That was also the major reason for Luther's belief in the Trinity in the Old Testament. What at first could appear as the result of an exegetical method, namely, the Christological-prophetic interpretation,[436] was in reality the expression of Luther's conviction underlying all his exegetical work, that his God is the God of the whole Scripture. What is at stake is not an unessential typological anticipation of a later and higher level of salvation history *(Heilsgeschichte),* but the uncovering of the reality of the whole, and that means triune, God in the Old Testament; a reality which is hidden at first but then visible to the eyes of faith. The exegetical documentation

433 *Table Talk,* 1531, *WA,* TR 2, 369:19 ff. (No. 2219). See also the conclusion above, p. 198.
434 *WA,* TR 2, 396:26 (No. 2271b).
435 *Lectures on Isaiah,* 1527–1530, *WA* 31^II^, 552:34. *On the Bondage of the Will,* 1525, *WA* 18, 775:19 ff.; Packer and Johnston (trans.), *op. cit.,* p. 301.
436 See above, pp. 101–20.

does not prove this conviction; instead, it presupposes it and, Luther was certain, renders it feasible, with linguistic and logical arguments, for every interpreter not so prejudiced as the Jews.

### *c. Christ—the Word of God and the Lord Sabaoth*

The presence of the entire triune God means the presence of the Son. Again: he was not only prophesied in the Old Testament; he was himself present everywhere. The God who turned to us, the Word that created the world and spoke to the patriarchs and to the prophets, is Jesus Christ. He spoke everywhere God's voice sounded in the Old Testament under cover of law or in secret contrast to it, and in the promises believed by only a few. We have already seen what it meant to Luther to have the greatest witnesses of the whole Bible (Moses, David, John, Paul) agree in their faith in the creation of the world through God's Word, that is, through Jesus Christ.[437] In spite of this, Luther showed great reserve in his application of this basic thesis in opposition to Augustine, which extended from his first until his last lecture.[438] Of all the intimate trinitarian problems of Augustine, the only one which remained for Luther was that in the one deity acting here, two person must be distinguished. It is not an accident that it says first, "God created," and then, "God said." God and his eternal Word must be held apart.

It does not say that he made creatures through the Word, but that he spoke the Word. God speaks, and through his speaking creation occurs. This means: God has the Word with himself and this Word created light in the beginning. This Word must be God himself, because he made creatures through this Word; thus the Word is God. This happens because he who speaks and the Word are two persons, yet one God. Although this is incomprehensible, it is still in Scripture; it also urges me to confess the truth because it says, "God spoke." Yet speaking and God are not one and the same thing.[439]

Luther developed his view neither on the basis of the concept of an intermediary, as was the case in the late Jewish and early Greek

[437] See above, pp. 118–19.

[438] On the lectures on Psalms, see Vogelsang, *Die Anfänge von Luthers Christologie*, pp. 165 ff.; *Sermons on Genesis*, 1523–1524, *WA* 14, 100:15 ff. (1527 edition: *WA* 24, 28:31 ff.); *Lectures on Genesis*, 1535, *WA* 42, 15:1; *LW* 1, 18.

[439] *Sermons on Genesis*, 1523–1524, *WA* 14, 100:22 ff. (1527 edition: *WA* 24, 29:7 ff.); *Lectures on Genesis*, 1535, *WA* 42, 14:32 ff.; *LW* 1, 18.

Logos doctrine, nor from the psychology of the divine thought process, as was the case in Augustine, but on the basis of the essence of the natural word, which first rests in the speaker and then comes forth. Thus the Word is one with the speaker in essence, and yet simultaneously separated from him existentially.

On the basis of this relationship of God and his Word, one should not really expect Luther to explain clearly that wherever God spoke in the Old Testament Jesus Christ spoke. That is obvious, and grounded in the unity of the Trinity. When God speaks, it means that he does so through his Word Jesus Christ. If one does not hold fast to this presupposition, one will search in vain for the specific mention of Jesus Christ in the interpretation of the pertinent passages. It required special reasons for Luther to do so. For instance, a question expressing doubt regarding the *Protevangelium* (Gen. 3:15) on the part of Melanchthon gave him an opportunity to do so. The similarity he found between this first and the last speech of Christ (Luke 24:47) strengthened him in his conviction.

> I believe that the Son of God himself spoke in the first prophecy. In the afternoon God spoke to Adam, and it is significant that Christ will assume flesh in the last days. The first speech is similar to Christ's mandate in Luke's last chapter [24:27] about the proclamation of penance and the remission of sins; for it has the same structure.[440]

Thus Christ is not only prophesied there,[441] he himself also speaks. The eternal Word there proclaims his future incarnation.

Thus Christ spoke everywhere in Scripture where there is a report about God's Word addressed to men. But he also spoke *through them.* All the passages in the Psalms or prophets that Luther, in his Christological-prophetic interpretation, put into Christ's mouth[442] were not meant in the same sense as in a play, where a specific person is given invented words to say. Rather, these words were to him, in absolute reality, the words of Christ himself, who spoke spiritually through the psalmists and prophets. For these sections of the Bible did not have a double meaning for him: a finite-historical and a figurative one, looking forward to Christ, but only

[440] *Table Talk* (from various years), *WA,* TR 5, 361:15 ff. (No. 5800). It is entitled, "On Philip Melanchthon's Scruples About the First Prophecy."
[441] See above, p. 101, n. 79.
[442] See above, pp. 96–101.

one. And they have only one speaker: Christ, who makes use of a human mouth and speaks words which the prophet or poet cannot find or understand in a natural way but only "in the Spirit." That is how Luther solved a problem like that found in the psalms of vengeance. There are two types of these: the ones in which the pious pray against their persecutors (such as Psalm 94),[443] and the ones in which Christ curses his enemies. The most striking example is his interpretation of Psalm 109. "David composed this psalm in the Spirit about Christ, who speaks the entire psalm in the first person against Judas, his betrayer, and against Judaism as a whole, proclaiming their ultimate fate."[444] The terrible prayer of vengeance becomes, in the mouth of Christ, a shocking word of judgment on the Jews.[445] Thus the scandal of the psalm of vengeance is also overcome for him. For Christ, who forbade man to curse and who prayed on the cross for his slanderers, pronounces this curse "not for the sake of his person, but for the sake of his office and his Word." He does it in this psalm "entirely for the sake of doctrine." Then faith must curse and call upon God's destructive vengeance, while love tolerates and forgives personal enmity.[446]

Christ is therefore always present in double measure, as it were, in all the Christological prophecies of the Old Testament, as the one who speaks and the one prophesied. But we may not tear the two sides apart, as though the eternal Christ would proclaim the future man Jesus of Nazareth. Instead, on the basis of the inseparability of the two natures, of the "communication of attributes," the whole God-man is everywhere present in the Old Testament. He is not symbolic and sensed in advance; rather, he is there in his own person and imparts himself wherever his promise is believed. The "if you believe, you have" which bears Luther's concept of the reality of God also applies to the Christ of the Old Testament. The passionate realism of this faith, which was of utmost importance to Luther, becomes most evident if one also includes the signs of the old covenant in the process of thought. Luther saw here, too, the same insoluble connection of Word and sign. The

443 *The Four Psalms of Comfort,* 1526, *WA* 19, 582:6; *LW* 14, 243.
444 *Ibid., WA* 19, 545:4; *LW* 14, 257.
445 See above, p. 6 and pp. 75–76.
446 Psalm 94, *The Four Psalms of Comfort,* 1526, *WA* 19, 595:24 ff.; 596:9; 597:2 ff.; *LW* 14, 257–58, 259.

Christ speaking as God's Word is present in the great signs of the grace of God. To clarify this, Luther could easily connect it with Paul's Christological use of these signs, particularly of the rock which provided water for the people of Israel in the wilderness (Exod. 17:6; I Cor. 10:4). "In this way he applies and relates all these figures and signs which have happened to the people of Israel through God's Word, to Christ. For wherever God's Word is, there is Christ."[447] Luther, in this connection, strongly maintained the relation to the coming historical Jesus; he did not just find the eternal divine Christ here.[448] That is why he also gave this passage a meaning that would have to be called allegorical if seen superficially: the solitary rock is the Christ, inconspicuous to the eyes of men; the wonderful water is the Spirit of God; the staff of Moses is the office of preaching.[449] But this is more than simple allegory or symbolic interpretation, as we distinguished allegorical and spiritual interpretation above.[450] Christ encounters the Jew spiritually-actually in this rock. For where faith in God's Word is alive, God is present for us; but that means Christ is present. That is why Luther explicitly drew the parallel between this passage and the words of the eucharist.[451] The exegetical rule which he used against

447 *Sermon on Septuagesima Sunday on I Cor. 9:24 ff., Lenten Postil,* 1525, *WA* $17^{II}$, 132:32; *LE* 3, 100. See also *On the Last Words of David,* 1543, *WA* 54, 66:28 ff.

448 At that time he still supported it through his translation of I Cor. 10:4, ". . . the rock following" (*Felsen der hernach kam*). *Lenten Postil,* 1525, *WA* $17^{II}$, 134:2; *LE* 3, 101. After the Bible edition of 1527, he gave it up: "... the rock that accompanied" (*der mitfolgte*). *The German Bible, WA,* DB 7, 112.

449 *Lenten Postil,* 1525, *WA* $17^{II}$, 135:7 ff.; *LE* 3, 103.

450 See above, pp. 88–91.

451 *Lenten Postil,* 1525, *WA* $17^{II}$, 134:10 ff.; *LE* 3, 102. This parallel helps clarify the relationship between symbol and reality in Luther's concept of the Lord's Supper. He sharply distinguished here, on the basis of the Pauline text (I Cor. 11:23 ff.), between the "bodily" and the "spiritual." The faith of the Jews was directed only to the "spiritual rock," that is, to the spiritually present Christ; and it was directly watered by him (*ibid., WA* $17^{II}$, 132:3; *LE* 3, 99). Luther, for the sake of the reality of the event, sharply rejected the merely symbolic interpretation of the rock in terms of Christ. Yet, in addition, the "bodily rock" is, according to the allegorical method developed above, a sign pointing to the coming Christ. The relationship between symbol and reality in Luther's concept of the Lord's Supper is exactly the same: the elements can be symbols of the spiritual, as Luther developed it especially in his sermons of 1519. But the spiritual reception of the Christ present in faith is an actual event, just as the nourishment of the Jews through Christ was an actual event. It is only complicated in the Lord's Supper by the fact that Christ is not only present spiritually—just as he is in the sign of the rock—but is simultaneously (because of the "communication of properties" [*communicatio idiomatum*]) present bodily in bread and wine. And yet the receiving faith is directed only to his spiritual presence, while the receiving mouth enjoys his bodily presence.

Zwingli for the Words of Institution also find their application to the understanding of the presence of Christ in the Old Testament signs.

This real presence of Christ in Word and sign, as well as in the whole history of the Old Testament, is crowned by the fact that Luther considered him completely unified with the acting God and named him by name. One cannot summarize the concrete points of this more impressively and at the same time express the passion of this faith more strongly than he did himself.

> Thus it follows powerfully and irrefutably that the God who led the people of Israel out of Egypt and through the Red Sea, who guided them in the wilderness through the pillars of cloud and fire, who nourished them with heavenly bread, and who performed all the miracles Moses describes in his book, who also brought them into the land of Canaan and then gave them kings and priests and everything is therefore God and no other than Jesus of Nazareth, the Son of the Virgin Mary, whom we call Christ our God and Lord.... Again, it is he who gives Moses the Ten Commandments on Mount Sinai, saying, "I, the Lord, am your God who led you out of Egypt; you shall have no other gods." Yes, Jesus of Nazareth, who died for us on the cross, is the God who says in the First Commandment, "I, the Lord, am your God." If the Jews and Muhammadans heard this, how they would rage! And yet it is true and must remain true eternally, and he who does not believe it should forever tremble and burn.[452]

This axiom, which precedes all other Christological pronouncements and which Luther here hurled out with concentrated power, extends so far that, next to it, his otherwise critical regard for the difference between Father and Son could give the impression of being a sign of theological correctness. He did not wish to criticize explicitly that one prays to Christ with the name "Father." "Nevertheless it is better if one keeps the order of persons and does not scorn it, as the apostles keep it, and as, following their example, the church does, since they name the person of the Father when invoking him or praying, as in the Lord's Prayer."[453] The unity of the trinitarian God here seems to make the differences of the persons unessential. And yet it would be false to argue this way. Luther would not think of giving them up. His whole Christological exegesis of the

[452] *On the Last Words of David,* 1543, *WA* 54, 67:1 ff.
[453] *Ibid.,* 69:17.

Old Testament was based on them; for it was certainly one of his noblest methods of proving Christ as second person next to the Father on the basis of the repetition of God's name or similar indications. Thus he found his name secretly added in innumerable passages, and acting in the Old Testament.[454] And at the same time the distinguishing of the persons was to him the given and necessary expression for the true humanity of the God become flesh.

One must therefore always add his thought of this separation of persons when one sees how Luther applied the Old Testament concepts of God to Christ. Unity and difference are insolubly and excitingly tied together in the paradox in which he saw the agreement between Moses and the New Testament "that Jesus Christ is Jehovah, God and man."[455] That is why he also defended, in a disputation in 1545, Christ's right to the name Jehovah.

> Jehovah joins Christ, just like the Word. The Word becomes flesh [John 1:19]. The Word is Jehovah, and Jehovah is the Word. What can be reduced to the Word, can be reduced to Jehovah. It is rightly said: the Word becomes flesh, and Jehovah becomes flesh. When, therefore, Jehovah signifies in Christ nothing but the being which is eternal, eternity itself becomes reality in the flesh. Consequently we debate according to grammatical rules.[456]

And he gave him the name of the Lord Sabaoth as well.[457] But, in any event, this happened less often than one would expect from the turn taken in "A Mighty Fortress," through which this title has become the popular expression of the unity of Father and Son.[458] Not without justification, as far as "subject matter" is concerned,

454 For example, on Exod. 34:8 ff., see *ibid.*, 84:10. See also above, pp. 102–03.
455 *On the Last Words of David,* 1543, *WA* 54, 79:29.
456 *Theses for the Licentiate Examination of Peter Hegemon,* 1545 *(Promotionsthesen zur Disputation von Petrus Hegemon), WA* 39II, 374:5 ff. What is important here is the mediating significance of the concept of the Word.
457 On Ps. 24:10, *Lectures on the First Twenty-five Psalms,* 1530, *WA* 31I, 373:26. In Isa. 54:5, Christ, the Lord Sabaoth, appears as the husband of the lonely, barren wife. "See the consolation for our barrenness, because we shall have a bridegroom who is able to propagate himself. This, however, happens through the Word. Thus our God, who was once called the God of Abraham, Isaac, and Jacob, is now called the Lord of all the lands of the earth." *Lectures on Isaiah,* 1527–1530, *WA* 31II, 444:20. See also *The Prophet Zechariah,* 1527, *WA* 23, 53:14 ff. Further material in Theodor Knolle, "Hebräische Heils-namen in Luthers Liedern," *Lutherjahrbuch,* XXII (1940), 64 ff.
458 The fact that Luther himself quoted the stanza of the hymn in the *Lectures on Genesis,* 1535–1545 (*WA* 43, 463:7; *LW* 5, 50)—Friedrich Loofs, *Leitfaden zum Studium der Dogmengeschichte* (4th ed.; Halle/Saale, 1906), pp. 724, 762, uses it—is probably due to the work of his editors. This is also the opinion of Meinhold, *op. cit.*, p. 153.

for this unity of Redeemer and Creator was the foundation of Luther's Christology. In the lectures on the Psalms (1513–1515) the application of the name Sabaoth to Christ is still the rule, in so far as the psalm can in any way be understood as a prayer to Christ and not, as in Psalm 69, a prayer of Christ. Here the "hosts" are the angels, sometimes broadened to include the spiritual powers of the church.[459] While Luther here generally understood Sabaoth as a name for the Creator, he later occasionally applied the "hosts" to the Christian people. "Scripture calls Christ the 'Lord of hosts' because his Christian people continuously wage war with the gospel. . . . The kings of these hosts are the apostles."[460]

Even though the name Lord Sabaoth for Christ occurred less frequently now in Luther than in his early days, it nevertheless remained the pertinent expression for his idea that there is no God outside of Christ. His Christology reached its apex in this equation. Thus, in the most comprehensive and most real sense, Christ is the sole true content of the whole Scripture. He is not only the focal point in whom all lines would one day meet. "He is the little point at the center of the circle, and all the stories in Holy Scripture, if viewed aright, point to Christ."[461] "Christ is the center of Holy Scripture."[462] He is the real center of Scripture, the promising Word of God and the promised earthly figure of the Word. Luther's well-known sentence, "Take Christ out of Scripture and what will be left to find there?"[463] was valid in a substantial sense. Christ is the substance of Scripture.

Naturally the person of Christ is not thereby evaporated into

[459] Ps. 46:8 in *Lectures on the Psalter,* 1513–1516; *WA* 3, 266:5; Ps. 48:9, *ibid.,* 269:14; Ps. 80:5 ff., *ibid.,* 604:4 ff. (Christ appears also in the role of the Son of Man, *ibid.,* 605:20); Ps. 84:2, *ibid.,* 640:4; Ps. 89:9, *WA* 4, 38:3. See also Ps. 68:12 (where Luther still had the Vulgate text before him, "king" [*rex*]; but see, on the other hand, the note in *WA* 3, 386:12; 394:1 ff.). The application of Isa. 6:3 to Christ (*ibid.,* 453:29), pointed out by Vogelsang (*Die Anfänge von Luthers Christologie,* p. 162, n. 3), had become apparent to Luther on the basis of John 12:41 already. That is perhaps the reason for the fact (mentioned above, p. 94, n. 55) that Luther added an elaborate allegory to his interpretation of this chapter and no other in his *Lectures on Isaiah,* 1527–1530, *WA* 31$^{II}$, 53.

[460] On Ps. 68:12, *German Exposition of Psalm 68,* 1521, *WA* 8, 13:25; *LW* 13, 13.

[461] *Sermons on John 3 and 4,* 1538–1540, *WA* 47, 66:23; *LW* 22, 339.

[462] *Table Talk,* 1532, *WA,* TR 2, 439:25 (No. 2383). See also *WA,* TR 1, 489:35 ff. (No. 967).

[463] *On the Bondage of the Will,* 1525, *WA* 18, 606:29; Packer and Johnston, *op. cit.,* p. 71.

the mythical sphere, and his true historicity is not annulled. As much as Luther used the natural word as parable for the relationship of the Son to the Father and his working in the world, he nevertheless at the same time emphasized the particularity of the biblical concept of the Word: it is substantive and personal.

> This is a new manner of speech, which has not been heard before in the world. Christ is not a mathematical or physical word, but the divine Word and uncreated; this means substance and person, because the divine Word is divinity itself. Christ is the divine Word. Therefore he is divinity, that is, substance and person itself.[464]

The indissoluble connection of Word and person in Luther's Christology protected it from degenerating in two directions: from a spiritualistic dissolution as well as from a view of Christ as a kind of semi-divine mediating being. The Christ of the Old Testament is by no means just another form of the Holy Spirit; but from the very beginning he is already bound to his future earthly body. And the historical Christ is not a finite hero, but eternally one with the Father, like the Word is with the Spirit who speaks it. The connecting of Old and New Testament in Luther helps to avoid the one-sided dissolution of this balanced relationship in his Christology. The unity of Moses and John, which Luther so emphatically asserted,[465] the unity of the Word of creation and the Word become flesh gives the figure of Christ its infinite divinity. And the historical person of Jesus gives to the revelatory action of God in the Old Testament a direction to a goal in time and thus its true historicity.

### *d. The Church of the Old and the New Testaments*

"Where the Word is, there is the church."[466] If the Word of God, that is, Christ himself, has from the beginning of the world shown men the way to God and has tried to keep them on this road through commandment and warning, consolation and promise,

[464] Theses for the disputation on the divinity and humanity of Christ, *Theological Disputation,* 1540 *(Disputatio theologica), WA* 39$^{II}$, 103:5.
[465] *Sermon of December 27, 1524, on John 1:1 ff., Sermons of 1524, WA* 15, 800:20 ff.; see also the edition in *Feast Postil,* 1527 (*Festpostille*), *WA* 17$^{II}$, 316:26 ff.; *On the Last Words of David,* 1543, *WA* 54, 55:18 ff.
[466] Thesis 24 of *The Licentiate Examination of John Machabeus Scotus,* 1542 (*Promotionsdisputation von Johannes Machabäus Scotus*), *WA* 39$^{II}$, 176:8. See also *On the Councils and the Church,* 1539, *WA* 50, 629:28 ff.; 631:27; *LW* 41, 150, 152; *Lectures on Genesis,* 1537, *WA* 42, 424:5; *LW* 2, 229.

then there has always been a congregation to listen to it. Even if it was ever so small and hidden, it was never completely lacking. For to the Word of God belongs the promise, which Luther loved so much and which he mentioned countless times from the beginning to the end of his life,[467] "The Word which goes forth from my mouth ... shall not return to me empty" (Isa. 55:11). To Luther, therefore, there had existed a unified church from paradise and it would exist until Judgment Day.

This church is not only evidenced in the secret hints of the coming congregation of Christ which Luther gathered from the Old Testament texts with the help of allegorical interpretation. We have already seen[468] that after he had overcome the excessive use of allegory following his first lectures, he still used it often enough. He used it for the church too. For example, the ark of Noah, with its one door (Gen. 6:16), can be applied to the body of Christ, the church, into which the pure and the impure enter through the depths.[469] One could also relate the ark to the actual body of Christ and the windows to the wound in his side. "These allegories, if not actually scholarly, are nevertheless harmless, inasmuch as they contain no error; and one may use them for the sake of embellishment, except in debates."[470] The sacrificial altar of Adam, the temple, and the ark of the covenant are indications that God desires to be honored in a specific place for the Christian faith incarnate in Christ.[471] And there are many other "figures" for the coming church in the Old Testament.[472]

But Luther meant not only allegorical hints but a direct reality when he found the church everywhere in the Old Testament already. That is the only issue here. The uninterrupted continuity through the centuries down to his day, which he saw and repeatedly documented, was a source of consolation in the soul conflict

467 *Lectures on the Psalter*, 1513–1516, *WA* 3, 259:15; *To the Saxon Princes*, 1545 (*Dem Kurfürsten zu Sachsen, und Landgraven zu Hessen, von dem gefangen H. zu Brunswig*), *WA* 54, 405:7; *LW* 43, 280.
468 See above, pp. 94–95.
469 *Lectures on Genesis*, 1536, *WA* 42, 310:8 ff.; *LW* 2, 68 ff.
470 *Ibid.*, *WA* 42, 310:13; *LW* 2, 68.
471 *Lectures on the Fifteen Gradual Psalms*, 1532–1533, *WA* 40^III, 405:6 ff.
472 Numerous comparisons and typological applications to the true and false worship of God are found in the glosses to the translation of the Bible; they are conveniently arranged in Knolle, *Luthers Glossen zum Alten Testament*, pp. 41 ff.

*(Anfechtung)* his work brought him. Although the mightiest kings, pharaohs, Sennacherib, and many others tried to exterminate the church, it "maintained itself time and again down to our own time, even though it was a small and weak little crowd compared to the mass and power of the world," he wrote in a copy of the Bible.[473] It has to wage and to survive an uninterrupted struggle against heresies of all kinds, against Canaanites and Esauites, false prophets and apostles, and now against the false teachers of the Roman church.[474] Thus the history of the church is the history of one trouble after another; and so Luther portrayed this emphatically in a sermon on the storm at sea (Matt. 8:23 ff.), which he preached in Eisleben shortly before his death.[475] The history of the church is also the history of constantly new and miraculous help from God; this was verified for Luther in the beginning of Psalm 90.[476] God's goodness has imparted itself to the church from generation to generation, and it has greatly preserved his punishing and promising Word.

> Beginning with Adam there is, and was continued, one church of God, in which God has made himself known through his tremendous goodness, and in which was always heard, and had to be heard, the voice of God proving the sins of mankind and promising the remission of sins because of the promised Son and the restitution of eternal life.[477]

Luther often listed the series of patriarchs, kings, and prophets who were bearers of the divine Word in the church in the old covenant.[478] His lectures on Genesis gave him the opportunity to elaborate upon this in a broad context; it virtually became to him an *Old Testament church history.* The church was founded when God first gave man a commandment: at the tree of paradise. It is

473 See Aurifaber's *Interpretation of Some Sayings of Consolation Which the Reverend Doctor Martin Luther Wrote in the Bibles and Postils of Many Good Lords and Friends,* 1547 *(Auslegung etzlicher Trostsprüche, so der Ehrwirdigt Herr, Doctor Martinus Luther, jinn seiner libben Herrn, und guten Freunden Bibeln und Postillen, mit eigener hand geschrieben), WA* 48, 84:5 ff.
474 *Lectures on the Fifteen Gradual Psalms,* 1532–1533, *WA* 40$^{III}$, 391:3.
475 *Sermon of January 31, 1546, on Matt. 8:23 ff., Sermons of 1546, WA* 51, 153:39 ff.
476 *Lecture on Psalm 90,* 1534–1535, *WA* 40$^{III}$, 504:11 ff.; *LW* 13, 88 ff. See also *Table Talk,* 1540, *WA,* TR 5, 23:27 ff. (No. 5242).
477 *The Licentiate Examination of John Marbach,* February 16, 1543 *(Promotionsdisputation von Johann Marbach), WA* 39$^{II}$, 206:4. See also Thesis 20 of *The Licentiate Examination of Heinrich Schmedenstede,* 1542, *WA* 39$^{II}$, 188: 26 ff.; *LW* 34, 304.
478 See, for example, the sermon and *Table Talk* cited in nn. 475 and 476 above.

therefore older and more important than family and state. God therewith announces that man is called to something higher than the other living beings.[479] "Thus the church was established first, because God wants to show by this sign that man was created for another purpose than the rest of the living beings."[480] If man had obeyed the commandment, this concise Word of God would have been his Bible. He would have had no need for another.[481] Just as the tree itself was the "church," that is, the place where Adam and Eve were to offer their praise,[482] so they continued to do after the Fall. Adam practiced his priestly office and offered his sacrifice by a tree or on a hill, and always proclaimed God's Word there, as did the later patriarchs.[483] Cain's fratricide then split the first pious congregation and created two churches: a hypocritical, bloodstained one which suppressed the other, the true and pure one.[484] Although Luther appealed to Augustine's famous interpretation of the Cain and Abel history to prove this, in reality he made something else out of it. Whereas Augustine saw Cain as the founder of the "earthly city,"[485] Luther traced the "hypocritical church" back to him; one can see the respective opponents against whom they were fighting. Undoubtedly Cain and his descendants are also in possession of political power and therewith suppress, like Duke George, whom he compared to Cain, the church of Christ.[486] In Cain is demonstrated a

479 *Lectures on Genesis,* 1536, *WA* 42, 79:3 ff.; 87:7, 11; *LW* 1, 104, 114–15.
480 *Ibid., WA* 42, 79:21; *LW* 1, 104.
481 *Ibid., WA* 42, 80:3; *LW* 1, 105.
482 *Ibid., WA* 42, 80:19; *LW* 1, 105.
483 *Ibid., WA* 42, 210:3; 183:34, 44; 635:4 ff.; *LW* 1, 284, 247.
484 *Ibid., WA* 42, 187:13 ff.; *LW* 1, 252.
485 *The City of God (De civitate Dei),* XV, 5, II, *MPL* 41, 441; *PNF*1 2, 286–87.
486 *Table Talk,* 1533, *WA,* TR 3, 151:12 ff. (No. 3038b); 4 (1539), 419:14 ff. (No. 4654) (in a series of other Cainite tyrants). At the news of Duke George's death in 1539, Luther remarked, "How could we pray for him? If we did, we would have to pray against Christ himself. He who wants to pray for Abel cannot pray for Cain." *WA,* TR 4 (1539), 365:12 ff. (No. 4532). Angry about Duke Moritz's behavior in the battles for the monastic property in Wurz *(Wurzener Stiftsfehde)* of 1542, Luther also used the invective name for him and for the "glittering bloodhounds of Meissen" in general. Letter to Nicholas Amsdorf, April 13, 1542, *WA,* BR 10, 48. Cain was to Luther the prototype of all enemies of justice and peace: "Every Abel has his Cain," *Table Talk* (from various years), *WA,* TR 5, 383:26 (No. 5860); "Cain kills Abel without end," Preface to *Lectures on Galatians,* 1531, *WA* 40I, 34:42; about Phocas, who killed the emperor, "this pious Cain," *On the Councils and the Church,* 1539, *WA* 50, 578:17; *LW* 41, 90.

little of God's law in history, that the godless outwardly appear as the blessed.

God wants the church to be in such a condition in this world that the curse of the ungodly appears to be transferred to it, and that, in contrast, the ungodly should appear to be blessed. Cain, therefore, built the city of Enoch while Seth was dwelling in tents.... Although the godly are oppressed in this world, they are nevertheless most certainly the heirs and sons of God. The ungodly, on the other hand, even though they flourish for a time, are nevertheless finally cut off and wither, as the psalms often declare [Ps. 94:3].[487]

But to Luther this possession of power alone was not the essential aspect. When Cain, cursed by God through the mouth of Adam and excommunicated from his congregation,[488] founded a city, he did it to gather a church there too.[489] It is a church of heretics,[490] more precisely, of works-righteous people. In the *Wartburg Postil* (1522) Luther pointedly and in detail described the Roman church, with its monasticism, fasting, mass, ceremonies, etc., as the church of the "Cainite saints."[491] For it was inconceivable to his

[487] *Lectures on Genesis,* 1535–1536, *WA* 42, 389:2, 9; *LW* 2, 180.
[488] *Ibid., WA* 42, 210:10; 214:35, 41; 217:13 ff.; 220:15; *LW* 1, 284, 290–91, 294, 298–99. God and Adam are mixed peculiarly as the persons who utter the curse (Gen. 4:9 ff.) in the lectures on Genesis. The explanation for this was obviously Luther's conviction—evident in some *Table Talk, WA,* TR 1 (1530), 313:1 ff. (No. 663); *LW* 54, 121 (No. 663); *WA,* TR 1 (1530), 336:31 ff. (No. 690); 2 (1531), 368:17 ff. (No. 2215); 3 (1533), 135:25 ff. (No. 2994)—that Adam himself talked to his son on God's orders, just as the prophets pronounced God's messages. Luther imagined what the conversation was like in *Table Talk* No. 663.
[489] *Lectures on Genesis,* 1535–1536, *WA* 42, 232:7; *LW* 1, 314.
[490] *Lectures on the Fifteen Gradual Psalms,* 1532–1533, *WA* 40$^{III}$, 36:4; 391:3; *Table Talk,* 1532, *WA,* TR 1, 121:19 (No. 291); *LW* 54, 40–41 (No. 291).
[491] *Sermon on the First Sunday after Christmas on Gal. 4:1 ff., Church Postil,* 1522, *WA* 10$^{I,1}$, 326:16; 327:5; 330:10, 21; 331:17; 332:19; 334:15, 19; 343:7 ff.; 368:8; 374:3; *LE* 1, 225–26, 228 ff., 244, 258, 261–62. Protestant Spiritualism, in which the opposition between the churches of Cain and Abel became a favorite theme, reversed the accusation later and ascribed to it, in a distortion of the doctrine of justification, an open rejection of good works. Thus Jacob Böhme, for example, wrote in his mystical interpretation of Genesis, *The Great Mystery (Mysterium Magnum),* chaps. 27–28, especially 27:58, "The Cainite church was never more powerful on earth than just now, when the great cry is heard, 'Come ye all. We have found the sacrifice of Abel in Christ!' Yes, dear Babylon, you certainly have found the coat of Christ. But only look at your Cainite heart, and you will see whether you sacrifice with Abel as a new creature or with the false spirit of fratricide. Where are your fruits? ... Prove then your Christian virtues. . . . Your mouth only gossips about the sacrifice, just as Cain's mouth only gossiped about the sacrifice. Yet his heart was a murderer." Will-Erich Peuckert (ed.), *Jakob Böhme's sämtliche Schriften* (reprint of 1730 ed.; 11 vols.; Stuttgart, 1955), VII, 226–27. The Cain

pious mind that Cain could have presented himself as godless; he was undoubtedly, as far as appearance was concerned, "a seemingly excellent world saint."[492] Therefore the slavish spirit of the law was to him a "Cainite spirit."[493] Then after Seth, the bearer of the promise,[494] and his son Enosh were born, Adam exercised his office as priest of his small church in a larger circle, and began to preach publicly (Gen. 4:26).[495] Among Adam's descendants it was the pious Enosh who above all served the church of Christ. Luther had much to tell about his preaching,[496] but even more about the mighty prophet Noah, whose sermon of repentance and exact prediction of the Flood—Luther again put the words of God into his mouth (Gen. 6:13)[497]—could qualify him for the name of the "second Adam and prince of the human race."

> But this prophecy of Noah surpasses all the others, because through the Holy Spirit he predicts a definite number of years when the entire human race will perish. He is worthy of being called the second Adam and prince of the human race, through whose mouth God speaks and calls the entire world to repentance.[498]

The church has been preserved in Noah and his family,[499] and he continued to exercise the inherited priestly episcopal office in it.[500] God's blessing continued through him and his sons down to their descendants, not only to the Semites but also through Paul to the Japhethites, among whom Luther, according to the interpretation of the table of nations, classified the Germans.[501] With Abraham,

---

motif had already been used by Paracelsus. See Karl Sudhoff, *Versuch einer Kritik der Echtheit der Paracelsischen Schriften* (2 vols.; Berlin, 1894–1899), II, 335.

492 *Table Talk,* 1532, *WA,* TR 3, 233:30 ff. (No. 3248). See also *ibid.,* 2 (1532), 257:19 ff. (No. 1904), and the *Sermon on the Second Sunday after Trinity on I John 3:13 ff., Summer Postil,* 1528 (*Sommerpostille*), *WA* 22, 10:3 ff.: "... he is the father of all hypocrites and false saints." See also Knolle, *Luthers Glossen zum Alten Testament,* p. 64.

493 *Sermon on the First Sunday after Christmas on Gal. 4:1 ff., Church Postil,* 1522, *WA* 10$^{I,1}$, 361:19; *LE* 1, 252.

494 *Lectures on Genesis,* 1536, *WA* 42, 239:15; *LW* 1, 324.

495 *Ibid., WA* 42, 241:5, 12 ff.; *LW* 1, 327.

496 *Ibid., WA* 42, 253:15 ff.; *LW* 1, 344–45.

497 See above, p. 211, n. 488.

498 *Lectures on Genesis,* 1536, *WA* 42, 280:13; *LW* 2, 26. On Luther's view of Noah, see also E. Seeberg, *op. cit.,* p. 39.

499 *Lectures on Genesis,* 1537, *WA* 42, 334:15; *LW* 2, 101.

500 *Ibid., WA* 42, 342:17 ff.; 378:5; *LW* 2, 112–13, 165.

501 *Ibid., WA* 42, 392:22; 393:16; *LW* 2, 184–85. Luther followed the Jewish interpretation, according to which Japheth's son Ashkenaz represents the Germans—the Goths, according to Eusebius (*WA* 42, 396:5; *LW* 2, 190). Since

God's tool tempered in temptation and proven in faith, God once again visibly separated his church from the pagans;[502] he strengthened and consoled it with his promise and his help, especially through the victory over the hostile kings (Genesis 14).[503] Abraham and his family and household were at that time the sole true congregation and therefore at the same time a prophecy of the coming church.[504] Abraham publicly preached God's Word in his simple temple at an altar under an oak, or in a tent on a hill.[505] That is why God made an eternal covenant with him, which not even Christ nullified; by abolishing circumcision, Christ only changed the sign of the covenant.[506] But the misfortune of a schism in the church was repeated in Abraham's family. While the true people of God is the only one that has the promise, under Ishmael as well as under Cain an embryonic church was formed from which the true church has to suffer much persecution.[507] "There is no people of God unless it has the promises and believes them."[508] It is true that Ishmael, the father of the Arabs, was a pious man and "great theologian";[509] but the decree through which the promise was denied him was stronger than he; of necessity his church became a church of superstition and of struggle against the true congregation.[510] Thus Ishmael became the first example of predestination. Luther made his sympathy for him quite obvious and hoped that he as well as many of his descendants had nevertheless been converted.[511] Isaac, on the other hand, the bearer of the promise, built a little wooden chapel under a tree and preached there about the mysteries of the Trinity, of the incarnation of Christ, of immortality, etc.[512] He converted Abimelech with his

---

he also appealed elsewhere to his descent from Noah and Japheth (*On the Jews and Their Lies,* 1543, *WA* 53, 426), this deduction cannot be ascribed to the editors of *Lectures on Genesis.*

502 *Lectures on Genesis,* 1537, *WA* 42, 430:18; *LW* 2, 236.

503 *Ibid., WA* 42, 542:5; *LW* 2, 389.

504 *Ibid., WA* 42, 446:29 ff.; 462:7; 653:11; 451:18; *LW* 2, 259, 280, 265; *LW* 3, 147.

505 *Ibid., WA* 42, 499:21 ff.; 500:18 ff.; *LW* 2, 382, 333.

506 *Ibid., WA* 42, 630:23 ff.; 631:3; *LW* 3, 116.

507 *Ibid., WA* 43, 159:10; 160:8, 16; *LW* 3, 34.

508 *Ibid., WA* 43, 158:21.

509 *Ibid., WA* 43, 371:40 ff.; *LW* 3, 327.

510 *Ibid., WA* 43, 372:24 ff.; *LW* 4, 328.

511 *Ibid., WA* 43, 165:34; 184:33; 372:11 ff.; *LW* 3, 42, 69, 327–28.

512 *Ibid., WA* 43, 483:8 ff., 16 ff.

preaching and made of him a defender of the church.[513] While he had to imagine the sermons of Noah or Isaac, Luther with both hands seized the opportunity presented to him when, as in the case of Jacob, he had the actual words of the patriarch. Thus he formulated a long exposition on the theme "Where God speaks, there is the church" out of the words Jacob spoke after his dream (Gen. 28:16 ff.).[514] And Jacob's commandment to his people to renounce idols (Gen. 35:2) was to him an extensive sermon about the reformation of the church.[515] The obedient and faithful congregation of the patriarch obeyed its bishop and teacher and separated itself from its idols.[516] Joseph, the beloved son, guided by God, took over the priestly office of proclamation from his father. He undoubtedly exercised it in his servitude too,[517] brought rich blessing upon Potiphar's household,[518] and preached his brothers a sermon about the wisdom of God, which Luther again described elaborately.[519] Nevertheless, God turned the main blessing, the promise directed toward Christ, not toward Joseph but toward Judah, a sign that we attain salvation out of grace, not out of merit.[520] A small line branched off from this main line of promise: from Nahor, who led his church like his brother Abraham, or from Esau, it led to Job, who partook of grace as a non-Jew.[521]

The faith of the patriarchs had become the faith of the people. We can therefore differentiate between *the church of the patriarchs,* the first part of Old Testament church history which Luther described with special breadth in his interpretation of Genesis, and the second part, *the church of the people.* The latter is the time between Moses and Solomon. Within this period the church was a people. The great memories of Jewish folk history, exodus from Egypt, Red Sea, the help of God in the wilderness, were signs on the road pointing to the church of the Jews.[522] We have already spoken of Moses and David as proclaimers of law and gospel in

513 *Ibid.,* 486:15.
514 *Ibid.,* 597:13–14.
515 *Ibid., WA* 44, 168:4—176:6.
516 *Ibid.,* 176:10; 237:25.
517 *Ibid.,* 342:27 ff.; 343:3 ff.
518 *Ibid.,* 344:19 ff.; 352:15 ff.
519 *Ibid.,* 599:34; 600:1—612:18.
520 *Ibid.,* 750:26.
521 *Ibid.,* 288:27 ff.
522 *Table Talk,* 1538, *WA,* TR 3, 665:16 ff. (No. 3862).

enough detail not to have to repeat here their significance for the Old Testament church. People and church once again separate in the later period of kings. The third part, *the church of the prophets,* was entirely a history of the hidden church. A chain of battle and rescue, contrary to external appearance, stretched from Elijah, who at times completely lost sight of the wretched church and thought he alone had remained true to God, whereas the Lord had rescued seven thousand believers (I Kings 19:10, 18),[523] to the writing prophets.[524] The moving temptation *(Anfechtung)* of the prophets was the seal for this.[525] God's Word never became entirely silent; there was always a small congregation.[526] It goes on in this way down to the days of the fateful turning point of the Jewish people when once again, as at the time of Elijah, one man alone—and yet, as a man of God, not really alone—stood up against the people and its leaders: John the Baptist, the "highest preacher." "It means not one man, but a man of God. Heroes are not one man."[527] But God, in his wrath against the unbelieving people, allowed him, like Jesus, to exercise his office for only a short time; and then he executed his judgment upon Israel.[528]

He introduced the gospel into all the world, confusing all the wise and those in power. And he said, "I will bring it to an end." That is why these two men exercised their office in the world in such a short time. Other prophets, bishops, and martyrs did not do it in such a short time. These, however, are the highest; thus they [preached] the shortest time.[529]

523 *Lecture on Psalm 90,* 1534–1535, *WA* 40$^{III}$, 505:2; *LW* 13, 89; *On the Bondage of the Will,* 1525, *WA* 18, 650:13 ff.; Packer and Johnston, *op. cit.,* p. 120. God often enough preserved the church through one person. For example, "It is wonderful how God preserves the universal church and the gospel itself through one person, Paul." *Lectures on Galatians,* 1531, *WA* 40$^{I}$, 203:6; *LW* 26, 113. See also *Table Talk,* 1540, *WA,* TR 5, 23:27 ff. (No. 5242).
524 *Lectures on Genesis,* 1537, *WA* 42, 423:18 ff.; *LW* 2, 228 ff.
525 See above, pp. 26–33.
526 Although Luther related the prophecies about the holy seed and remnant in his exegesis mostly to the future Christian church (on Hos. 2:23, see *Lectures on the Minor Prophets,* 1524, *WA* 13, 13:3 ff.; on Isa. 6:13, see *Lectures on Isaiah,* 1527–1530, *WA* 31$^{II}$, 52:36 ff.), he also used them for the Old Testament period. See *On the Bondage of the Will,* 1525, *WA* 18, 650:29; Packer and Johnston, *op. cit.,* p. 120; *Lectures on Genesis,* 1537, *WA* 42, 424:11; *LW* 2, 229; gloss to Hos. 2:22–23, Knolle, *Luthers Glossen zum Alten Testament,* p. 61.
527 *Table Talk, WA,* TR 4 (1538), 128:9–10 (No. 4087); 5 (from various years) 571:18 ff. (No. 6279).
528 *Sermon of June 24, 1534, Sermons of 1534, WA* 37, 464:3 ff.
529 *Ibid.,* 464:12.

The new church grew out of this; whatever preceded it was mere child's play.

The significant aspect of Luther's view of the Old Testament church history was that the Jewish cultic community was not the prototype of the Christian church. He did not make great efforts to uncover agreements and typological connections between the two, as the exegesis of the early church had done. Above all he repudiated, together with the concept of priesthood in general, the conviction, held by the Catholic church to this day, that the Old Testament priesthood has been continued in the Christian church. "Here He casts down the outward and bodily priesthood, which had existed before in the Old Testament, as well as the outward church—all this he casts away."[530] Luther even mentioned that the church fathers would never have used the word "priest" for the servants of the Word if it had not already been used parabolically in the New Testament.

The name "priests" [*sacerdotes*] began to be applied to our rulers quite early, taken from Hebrews 5 [:1], where it is written, "every priest taken from among men," etc. This is said of the Old Testament and is applied by way of analogy to the New Testament. If the good fathers had been compelled to write about this, they would probably have found some other name in accord with Scripture rather than wickedly defending the name they used.[531]

And he emphasized sharply, against the Roman viewpoint, how often God's Word, in the mouth of the prophets, attacked the authority of the old priesthood.[532] Luther found it expressed by God himself in Mal. 2:7 that not everyone who is consecrated is a priest, but rather only he who is the messenger of God, whose "lips preserve the doctrine that one should seek the law from his mouth"; and he thus defended himself strongly against the Roman concept

[530] On I Pet. 2:5, *St. Peter's Epistles, Preached and Interpreted,* 1523, *WA* 12, 306:26; *LE* 3, 91. See also *Propositions Concerning the Abrogation of the Private Mass,* 1521 (*De abroganda missa Privata Sententia*), *WA* 8, 415:15 ff. The priests of the Old Testament are allegorically also related only to the Christians. See the passage quoted below, p. 218.

[531] *Answer to the Super-Christian, Super-Spiritual, and Super-Learned Book of the Goat Emser at Leipzig; with a Side Glance at His Comrade Murner,* 1521 (*Auf das ubir christilich ubir geystlich und ubirkunstlich buch Bocks Emszers zu Leypczick Antwortt, Darynn auch Murnarrs zeynsz gesellen gedacht wirt*), *WA* 7, 633:34; *PE* 3, 327.

[532] *Ibid., WA* 7, 663:20 ff.; *PE* 3, 367. See also above, pp. 28–29.

of priesthood.[533] It is true that for him, too, the original, genuine cultic institutions of Israel had been instituted by God. During the time in which the people walked in the ways of God, the tabernacle was "like a parish church or religious foundation, where the people of Israel should come and hear God's Word so that they would not, according to their own religious desires, run here and there, on mountains, into fields and other places, to sacrifice to God."[534] At first true worship, as God had ordained for the time of law and of sacrifice, was performed here, and later in the temple.

Here you see that He does not want to have independent and self-chosen worship outside his instituted worship.[535]

In the synagogue there existed that which was celebrated first with distinction: the legitimate priesthood of Aaron, instituted by God [Exod. 28:1 ff.].[536]

So now we say that all true Christian believers are true priests in the Christian congregation, as the Levitical priests were in the synagogue. The bishops and the canons are priests of Beth-Aven. The old monks and hermits are priests of the high places. But the new monks and mendicant orders are Baalites. Molech is the universities.[537]

But to the extent that they were misused for self-aggrandizement of the Jewish people rather than for real worship of God, the split between their hypocritical piety and the faith of the hidden church became greater and greater; finally it was so incurable that one messenger of God after another was rejected and killed.

Luther's view of the Old Testament church conformed exactly to that of the New Testament; both historical halves fitted into each other. The church was to him never anything else but the hidden community of saints, the people of God living from the Word of God. When reference is made to the people of God in

533 *The Babylonian Captivity of the Church,* 1520, *WA* 6, 564:17; *LW* 36, 113.
534 Gloss to Exod. 27:21, Knolle, *Luthers Glossen zum Alten Testament,* p. 43.
535 Gloss to Lev. 17:3–4, *ibid.,* p. 43.
536 *Propositions Concerning the Abrogation of the Private Mass,* 1521, *WA* 8, 470:11. See also the German edition, *The Misuse of the Mass,* 1521 (*Vom miszbrauch der Messe*), *ibid.,* 554:32; *LW* 36, 219.
537 *Ibid., WA* 8, 555:7 ff. (Latin: 470:19 ff.); *LW* 36, 220. In this connection Luther applied, in an amusing allegorical game, the blasphemous cults of Israel to the institutions of the Roman church. He then elaborated on them.

the Old Testament, it does not mean the Jewish people as such, though blessed and elected by God while a large proportion of them do not really believe. Rather, it means the same people which in promise and anticipation is later called Christianity, namely, those who live from the Holy Spirit,

> who daily sanctifies them, not only through the forgiveness of sins which Christ earned for them (as the Antinomians rant), but also through the removal, sweeping out, and killing of sins; that is why they are called a holy people. And if now the holy, Christian church is the same as a people who are Christians and holy or, as one usually says, holy Christianity, that is the whole of Christendom, in the Old Testament it is called the people of God.[538]

Just as, according to Luther, not the Jewish rites but the signs of God in the Old Testament are the precursors of the Christian sacraments,[539] so it is not the Jewish cultic community but the old covenant community of faith which is the prefiguration of the church of the new covenant. Sacrament and church are functions of the Word, sign and fruit. Luther never thought institutionally, from one cultic association to another, but always from divine action, from the Word also effective in the sign, and from the faith resulting from it.

[538] *On the Councils and the Church,* 1539, *WA* 50, 624:30 ff.; *LW* 41, 143–44.
[539] See above, pp. 181–87.

# 5

# LUTHER'S CHRISTIAN TRANSLATION OF THE OLD TESTAMENT

Luther saw unity-in-tension between the testaments. Accordingly, he made Moses the Lawgiver a Christian. Luther often saw Christ in the Old Testament, speaking and also foretold there. This understanding was bound to affect Luther's translation. He maintained the principle of "rhyming" with the New Testament throughout his interpretation and translation. Our survey of his concept of the entire Old Testament prevents our classing this principle of his as unscholarly theorizing or careless invention. It was so basic to his understanding of the Old Testament that it was the guiding principle of his work. As he bound himself to this principle, he bound his colleagues to it, too.

"When he [Forster] said, 'Ah, the rabbis interpret it this way,' I said, 'Could your grammar and points allow you to render the sentence so that it rhymes with the New Testament?'

"Answer: 'Yes.'

" 'Then take it!'

"The result was that they themselves marveled and said they never in their lives would have believed it."[1]

The incessant translation of Old Testament ideas into the Christian thought world—as into a foreign language—involves not so much a shift in concepts which can be precisely specified as a change in atmosphere which often can only be sensed. Such translation is not a matter of conscious and intentional change, but rather a natural process of recasting, which involves every part. It is hard

[1] *Table Talk,* 1542–1543, *WA,* TR 5, 218:25 ff. (No. 5533), quoted also in Hirsch, *Luthers deutsche Bibel,* p. 49; *LW* 54, 445–446 (No. 5533). See also *WA,* TR 5, 220:7 ff. (No. 5535).

to describe in detail, but is very deep and far reaching. When Luther interpreted and translated the Old Testament he injected the gospel into its bloodstream so that it spread into the smallest capillaries almost by itself. Just as familiarity with German linguistic style reveals the beauty of his translation, so, too, only someone who is at home in the world of the New Testament can fully sense this illumination with the gospel. It is necessary to compare his translation with the original meaning of the text to see if there is a contradiction between the original meaning and the New Testament language which appears in the translation. Such comparison will also show where the New Testament language used corresponds with the original meaning, as in many psalms and in Deutero-Isaiah.

This transposition into a new key naturally becomes clearest in those areas of thought which are more characteristic for Luther's understanding of the New Testament. I shall attempt to arrange a series of examples under a few general headings.[2]

## 1. TEMPTATION AND CONSOLATION

The classic passages on temptation *(Anfechtung)* in Luther's translation of the Old Testament show his magic hand most clearly. We will compare the literal translation of modern exegetes with that of Luther against the Vulgate text. In this way we will see the extent to which he was indebted to the Vulgate and where he was independent of it.

[2] This process would deserve a more comprehensive description, which should also draw upon Luther's change of expression in the various editions of his translation as well as upon his interpretations. It is very gratifying that *WA*, in its printing of the translation of the Old Testament (*WA*, DB 9[I] [1939]), now has begun to offer material for it in a theological commentary, which unfortunately is otherwise everywhere missing. Besides a few hints (especially in Hirsch, *Luthers deutsche Bibel*), there is, up to now, only one valuable study available—but only for a portion of the Bible—namely, F. Hahn, "Zur Verchristlichung der Psalmen durch Luthers Übersetzung," *Theologische Studien und Kritiken*, CVI (1934–1935). That is why I prefer evidence from other Old Testament books. The study of Luther's sources regarding his translation of the Psalms (Pahls, *Quellenstudien zu Luthers Psalmenübersetzung*) treats only the linguistic questions and the relationship to the exegetical tradition, but not the theological motifs, without which Luther's translation and its revisions cannot be understood. On these questions the edition of Heinrich E. Bindseil and Herman A. Niemeyer (eds.), *Dr. Martin Luthers Bibelübersetzung nach den letzten Originalausgaben*, Teil 1–7 (Halle, 1845–1855), is still indispensable.

| MODERN TRANSLATION | LUTHER | VULGATE |
|---|---|---|
| *Isa. 28:19* It will be pure horror to interpret oracles.[3] Then it is sheer dread to understand revelation.[4] | Only conflict teaches us to pay attention to the Word. [This version in the revision of 1541 and after; until 1534: "accident"; then: "punishment."] | *Tantummodo sola vexatio intellectum dabit auditui.* |
| *Isa. 38:17* See, for my salvation the bitter is bitter to me [Duhm: "I am troubled for my peace"][5] but you have kept back [changed for: "have loved"] my soul from the pit of extermination.[6] | See, I was very frightened about consolation, but you have heartily taken on my soul. [This version in the revision of 1534 and after; before: "about peace."] | *Ecce in pace amaritudo mea amarissima, tu autem eruisti animam meam, ut non periret.* |
| *Jer. 15:16* Yet your Word proffered me delight and joy to my heart.[7] | Your Word is my heart's joy and consolation. | *Factum est mihi verbum tuum in gaudium et in laetitiam cordis mei.* |
| *Jer. 17:9* The heart is more deceitful than every other thing, and it is malicious.[8] | The heart is a spiteful and cowardly thing. | *Pravum est cor omnium et inscrutabile.* |

For Luther temptation and need for consolation were so much the natural fate of man that his method of expression was quite naturally colored. He translated the Hebrew conjunction *ḥazaq we'emeth* ("be strong and brave": Deut. 31:6, 7, 23; Josh. 1:6,

[3] Bernhard Duhm, *Das Buch Jesaiah übersetzt und erklärt* ("Göttinger Handkommentar zum Alten Testament," III, 1, ed. W. Nowack [4th ed. rev.; Göttingen, 1922]).

[4] Hermann Guthe in *Die Heilige Schrift des Alten Testaments*, trans. Emil Kautzsch, ed. Alfred Bertholet (4th ed.; Tübingen, 1922–1923).

[5] Duhm, *op. cit.*

[6] Otto Eissfeldt in Kautzsch, *op. cit.* He, like other modern interpreters, eliminates the first part of the verse.

[7] Rothstein in Kautzsch, *op. cit.*

[8] *Ibid.*

7, 9, 18; 10:25; I Chron. 22:13; 28:20; II Chron. 32:7, Ps. 27:14; 31:24) regularly with "be consoled and undaunted" or ". . . and joyful," "and fresh," and the like, but "consoled" is never missing in any passage or in any edition of his translation (Vulgate always: *confortari*). It acquires its peculiar quality because Luther not only used it here and in several other passages (for example, Num. 13:20; I Sam. 4:9; II Sam. 10:12; I Kings 2:2, and others) as an expression of courage, but also for the real situation of temptation, for example, "his heart is consoled [literally: "unswerving"] and unafraid," Ps. 112:8; "The righteous is consoled even in death," Prov. 14:32; and "Tell the fainthearted, 'Be comforted, fear not,'" Isa. 35:4.

## 2. FAITH AND JUSTIFICATION

Luther was in close agreement with New Testament thought in translating *emunah* as "faith" when it applies to man. Only once did he translate it as "truth" (Jer. 9:3); and at times when used adverbially he translated it as "loyally" (II Chron. 19:9; 31:18;[9] Isa. 59:4; see also Prov. 28:20). Thus he arrived at a whole series of impressive directives to faith in the Old Testament, even in cases in which the meaning "loyalty" would have suggested itself, for instance, "The Lord will judge every man according to his righteousness and his faith" (I Sam. 26:23; "loyalty" was written in the manuscript);[10] "Lord, your eyes look after faith" (Jer. 5:3, although used in contradistinction to false swearing); "Righteousness will be the girdle of his loins, and faith the girdle of his kidneys" (Isa. 11:5, although "loyalty" would fit precisely for the Messiah); ". . . the righteous people who preserve the faith" (Isa. 26:2, although here too "loyalty" as against the "disloyalty" often reproved by the prophets would suggest itself). Even for God's covenant with the people in Hos. 2:19, Luther says, "in faith shall I betroth myself to you," although God's loyalty there stands in contrast to the people's disloyalty.[11] This consistent use of the con-

[9] In these two passages "in faith" is changed to "upon their faith" only after the revision of 1541.

[10] *The German Bible,* 1545, *WA,* DB $9^{I}$, 280. I quote, by the way, according to the modern text of the Bible, in so far as it agrees in essence with the original edition. To be phonetically loyal here would be senseless.

[11] See also Jer. 7:28 and Isa. 33:6 ("safety, undisturbed peace," according to E. Robinson *et al.* [eds.], *William Gesenius, a Hebrew and English Lexicon of the Old Testament*).

cept of faith in place of loyalty, which was often more apt and not unknown to Luther, is only comprehensible because to him "faith" expressed the sole possibility of existence before God, and precisely because he heard in it the accord between the Old and New Testaments in a marvelous way. The saying, "The righteous shall live by faith" (Hab. 2:4; Rom. 1:17), which had become dear to him through hard inner struggle, was to him one of the brackets around the whole of Scripture. Of course in Luther's mouth it also had a New Testament sound; less in the shadings of *emunah* than in the inimitable genitive, which transforms the Old Testament thought "to live through the loyal clinging to God" into the New Testament "to have one's life solely in faith."[12] That Abraham, the great model of faith, bore for him features given to Abraham by Paul can be seen in his translation, "Abraham believed the Lord, and that was reckoned to him as righteousness" (Gen. 15:6); especially when one takes Gunkel's translation as comparison, "He believed Yahweh this time too; He, however, recognized therein his piety."[13]

Luther added depth and direction to faith, the sum total of human behavior before God, by translating *emunah,* in so far as it is used by God, as "truth," to the extent that "loyalty" did not suggest itself. The great transformation which he undertook in the Psalter after the revision of 1531 demonstrates particularly that it was done with care. Only a minority of the numerous passages[14] in which we today read "truth" were contained in Luther's translation from the very beginning. The great majority have been changed from the original "faith"[15] or "loyalty."[16] By basing the

12 Here Luther stayed close to the Vulgate (*iustus in fide sua vivet*), which he had followed literally earlier. See his *Epiphany Sermon of January 6, 1521, A Useful Sermon of D. Martin Luther, Augustinian at Wittenberg, Preached in the Afternoon on the Day of the Holy Three Kings, on the Kingdom of Christ and Herod (Ain nutzliche sermon Dictor Martini Luthers Augustiner zu Wittenberg, geprediget an dem hailigen drey Künig tag nach mittag von dem reich Christi unnd Herodis), WA* 7, 240:14. He rejected the rabbinical translation of *emunah* as "truth." *The Prophet Habakkuk,* 1526, *WA* 19, 395:22 ff.

13 *Genesis, übersetzt und erklärt,* p. 180. See also the explanation of Holzinger in Kautzsch, *op. cit.*

14 Ps. 15:2; 26:3; 43:3; 45:4; 51:6 (substituted for "wisdom" in 1528); 86:11; 111:7; 119:43.

15 Ps. 40:11; 89;1, 2, 5, 8, 24, 33, 49; 92:2; 96:13; 98:3; 100:5; 119:88, 138; 143:1.

16 Ps. 25:10 (already since 1528); 36:5; 57:10; 89:14, 25 (in 1528: "faith"); 91:4; 108:4; 115:1; 117:2. In addition, in 1531 Luther substituted "truth" *(Wahrheit)* for "constant" *(beständig)* (Ps. 119:142, 160) and "certain" (*gewiss*) (Ps. 119:20).

whole relationship between God and man on "truth" and "faith," Luther already filled the Old Testament with the spirit of the gospel, in which the contrast of promise and faith is contained.

The words which are connected with justification have a New Testament ring, and even as was true of the words dealing with faith, Luther did not always translate *hiṣdiq* the same way.[17] Rather he applied different shades of meaning. Comparison shows that these words are related to the process of justification, though he does not slavishly borrow from the various words used in the Vulgate: "to let be just" (Exod. 23:7); "to help toward justice" (II Sam. 15:4; Ps. 82:3); "to agree" (Job 27:5); "to keep justice" (Ecclus. 42:2); more generally, "to point to righteousness" (Dan. 12:3; Vulgate: *ad iustitiam erudire*). Note the rest, which Luther rendered with: "to justify" (II Chron. 6:23); "to declare righteous" (Luther says "to acquit," Deut. 25:1; I Kings 8:32; Isa. 5:23; 50:8; Prov. 17:15) or "to make righteous" (Isa. 53:11). The text shows that these are related to the process of justification. However, for a Christian they gain the character of a suspended sentence: "You should hear it in heaven and create justice for your servants . . . to declare the righteous righteous, to reward him according to his righteousness" (I Kings 8:32; II Chron. 6:33); "He is near who declares me righteous; who will dispute me?" (Isa. 50:8). This is, of course, not translated falsely; but the New Testament meaning cannot be ignored (see Karl Budde in Kautzsch, *op. cit.,* "He who creates justice for me"; Duhm, *op. cit.,* "He who is the creator of my righteousness").

But much more significant than such terminological shifting is the fact that "righteous" and "righteousness" have a completely different meaning in Luther than in the Old Testament. No matter how aptly he may have translated literally, it sounds different and is different. To the extent that a text is not directed against a false self-righteousness, "righteous" meant to him, as to Paul, the "believer"; and God's righteousness is the *iustitia dei,* a meaning he had gained in a difficult personal struggle. How different the effect is can be illustrated in a passage in which Luther added nothing

[17] In the first complete edition of 1534 he substituted "to justify" (*rechtfertigen*), frequently used earlier with other shades of meaning (Exod. 23:7; Deut. 25:1; I Kings 8:32; Isa. 50:8).

even subconsciously, but rather translated literally, like the Vulgate, whereas a modern translator consistently avoids all these presupposed concepts of "righteousness" to freely elaborate the actual meaning of the text.

| MODERN TRANSLATION | LUTHER |
|---|---|
| *Isa. 45:21–25* There is no God besides me who brings salvation and rescue! ... I swear by myself that out of my mouth comes truth, a word that does not reverse, so that every knee will bend to me and every tongue will swear, "Only in Yahweh do I have"; one will say, "success and power!" To him must come, to feel ashamed, all those who were angry with him, to have victory in Yahweh and boast of all the seed of Israel.[18] | And there is no other God but me [*ausser mir*],[19] a just God and Savior; and there is no one besides me.... I swear by myself, and a word of righteousness proceeds from my mouth; let it stay that way: all knees should bend to me, and all tongues swear and say, "In the Lord do I have righteousness and strength." Such will also come to him; but all who resist him must come to nought. For in the Lord all the seed of Israel will be righteous and will boast of it. |

## 3. GOD AND CHRIST

In Luther's translation the whole Old Testament view of God is painted with New Testament colors, inconspicuously, but all-permeating. This is seen in his translation, already dealt with,[20] of the name of God with Christian concepts. Luther thus only continued the avoiding of pronouncing the name of God as done by the Septuagint and by the rabbinic vocalization of the word Lord for the name Yahweh. This was followed then by the Vulgate and all the other Christian translations of the Old Testament. This namelessness of God makes him the true God. His work is the same at all times: redemption and salvation for men. That is why even in Luther's choice of words the varied rays of divine deliverance are seen shining through the Old Testament.

Only the Old Testament God bears, in Luther's German Bible, the name "Redeemer" (especially for the term *go'el,* occurring in

[18] Budde in Kautzsch, *op. cit.*
[19] Luther: "without me" (*ohne mich*). I chose the modern biblical text to avoid small antiquities here.
[20] See above, pp. 195–96.

II Isaiah and III Isaiah and in later writings).[21] It was mostly applied by Luther to the working or promised Christ, but not always.[22] And Christ too is certainly hidden from the Old Testament believers, behind the mask of their God.

The Christological motif is strengthened by the repeated use of the New Testament concept of "savior." Luther here followed a path indicated to him by the evidence before him. For he found the *moshia'* of the Hebrew text (or else some derivative of *yasha'*) almost regularly rendered in the Vulgate with *salvator* (sometimes also *salvans* or *salutaris*). Luther followed this translation from the very beginning, even where it is used of men (Judg. 3:9, 15; II Kings 13:5; Obad. 21). Even in the rare cases in which he gave up the translation "savior" again, it was done in agreement with the Vulgate (I Sam. 11:3 since the revision of 1539 and 1541, "Is there then no savior?" Vulgate: *qui nos defendit*).[23] On the other hand, he often liberated himself from the Vulgate[24] in the Psalter after his revision of 1531, and not by accident strengthened the New Testament tone in his beloved "little Bible" by the name "savior" (instead of "God of my salvation"). See Ps. 85:4, 88:1, and especially Ps. 51:14, which in other ways too presents a beautiful example of Luther's work on his translation:

*Psalms of Penance, 1517:*

O God, God of my salvation, deliver me from the bleeding [*Gebluten*] and let my tongue preach your righteousness with joy.

*Personal Prayer Book, 1522:*

But my God, God of my salvation, save me from the bloody ones [*Blutigen*], so that my tongue may joyfully preach how you make people pious.

*Psalter translation up to 1531:*

Save me from the blood-guilty [*Blutschuldigen*; 1528: *Blut-*

[21] Otherwise used by Luther only in Ecclus. 29:17 for the guarantor and in Acts 7:35 for Moses.

[22] For example, Ps. 19:14, *A Very Brief Christian Exposition of Psalm 19,* 1531, *WA* 31^I^, 586; *LW* 12, 144; Ps. 78:35, *Defense of the Translation of the Psalms,* 1531–1533, *WA* 38, 46.

[23] *The German Bible, WA,* DB 3, 375:15; 9^I^, 532; Ps. 67:2 too shows a change which grasps much better the Hebrew text as well as that of the Vulgate. *Personal Prayer Book,* 1522 *(Eyn bett buchlin):* ". . . so that we may know on earth what is His deed and who is His savior." After 1524: ". . . that we know His way on earth, among all pagans His salvation." See F. Hahn, "Zur Verchristlichung der Psalmen," p. 198.

[24] Conversely, even in the rare cases where the Vulgate offers him *salvator* in the Psalter (Ps. 25:5; 62:7), he did not follow it, because of his even closer dependence upon the original text, either before or after the revision.

*schulden*], O God, who are the God of my salvation, so that my tongue may praise your righteousness.

*Psalter translation after 1531:*

Save me from blood-guilt [*Blutschulden*], O God, who are my God and Savior, so that my tongue may praise your righteousness.

*Bertholet:*[25]

Save me from the bloodbath, Yahweh; my tongue shall be joyful over your righteousness.

*Vulgate:*

*Libera me de sanguinibus Deus, Deus salutis meae, et exultabit lingua mea iustitiam tuam.*

Almost every one of the passages in the psalms and prophets (for example, Isa. 43:11; 45:21; 49:26; 63:8; Hos. 13:4; Ps. 17:7; II Sam. 22:3) shows what Christian overtones the Savior concept in Luther's translation brings, up to the one that like no other encompasses his whole concept of God: "Truly you are a hidden God, you God of Israel, the Savior" (Isa. 45:15; Vulgate: *Vere tu es deus absconditus, deus Israel salvator*).

Wherever Luther found Christ prophesied in a certain manner in the Old Testament, his translation was also influenced by it. This is the case in the very controversial *shiloh* passage, Gen. 49:10, in which he translated, from the very beginning, straying from the Vulgate *(qui mittendus est),* "until the hero comes."[26] The equally puzzling passage for Luther, as well as for other interpreters, II Sam. 7:19, attained its final form because he found a documentation for the doctrine of two natures in it.[27]

| *1524–1540* | *1541–1543* | *1545* |
|---|---|---|
| Is that human law, Lord, Lord? | O Lord, Lord, do you show yourself thus to a human being? | That is a way of a man who is God the Lord. |

25 In Kautzsch, *op. cit.*

26 See above, p. 102, n. 84. The interpretation in the *Lectures on Genesis* mentioned there did not make its way into the translation of the Bible. Bindseil and Niemeyer (*op. cit.,* 1, 115) suppose that Luther interpreted *shiloh* as "pacifier, bringer of peace" *(Beruhiger, Friedebringer)* and accordingly translated it freely with "hero" *(Held).*

27 *The German Bible, WA,* DB $9^{I}$, 318–19. See also the explanation of Schleiff in *WA,* DB $9^{I}$, 547. Here Luther could not do anything with the Vulgate. See *On the Last Words of David,* 1543, *WA* 54, 47:35; 54:27. Today the Masoretic text is regarded as corrupted ("and that is the instruction of man, O Lord Yahweh"). See Kittel in Kautzsch, *op. cit.*

The Psalter in particular contains many Christological allusions.[28] There could be no doubt for Luther that he would have to render the difficult passage Ps. 2:12 as "kiss the Son," since he thus conveyed both the most literal translation and the allusion to Christ. Consequently, he, together with Lyra, frequently and with explicit arguments rejected the Vulgate's rendition, based on the Septuagint, "employ discipline" *(apprehendite disciplinam),* and Jerome's "pray purely" *(adorate pure).*[29] On the other hand, the Vulgate and Heb. 10:7 showed him the way in Ps. 40:7:

| MODERN TRANSLATION | LUTHER | VULGATE |
|---|---|---|
| In a scroll a prescription is given to me.[30] | Something is written about me in a book. | *In capite libri scriptum est de me.* |

This is also the case in Ps. 68:18, related to the ascension in Eph. 4:8:

| MODERN TRANSLATION | LUTHER | VULGATE |
|---|---|---|
| You ascended, you took away prisoners, you took gifts from among men.[31] | You have gone to the height and you have caught the prison; you have received gifts for the people. | *Ascendisti in altum cepisti captivitatem, acceptisti dona in hominibus.* |

How a whole psalm can receive a completely new face through Christological interpretation is strikingly shown in Psalm 8: the basic text is a hymn of praise to God for his creation, especially his most glorious work, man; according to Luther (Heb. 2:6 ff. and I Cor. 15:27) it is "a prediction of Christ, his suffering, resurrection, and kingdom over all creatures."[32] Luther therefore put

[28] The subsequent examples are thoroughly discussed in F. Hahn, "Zur Verchristlichung der Psalmen," pp. 179 ff., and explained in terms of Luther's own interpretations. Two further examples (Ps. 118:27 and Ps. 22:16) I have already introduced in another context (see above, p. 97).
[29] *Lectures on the Psalter,* 1513–1516, *WA* 3, 34:1; *Works on the Psalms,* 1519–1521, *WA* 5, 72:1 ff.; *LW* 14, 346; *Lecture on Psalm 2,* 1532, *WA* 40$^{II}$, 297:5 ff.; *LW* 12, 82.
[30] Bertholet in Kautzsch, *op. cit.*
[31] *Ibid.*
[32] *Defense of the Translation of the Psalms,* 1531–1533, *WA* 38, 20:31.

all verbs into future tense, going beyond the model of the Vulgate. Compare Ps. 8:3–6:

| MODERN TRANSLATION | LUTHER | VULGATE |
| --- | --- | --- |
| When I look at your heaven, the work of your fingers, the moon and the stars which you have prepared—what is man that you are mindful of him, and the son of man, that you care for him? You have made him a little less than angels, you crown him with glory and majesty, you make him the ruler over your handiwork. You have placed everything at his feet.[33] | For I shall see the heavens, the work of your fingers, the moon and the stars which you prepare. What is man, that you are mindful of him, and the son of man, that you care for him? You will let him be deserted by God for a little while, but you will crown him with honors and adornments. You will make him the Lord over your handiwork; you have put everything under his feet.[34] | *Quoniam videbo caelos tuos, opera digitorum tuorum, lunam et stellas, quae tu fundasti. Quid est homo, quod memor is eius? Aut filius hominis, quoniam visitas eum? Minuisti eum paulo minus ab angelis, gloria et honore coronasti eum et constituisti eum super opera manuum tuarum. Omnia subiecisti sub pedibus eius.* |

The view toward the hidden Christ can be seen in very insignificant stylistic means. When Luther translated Isa. 53:4, "But we considered him the one who was persecuted and beaten and martyred by God," it was but a small variation from the literal translation ("While we counted him as afflicted, as beaten by God, and as humbled"),[35] a variation which was not offered to him by the Vulgate either ("We regarded him as a leper, as it were, and as beaten by God" [*putavimus eum quasi leprosum et percussum a*

33 Bertholet in Kautzsch, *op. cit.*

34 Luther's translation does not show essential variations at any point from 1524 to 1545. The tenses in verses 6 and 7 are influenced by the Vulgate only in the use of some writings. On this passage, see Bindseil, *Verzeichnis der Original-Ausgaben der Lutherischen Übersetzung sowohl der ganzen Bible.* The biblical revision, finished in 1892, eliminated Luther's interpretation and produced a more faithful translation. See Willibald Grimm, *Kurzgefasste Geschichte der lutherischen Bibelübersetzung* (Jena, 1884), p. 61.

35 The translation of Duhm, *op. cit.*

*deo*]). But every Christian reader knows whom Luther meant by the added determinative pronoun.

## 4. SALVATION, REDEMPTION, GRACE, BLESSEDNESS

The most common of all concepts for God's work of salvation, "salvation" *(Heil),* contributes very little to our question. Luther translated the Hebrew *yeshu'ah* (in the Vulgate mostly *salutare*) as "salvation" in a number of passages where it was clearly used to indicate outside help, for example in Exod. 14:13; I Sam. 14:15; II Chron. 20:17. But he did not do this to impose New Testament ideas of salvation upon these passages; rather, he did it because for him the broad meaning of "salvation" included outside help and protection, for example, "We have a strong city; walls and defenses are salvation" (Isa. 26:1). On the other hand, Luther, after the revision of 1531, made changes in the Psalter with a consistency similar to that which we observed above with the concept of truth,[36] and in a large number of passages distinguished carefully between "salvation" and "help" *(Hilfe)* in the sense of the original text.[37] Of the thirty-eight passages in which the Luther Bible today renders "help," he at that time changed half from "salvation."[38] Naturally the more restricted use of salvation for deliverance lifts the remaining passages that much more into the realm of timelessness and thus contributes to the New Testament tone of the Psalter (see Ps. 50:23; 67:2; 91:16; 98:2–3; 119:81, 123, 155, 166, and others).[39]

"To redeem," like "salvation," had a wide range of meaning. Luther used it for the Hebrew *ga'al* and *padah*[40] in many contexts, as

[36] See above, pp. 223–24.

[37] This distinction was already pointed out by F. Hahn ("Zur Verchristlichung der Psalmen," p. 199), who also quoted several examples. The reverse of his description is the case in Ps. 116:13. Luther changed the phrase in the Psalter "cup of salvation" *(calix salutis),* familiar to him through the Vulgate and thus constantly on his mind, into "wholesome chalice" *(heilsamer Kelch),* obviously because the other phrase appeared un-German to him. "Cup of salvation" made its way back into the Luther Bible only after the edition of 1893.

[38] Ps. 9:14; 12:5; 21:2, 6; 22:1; 35:3, 9; 38:22; 42:11; 51:14; 62:2, 7; 69:29; 78:22; 85:9; 106:4; 119:41; 140:7. Ps. 27:9 and 46:1 do not count here, because there *'ezrah* had to be translated, not *yeshu'ah.* Luther did not need to introduce this change in the rest of the Old Testament writings; instead, he put the emphasis differently in the first place.

[39] The Hebrew basis there is partially *yesha'* and partially *yeshu'ah.*

[40] Ps. 14:7, exceptional also for *shubh shebhuth* in 1531 and after, which he rendered with "transform a prison" before as well as on other occasions.

much for redemption from external slavery as from distress and sinful guilt, and on the whole he rendered the sense of the original text. But in a series of passages the Christian meaning of the word interjects another tone, as in connection with *nephesh:* ". . . who delivered my soul from all trouble" (II Sam. 4:9; I Kings 1:29), instead of "who has delivered my life [or me] out of all distress" (see also Job 33:28 and others). Small accents also mean something here. Like the Vulgate, but different from some more recent interpreters (Duhm, Budde), Luther served the New Testament idea of prevenient grace (and thus the use of this passage at baptism) when he rendered the perfect tense of Isa. 43:1 as a perfect tense, "Fear not, for I *have* redeemed you. . . ." The motif of salvation history *(Heilsgeschichte)* is particularly strong in the use of the abstract "redemption" (Ps. 111:9; 130:7; Isa. 45:17). And Luther, like Paul (I Cor. 15:55) and the Vulgate, transformed God's question threateningly directed to Ephraim in Hos. 13:14 into a mighty promise:

| MODERN TRANSLATION | LUTHER | VULGATE |
|---|---|---|
| Should I free them from the underworld, redeem them from death? Where are your plagues, O death? Where are your agonies, O underworld?[41] | But I shall redeem them from hell. Death, I shall be poison to you. Hell, I shall be a pestilence to you. | *De manu mortis liberabo eos, de morte redimam eos. Ero mors tua, o mors, morsus tuns ero, inferne.* |

The words related to "redemption" naturally have a particularly timeless force in the personal piety of the Psalter.[42] Luther used them here too for liberation from external distress, tyranny, enemies, etc.; and its distinction from "rescue" is based on other Hebrew verbs *(hiṣṣil, ḥilleṣ),* not on a distinction in subject matter, as with "salvation" and "help"; nor was this differentiation in general influenced by the revision. Nevertheless, some psalms acquired a new or Christian meaning, for example, Ps. 71:23, 74:2, 103:4, and particularly Ps. 49:8–9 and 49:14, where the transformation of Sheol, the world of death, into hell is added. More will have to be said about that.

41 Guthe in Kautzsch, *op. cit.*
42 See F. Hahn, "Zur Verchristlichung der Psalmen," pp. 200–01.

The concept of "redemption" produces only a subconscious and atmospheric assimilation of the New Testament into the Old. While a modest degree of self-correction can be discerned in Luther regarding "salvation," he did carry over one of the essential traits of New Testament language into the Old Testament through the conscious introduction of the concept "grace." It has already been pointed out several times that Luther's translation of the Psalms here underwent a strange development.[43] At first Luther rendered *ḥesedh,* corresponding to the *misericordia* of the Vulgate, as "mercy"; but then, as the manuscript shows, he went on in his work on the translation of the Psalter (perhaps from Psalm 36 on) to replace it with "goodness," which then appeared everywhere in the printed version (1524). He explicitly justified it in his preface to the 1524 Psalter and even more often afterward.[44] The incisive Psalter revision of 1531 brought about a transformation here too. In about one-half of the passages Luther changed "goodness" into "grace," already used in the *Personal Prayer Book*[45] and in some individual passages outside the Psalter. Luther thus attained not only a mere change of expression, certainly sometimes very welcome to him, but also a finer differentiation of the divine demonstrations of love. "Goodness" becomes the expression for the concern of the Creator for man and the whole world (Ps. 33:5; 36:5, 7, 10; 57:10; 119:64; 145:8–9) and for God's love and desire to help (for example, Ps. 6:4; 17:7; 21:7; 31:7, 16, 19, 21; 66:20; 86:5; 106:45; 143:12). Thus Luther translated *ḥesedh we'emeth* as "goodness" and "loyalty" in those passages (Ps. 40:10–11; 57:3; 61:7; 86:15) in which God's protective power is praised in song. On the other hand, "grace," which is used only for God, is marked mostly by its contrast to the wrath that punishes sin (Ps. 56:7; 59:13; 77:8; 85:7; 89; 90:14), or as the sum total of the justifying action of God (Ps. 5:12; 103:4, 11, 17; 130:7). Grace is the refuge of him who is being tempted

43 First by Pahls (*Quellenstudien zu Luthers Psalmenübersetzung,* pp. 55, 82, 85, 114); then by F. Hahn ("Zur Verchristlichung der Psalmen," pp. 192 ff.), in the context of a discussion of the theological motifs.

44 Bindseil, *op. cit.,* pp. 7, 329; *Psalm 118, the Beautiful Confitemini,* 1530, *WA* 31$^{I}$, 75:6 ff.; *LW* 14, 50; *Lecture on Psalm 51,* 1532, *WA* 40$^{II}$, 345:9 ff.; *LW* 12, 323.

45 Pahls, *Quellenstudien zu Luthers Psalmenübersetzung,* p. 21.

(Ps. 109:21). The translation of the expression *hesedh we'emeth* (sometimes separated by a half verse) was changed to "grace and truth" where God's disposition to salvation in general is praised (Ps. 89:14, 24; 92:1–2; 98:3; 100:5; 115:1; 117:2). Luther also translated *raṣon* as "grace," particularly in those passages (Ps. 5:12; 51:18; 89:17; 106:4) where it is also more narrowly defined in the context as a concept of justification or of God's loyalty to his promise, in the same sense as it appears in the New Testament.

The evidence in the translation of the Psalms is also confirmed in the other Old Testament writings. While Luther usually translated *ḥen* and other cognate words as "grace" in the sense of divine or human favor and goodwill ("He found favor in his eyes"), in the books published before the great revision of the Psalter the translation of *hesedh* as "grace" is a rare exception (Exod. 34:6–7). Its occasional appearance in the prophets after the translation of Isaiah in 1528 (Isa. 54:8, 10; 55:3), more often in the edition of the prophets in 1532 (Jer. 16:5; Dan. 9:4; Hos. 2:19; Jonah 2:9 [until 1526: "mercy"]; Mic. 7:20), and throughout the changes in the complete edition of the Bible in 1534 (Jer. 16:5 changed from "goodness"; Isa. 60:10, *raṣon* changed from "goodwill") shows once again the direction of the whole development.[46] The climax of this conscious interpretation of the divine behavior as grace is the translation of even *sedhaqah* as "grace" in Mic. 7:9.

| MODERN TRANSLATION | LUTHER | VULGATE |
|---|---|---|
| I bear the wrath of Yahweh because I sinned against him. Finally he will fight for me and create justice for me. He will lead me into the light; I shall refresh myself in his righteousness.[47] | I want to bear the Lord's fury, for I have sinned against him, until he settles my problem and creates justice for me. He will bring me to the light, so that I may see my delight in his grace. | *Iram domini portabo, quoniam peccavi ei, donec causam meam iudicet et faciat iudicium meum, educet me in lucem, videbo iustitiam eius.* |

[46] "Grace" was still contained in the biblical revisions of the nineteenth century, obviously because of stylistic reasons; for example, Job 37:13 (*Experimental Bible* of 1883 for "merciful" [*barmherzig*]) and Isa. 63:7 (in the Revised Bible of 1893, twice for "goodness" [*Güte*]).
[47] Guthe in Kautzsch, *op. cit.*

Wherever the original text balances knowledge of sin and knowledge of one's own rights, which Yahweh will sometime acknowledge, there the appeal of the penitent sinner to the grace of God comes directly from Luther's translation. Small translation aids from the Vulgate cannot be overlooked, but with "grace" Luther freely introduced his knowledge of the righteousness of God into the text.[48]

Thus Luther, in his entire translation of the Bible, took pains to select a number of passages in which he established, in a particular manner, harmony with the New Testament message of grace. This translation certainly cannot be called false. The more recent translators also make use of the word in these passages almost regularly—without, it seems to me, being sufficiently aware that grace is a concept filled with its New Testament content which often does not render the pure meaning of the original text. Luther, on the other hand, heard this sound in the Hebrew text itself; for it was to him the voice of Christ. He therefore determined the tone of the whole verse, often even of a whole psalm, particularly the concepts "righteous one" and "righteousness" often connected with it, through this sign of the new covenant: grace.

In Jer. 31:3 Luther translated *ḥesedh* as "goodness." Any addition to the Hebrew text here, as in some other cases, should be traced to the Vulgate and its dependence on the Septuagint.

| LITERAL TRANSLATION | LUTHER | VULGATE |
|---|---|---|
| I have loved you with everlasting love; therefore long I have kept for you my goodness [actually: "stretched"].[49] | I have loved you again and again; that is why I have drawn you to me out of sheer goodness. | *In caritate perpetua dilexi te, ideo attraxi te miserans.* |

The examples of an opposite development repeatedly demonstrate that Luther did discipline himself against unjustified intru-

[48] It can no longer be determined how aware he still was of the Vulgate's similar confusion at another place (see above, pp. 158–59).

[49] Rothstein (in Kautzsch, *op. cit.*) emends this passage on the basis of the Septuagint, whereas Rudolph in Kittel maintains the Masoretic text. See also *Jeremiah* ("Handbuch zum Alten Testament," ed. Otto Eissfeldt *et al.*, 12 [2nd ed. rev.; Tübingen, 1912]).

sions of New Testament expressions. His careful work becomes even plainer with "blessed" and "blessedness" than with "salvation"[50] In the *Psalms of Penance* (1517) he had regularly translated *ashre* (Vulgate: *beatus*) with "blessed" and thus raised it to the level of the New Testament *makarios*. After the translation of 1524,[51] Luther almost everywhere substituted "well-being to him" for it, and went on doing so consistently, so that the word "blessed" does not appear anywhere in the Psalter today. In the other Old Testament books too he used "blessed" almost exclusively in the sense of "consider blessed," "to congratulate" (Gen. 30:13; I Kings 10:8; II Chron. 9:7; Job 29:11; Prov. 31:28; Mal. 3:12; Wisd. of Sol. 3:13),[52] and in a deeper, but basically similar sense in Job 5:17 and Prov. 3:18. That is why the two passages in which the word is given an independent meaning gain so much more weight.

*Deut. 33:29:*

| MODERN TRANSLATION | LUTHER | VULGATE |
|---|---|---|
| Hail to you [*Heil Dir*], Israel! Who is like you?—a people, victorious through Yahweh! He is the shield which protects you, and the sword which brings you elevation![53] | Well being to you [*Wohl dir*], Israel, who is equal to you? O people that becomes blessed through the Lord, who is the shield for your help and the sword for your victory. | *Beatus tu, Israel, quis similis tui? Popule, qui salvaris in Domino, qui est scutum auxilii tui et gladius gloriae tuae.* |

With a certain amount of help from the Vulgate, a promise of blessedness develops from the promise of victory.

50 See above, p. 230.

51 Pahls, *Quellenstudien zu Luthers Psalmenübersetzung*, p. 46, n. 1; not 1522, as F. Hahn ("Zur Verchristlichung der Psalmen," p. 201) suggests. That Luther here made a decision concerning subject matter and did not just follow Reuchlin's *Rudimenta*—as Pahls obviously thinks—becomes clear from the fact that Reuchlin offered a choice of both translations ("well or blessed" [*bene vel beatus*]).

52 In Wisd. of Sol. 18:2 "to consider blessed" *(selig preisen)* is substituted for "laud" *(loben)* again only after 1883.

53 Marti in Kautzsch, *op. cit.*

*Isa. 45:22:*

| MODERN TRANSLATION | LUTHER | VULGATE |
|---|---|---|
| Turn to me and let yourselves be saved, all corners of the earth. For I am God and there is no other.[54] | Turn to me and you will become blessed, ends of all the world. For I am God and no other. | *Convertimini ad me et salvi eritis, omnes finis terrae, quia ego deus et non est alius.* |

Again, as Luther interpreted it,[55] and as the Christian reader clearly discerns it in the Vulgate and in the whole context,[56] a promise of justification through Christ developed out of a prophecy of the deliverance of nations.

The same situation exists in the two passages in which the Luther Bible today offers "blessedness," Wisd. of Sol. 5:2 and II Macc. 12:45. Luther came upon this translation because of the eschatological character of these two texts, in the latter in perceptible opposition to the Vulgate, from which Catholic doctrine derives scriptural support for purgatory and sacrifice for the dead:[57]

| MODERN TRANSLATION | LUTHER | VULGATE |
|---|---|---|
| Then he considered that the most glorious wage of grace is preserved for those who died in piety.[58] | But because he remembered that those who die in the true faith may have hopes of joy and blessedness. . . . | *Quia considerabat, quod hi, qui cum pietate dormitionem accepterant, optimam haberent repositam gratiam. . . .* |

When Luther applied the promised redemption and blessedness to the believers who, secretly in the old covenant, in open recognition in the new, placed their hope on Christ, then the universality of this salvation, no longer limited to Israel, had to find expression in his translation. Therefore, when in Jer. 23:5 (33:15) a seed of David is promised "who is to rule as king and deal wisely and

[54] Budde in *ibid.*
[55] "Thus he secretly returns from Cyrus to Christ and his gospel." *Lectures on Isaiah,* 1527–1530, *WA* 31<sup>II</sup>, 368:1. See also *ibid.*, 367:17 ff.
[56] See above, pp. 224–25.
[57] See, for example, Karl Adam, *The Spirit of Catholicism,* trans. Dom McCann (New York: Macmillan, 1955), p. 141.
[58] Kamphausen in Kautzsch, *op. cit.*

who is to exercise justice and righteousness in the land,"[59] then in Luther this became "on earth." He translated "earth" in other passages (for example, Jer. 9:24), but in Jeremiah this conveyed the Christological sense. Equally clearly in Ps. 24:7:

| MODERN TRANSLATION | LUTHER | VULGATE |
|---|---|---|
| Lift up your heads, you gates! Rise, you ancient doors. . . .[60] | Open the gates wide and the doors in the world high. . . . | *Attolite portas principes vestras et elevamini portae aeternales. . . .* |

Luther's use of the late Jewish meaning *'olam,* "world," which is occasionally found elsewhere (for example, Gen. 6:4; 49:26; Ps. 73:12), as well as the call to men rather than gates, gave the word its overtone of Advent.[61]

## 5. WORD, PROPHECY, PREACHING

"O man, what is good is told to you . . . namely, to keep God's Word . . ." is the way Luther translated the great rule for a pious life in Mic. 6:8, although he knew quite well that the original text really says "to do right" (Vulgate: *facere iudicium*). The protocol of the revision of 1541 gave the reason for this: "*facere iudicium,* 'to do right,' applies equally to the verb, which means 'right according to God' *(iudicium coram deo)*."[62] This is a classic example of the transformation of Old Testament moralism into the Christian's stance of faith. The translation of Micah, in particular, provides further evidence for basing man's relationship to God solely upon the Word. Luther subconsciously altered the disagreement with the false prophets along the lines of his struggle against the enthusiasts *(Schwärmer).* When the prophet warned them that the "divine answer" would not come to them (Mic. 3:7; Vulgate: *quia non est responsum dei*), Luther translated, "because there will be no Word of God." The missing prophetic audition becomes the missing testi-

59 Rothstein in *ibid.*
60 Bertholet in *ibid.*
61 F. Hahn ("Zur Verchristlichung der Psalmen," p. 190) strikingly comments, "Luther makes an Advent of Christ out of the Advent of Yahweh."
62 *The German Bible,* 1545, *WA,* DB 4, 251. Luther's translation was well established after the first edition of the prophets (1532). He still followed the text of the Vulgate in his lectures on Micah in 1525. *Lectures on the Minor Prophets. The Prophet Micah,* 1525, *WA* 13, 291:3 ff.

mony from God's Word, a formulation hinting at the Word of Scripture which the enthusiasts lack. The relationship to both the original text and to the Vulgate in Mic. 7:11 is also very characteristic:

| MODERN TRANSLATION | LUTHER | VULGATE |
|---|---|---|
| . . . then, when my walls are built and my boundary extends.[63] | At that time your walls will be built and God's Word will spread widely. | *Dies, ut aedificentur maceriae tuae, in die illa longe fiet lex.* |

Luther obviously did not consider "boundary" for *ḥoq,* but rather considered the Vulgate translation correct. But, in a context which he illuminated evangelically elsewhere too,[64] the law became for him the Word of God in which a wide mission was inherent.[65]

Luther's love of the formula "God's Word" increased with his constantly new revision of the Bible. Thus the marvelous Reformation translation of 1531, "My heart holds before you your Word, 'You shall seek my face'" (Ps. 27:8) is the result of many efforts to which the earlier preliminary forms, rendering the original text literally (1524: "My heart has told me about you"; 1528: "... says about you"; Vulgate: *Tibi dixit cor meum, exquisivit te facies mea*), and the detailed protocol of the revision testify. "I call upon you, clinging to your mandate and promise.... It is truly a fine assurance, and it has a fine way of reasoning: you give me your commandment and I choose you. . . . Your Word is both commandment and promise, spoken simultaneously."[66] Or observe the development in Ps. 93:5:

| MODERN | *1524–28* —LUTHER | *1531*—LUTHER | VULGATE |
|---|---|---|---|
| Your testimony is quite trustworthy.[67] | Your testimony is very certain. | Your Word is a true doctrine. | *Testimonia tua credibilia facta sunt nimis.* |

[63] Guthe (in Kautzsch, *op. cit.*), with some unessential textual alterations.
[64] See above, p. 233.
[65] Luther, in his interpretation of Micah in 1525, did not yet interpret "law" *(lex)* in terms of the Word, but in terms of the restoration of an independent political order after the Assyrian rule was broken. *Lectures on the Minor Prophets, WA* 13, 297:2 ff.
[66] *The German Bible,* 1531, *WA,* DB 3, 19 ff.
[67] Bertholet in Kautzsch, *op. cit.*

The 1531 protocol of the revision shows that Luther gave a detailed account of his reasons for the change. He wanted to find a strong word of consolation; and thus the doctrine of the church appeared to him to be the strongest support.

I would rather wish consolation were "strong, honest, loyal." I don't like "certain"; I don't like "truly" because it sounds like the opposite of hypocrisy. . . . The teaching of hypocrites is not faithful; it does not endure. . . . But what you teach in the church is true and holds up.[68]

His work on Psalm 119 is especially revealing. Wherever Luther translated independently or changed his earlier text, he always ended up by putting in "your Word" in 1531, so that today it appears forty times (and five times "your words") in the psalm. In the Hebrew text he changed the plural previously used frequently in the Vulgate into the singular (for example, vss. 17, 28, 42, 101, 107) and replaced *imra,* previously translated as "speech," regularly with "Word" (for example, vss. 11, 38, 41, 50, 57, 116, 154). He now also translated terms with different meanings in this same way, such as *mishpaṭ, ordinatio* (for example, vs. 91), and *piqqudhim, mandata* (for example, vs. 104).[69] The psalm receives its homogeneous feature only through this editing, and shifts from praise of the law to praise of the "glory of the Word of God," as it is later entitled in Luther Bibles. "But it is especially created for the purpose of stimulating us to the Word of God, which praises thoroughly."[70]

The same style can also be found elsewhere. For example, the singular "Word," placed in Jer. 15:16a against the Hebrew and Latin texts, is not an insignificant factor in the comforting character of the verse, the continuation of which I have already mentioned in another context.[71] And a large part of the power of Jer. 23:29 ("Is not my Word like a fire . . . and like a hammer that smashes

[68] *The German Bible,* 1531, *WA,* DB 3, 119:9 ff.

[69] The revision of 1531 also singled out several passages. *Ibid.,* 148 ff. The brief explanation of 1529 still differentiated and explained the differences between "word," "speech," "commandment," etc. *WA* 31$^{I}$, 2–3.

[70] *Defense of the Translation of the Psalms,* 1531–1533, *WA* 38, 57:10.

[71] See above, p. 221. Luther translated, "Yet keep away your Word from us when we receive it." The modern text, "Your Word was my nourishment when I received it," represents an improvement from that of 1883.

rocks?") depends on this singular, not introduced until 1539, conforming to the Hebrew but opposed to the Vulgate text.

Luther was convinced that this prophetic prediction points to Christ. This conviction also becomes noticeable in his translation; not only because the figure of Christ shines through, but also in the chronological dating and the description of the prophecy as a whole. For example, while according to the original text the prophet in Hab. 2:3 receives a promise from Yahweh that although His attack on the tyrant would be delayed, it would nevertheless take place in his own time, Luther saw in this verse a promise of the coming Christ,[72] which, when combined with verse 4, becomes a mighty witness to justification by faith:

| MODERN TRANSLATION | LUTHER | VULGATE |
|---|---|---|
| Revelation still has its time limit; but it hurries to its end and does not deceive.[73] | Indeed, the prophecy will be fulfilled still at its own time, and will finally come out into the open freely. | *Quia adhuc visus procul et apparebit in finem et non mentietur.* |

Prophets are proclaimers, not fortune-tellers.[74] That is why Luther loved to let them, like the patriarchs whose history he already showed us,[75] "preach." The Word gained its impact because he summarized concepts of different meanings therein: pale expressions like *amar, dibber, sipper, higgidh* (in the Vulgate usually *dicere, loqui;* for example, Isa. 3:10; Jer. 23:25, 28; 26:2; Ps. 2:7; 22:22, 31; 26:7; 87:3), as well as *bissar,* promising a joyful message (*praedicare* in Isa. 52:7, *evangelizare* in Isa. 40:9, *annuntiare* in Isa. 61:1; Ps. 40:10; 96:2). Again, one can see that Luther con-

[72] See the interpretation of 1526, *The Prophet Habakkuk,* 1526, *WA* 19, 391 ff. Luther did not know at all the term "revelation" *(Offenbarung)* for the Christological prediction in the Old Testament. Indeed, he did not even use it in the New Testament in an absolute sense, but only as "revelation of something" (corresponding to *apokalypsis*). Even the only passage in which Luther used the word for God in the Old Testament (Num. 24:4, 16, changed from "countenance" [*Gesicht*] in 1534) is not based Christologically, since Luther did not apply the prophecy of Baalam, as that of an unworthy prophet, to Christ, but rather to David. *Sermon of October 18, 1528, Sermons on Leviticus and Numbers,* 1527–1528, *WA* 25, 500:1 ff.

[73] Guthe in Kautzsch, *op. cit.*

[74] See above, pp. 34–35.

[75] See above, pp. 209–16.

sciously strengthened the term "preaching" in his translation by changing his earlier literal rendering of the Hebrew text "to invoke His name" (Gen. 4:26; 12:8; 13:4; 21:33; 26:25; Ps. 105:1; 116: 13, 17; and the like) into "to preach His name" in the 1531 Psalter and then in the 1534 Bible (see also Isa. 12:4). The striking change of 1534 in Isa. 42:20, "one undoubtedly preaches much" instead of the earlier literal, "there is undoubtedly much to see" (Vulgate: *qui vides multa*), also shows that Luther considered the essential task of the prophet to be proclamation, not visions. The "preaching" messengers of peace (Isa. 52:7) and, above all, the "sermon" at the beginning of Isaiah 53 strengthen the application of these passages to the gospel and to Christ. A small alteration can be decisive, for example, in Ps. 87:3:

| MODERN TRANSLATION | LUTHER | VULGATE |
|---|---|---|
| Glorious things are spoken of [*von*] you, you city of God.[76] | Glorious things are preached in you, you city of God. | *Gloriosa dicta sunt de te, civitas dei.* |

The application of the city of God in the psalm to the church guided Luther's pen.[77] And when he translated Ps. 68:11, "The Lord gives the Word with great flocks of evangelists"—it is the only passage where he let the concept[78] stand, though it is used four times in the Vulgate—no one believes he is still in the Old Testament.

The outline of Old Testament "church history" in the previous section has demonstrated how closely preaching is interwoven with the application of the New Testament concept of church.

Eccles. 12:12 offers an amusing example of how Luther's translation grew out of his total interpretation of an Old Testament book: "much preaching tires the body." Since Luther did not conceive of the author as the melancholy character he is usually thought to be, but rather as a man quite experienced in calm liv-

76 Bertholet in Kautzsch, *op. cit.*
77 F. Hahn ("Zur Verchristlichung der Psalmen," p. 200) also indicates this example. Luther not only applied this psalm to the church in his first lectures on the Psalms, but also later. *Defense of the Translation of the Psalms,* 1531–1533, *WA* 38, 48.
78 In Isa. 40:9 Luther translated "female preacher" (*Predigerin*); in Isa. 41:27, (*evangelista*) "preacher" (*Prediger*); in Nah. 1:15, "good messenger" (*guter Bote*).

ing, his own fatigue cannot be meant; rather, it must be that of others. But then "meditation," with which the Vulgate translates *lahag* (which appears only here), does not quite fit. And so he arrived at "preaching."[79]

## 6. HOLY

To call God and God's name, deeds, temple, etc., "holy" *(heilig)* was suggested to Luther through the wording of the Hebrew text and the Vulgate. Only in one passage, which however is significant in showing his use of this word, did he make an exception. In 1534 he changed the cry of Jacob awakening from his dream, "How terrible this place is!" (Gen. 28:17; Vulgate: *terribilis*), into, "This must be a holy place." While he usually translated the original *nora'* with expressions indicating awe,[80] he softened it here, because for him the passage contained not only a glorious promise to Jacob but also pointed to the true church.[81] Thus the holiness of this place does not only arise out of the fright of the ancient narrator by the nearness of God, but also out of something frightening (Jacob "was afraid") and at the same time comforting.

Luther's rendering of *qadosh* as well as *ḥasidh* as "holy" simply followed the Vulgate, as was so often the case. Naturally the prophetic name of God, often recurring especially in Isaiah, "the Holy One of Israel" *(qedosh Yisra'el)*,[82] or just "the Holy One," had a Christological ring for him.[83] This does not mean that Christ as a specific person is always meant. Instead, what Christ is to us Christians, God is as "the Holy One" to the believers of the old

79 See the *Preface to Ecclesiastes, with Notes,* 1532, *WA* 20, 8:19 ff., and the interpretation of Eccles. 12:12, *ibid.,* 201:9 ff. The revision of the nineteenth century inserted the literal translation "studying" (*studieren*), after the objection that the passage could serve as biblical evidence for the forced retirement of senile clergymen was refuted through Luther's interpretation. See Grimm, *op. cit.,* pp. 61–62.

80 "Terrible" (*schrecklich*): Exod. 15:11; Deut. 7:21; 28:58; Job 37:22; Ps. 47:2; Joel 2:11, 31; Hab. 1:7, and others. "Horrible" (*greulich*): Isa. 18:2, 7. "Cruel" (*grausam*): Deut. 1:19. Only the "wonderful name" (*wunderbarliche Name*) of God (Ps. 99:3) shows a similar softening.

81 Already in *Sermons on Genesis,* 1523–1524, *WA* 14, 385–86 (1527 edition: *WA* 24, 496 ff.); and more elaborately in *Lectures on Genesis,* 1542, *WA* 43, 597 ff.

82 See in addition II Kings 19:22; Ps. 71:22; 78:41; 89:18.

83 See for example the explicit comments on Isa. 12:6 and 43:3 in *Lectures on Isaiah,* 1527–1530, *WA* $31^{II}$, 93:26; 329:13 ff.

covenant—for us, the God who is not yet revealed. For God is not called "holy" as such, but "on the basis of his action" as the one who sanctifies us and thus excludes the self-sanctification of man.

For they were sanctified through their God and through nothing else, as he says in Leviticus [20:8], "I am the one who sanctifies"; just as we now become Christians, that is, saints, through Christ, and not through our own work or merit. . . . One should be used to the fact that God is called "the Holy One." For wherever he is, he sanctifies through his Spirit.[84]

He is called "the Holy One" on the basis of his work. Our "Holy One" is Christ who sanctifies us through the Word of truth. But some attack this true and unique sanctification on the basis of a fabricated and false sanctification. . . . Hypocrites want to sanctify God.[85]

Luther's translation and interpretation of *ḥasidh* in Ps. 16:10 was also determined by the direct Christological prophecy which he found used in the New Testament (Acts 2:27; 13:35).[86] While the believer expresses his confidence in deliverance from fatal danger in the Hebrew text, Luther here obtained scriptural evidence for the resurrection of Christ particularly important to him.[87]

| MODERN TRANSLATION | LUTHER | VULGATE |
|---|---|---|
| You do not give up my soul to the underworld; you do not let your believer look into the pit.[88] | You will not let my soul go to hell, and you will not allow your holy one to rot [before 1531: "see the pit"]. | *Non derelinques animam meam in inferno nec dabis sanctum tuum videre corruptionem.* |

From the beginning and without wavering Luther also translated the plural (that is, *qedoshim* as well as *ḥasidhim*, used above

[84] On Hab. 1:12 and 3:3, *The Prophet Habakkuk,* 1526, *WA* 19, 377:1; 427:20.
[85] On Isa. 1:4, *Lectures on Isaiah,* 1527–1530, *WA* $31^{\text{II}}$, 6:17; 109:31.
[86] F. Hahn's data ("Zur Verchristlichung der Psalmen," pp. 195 ff.) are not correct here. The "Holy One" in Ps. 89:18 was to Luther, according to I Sam. 13:14, David, not Christ. *Defense of the Translation of the Psalms,* 1531–1533, *WA* 38, 48:24 ff. See also the revision of the Psalter in *The German Bible,* 1531, *WA,* DB 3, 112:17. Moreover, Ps. 71:22 and 78:41 read *qadosh;* only in Ps. 16:10 is *ḥasidh* interpreted Christologically.
[87] F. Hahn ("Zur Verchristlichung der Psalmen," pp. 173 ff.) has collected additional material.
[88] Bertholet in Kautzsch, *op. cit.*

all in the Psalter) as "the saints."[89] Like the Vulgate, he thus established the harmony between them and the saints of the new covenant, the believers in Christ. If one also considers the meaning of the holiness of God to be giving, then the transformation of the "believers" of the Psalter into the "saints" radically alters the subject of these psalms. If Luther's concept of holiness were more familiar to the reader of the Bible, he would clearly feel that this was one of the most effective methods by which Luther interpreted the Psalms in a Christian way. The liberal editing of Ps. 12:1 in the *Personal Prayer Book of* 1522 demonstrates what he meant: "Help, God! How few Christians remain" (in the Bible translation: "Help, Lord, the saints have been reduced").[90]

One could continue giving examples. Often they are words which quite naturally came to Luther and yet had a new sound and content, as, for example, "hell," "the place of punishment," instead of "Sheol," "the world of death,"[91] especially in Ps. 49:15:

| MODERN TRANSLATION | LUTHER | VULGATE |
|---|---|---|
| Yahweh will redeem my soul; he will surely take me to himself out of the power of Sheol.[92] | God will redeem my soul from the power of hell, for he has accepted me [before 1531: "out of the hand of hell if he accepts me"]. | *Deus redimet animam meam de manu inferi, cum acceperit me.* |

[89] See F. Hahn, "Zur Verchristlichung der Psalmen," p. 196. He asserts that after 1531 Luther always translated *ḥasidim* as "saints" (*Heilige*) and *yesharim* as "pious" (*Fromme*). He is right only in the latter case. Luther in later revisions generally used "pious" for "honest" (*aufrichtig*). See also Pahls, *Quellenstudien zu Luthers Psalmenübersetzung,* p. 115. Luther's use of "the saints" (*die Heiligen*), however, never changed. The only variation is the edition of Ps. 12:1 in the *Personal Prayer Book,* 1522, also cited by Hahn. See below, n. 90.
[90] *Personal Prayer Book,* 1522, *WA* 10$^{II}$, 410:3.
[91] For examples from the Psalter, see F. Hahn, "Zur Verchristlichung der Psalmen," pp. 201–02. Luther strengthened the significance of "hell" in the passages and thus emphasized, by differentiating more strongly through changes in his translation, differences between "hell" (*Hölle*) and "pit" (*Grube*); and he did so without differentiating regularly between *sheol* and *bor.* (Compare Gen. 37:35; 42:38; 44:29, 31 with Ps. 28:1.) So much for the correction of Friedrich Jehle, "Die Hölle in Luthers Bibelübersetzung," *Neue Kirchliche Zeitschrift,* XXXIV (1923), 720 ff., where also evidence is found concerning changes in the biblical revisions.
[92] Bertholet in Kautzsch, *op. cit.*

Besides the contrast between the deliverance from death and from damnation, the correction of 1531, as against the Vulgate which at other times served as a model, also shows how Luther translated out of his understanding of justification: the believer was long ago graciously accepted in Christ. In the concept "eternity," too, something other than the unlimited duration of the Hebrew *'olam* arises out of Luther's translation (for example, II Sam. 7:25; Ps. 103:17; 117:2; Mic. 5:2).[93]

Luther substituted, after 1531, "to promise" in passages of grace in the Psalter for *ṣiwwah (mandare, praecipere),* which he himself previously had rendered as "to command" or "to order" (Ps. 42:8; 44:4; 105:8; 106:4; 111:9; 133:3).[94] He thus drew, as it were, the situation into the verb, although his sharp ear did not miss the subtle distinctions in the original text. "'Commanded,' 'promised,' although it means a bit more than 'to promise.'"[95] But he thus obtained, in each individual case, an expression which sharply reflected his view of God.

In the course of time Luther strengthened the use of "sin"[96] as a term to express a condition, in addition to "misdeed," "mischief," "transgression," etc. And he even drew the idea of original sin from Ps. 51:5, by slightly changing his original, literal translation of the Hebrew text and the Vulgate, "I was born in unrighteousness; my mother conceived me in sin" (1517), to "I was made in the womb by sinful seed, and my mother conceived me from sinful seed."[97]

It should also be remembered that Luther's regular translation of *goyim* as "pagans" introduced a note which was justified only after the time of Hosea.[98]

But even if one were to gather very much evidence, and take into consideration terms, sentence structure, verb tenses, attributes of

93 Luther himself distinguished between a human *le'olam* ("unlimited duration") and a divine one. *A Letter of Martin Luther Against the Sabbatarians,* 1538, *WA* 50, 324 ff.
94 See Pahls, *Quellenstudien zu Luthers Psalmenübersetzung,* pp. 114–15.
95 Psalter revision of Ps. 133:3, *The German Bible,* 1531, *WA,* DB 3, 159:4. The difficulty of translating these passages becomes evident in the not very fortunate choice of Bertholet (in Kautzsch, *op. cit.*), "to summon" *(entbieten).*
96 Pahls, *Quellenstudien zu Luthers Psalmenübersetzung,* pp. 54–55, 115.
97 *Personal Prayer Book,* 1522, *WA* $10^{II}$, 412:12. For a survey of the various changes up until the final version of 1545, see F. Hahn, "Zur Verchristlichung der Psalmen," pp. 177–78, and Bindseil (*op. cit.*) on this passage.
98 Kind information from Albrecht Alt.

God, and whatever else there may be, the sum of the details does not equal the whole even here. Each detail is but an indication of how the sum total was transformed inimitably into a warm consoling language, filled with promise. This language forges the substance of the unity which Luther saw hidden behind all the tensions.[99]

[99] One of the effects of this New Testament transformation of the Old Testament world of thought is the use of Hebrew names of salvation in Luther's hymns. See Knolle, "Hebräische Heilsnamen in Luthers Liedern," *Lutherjahrbuch,* XXII (1940), 46 ff.

# 6

# THE UNIQUENESS OF LUTHER'S VIEW OF THE OLD TESTAMENT

There is a consistency to Luther's Old Testament translation and interpretation. Even his deviations from the original texts, where they occur, are so obvious that they can be recognized and set aside without modern Hebrew philology. Nevertheless, Luther could always justify his translation of such passages as an exegete of the whole Bible. He applied his basic premise thoroughly and consistently: exegesis and translation of individual passages must derive from an understanding of the text as a whole. This premise is just as important today in understanding and conveying any message. His interpretation and translation were the result of his life's work, his biblical studies and lectures in Wittenberg after 1512. This contribution is quite in addition to whatever significance Luther has for theology, church, and society. Modern historical biblical study has made this great body of Luther's work more distant from us. It seems to belong on the far shore of ancient and medieval ecclesiastical exegesis. Therefore it is necessary to draw together the main strands again and to inquire into particulars of Luther's view of the Old Testament.

The Old Testament was never the undisputed property of the church. Rather the church has always had to struggle to bring itself into ever new relation to the ancient word.[1] The Jews were the

[1] This is the impression one receives from the still excellent book of Ludwig Diestel, *Die Geschichte des Alten Testaments in der Christlichen Kirche* (Jena, 1869), which leads one through an enormous amount of source material with a fine sagacity for that which is significant and different. See also Nathanael Bonwetsch, "Das Alte Testament in der Geschichte der Kirche," *Allgemeine evangelische lutherische Kirchenzeitung,* LVI (1923), 50 ff., 60 ff. Von Dobschütz ("Vom vierfachen Schriftsinn," *Harnack Ehrung*) also traces a significant piece of the history of exegesis. For a comprehensive collection of material concerning the interpretation of the Old Testament in the early

first to contest its use, not willing to leave their Holy Scripture to their arch enemies the Christians. Others from the outside have argued against the church's use of the Old Testament. Even within the Bible, though it was compiled by the church itself, there is considerable diversity concerning the acceptance of the Old Testament among Christians. Thus the extreme judgments which have been made in the course of history are really not surprising, although the New Testament's use of the Old really precluded the church from rejecting the latter altogether.

Luther also was limited by this preclusion. One would only have to enumerate the different ways in which the Old Testament is used in the New Testament[2] to discern the basic features of Luther's attitude toward the Old Testament: the harsh contrast of law and gospel; conscious and intentional allegorizing; the appeal to examples of faith (Romans 4, Galatians 3, Hebrews 11) and to Christological predictions in the prophets and Psalms; the conviction that the Spirit of Christ had already spoken in the prophets themselves (I Pet. 1:11), etc. But Luther did not merely deduce exegetical principles for his interpretation of the Old Testament on the basis of this New Testament evidence.[3] Rather his method of interpretation developed from his disagreement with the methods of earlier interpreters who stood between him and the New Testament and blurred his clear picture of it.

---

church (up to Irenaeus), see the index in J. L. Koole, "De overname van het Oude Testament door de christlijke Kerk," pp. 16 ff. Here the material is conveniently arranged and worked into a systematic presentation. This work serves to illustrate, for the history of Christian exegesis and hermeneutics, the position of the church with regard to the Old Testament in a period which still lay before the complete victory of the allegorical method among the Alexandrian theologians. Thus it becomes evident that Luther's interpretation was in closer contact with this exegesis of the Apostolic Fathers, of the Apologists, and of Irenaeus, only partially known to him and hidden through the ecclesiastical tradition, than with the later one. Regarding the complementation of the subsequent sketch, which limits itself to the most significant basic traits, I can now refer to the elaborate study in which Ebeling (*Evangelische Evangelienauslegung*, pp. 90 ff.) integrates, in a gratifying manner, Luther's interpretation of the gospels into the history of the hermeneutical and exegetical tradition.

2 For this enumeration, see especially Leonhard Goppelt, *Typos. Die typologische Deutung des Alten Testaments im Neuen* ("Beiträge zur Förderung christlicher Theologie," 2 [1939]), p. 43.

3 Thus Luther was in agreement with the entire history of Christian exegesis, in which Ebeling (*op. cit.*, p. 102) observes this basic element: "As much as the New Testament was from the very beginning the norm for the Christian interpretation of both testaments, so little was it ever attempted within Christianity to let the New Testament be normative for the methods of Christian biblical interpretation."

Allegory was a very influential late pre-Christian method. It recommended itself in the first centuries of the church as a contemporary and total solution of the problem. Through this pseudo-solution ecclesiastical exegesis took over total control of the entire Old Testament. Luther's greatest achievement in the history of biblical interpretation is his mistrust of this sham. His conquest of allegorization as a significant key to Scripture does not ignore the fact that from time to time he could make use of allegory. His use of it only shows that he knew the possibilities of imaginative interpretation that he thus rejected. His opposition to allegory did not originate from historical considerations. Yet, historical considerations surely played a role in this opposition. Because of his understanding of the subject matter he realized that allegory destroys true history, namely, the history of Christ and the history of faith in the Old Testament; it abrogates the real meaning of the text in favor of some supposed lofty meaning.[4] Luther clearly saw that the history of Israel thereby lost its value and attraction. If one did not see the role of faith in Israel's history, then events in the history of other peoples would seem much more significant and enthralling.

> If you omit dealing with faith in the sacred histories (Origen is a true master in this matter), then the histories of other peoples will be much greater and much more illustrious. Thus a mind which is without faith and is guided only by natural reason must necessarily abhor and despise the sacred histories as minute matters if compared to the fabulous and great deeds of emperors.[5]

He could have added to these objections, from closer study of Origen, that allegory destroys the true gospel as well as the meaning of the law. What Luther valued as Jewish national law, which wrote the will of God into the hearts of that time, Origen declared to be in part senseless; the Israelites should have learned to seek a higher meaning beyond it.[6] Thus Luther was capable of acknowledging a true historicity, a preservation of faith and past significance of the law of that time, while the allegorical method was dissolving that which was historical into something timeless.

The rival of allegorical exegesis, the typological method of the

[4] See above, pp. 88–91.

[5] Preface to Justus Menius' *Exposition of I Samuel,* 1532 *(In Samuelis Librum Primorem Enarratio. Iusto Menio Autore), WA* 30$^{III}$, 540:1.

[6] Origen, *On Principles (De Principiis),* IV, 29; *MPG* 11, 374; *ANF* 4, 368.

Antiochians, had tried to correct this fault. Events and institutions which seemed to be types of coming New Testament events were valued as having contemporary importance. Sacrifices and rites of purification are examples.[7] But Luther criticized this method just as he had the allegorical method. Shadowy anticipation of that which was to come meant nothing to him. It existed for him, still veiled, but nonetheless real. Christ is actually present for the prophets of the old covenant through his Word and is received in faith. He is not represented through a type characterized, according to the definition of Theodore of Mopsuestia, by a "model" *(mimesis)* of his original image;[8] instead, he is truly present. While allegory eradicates the historicity of the Old Testament events, typology annuls the historical presence of Christ in the Old Testament. Typology can even lead to a double meaning in which the typological passages would have one meaning for the present and one for the future; Ephraim the Syrian is a clear example of this double meaning.[9]

For Luther all passages within the Old Testament, including the ones he interpreted Christologically, had only *one* meaning. That is why he aimed at something quite different from allegory or typology: to find not only the shadows of the New Testament in the Old Testament, but also to find the direct testimony, indeed, the work of Christ already in the Old Testament. Thus he directed his attention to quite different things in the Old Testament, not to cultic or historical circumstances and persons, but to those passages in which he thought he actually found Christ, which explains why Theodore, the most severe of the Antiochians, found few direct prophecies of Jesus, and no indications whatsoever of his being the Son of God or of the Trinity in the Old Testament,[10] while Luther collected his

[7] See Diestel, *op. cit.*, pp. 129 ff., and Goppelt, *op. cit.*

[8] "One particular type [*typos*] has a certain model [*mimesis*] for that to which it is said to be a type." Theodore of Mopsuestia, *Commentary on the Twelve Minor Prophets*, ed. A. von Wegnern (Berlin, 1843), I, 343; quoted by Diestel, *op. cit.*, p. 131. See also Eduard Schweizer, "Diodor von Tarsus als Exeget," *Zeitschrift für neutestamentliche Wissenschaft*, XL (1941), 60–61.

[9] In Isa. 9:7, for example, something is to be related to Hezekiah, something to Jesus. Ezek. 37:21 ff. already applies in part to Zerubbabel, but on the whole to Christ. The tower of Babel was certainly built; yet at the same time it points to the mediator who connects heaven and earth. See Diestel, *op. cit.*, pp. 138–39; Otto Bardenhewer, *Geschichte der altkirchlichen Literatur* (5 vols.; reprint of 1924 ed.; Darmstadt, 1962), IV, 358.

[10] Diestel, *op. cit.*, p. 133.

strongest arguments for his Christological interpretation precisely therein. The astonishing critical acumen Theodore demonstrated at this point stands over against Luther's completely different critical prudence, which refused to look for types of Christ and New Testament events in sacrifices, rites, and persons of the Old Testament. The difference again lies in the fact that Luther sought real history in the Old Testament—the history of God and faith, which means the universal history of Christ. It must have its concrete result in the testimony of the Old Testament itself. That is why Luther carefully collected everything which appeared to him to be evidence of Christ, not an allegory or typology of Christ. He did not distinguish the obvious from the more distant; instead, he saw only one, always the same, reality, which was there although it remained a puzzle or was only sensed at that time, while it is revealed to the eye looking backward since Christ.

The remaining exegetical methods of the early and medieval church are, on the whole, only variations of these two basic forms of exegesis of the early church; they were later summarized, with interpretations derived from them, in the awkward yoke of the fourfold sense of Scripture. And since allegory and typology both sought a higher or spiritual meaning in the text, the whole exegesis of the early church moved essentially on the same level. No exegete overcame the dualism inherent in both methods, neither the allegorists, who canceled the literal sense through the spiritual sense, nor the typologists, who accepted a double meaning of the type *(typos)*, a contemporary and a future one. And this is how it was in the Middle Ages too. Even Lyra did not break with the manifold sense of Scripture; he only strengthened the gravity of the literal sense and decided in its favor in controversial questions.[11]

[11] Diestel (*op. cit.*, p. 198) correctly draws attention to the fact that this method represents only an intensification of insights already apparent earlier, and not a basic break with the hitherto existing dualism. Ebeling (*op. cit.*, p. 131, n. 81) draws attention to Lyra's dependence upon Thomas Aquinas; yet this dependence does not fully explain his peculiar concern, which, however, is offered with strange hesitation. This concern also became evident in the rules of his successor, Paul of Burgos; Ebeling (*op. cit.*, pp. 123 ff.) presents a fine survey of them. The judgment of Ernst von Dobschütz (*op. cit.*, p. 13) that Lyra's theory is only "a bashful way of asserting allegory as a higher literal sense" goes too far in its attempt to contest Lyra's relatively exceptional position within medieval exegesis. He did not basically change the scholastic interpretation of Scripture. See also Ebeling, *op. cit.*, p. 134. It is, however, misleading when Ebeling *(ibid.)* ascribes an understanding of Scripture to this

To see how pressing was the question of a sound exegetical method for Luther, we must not only see the discrepancies in the exegetical traditions out of which he grew, but also see what humanistic exegesis, the best scholarship of his time, offered him as an alternative. Even Erasmus knew of no other way than allegory to gain meaning from large parts of the Old Testament.[12] Just like his model Origen, whom he admired as an exegete as much as Luther rejected him as one, he found the literal meaning of the text quite senseless, indeed, often enough, repulsive and ridiculous.

> Thus you should observe in all your reading those things consisting of both a simple and a hidden sense, comparable to body and spirit, so that indifferent to the merely literal sense you may examine most keenly the hidden sense.[13]

> Allegories are to be treated with special care because Holy Scripture, through which eternal wisdom stammers with us, as it were, consists almost entirely of them. Unless they assist the reader, especially in the books of the Old Testament, the greatest part of the fruit is lost to him. It is certainly false, and sometimes even ridiculous and absurd, when the literal sense is simply accepted.[14]

Thus Luther stood encircled by the same walls.

His antithesis to the allegory and typology of the early church can also be traced in detail in his concept of the Old Testament. First, in the *difference between the testaments.* The exegetes of the early church in general saw only gradual differences. The Logos

---

scholastic hermeneutics "in which the historical factor has its decisive significance." What he means by this is the contemplation of the historical Christ, so vivid in the Middle Ages, his suffering, his relics, the urge for a sensory representation of the life and world around Jesus during the crusades, but not (as this formulation could easily be understood to mean) an overcoming of the spiritual interpretation of Scripture through a literal-historical one.

[12] This is pointed out by Holl, "Luthers Bedeutung für den Fortschritt der Auslegekunst," in *Gesammelte Aufsätze zur Kirchengeschichte,* I, 552. That Erasmus handled allegory better than most of the exegetical representatives between Origen and him does not change the fact that he was unable to go beyond this pseudo-solution. See Hermann Schlingensiepen, "Erasmus als Exeget. Auf Grund seiner Schriften zu Matthäus," *Zeitschrift für Kirchengeschichte,* XLVIII (1929), 31.

[13] Erasmus, *Enchiridion,* 1503. See Hajo and Annemarie Holborn (eds.), *Desiderius Erasmus Rotterdamus. Ausgewählte Werke* ("Veröffentlichungen der Kommission zur Erforschung der Geschichte der Reformation und Gegenreformation" [München, 1933]), p. 70:12; *The Enchiridion of Erasmus,* trans. Raymond Himleick (Bloomington: Indiana University Press, 1963), p. 105.

[14] Erasmus, *The Method of True Theology,* 1519–1522 *(Ratio seu methodus compendio perveniendi ad veram theologiam),* Holborn, *op. cit.,* p. 274:24.

did not just appear suddenly; rather it offered itself more fully and more purely in the revelation of the new covenant than in the perceptions of the old covenant. This idea can be expressed in a great variety of images, which all amount to a systematic education from the law to the gospel. According to the model of the Apologists and Alexandrians, the whole early church seemingly had a completely different view of the schoolmaster of Gal. 3:24–25 than Paul apparently had,[15] and certainly different than that of Luther, who rendered it "taskmaster," including the idea of "executioner." Luther elucidated it with *lictor,* and if he expressed it by the image of the teacher, then only in the sense that he reported the hatred of the pupil for him.

> Show me a pupil who loves his schoolmaster [*paedagogus*]. Did the Jews love Moses very much and do with pleasure and love what he commanded? They would have stoned him! It is impossible for a boy to love his schoolmaster, because he uses the whip and locks him up. . . . He is his *lictor.*[16]

Wherever Luther described the law's office of executioner and death,[17] the early church saw the loving, if need be also the punishing, pedagogical guidance. The images Irenaeus used, the steps leading to God,[18] and the proliferation of grace in the New Testament over against the Old Testament,[19] or the parable of Jerome, who described the Old and New Testaments as seed and harvest,[20] show

[15] I Cor. 4:15. See Hans Lietzmann, *An die Korinther* I–II ("Handbuch zum Neuen Testament," 9 [2nd ed. rev.; Tübingen, 1923]), p. 21.

[16] *Lectures on Galatians,* 1531, *WA* 40I, 529:2 ff.; 530:2; *LW* 26, 345, 346. The word here translated "stone" must read *lapidassent,* according to the printed version, instead of the nonsensical *lapsi.* See also *Lectures on Galatians,* 1519, *WA* 2, 528:20 ff.; *LW* 27, 278–79. A *lictor* was one of the public attendants of the principal Roman magistrate, who bore the whips (*fasces*) as emblems of criminal jurisdiction. He also executed the sentence of the magistrate.

[17] See above, pp. 144–46.

[18] "For there is one salvation and one God; but the precepts which form man are numerous, and the steps which lead man to God are not few." Irenaeus, *Against Heresies,* IV, 9, 3, ed. Harvey, II, 171; *ANF* 1, 473. See also Diestel, *op. cit.,* pp. 56 ff.

[19] "Thus the one and the same Lord granted, by means of his advent, a greater gift of grace to those of a later period than what he had granted to those under the old covenant." Irenaeus, *Against Heresies,* IV, 11, 3, ed. Harvey, II, 175; *ANF* 1, 474.

[20] "In speaking thus I do not mean to sever the law from the gospel, as Marcion falsely does. No, I receive one and the same God in both, who, as time and cause vary, is both the beginning and the end, who sows that he may reap, who plants that he may have something to cut down, and who lays the

a cohesive development, while Luther saw only the severest antitheses. The development in which the early church believed naturally did not proceed in a historical unfolding of original buds to later ripe forms; rather, it was an ideal occurrence, through which the Logos then fulfilled its originally only shadowy form in a completely different way. The unity is in the Logos, not in the things or thoughts in which it reveals itself. These—for instance the Jewish rules for purification and the purity of heart demanded by Christ, the blood of passover and the blood of Christ, the prohibition of pork and Christian abstinence—have nothing to do with each other objectively; at best they show a superficial resemblance here and there. And yet the one is the first step to the other; they are held together by the planned unfolding of the Logos. The whole exegesis of the early church was in agreement on this comparative relationship of old and new covenant.

Luther distinguished absolutely, not relatively, between the old and new covenant. Law and gospel are deadly enemies. Although the law must serve the gospel, the law does so against its will and against its real meaning. That is why it dies in the process. The same happens to man who lives from it. He is not prepared for the gospel pedagogically; instead, he must tear himself away from his executioner and "beat Moses to death," even if he appears in the mask of Christ.[21] Thus the difference between Luther and the earlier exegetes rests in their attitude toward the law. In the exegesis of the early church one adapted oneself to the law by differentiating between ceremonial law and moral law. The former was as good as abolished, but was allegorized and typologized as secret witness to the coming revelation.[22] This was the first step of the full gospel which the Logos brings. For Luther the ceremonial and national law, as the Jewish code of law, did not bind the pagans, even without the coming Christ. But Christ is the end of precisely the customary law, which the whole world felt in its accusing conscience.[23]

foundation that in the fulness of time he may crown the edifice." Jerome, *Epistola,* 123, 13; *MPL* 22, 1054; *PNF*2 6, 235. See also Diestel, *op. cit.*, p. 109.

[21] See above, p. 146.

[22] See, for example, the quotations from Justin and Origen in Diestel, *op. cit.*, pp. 55, 62.

[23] See above, pp. 135–49.

The old covenant, which depended upon obedience to the law, was annulled through God.

We see the same contrast between Luther and the earlier exegetes in the problem of the unity of the testaments as we saw in their differences. The unity for Luther consisted in that the new covenant was already recognized and followed in the time of the Old Testament. Although the new covenant was insolubly bound to the once-and-for-all historical appearance of Jesus Christ, it was efficacious wherever someone trusted in faith solely in the grace of God in view of the coming Christ.

> All history and Word of God are always directed to the coming Christ who came and in whom everyone had to believe, just as Abraham saw the ram behind the thicket [Gen. 22:13], took it, and sacrificed it—that is, he believed in Christ who was to come afterward and was to be sacrificed.[24]

Thus the new covenant did not break into the world at the time of Christ's birth; rather, it had already existed secretly since the expulsion from paradise, in the expectation of this promised event of salvation, and was recognized by believers and prophets. The old covenant was not the predecessor of the new covenant, either in time or in content. It was the exclusive antithesis to the new covenant, but both existed side by side from the very beginning in the history of the people of God. The one was destined for death from the very beginning; to the other belonged the promise of victory recognized at first by only a few people. Luther thus demolished the whole scheme of salvation history *(Heilsgeschichte)* in the exegesis of the early church. The early church saw salvation history as a parallel to world history. Salvation history to the early interpreters prepared the way for a particular historical event. For Luther, on the other hand, the history of God could not be compared with the history of the world. The incarnation of Christ is a truly historical event. Yet it only reveals the grace which God had already been showing to believing hearts from the beginning. Its link with history and freedom from it are intertwined in a paradoxical way which cannot be explained on the basis of the usual coherent course of history. The work of Christ in the Old Testament depended on the fact that

[24] *Sermon on Septuagesima Sunday on I Cor. 9:24 ff., Lenten Postil,* 1525, *WA* $17^{II}$, 134:5.

he would one day become man; the incarnation, as the center of all events of salvation, radiated just as much back into the past as forward into the future. But it was not the fulfilment of a development progressing in the course of time. It could not be interpreted with any finite concept alone; beginning, middle, and end all may be applied to it. It could not be otherwise with the breaking-in of eternity into the realm of time.[25]

Therefore the Christ event was not evident to Luther in so many prefigurations of Old Testament history; rather, it was in the midst of them. That was why he pressed so hard for an understanding of what really occurred. All of one's attention should be directed to the factual occurrences of Jewish history, in which God saved his people contrary to merit and hope, in the real experiences of temptation *(Anfechtung)* and consolation in the life of individual believers and prophets. They were not just images for a later Christ event; they were already Christ events themselves. Faith cannot build upon images, but only upon events. It is true that faith can afterward play with symbols, as Luther did himself in his allegories, but only because faith has become confident on the basis of historical experience.

The individual results, in which the difference between Luther's interpretation and that of the early church and of scholasticism become clear to us, originate from this fully transformed understanding of the Old Testament, especially in regard to the sacraments and the church of the Old Testament. Old Testament sacraments were to him not the rites of the Jewish cult, shadowy anticipations of later Christian rites, but rather the great signs with which in the old covenant God confirmed his promise and came to the aid of faith, as he did with the New Testament miracles and signs. Thus Luther did not look for a figurative application but for real events of God's history in the Old Testament.[26]

The Old Testament church was not the Jewish cultic congregation, but the hidden community of believers often persecuted by the official "church," the people of God which in the time of the promise already sensed and lived by the same faith as did believers later

[25] The study of Luther's understanding of time still remains a significant task. See Bornkamm, *Das Wort Gottes bei Luther,* pp. 38 ff., and the small amount of literature cited there.
[26] See above, pp. 184–87.

in the time of fulfilment. Here too Luther saw at that time the real fruit of the divine work in history and not just a symbolic hint of a future establishment of God.[27]

But still more: if Christ is already present in veiled form in the old covenant, if God already performed his signs and created his congregation in hidden form at that time, then there were Christians even in the Old Testament. For whoever believed in Christ, be it only in the promised Christ, was a Christian. That was why Luther unhesitatingly called Moses and the patriarchs Christians whenever he spoke of their faith in the promise of the future Redeemer. The peculiarity of his conception became particularly clear in that he once thought he could refer to one of the fathers of the church for evidence. He voiced his agreement with Anselm's opinion that Adam and Eve also participated in salvation.[28] But if one takes a closer look, the difference becomes obvious precisely in this apparent agreement. Anselm, through a parable (a king forgives all the inhabitants of a guilty city for the sake of the expiatory death of a single innocent person) and through a logical conclusion (God was forced to re-establish the number of citizens in the kingdom he desired, if he did not want to declare his work ruined, by substituting them for the fallen angels), tried to offer intricate proof that Adam and Eve were saved, even though Scripture does not say so.[29] He thought of this salvation as a kind of distant benefit issuing from Christ's death into the past and into the future.

> Since all men who are to be saved could not be present when Christ made that redemption, yet such virtue is there in the power of his death that its power is extended even to those far removed in place or time.[30]

Since it cannot be assumed that mankind at any one time was entirely without fruit for God's eternal goal, the first set of parents, at that time all of mankind, must have been saved too. "For it seems unfitting that God should even for a moment allow the

[27] See above, pp. 216–17.
[28] *Lecture on Psalm 90,* 1534–1535, *WA* 40$^{III}$, 507:3 ff.; *LW* 13, 90.
[29] Anselm, *Why Did God Become Man? (Cur deus homo?),* II, 16; Franciscus Schmitt (ed.), *Cur deus homo* (Darmstadt, 1960), pp. 125 ff.; S. W. Deane (trans.), *Saint Anselm: Basic Writings* (2nd ed.; La Salle, Ill.: Open Court Publishing Co., 1962), pp. 265 ff.
[30] Anselm, *Why Did God Become Man?* II, 16; Schmitt, *op cit.,* p. 126; Deane, *op. cit.,* p. 267.

human race, made to complete the heavenly state, and those creatures which he made for their use, to exist in vain."[31] Luther made something quite different out of Anselm's train of thought. Adam and Eve were not only participants in the salvation achieved by the chronologically remote saving death of Christ; they themselves immediately experienced justification in their faith. After the law and the fall shattered them, God himself ran after them and brought them back. Thus they became Christians in their faith in the promise of the *Protevangelium,* and the two of them constituted the church at that time.

> Elsewhere Anselm draws the conclusion that Adam and Eve were Christians and that they were called back to life immediately after the fall; they were shattered by the law and the fall. Then their sin was repaid because when they fled from God they were not displeasing to God; instead, he brought them back even after the fall. Thus he [Anselm] says that they had to be justified so that the church could remain. . . . This is a good syllogism: where there is the church, there must be two or three. Consequently, if there were as many as two, there was the church. Thus the church always remains, not through human, but through divine conservation.[32]

Luther's concern for the historicity of God's action in the Old Testament and for the irrevocability of independent faith once again becomes plain. God really justified Adam and Eve by awakening faith in them and not only took them up into his eternal kingdom but also let the church on earth begin with them.

> Look at Adam and Eve: they are full of sin and death. And yet, because they bear the promise concerning the Seed who will crush the serpent's head, they have the same hope we have, namely, that death will be removed, that sin will be abolished, and that righteousness, life, peace, etc., will be restored. In this hope our first parents live and die, and because of this hope they are truly holy and righteous.[33]

In view of the difference and unity of the testaments, the same thing that divided Luther from the earlier exegesis repeatedly becomes apparent: he sought the deeds of God, the tracks of Christ,

[31] Schmitt, *op. cit.,* p. 128; Deane, *op. cit.,* p. 268.
[32] *Lecture on Psalm 90,* 1534–1535, *WA* 40$^{III}$, 507:3 ff.; *LW* 13, 90. In addition, see Rörer's supplements: "Then He ran after them and called them back. Thus Adam and Eve had to be justified immediately." I corrected some of the many meaningless readings in A. Freitag's *WA* edition.
[33] On Gen. 3:15, *Lectures on Genesis,* 1538, *WA* 42, 147:10; *LW* 1, 197.

the evidence of true Christian faith in the Old Testament, not just the shadowy hints of a future event. While his assumption of a large number of Christological prophecies joined him with the exegesis of the early and medieval church, this compulsion for true historicity constituted his peculiarity. *His interest in the Old Testament is not historical* [historisch] *in the sense of a modern science of history, but rather historical* [geschichtlich] *in the sense of a true history of God.* Thus even the events of Israelite history attained a significance for the believer; they were not just transparencies for a higher future event. They were, as Luther once classically formulated it, the visible Word of faith, and teach nothing that Scripture does not otherwise teach with words. The art of interpretation therefore consists in how, through a kind of baptism, they undergo a rebirth, making them new for the present, indeed, how they are presented as eternal examples of faith.

> For if you compare this interpretation with previous ones, you will see that these histories are reborn through a kind of baptism, as it were, through the application of faith; thus they become new even for us and also for our own time, indeed, they live forever and serve as magnificent and clear examples of faith for our own discipline, censure, instruction, consolation, and all that of which Paul writes [II Tim. 3:16] about the Word of faith being helpful. For what else is holy history than the visible Word of faith, or a work of faith which it teaches us through fact and deed, and the other things Scripture hands on through word and speech?[34]

This interpretation was the application of his realistic theology as a whole, as differentiated from any symbolism. We have frequently seen how Luther's concept of the Old Testament conformed to his basic theological views. The Old Testament church as the community of believers corresponds to his understanding of the church as a whole. The sacraments as signs of divine promise are differentiated from those of the New Testament only in external form, not in essence. It is the same image of God, of the wrathful one and the gracious one, of the God permeating nature and the one turning to man in the Word, of the one God, yet working in trinitarian fulness. It is the image of man, to whom the natural law, which Moses clarified in the Decalogue, speaks in conscience, but

[34] This comment is Luther's praise in the Preface to Justus Menius' *Exposition of I Samuel,* 1532, *WA* 30$^{III}$, 539:30 ff.

who can never cope with it on his own strength. Therefore, the Old Testament, like the New Testament, teaches that man can only be led into communion with God through the contrast of law and gospel, through death to life. It is the same faith which, contrary to all appearances and in spite of all temptation *(Anfechtung),* must dare to cling to God's promise. Whatever Luther said about the power of the Word is also taken from the Old Testament, judging and comforting, spirit-awakening, life-creating, revealing the depths of God, and pressing from the outside into the inner life of man.[35] This Word was even at that time the same Christ who spoke everywhere where God spoke graciously to men. Luther's Old Testament theology was only an application of his faith in the omnipresence of Christ, which, in a special manner, is also applied in his doctrine of the sacraments. For Christ is "God for us." Wherever God turned his face toward men, be it ever so veiled, it was the face of Christ. Thus the Old Testament encompasses a mighty tension: to the extent that it is testimony of the old covenant, God himself has annulled it completely in the course of history; to the extent that the new covenant was prophesied in it, indeed, even realized here and there in the awareness of faith, he confirmed and fulfilled it in the New Testament.

[35] See my study, *Das Wort Gottes bei Luther.*

# POSTSCRIPT

Recent Old Testament study has set us a world apart from Luther's point of view. We are unable to bridge this gap. Yet it should disturb us. Having concluded our topic here, we should like to indicate some points at which the results of our investigation could serve future consideration of this difficult, but very pressing problem.[1]

1. Luther ascribed to the actual history of the Old Testament a real significance for faith. His point of view leaves historical research the indispensable freedom required for all scholarly Old Testament work. Old Testament research cannot be absolved of its clear obligation to truth and to historically verified facts. Nor would an appeal to Luther give it any such right. He, too, freed himself from earlier attempts to find a superhistory or metahistory behind the actual events, and, through his exegesis, strove to appreciate only that which actually happened. No matter how many of Luther's individual views must thereby be discarded, pure historical research, in the final analysis, is led to the same theological goal that also concerned Luther: to recognize the encounter of the people of Israel with God in their history. Luther's axiom, "Faith rests upon history,"[2] requires the absolute truthfulness of historical research. A conservative picture of history serves this goal no better than a critical one. The most convincing one serves best.

2. Exegetical methods Luther had already surmounted have no right to survive in the evangelical interpretation of Scripture. Any Protestant allegorizing and typologizing or Catholic symbolical

[1] This is neither the place nor am I specialist enough for a critical discussion of the voluminous literature; thus I forego taking any position regarding it. It is conveniently collected and vividly characterized in the report of Rudolf Abramowsky in *Theologische Rundschau,* Neue Folge, IX (1937), 65 ff.

[2] See above, p. 91.

interpretations simply throw us back to a pre-Luther level of consideration of the Old Testament and thereby destroy Luther's greatest accomplishment in the history of exegesis. The occasional "game" Luther could still play with allegory changed nothing, as we have seen,[3] in this break from a tradition of fourteen hundred years, for Luther did not play the game with the idea of really interpreting with it. Instead, when he interpreted he sought to uncover the actual occurrence or the actual thoughts of the authors. This discipline is basic to evangelical interpretation of Scripture. It must never be surrendered. It must rather be joined with the requirements of conscientious attentiveness to historical sense and context.

3. Modern historical research differs from Luther's interpretation of the Old Testament especially in that it can no longer revive the radical prophetic-Christological interpretation of many parts of the Old Testament which were self-evident to Luther. Such study cannot escape the historical meaning of the text when it was written. Therefore, it is not governed by a direct connection with the coming Christ. Double exegesis was prohibited by Luther himself. This is the essential and necessary crisis over Luther's view of Scripture; it cannot be resolved by repristination. Rather, any research which thinks historically will have to give up, without hesitation or reservation, Luther's scheme of Christological prediction in the Old Testament.

4. However, in the course of our study it became clear that Luther's conception does not spend itself entirely in this scheme. Rather, he illumined the whole content of the Old Testament from within by contrasting law with gospel. He thereby taught us to distinguish folk law from natural moral law and to see the unity of the natural law and the Decalogue. He uncovered the deadly distress into which man must fall under the law, and thus looked toward the end and the abrogation of the law, to which the law itself points. From this viewpoint he could see the marvelous intertwining of command and promise in the First Commandment, in which the whole gospel is already contained in the Old Testament in a nutshell. He discovered with this divining rod of "law and

[3] See above, pp. 92–96.

gospel" the great examples of faith in which the ancient patriarchs out of the trust of their hearts found the true God, albeit still without His name, in the midst of terrible temptation *(Anfechtung),* and the words of faith with which the psalmists and the prophets spoke of him. And he saw the hidden community of believers already present in the Old Testament, which links itself to the church of the new covenant in a unity before God surpassing the differences of the times. Because of the clarity of the revelation, he believed that he understood the patriarchs better than they had understood themselves; and he could give a name and a concept to that which they sensed and felt. For all the experiences reported by the Old Testament under the yoke of the law were, in the final analysis, experiences of Christ, because Christ is not just bound to the earthly life of Jesus of Nazareth, but is present wherever God's mercy overcomes a human heart. Our task of seeing the Old Testament through the eyes of Luther, it seems to me, still lies before us and is possible even in the face of the most severe historical research. I would like to call it, as I have formulated it once before,[4] a Christocentric interpretation, in contradistinction to a Christological prophecy, which a truly historical exegesis really could not find in the Old Testament. The methodological difference lies in the fact that the Christological-prophetic interpretation is forced to carry the concepts of the New Testament revelation into the Old Testament and put them in the mouths of the patriarchs and writers. A Christocentric understanding must strongly beware of doing this; it may only induce the exegete to use the view of the Christian, enlightened through the New Testament, to illumine the situation of man and his encounter with God on the manifold Old Testament levels. If the Old Testament is understood in the light which falls back on it from its end, then true historical understanding is not contradicted. For no historical epoch can be understood through itself; rather, in a different and deeper sense, it can only be understood from the goal at which it arrives.

5. However, the interpretation of the Old Testament resulting from a critical consideration of Luther should not be equated with

[4] See above, p. 121.

a concept of development which traces all lines to the goal based on contrast and on the seeds of that which is to come. As justified and necessary as this concept is, even here, in the historical framework, it has little to do with the task of a theological concept of the Old Testament. Yet, this is indispensably required by the subject. A series of three presuppositions are necessary for this:

a) A theological interpretation of the Old Testament demands clarity regarding the relationship of law and gospel in two ways. First, the law which found its end in Christ is not only, according to Paul, the ceremonial law of the Jews, but also the moral law testified to by the conscience of every man. Without clarity concerning the antithesis, the relationship of law and gospel cannot be used as a key to the question regarding the relationship of the two testaments. Second, this antithesis is not resolved by equating the Old Testament with law and the New Testament with gospel. If one formulates the contrast in this way, one can see only the break and not the fulfilment, of which the New Testament itself speaks so much. The New Testament examples of faith taken from the Old Testament, or even just Luther's view of the First Commandment, should open one's eyes to the correct use of the antithesis of law and gospel. No doubt the weight of the law in the Old Testament, contrary to Luther's view, will be strongly fortified, if only because of the renunciation of the direct Christological pronouncements he found there. But the antithesis will never be resolved in a mere comparison of the two testaments.

b) A theological concept of the Old Testament further presupposes that the God who speaks and acts in the Old Testament is God himself, the Father of Jesus Christ. This of course does not mean that all conceptions which the people in the Old Testament had of God, originating in part in very primitive levels of the history of religion, were justified. The study of this cultic God and the use of his name "Yahweh" is a demand of historical analysis which can no longer be ignored. The gulf between the Yahweh of modern translations and interpretations and the name "God" employed by Luther's translation and whole exegesis can no longer be bridged. But it shows what the task is. The Bible seems to fall into two separate periods of the history of religion, the period of a Jewish cultic God, and that of a Christian God. This raises the question of why we still pay any attention at all to the first. The decisive theological task is to see with New Testament eyes the guiding hand of God in the history of Israel's complicated struggle as it searched for clarity. In the final analysis, it is this hand of God which builds his work, about which the Bible informs us, into a unity despite all differences. But a view that just compares religions will have to beware of seeing this connection based on any superiority of the Jewish religion or of the Jewish people. That Jesus Christ came from Israel is due to the sovereign freedom of God, who elected to give revelation to this people and prepared them from their early days for his decisive historical hour. Then they, except for a tiny remnant, missed it completely. The path of the message of Christ to other religions shows that there are also ways from them to him. Luther's supposition that the city of Nineveh could be called to repentance because of its strong natural knowledge of God[5] is an indication that God had not left himself without witness among the pagans either, from whom, as Luther often expressed it, we descend. Naturally the call had to come from where God had given his Word, from a prophet of Israel. Thus the uniqueness of the biblical history of revelation and of the path of God in the history of religions must be seen in their correct relationship to each other.

c) Finally, we must again find an expression for what Luther meant when he equated the Word of God, also efficacious in the Old Testament, with Jesus Christ. The theological question of the Old Testament is first of all a question addressed to our Christology. Luther, in his concept of the Word so comprehensively thought out, possessed a means of grasping God's dealings with humanity throughout history as a unity. This unity gains its face and name in Jesus Christ. He is "God for us," and his name discloses to the Christian all the encounters with God of previous times, which remained a mystery for those who experienced them. Access to this knowledge has been made extraordinarily difficult for us today because of the speculative forms of early Christology and the doctrine of the Trinity. But this access must be rediscovered. And Luther's doctrine of the Word seems to me to open it to us most

[5] See above, p. 54.

easily and to help us very quickly to a mode of expression which would express this basic insight with new originality and vitality.

It is an urgent matter for Christians to interpret the Old Testament correctly. Today it is even more urgent than before because of the crisis that overshadows our relationship to it. Yet, our use of Luther's work has made this proper interpretation more important now than ever. His work has Christianized the Old Testament thoroughly, as we have seen. We cannot use it with a clear conscience much longer if we cannot give clear and new reasons to justify such an interpretation. If we take this task just as seriously as we take the inviolable truthfulness of historical research, then we can let go of the "swaddling clothes"[6] of Luther's interpretation of the Old Testament and once again salvage the treasure in the manger.

[6] *Preface to the Old Testament,* 1523, *WA,* DB 8, 13. "The swaddling clothes are nothing else than the Holy Scripture, in which the Christian truth lies wrapped; faith is described in it. For the Old Testament contains nothing else than Christ as he is preached in the gospel." *Sermon on Christmas Day on Luke 2:1 ff., Church Postil,* 1522, *WA* $10^{I,1}$, 80:3 ff.; 81:8; *LE* 10, 150.

# APPENDIX, BIBLIOGRAPHY, INDEXES

# APPENDIX

## *Luther's Old Testament Interpretations*

| TEXT | DATE | Transmission[1] copy dictation edited | WA | ENGLISH |
|---|---|---|---|---|
| **Genesis** | | | | |
| Lectures (*scholia*) | | | | |
| 1–34 | 1519–1521 (?) | E | 9, 329–415 | |
| Sermons | | | | |
| 8–28 | 1519–1521 | C | 9, 416–99 | |
| 29 | | C | 9, 500–04 | |
| 29 | | E | 9, 535–54 | |
| 30 | | C | 9, 505–08 | |
| 30 | | E | 9, 558–78 | |
| 31 | | C | 9, 508–13 | |
| 31 | | E | 9, 579–616 | |
| Sermons | 1523–1524 | C | 14, 92–488 | |
| Printed editions: | | | | |
| a) *In Genesin Declamationes* | 1527 | E | 24, 1–710 | |
| b) *Über das 1. Buch Mose* | 1527 | E | | |

| TEXT | DATE | Transmission[1] copy dictation edited | WA | ENGLISH |
|---|---|---|---|---|
| Lectures | | | | |
| 1–17 | | | 42 | *LW* 1–3, 175 |
| | | | | *LE* 2 (chaps. 1–4) |
| 18–30 | 1535–1545 | E | 43 | *LW* 3, 175 ff. |
| 31–50 | | | 44 | *LW* 5 ff. |
| **Exodus** | | | | |
| Sermons | 1524–1527 | C, E | 16 | |
| Glosses to the Decalogue | 1530 | | $30^{II}$, 357–59 | |
| **Leviticus** | | | | |
| Sermons | | | | |
| 9–10 | 4/7/1527 | C | 25, 411–14 | |
| 11 | 5/19/1527 | C | 25, 414–16 | |
| 12–15 | 5/26/1527 | C | 25, 416–19 | |
| 18 | 7/2/1527 | C | 25, 420–22 | |
| 19:1–15 | 7/21/1527 | C | 25, 423–26 | |
| 19:16 ff. | 10/13/1527 | C | 25, 427–29 | |
| 23, 25, 27 | 11/24/1527 | C | 25, 429–32 | |
| 27 | 12/1/1527 | C | 25, 432–36 | |

| | | | | |
|---|---|---|---|---|
| **Numbers** | | | | |
| 6:24–26 | 1532 | | $30^{III}$, 572–82 | |
| Sermons | | | | |
| 6 | 1527–1528 | C | 25, 436–39 | |
| 11–31 | 1527–1528 | C | 25, 439–517 | |
| **Deuteronomy** | | | | |
| Lectures | 1523–1524 | C | 14, 545–744 | *LW* 9 ff. |
| *Deuteronomion Mosi cum annotationibus* | 1525 | | | |
| Sermons | | | | |
| 9 | 1529 | C, E | 28, 509–763 | |
| **Judges** | | | | |
| Lectures | | | | |
| 1–18 | 1516 ff. (?) | E | 4, 527–86 | |
| Sermon | | | | |
| 14:14 | late March 1516 | | 1, 58–60 | |
| **II Samuel** | | | | |
| 23:1–7 | 1543 | | 54, 16–100 | |

| TEXT | DATE | Transmission[1] copy dictation edited | WA | ENGLISH |
|---|---|---|---|---|
| **Psalms** | | | | |
| *Summarien über die Psalmen* | 1531–1533 | | 38, 18–69 | |
| *Dictata super Psalterium* | 1513–1516 | | 3, 11—4, 462<br>9, 116–121 | |
| *Operationes in Psalmos* | | | | |
| 1–22 | 1519–1521 | | 5 | *LW* 14, 287–349 (Psalms 1–2)<br>*LE* 1, 25–420 (Psalms 1–8) |
| 1–25 | 1530 | D | $31^{I}$, 258–383 | |
| 1 | 1530–1532[3] | | $31^{I}$, 482–84 | |
| 1 (sermon) | 1541 | C | 49, 223–28 | |
| 1 (sermon) | 1541 | C | 49, 228–33 | |
| 2 | 1530–1532 | | $31^{I}$, 484–88 | |
| 2 | 1530–1532 | E | $31^{I}$, 563 | |
| 2 | 1532 | C, E | $40^{II}$, 192–312 | *LW* 12, 3–93 |
| 3 | 1530–1532 | | $31^{I}$, 488–91 | |
| 4 | 1530–1532 | | $31^{I}$, 491–94 | |

| | | | | |
|---|---|---|---|---|
| 4 (sermon) | 9/15/1536 | C | 41, 668–75 | |
| 4 (sermon) | 12/21/1536 | C | 41, 736–739 | |
| 4–5 | 1518–1519 | C | Vogelsang[4] | |
| 5 | 1530–1532 | | $31^{I}$, 494–97 | |
| 5 (sermon) | 1/26, 28/1525 | C | $17^{I}$, 32–38 | |
| 5 (sermon) | 1/17/1535 | C | 41, 8–17 | |
| 6 | 1517 | | 1, 158–66 | |
| | 1525 | | 18, 479–84 | *LW* 14, 139–46 |
| 6 | 1530–1532 | | $31^{I}$, 498–501 | |
| 7 | 1530–1532 | | $31^{I}$, 501–03 | |
| 8 | 1530–1532 | | $31^{I}$, 503–07 | |
| 8 | 1530–1532 | | $31^{I}$, 535–37 | |
| 8 (sermon) | 11/1/1537 | C, E | 45, 204–50 | *LW* 12, 97–136 |
| 9 | 1525 | | 18, 226–29 | |
| 9 | 1530–1532 | | $31^{I}$, 515–16 | |
| 11 (sermon) | 2/21/1525 | C | $17^{I}$, 52–56 | |
| 13 (sermon) | 11/1/1533 | C | 37, 183–88 | |
| 14 (sermon) | 11/8/1533 | C | 37, 190–95 | |
| 16 | 1530–1532 | | $31^{I}$, 516–22 | |
| 19 | 1531 | E | $31^{I}$, 578–86 | *LW* 12, 139–44 |
| 19:2 (sermon) | 12/21/1516 | | 1, 111–15 | |
| 22 | 1530–1532 | | $31^{I}$, 522–23 | |
| 23 | 1530–1532 | | $31^{I}$, 523–25 | |

| TEXT | DATE | Transmission[1] copy dictation edited | WA | ENGLISH |
|---|---|---|---|---|
| 23 | 1536 | E | 51, 265–95 | *LW* 12, 147–79 |
| 23–25 (*scholae*) | 1516(?) | | $31^{I}$, 462–80 | |
| 25 (sermon) | 5/3/1536 | C | 41, 569–73 | |
| 26 (sermon) | 5/12/1525 | C | $17^{I}$, 228–43 | *LW* 12, 183–94 |
| 27 (sermon) | 9/9/1542 | C | 49, 269–70 | |
| 29 | 1530–1532 | E | $31^{I}$, 550–51 | |
| 29 | 1530–1532 | E | $31^{I}$, 551–53 | |
| 31 | 1530–1532 | | $31^{I}$, 525 | |
| 32 | 1517 | | 1, 166–74 | |
| 32 | 1525 | | 18, 485–91 | *LW* 14, 147–54 |
| 32 | 1530–1532 | | $31^{I}$, 525–28 | |
| 34 | 1530–1532 | E | $31^{I}$, 557–58 | |
| 37 | 1521 | | 8, 205–40 | |
| 37 | 1526 | | 19, 554–71 | *LW* 14, 211–29 |
| 37 (sermon) | 5/17/1535 | C | $17^{I}$, 334–36 | |
| 38 | 1517 | | 1, 174–84 | |
| | 1525 | | 18, 491–98 | *LW* 14, 155–63 |
| 42 | 1530–1532 | E | $31^{I}$, 553–55 | |
| 45 | 1532 | C, E | $40^{II}$, 471–610 | *LW* 12, 197–300 |

| | | | | |
|---|---|---|---|---|
| 45 | 1533(?) | | $31^{I}$, 565–71 | |
| 45:3 (sermon) | 1518 | | 1, 340–45 | |
| 45:5 (sermon) | 12/4/1515(?) | | 4, 639–44 | |
| 51 | 1517 | | 1, 184–94 | |
| | 1525 | | 18, 498–507 | *LW* 14, 165–75 |
| 51 | 1530–1532 | | $31^{I}$, 510–14 | |
| 51 | 1530–1532 | | $31^{I}$, 538–43 | |
| 51 | 1532 | C, E | $40^{II}$, 313–470 | *LW* 12, 303–410 |
| 56 | 1530–1532 | E | $31^{I}$, 560–61 | |
| 60:10 (sermon) | 1514(?) | | 3, 342–46 | |
| 62 | 1526 | | 19, 571–82 | *LW* 14, 231–41 |
| 65 (sermon) | 6/15/1532 | C | 36, 217–19 | |
| 65 (sermon) | 6/5/1534 | C | 37, 425–50 | |
| 68 | 1521 | | 8, 1–35 | *LW* 13, 3–37 |
| 68:19 (sermon) | 5/31/1527 | C | 23, 696–725 | |
| 72 | 1530–1532 | | $31^{I}$, 509–10 | |
| 72 (sermon) | 5/28/1533 | C | 37, 83–87 | |
| 72:1 (sermon) | 1/5/1540 | C | 49, 11–15 | |
| 72:2–5 (sermon) | 1/6/1540 | C | 49, 15–20 | |
| 72:6 (sermon) | 1/11/1540 | C | 49, 21–25 | |
| 72:7–11 (sermon) | 2/15/1540 | C | 49, 30–35 | |
| 72:10–14 (sermon) | 2/22/1540 | C | 49, 35–40 | |
| 72:15–20 (sermon) | 3/7/1540 | C | 49, 45–49 | |

| TEXT | DATE | Transmission[1] copy dictation edited | WA | ENGLISH |
|---|---|---|---|---|
| 81 | 1530–1532 | | $31^{I}$, 528–30 | |
| 82 | 1530 | | $31^{I}$, 183–218 | *LW* 13, 41–72<br>*PE* 4, 287–323 |
| 83 | 1529 | | $31^{I}$, 30–33 | |
| 89 | 1530–1532 | E | $31^{I}$, 574–77 | |
| 90 | 1534–1535 | C, E | $40^{III}$, 476–594 | *LW* 13, 75–141 |
| 91 | 1530–1532 | E | $31^{I}$, 561–62 | |
| 93 | 1530–1532 | | $31^{I}$, 530–31 | |
| 94 | 1526 | | 19, 582–94 | *LW* 14, 243–56 |
| 94 | 1530–1532 | | $31^{I}$, 543 | |
| 101 | 1534–1535 | | 51, 197–264<br>53, 659–78 | *LW* 13, 145–224 |
| 102 | { 1517<br>{ 1525 | | 1, 195–206<br>18, 507–16 | <br>*LW* 14, 177–87 |
| 109 | 1526 | | 19, 595–615 | *LW* 14, 257–77 |
| 110 | 1518 | E | 9, 180–202; 689–710 | |
| 110 | 1530–1532 | | $31^{I}$, 508–09 | |
| 110 | 1530–1532 | | $31^{I}$, 531–34 | |
| 110 | 1530–1532 | E | $31^{I}$, 563 | |

| | | | | |
|---|---|---|---|---|
| 110:1 (sermon) | 5/8/1535 | C | 41, 79–121 | *LW* 13, 227–348 |
| 110:1 ff. (sermon) | 4/20/1534 | C | 37, 387–90 | |
| 110:2 ff. (sermon) | 5/10/1535 | C | 41, 122–53 | |
| 110:3 (sermon) | 5/29/1535 | C | 41, 153–67 | |
| 110:4 (sermon) | 5/30/1535 | C | 41, 167–82 | |
| 110:4 (sermon) | 6/5/1535 | C | 41, 182–203 | |
| 110:4 (sermon) | 6/9/1535 | C | 41, 204–15 | |
| 110:5 ff. (sermon) | 6/12/1535 | C | 41, 215–29 | |
| 110:7 (sermon) | 6/13/1535 | C | 41, 229–39 | |
| 111 | 1530 | | $31^{I}$, 384–426 | *LW* 13, 351–87 |
| 112 | 1526 | C | 19, 294–336 | *LW* 13, 391–420 |
| 112:1–3 (sermon) | 6/9/1526 | C | 19, 298–315 | |
| 112:4–8 (sermon) | 6/16/1526 | C | 19, 315–26 | |
| 112:5 (sermon) | 5/1/1515 | | 1, 44–52 | |
| 113 | 1530–1532 | E | $31^{I}$, 558–59 | |
| 116:10–11 (sermon) | 6/1/1534 | C | 37, 419–24 | |
| 117 | 1530 | | $31^{I}$, 219–57 | *LW* 14, 3–39 |
| 118 | 1529–1530 | | $31^{I}$, 34–182 | *LW* 14, 43–106 |
| 119 | 1521 | | 8, 186–204 | |
| 119 | 1529 | | $31^{I}$, 1–29 | |
| 119 | 1530–1532 | E | $31^{I}$, 571–74 | |
| 120 | 1532 | C, E | $40^{III}$, 15–45 | *SM*, 111–32[5] |
| 121 | 1532 | C, E | $40^{III}$, 46–73 | *SM*, 133–57 |

| TEXT | DATE | Transmission[1] copy dictation edited | WA | ENGLISH |
|---|---|---|---|---|
| 122 | 1532 | C, E | $40^{III}$, 74–119 | *SM*, 157–83 |
| 123 | 1532 | C, E | $40^{III}$, 119–33 | *SM*, 184–92 |
| 124 | 1532 | C, E | $40^{III}$, 134–51 | *SM*, 193–204 |
| 125 | 1533 | C, E | $40^{III}$, 152–73 | *SM*, 204–19 |
| 126 | 1530–1532 | | $31^{I}$, 545–46 | |
| 126 | 1533 | C, E | $40^{III}$, 174–201 | *SM*, 219–39 |
| 126:1–3 (sermon) | 12/1/1536 | E | 41, 720–23 | |
| 126:4 (sermon) | 12/2/1536 | E | 41, 724–28 | |
| 127 | 1524 | | 15, 348–79 | *LW* 45, 317–34 |
| 127 | 1530–1532 | | $31^{I}$, 546 | |
| 127 | 1533 | C, E | $40^{III}$, 202–49 | *SM*, 240–91 |
| 128 | 1530–1532 | | $31^{I}$, 507–08 | |
| 128 | 1533 | C, E | $40^{III}$, 269–309 | *SM*, 292–323 |
| 129 | 1533 | | $40^{III}$, 309–35 | *SM*, 324–45 |
| 130 | { 1517<br>{ 1525 | | 1, 206–11<br>18, 516–21 | <br>*LW* 14, 189–94 |
| 130 | 1530–1532 | | $31^{I}$, 547 | |
| 130 | 1533 | C, E | $40^{III}$, 335–76 | *SM*, 345–78 |
| 130 (sermon) | 8/24/1534 | E | 37, 520–26 | |
| 131 | 1533 | C, E | $40^{III}$, 377–90 | *SM*, 379–91 |

| | | | | |
|---|---|---|---|---|
| 132 | 1530–1532 | | $31^{I}$, 547 | |
| 132 | 1533 | C, E | $40^{III}$, 390–458 | *SM*, 391–438 |
| 133 | 1530–1532 | | $31^{I}$, 547–49 | |
| 133 | 1533 | C, E | $40^{III}$, 459–69 | *SM*, 438–45 |
| 134 | 1533 | C, E | $40^{III}$, 469–75 | *SM*, 446–50 |
| 137 | 1530–1532 | E | $31^{I}$, 562–63 | |
| 143 | 1517 | | 1, 211–20 | |
| | 1525 | | 18, 521–30 | *LW* 14, 195–205 |
| 145 (sermon) | 10/27/1534 | C | 37, 564–71 | |
| 147 | 1532 | | $31^{I}$, 427–56 | *LW* 14, 109–35 |
| 147 | 1530–1532 | | $31^{I}$, 543–45 | |
| 148 | 1530–1532 | E | $31^{I}$, 555–57 | |
| 150 | 1530–1532 | E | $31^{I}$, 563–64 | |
| **Ecclesiastes** | | | | |
| Lectures | 1526 | C | 20, 1–203 | |
| *Annotationes* | 1532 | E | | |
| **Song of Solomon** | | | | |
| Lectures | 1527–1530 | C | $31^{II}$, 586–769 | |
| **Isaiah** | | | | |
| Lectures | 1527–1530 | C | $31^{II}$, 1–585 | |
| | 1532–1534 | E | 25, 79–401 | |
| 7:10 ff. (sermon) | 3/18/1540 | C | 49, 58–62 | |

| TEXT | DATE | Transmission[1] copy dictation edited | WA | ENGLISH |
|---|---|---|---|---|
| 7:12 ff. (sermon) | 3/25/1540 | C | 36, 145–53 | |
| 7:14 (sermon) | 12/26/1539 | C | 47, 867–71 | |
| 9 (lectures) | 1543–1544 | C, E | $40^{III}$, 595–682 | |
| 9:2–7 (sermon) | 12/25, 26/1525 | C | 19, 126–68 | |
| 9:2 (sermon) | 1/8/1541 | C | 49, 205–11 | |
| 9:2 (sermon) | 12/25/1525 | C | $17^{I}$, 500–04 | |
| 9:2 ff. (sermon) | 12/24/1537 | C | 45, 341–45 | |
| 9:2 ff. (sermon) | 12/31/1539 | C | 47, 871–75 | |
| 9:2 ff. (sermon) | 1/1/1541 | C | 49, 191–96 | |
| 9:2 ff. (sermon) | 1544 | E | 52, 578–87 | |
| 9:5 (sermon) | 12/24/1531 | C | $34^{II}$, 490–500 | |
| 9:5 (sermon) | 12/25/1531 | C | $34^{II}$, 508–14 | |
| 9:5 (sermon) | 12/26/1531 | C | $34^{II}$, 515–23 | |
| 9:5 (sermon) | 12/26/1531 | C | $34^{II}$, 523–30 | |
| 9:5 (sermon) | 12/27/1531 | C | $34^{II}$, 530–36 | |
| 9:6 ff. (sermon) | 12/26/1525 | C | $17^{I}$, 504–07 | |
| 9:6 ff. (sermon) | 11/1537 | | 45, 426–27 | |
| 9:6 ff. (sermon) | 1/5/1541 | C | 49, 196–200 | |
| 9:6 ff. (sermon) | 1/4/1545 | C, E | 49, 660–67 | |
| 53 (lectures) | 1544 | C, E | $40^{III}$, 683–746 | |

| | | | |
|---|---|---|---|
| 53:2 (sermon) | 1518 | | 1, 336–40 |
| 60:1 ff. (sermon) | 1522 | | $10^{I}$ 1, 519–55 |
| 60:1 ff. (sermon) | 1/6/1536 | C | 41, 503–07 |
| 60:1 ff. (sermon) | 1/6/1541 | C | 49, 201–05 |
| 60:1 ff. (sermon) | 1/6/1545 | C | 49, 667–74 |
| **Jeremiah** | | | |
| 23:5 (sermon) | 11/18/1526 | C, E | 20, 547–61 |
| 23:6–8 (sermon) | 11/25/1526 | C, E | 20, 561–80 |
| **Ezekiel** | | | |
| 1:5–6 | 1519(?) | | 4, 635 (9, 439) |
| 38–39 (preface) | 1530 | | $30^{II}$, 120–236 |
| **Daniel** | | | |
| 4:24 (theses) | 10/16/1535 | | $39^{I}$, 63–75 |
| **Hosea** | | | |
| Lectures | 1524 | C | 13, 1–66 |
| 13:12–14 | 1545 | | $40^{III}$, 760–75 |
| **Joel** | | | |
| Lectures | 1524 | C | 13, 67–87 |
| | | E | 13, 88–122 |
| **Amos** | | | |
| Lectures | 1524 | C | 13, 124–57 |
| | | E | 13, 158–206 |

| TEXT | DATE | Transmis-sion[1] copy dictation edited | WA | ENGLISH |
|---|---|---|---|---|
| **Obadiah** | | | | |
| Lectures | 1525 | C | 13, 207–14 | |
| | | E | 13, 215–23 | |
| **Jonah** | | | | |
| Lectures | 1525 | C | 13, 224–40 | |
| | | E | 13, 241–58 | |
| Exposition | 1526 | | 19, 169–251 | |
| **Micah** | | | | |
| Lectures | 1525 | C | 13, 259–98 | |
| | | E | 13, 299–343 | |
| **Nahum** | | | | |
| Lectures | 1525 | E | 13, 344–70 | |
| | | E | 13, 371–94 | |
| **Habakkuk** | | | | |
| Lectures | 1525 | C | 13, 397–423 | |
| | | E | 13, 424–48 | |
| Exposition | 1526 | | 19, 337–435 | |
| **Zephaniah** | | | | |
| Lectures | 1525 | C | 13, 449–79 | |
| | | E | 13, 480–509 | |

| TEXT | DATE | Transmission[1] copy dictation edited | WA | ENGLISH |
|---|---|---|---|---|
| **Haggai** | | | | |
| Lectures | 1525 | C | 13, 510–31 | |
| | | E | 13, 532–44 | |
| **Zechariah** | | | | |
| Lectures | 1525–1526 | E | 13, 545–674 | |
| Exposition | 1527 | | 23, 485–664 | |
| 9:9 (sermon) | 3/18/1540 | C | 49, 62–66 | |
| **Malachi** | | | | |
| Lectures | 1526 | E | 13, 675–703 | |
| 3:1 ff. (sermon) | 2/2/1517 | | 1, 130–32 | |
| **Ecclesiasticus** | | | | |
| 15:1 ff. (sermon) | 12/27/1516 | | 1, 115–17 | |
| 15:1 ff. (sermon) | 12/27/1517 | | 1, 37–43 | |
| 24:11 ff. (sermon) | 8/15/1520(?) | C | 4, 645–50 | |

[1] The form of transmission is designated by: C = Copy; D = Dictation; E = Edited. If there is no indication of transmission, it is Luther's original text. See also above, p. 7, n. 24.

[2] On the dating of Luther's earliest sermons, see Erich Vogelsang, "Zur Datierung der frühesten Lutherpredigten," *Zeitschrift für Kirchengeschichte,* L (1931), 112 ff.

[3] Luther's greatly varying small studies on the Psalms collected from the years 1530 to 1532 in *WA* 31[I], 481–577, are cited—insofar as they are not edited *Table Talk* (E)—as Luther's original texts without regard to their process of transmission, which is frequently uncertain. Consult *WA* for details. Some very small pieces have been excluded.

[4] Erich Vogelsang (ed.), *Unbekannte Fragmente aus Luthers zweiter Psalmenvorlesung 1518* ("Arbeiten zur Kirchengeschichte," 27 [Berlin, 1940]), pp. 31–94.

[5] W. Simpkin and R. Marshall (trans.), *A Commentary on the Psalms, Called Psalms of Degrees* (London, 1819).

# BIBLIOGRAPHY[1]

BARDTKE, HANS. *Luther und das Buch Esther.* ("Sammlung gemeinverständlicher Vorträge," Vols. 240–41.)

BEISSER, FRIEDRICH. *Claritas scripturae bei Martin Luther. Theologische Dissertation, Erlangen, 1964.* ("Forschungen zur Kirchen- und Dogmengeschichte," Vol. 18.) Göttingen, 1966.

BLUHM, HEINZ. "The Biblical Quotations in Luther's German Writings. A Preliminary Statistical Report," *Archiv für Reformationsgeschichte,* XLIV (1953), 103–13.

———. *The Creative Translator.* St. Louis, 1965. See the chapter "Translating of the Twenty-third Psalm," pp. 78–113.

BRINKEL, KARL. "Luthers Hermeneutik in seiner Übersetzung des Alten Testaments und die gegenwärtige Revision der Lutherbibel," *Luthertum,* XXIV (1960).

EBELING, GERHARD. "Die Anfänge von Luthers Hermeneutik," *Zeitschrift für Theologie und Kirche,* XLVIII (1951), 172–230.

———. "Luthers Auslegung des 44. (45.) Psalms," in *Referate und Berichte des 1. Internationalen Lutherforschungskongresses Aarhus (1956).* ("Lutherforschung heute.") Berlin, 1958. Pp. 32–48.

———. "Hermeneutik" in *Die Religion in Geschichte und Gegenwart* (3rd ed.), III, 251–53. See also the bibliography there, pp. 259–60.

GERDES, HAYO. "Luthers Streit mit den Schwärmern um das rechte Verständnis des Gesetzes Mose." Unpublished Theological Dissertation, Göttingen, 1955.

HAHN, FRIEDRICH. "Die heilige Schrift als Problem der Auslegung bei Luther," *Evangelische Theologie,* Vol. X (1950), No. 1, pp. 407–24.

HERMANN, RUDOLF. *Die Gestalt Simsons bei Luther. Eine Studie zur Bibelauslegung.* ("Theologische Bibliothek Töpelmann," Vol. 2.) Berlin, 1952. Reprinted in RUDOLF HERMANN. *Gesammelte Studien zur Theologie Luthers und der Reformation.* Göttingen, 1960. Pp. 427–46.

HILBURG, JOHANNES. "Luther und das Wort Gottes in seiner Exegese

[1] I have not included a bibliography concerning Luther's *First Lecture on the Psalms,* 1513–1515, since the present work deals primarily with the exegesis of the mature Luther. See above, pp. vii–viii.

und Theologie, dargestellt auf Grund seiner Operationes in Psalmos 1519/21 in Verbindung mit seinen früheren Vorlesungen." Unpublished Theological Dissertation, Marburg, 1948.

KRAUS, HANS JOACHIM. *Geschichte der historisch-kritischen Erforschung des Alten Testaments von der Reformation bis zur Gegenwart.* Neukirchen, 1956.

KRAUSE, GERHARD. *Studien zu Luthers Auslegung der Kleinen Propheten. Theologische Dissertation, Zürich, 1960.* ("Beiträge zur historischen Theologie," Vol. 33.) Tübingen, 1962.

KOOIMAN, WILLEM JAN. *Luther and the Bible.* Translated by John Schmidt. Philadelphia, 1961.

KRUMWIEDE, HANS-WALTER. *Glaube und Geschichte in der Theologie Luthers.* Göttingen, 1952.

———. "Usus legis und usus historiarum. Die Hermeneutik der Theologia crucis nach Luthers Auslegung von Jesaja 13," *Kerygma und Dogma,* VIII (1962), 238–64.

LERCH, DAVID. "Isaaks Opferung christlich gedeutet. Eine auslegungsgeschichtliche Untersuchung," in *Beiträge zur historischen Theologie,* Vol. 12. Tübingen, 1950. Pp. 156–202.

MÜLHAUPT, ERWIN. "Luthers Übersetzung und Auslegung des 37. Psalms, ein Beispiel zunehmender Verchristlichung aber nicht Christologisierung," in *Luther. Zeitschrift der Luthergesellschaft,* Vol. 34. 1963. Pp. 49–60.

OESTERGAARD-NIELSEN, HARALD. *Scriptura sacra et viva vox. Theologische Dissertation, Aarhus.* ("Forschungen zur Geschichte und Lehre des Protestantismus,' Vol. 10, No. 10.) München, 1957.

PEDERSEN, E. THESTRUP. *Luther som Skriftfortolker. I. En studie i Luthers skriftsyn, hermeneutik og eksegese.* Copenhagen, 1959.

PELIKAN, JAROSLAV. *Luther the Expositor.* Companion volume to *Luther's Works,* American Edition, Vols. 1–30. St. Louis, 1959.

———. "Die Kirche nach Luthers Genesisauslegung," in *Referate und Berichte des 1. Internationalen Lutherforschungskongresses Aarhus (1956).* ("Lutherforschung heute.") Berlin, 1958. Pp. 102–10.

QUANBECK, WARREN A. "The Hermeneutical Principles of Luther's Early Exegesis." Unpublished Theological Dissertation, Princeton, 1948.

RAEDER, SIEGFRIED. *Das Hebräische bei Luther, untersucht bis zum Ende der ersten Psalmenvorlesung. Theologische Dissertation, Zürich.* ("Beiträge zur historischen Theologie," Vol. 31.) Tübingen, 1961.

———. *Die Benutzung des masorethischen Textes bei Luther in der Zeit zwischen der ersten und zweiten Psalmenvorlesung (1515–1518).* ("Beiträge zur historischen Theologie," Vol. 38.) Tübingen, 1967.

SCHILD, MAURICE E. "Abendländische Bibelvorreden bis zur Lutherbibel." Unpublished Theological Dissertation, Heidelberg, 1964.

SICK, HANSJÖRG, *Melanchthon als Ausleger des Alten Testaments. Theologische Dissertation, Heidelberg, 1954.* ("Beiträge zur Geschichte der biblischen Hermeneutik," Vol. 2.) Tübingen, 1959.

STÖHR, MARTIN. "Luther und die Juden," *Evangelische Theologie,* XX (1960), 157–82.

VOLZ, HANS. "Melanchthons Anteil an der Lutherbibel," *Archiv für Reformationsgeschichte,* XLV (1954), 196–233.

———. "Neue Beiträge zu Luthers Bibelübersetzung: Luthers Arbeiten am Propheten Daniel," in *Beiträge zur Geschichte der deutschen Sprache und Literatur,* Vol. 77. 1955. Pp. 393–423.

———. "Luthers Arbeit am lateinischen Psalter," *Archiv für Reformationsgeschichte,* XLVIII (1957), 11–46.

———. "Luthers Stellung zu den Apokryphen des Alten Testaments," *Lutherjahrbuch,* XXVI (1959), 93–108.

———. "Zur Überlieferung des Gebets Manasse," *Zeitschrift für Kirchengeschichte,* LXX (1959), 293–307.

WÖLFEL, EBERHARD. *Luther und die Skepsis. Eine Untersuchung zur Kohelet-Exegese Luthers. Theologische Dissertation, Erlangen.* ("Forschungen zur Geschichte und Lehre des Protestantismus," Vol. 10, No. 12.) München, 1958.

# INDEXES

*Prepared by David J. and Joyce C. Wartluft*

## GENERAL INDEX

# INDEX TO SCRIPTURE REFERENCES

# INDEX TO LUTHER'S WRITINGS

# INDEX TO REFERENCES TO THE AMERICAN EDITION OF LUTHER'S WORKS

[*LW* volume numbers are in bold type. Thus 1, 9 — 116 means that *LW* volume 1, p. 9, is referred to on p. 116 of this book.]

# INDEX TO REFERENCES TO THE WEIMAR AUSGABE

[*WA* volume numbers are in bold type; line references are preceded by a colon. Thus 1, 112:24 — 9 means *WA* volume 1, p. 112, l. 24, is referred to on p. 9 of this book.]

"Toledot Yeshu"

Scriptura sacra sui ipsius interpres.

- think about L: Luther his own best interpreter.
    - even Scripture is subject to Gospel

Luther may not have understood all implications of thought.

✓ OT as perennial problem

?has Marcion won?